THE ADVENTURES OF HUCKLEBERRY FINN

《哈克贝利·费恩历险记》精读与鉴赏

主编 单俊 张锦红 熊焕力
参编 余嘉 王慧

重庆大学出版社

图书在版编目（CIP）数据

《哈克贝利·费恩历险记》精读与鉴赏：英文/单俊，张锦红，熊焕力主编. -- 重庆：重庆大学出版社，2020.6（2024.6 重印）

ISBN 978-7-5689-2117-6

Ⅰ.①哈… Ⅱ.①单…②张…③熊… Ⅲ.①英语—阅读教学—高等学校—教学参考资料②《哈克贝利·费恩历险记》—文学欣赏 Ⅳ.①H319.4：1

中国版本图书馆 CIP 数据核字（2020）第067667号

《哈克贝利·费恩历险记》精读与鉴赏

HAKEBEILI FEIEN LIXIANJI JINGDU YU JIANSHANG

主 编 单 俊 张锦红 熊焕力

责任编辑：张春花 版式设计：张春花

责任校对：刘志刚 责任印制：赵 晟

*

重庆大学出版社出版发行

出版人：陈晓阳

社址：重庆市沙坪坝区大学城西路 21 号

邮编：401331

电话：（023）88617190 88617185（中小学）

传真：（023）88617186 88617166

网址：http：//www.cqup.com.cn

邮箱：fxk@cqup.com.cn（营销中心）

全国新华书店经销

POD：重庆新生代彩印技术有限公司

*

开本：787mm×1092mm 1/16 印张：20.75 字数：615 千

2020 年 7 月第 1 版 2024 年 6 月第 3 次印刷

ISBN 978-7-5689-2117-6 定价：59.00 元

序　言

有人说:"读书,即使没有富庶的生活,仍有富庶的生命,让我清贫至今也朴素至今,平凡至今也善良至今。"书籍里藏着人生哲学。对一个人价值观的培养应该从阅读开始。可以这样说,一个人的精神发育史就是他的阅读史。

中小学语文部编版教材的推出和语文教学的改革,让我们看到了不少变化。一方面是大大提高了中国古诗文的阅读量。小学从一年级开始就有古诗文,整个小学六年级12册教材中,共选有古诗文124篇,占所有选篇的30%,比原有人教版教材增加55篇,增幅达80%。语文教学中更加重视传统经典文化的学习。语言的学习与经典阅读是密不可分的。我们也看到了喜人的成绩,2020年初,第五届诗词大会上有不少少年选手崭露头角。大赛的亚军韩亚轩就是一个11岁的小学生。另一方面,部编版教材更加重视扩大学生的课外阅读量,重视学生自主阅读实践,努力做到课标所要求的"多读书、读好书、好读书、读整本的书"。注意这里提出的是要读整本书,而不只是拘泥于课本上的各种短篇或长篇节选。我们已经充分认识到了,语文教学中若是没有题材广泛的阅读,没有大量的阅读积累,语文的核心素养是很难得到提升的。

再来看看英语学习,其本质和语文学习并无差异。我们的英语教学也不应该只停留在知识点层面,同样也应该重视阅读经典,传承文化,引导学生领略文学之美,感受刻印在文化中的深沉基因。让我们回到最初的几个问题去探索语言学习的本质,去思考语言教学的改革吧。

何为经典?经典,它取消了知识和意见的界限,成为了永久的传承工具。经典的作品展现出娴熟的形象语言、原创性、认知能力、知识以及丰富的词汇。

为什么要阅读经典?阅读经典可以提高我们个人修养,增强我们对文学、对艺术、对生命的感受力,从而更好地认识自己,提升自己。

怎样阅读经典?想要更好地理解经典作品,就要走进文学作品中去,主动思考以产生共鸣。语言专业的大学生在阅读经典的时候不应该满足于只是获得某些零星的感悟,而是需要通过深入思考,仔细研究,形成更加系统的认知。于是我们需要关注另一门学问——文学批评。文学批评是一门古老的艺术,文学批评与诗歌、散文、小说、戏剧一样,都是富有创造性的文学产品的主要形式之一。有着一定造诣的批评家在文学舞台上可以扮演与创作作家同样重要的角色。学习文学批评让我们可以更好地走进经典，走近那些伟大的作家。

最后，为什么要阅读长篇的经典作品呢？莫言在《捍卫长篇小说的尊严》中曾这样评价长篇小说：“长度、密度和难度，是长篇小说的标志，也是伟大文体的尊严。”优秀的长篇小说不是简单的字数累加，“而是一种胸中的大气象，一种艺术的大营造。那些能够营造精致的江南园林的建筑师，那些在假山上盖小亭子的建筑师，当然也很了不起，但他们大概营造不来故宫和金字塔，更主持不了万里长城那样的浩大工程。”不少外语学习者可能有过这样的亲身体验，曾经在学习期间花了一个假期的时间精读了一本长篇小说，突然感觉茅塞顿开，阅读理解能力大幅提升。无论从各个角度来看，长篇经典作品的艺术魅力，文化价值都是不言而喻的，精读长篇作品的意义自然也非常重大。

我们发现，纵观小学到大学，语文到英语各类教材都很少把长篇作品作为课堂上的教学内容。长篇作品的学习基本采用的还是选读、导读的形式，老师只能给予零星的、宏观的指导。即使非常重视阅读量的部编版教材，长篇作品的阅读仍然放在了课外阅读实践中，当然这与中小学课程教学目标，课时安排等诸多方面原因有关。同时我们也调查了在中国大学慕课网上的情况，外语类的各种文学、阅读课程中主要还是文学史、短篇小说分析，我们只找到了一门关于长篇小说的课程：《理智与情感》的生活智慧——英国文学名著多维导读。可见，如何将长篇经典作品转化为教学资源有着很大的探索空间。我们编写这本教材就是想将长篇经典作品转化成教学资源，引导学生去细读一本长篇作品，并能有所收获。

那么，我们为什么选择《哈克贝利·费恩历险记》这本书呢？

海明威这样评价道：“现代美国文学，全都来源于马克·吐温写的一本书，书名叫作《哈克贝利·费恩历险记》，它是我们所有的书中最好的一本书(美国评论家认为，美国文学中只有两三部杰作，《哈克贝利·费恩历险记》就是其中之一)。在这以前没有过，打它以后也没有这么好。”一百多年来，哈克和他的故事早已根深蒂固地扎根在美国人的民族意识中。可以这样说，每个美国人的血脉里或多或少地有着哈克的基因。一百多年过去了，人们对《哈克贝利·费恩历险记》依然情有独钟。

在给这本书写精华赏析时，我们对这本书越来越爱不释手，好像发现了一个巨大的宝库，里面有取之不尽、用之不竭的资源。有的美国评论家甚至还这样预言说：只要我们这个星球上依然存在着贫困、仇恨、种族主义、溺爱儿童、兽行、暴力、伪善、压迫、苦工，以及奴役——不言而喻，人们还得一遍一遍地仔细捧读《哈克贝利·费恩历险记》。在不断的阅读和思考中，我们却发现这本书绝不仅仅是在揭露当时社会的种种黑暗，正如我在本书第22章精华赏析中写道的那样：马克·吐温对陆地上的人和事进行了无情的批判，揭露了社会生活中种种丑恶现象，尔虞我诈，贪生怕死，冷漠无情等。可是小说不只是揭露丑恶，它还给了我们一个希望，那就是哈克。哈克纯洁、诚实。哈克用他儿童的眼睛看遍陆地上种种丑恶，却仍以一颗真诚善良的心对待他人，帮助他人，这是多么的难能可贵。经典文学作品最可贵之处不是揭露黑暗，而是让人们看到光明和希望。正如威廉·福克纳在诺贝尔奖颁奖典礼上的致辞所说"当最后一块无用的礁石在血红色的、死气沉沉的黄昏中伫立，世界末日的钟声在它上空渐渐远去时，仍然会有一个声音，那是人类仍然在用微弱但永不停息的声音说话。我拒绝接受这种情景。我相信人类不会仅仅存在，他还将胜利。人类是不朽的，这不是因为万物当中仅仅他拥有发言权，而是因为他有一个灵魂，一种有同情心、牺牲精神和忍耐力的精神。诗人、作家的责任就是书写这种精神。他们有权力升华人类的心灵，使人类回忆起过去曾经使他无比光荣的东西——勇气、荣誉、希望、自尊、同情、怜悯和牺牲，从而帮助人类生存下去。诗人的声音不应该仅仅成为人类历史的记录，更应该成为人类存在与胜利的支柱和栋梁。"这就是经典、伟大作品的力量。

对于这样一本优秀的经典作品，我们花了大力气给每一章都写了一篇精华赏析，每一篇精华赏析都可以说是短小的文学评论。我们采用了不同的分析方法去研究这本小说，包括符号学、叙述学、文体学、结构主义、女性主义、生态主义、原型批评，不一而足。即使这样，我们仍然觉得眼前是一座连绵起伏的大型山脉，无论怎样也只能窥其一二，难以纵览其全貌。我们希望让学生意识到经典长篇文学作品的魅力正在于此。用一句诗来形容阅读经典长篇作品的感受，那绝对是"横看成岭侧成峰，远近高低各不同"。

除了精读经典长篇小说，鉴赏经典长篇小说，我们还希望能够引导学生通过阅读走向语言产出，达到学以致用的目的。在这本书中，我们每六章设计了一套练习题，题型包括口语表达，词汇活用，思考问答，翻译和写作等，将外语学习中的各种产出形式都囊括其中。

此时编写这本书的初衷已经不言自明了，我们想借助经典长篇小说的阅读和鉴赏，改变新媒体时代下碎片化阅读的浅尝辄止；立足于语言的融合性产出，改变学用分离的语言学习模式。让经典活起来，把语言用起来。

有的评论家指出，《哈克贝利·费恩历险记》除了小说结尾处汤姆·索亚式的营救吉姆那一部分以外，是十全十美的，堪称一幅令人难忘的美国边疆少年图画（来自英国评论家马库斯·坎利夫的《美国幽默和西部的兴起》）。在第31章中，哈克撕掉写给沃森小姐的信，决定营救吉姆，"我打算想想办法，把吉姆给偷出来，免得他重新当奴隶；我要是还想得出更坏的事情来，我照样也会干的，因为反正是一不做，二不休，既然要干，我就索性干到底。”此时哈克的道德进化已经全部完成，小说之后的章节反倒偏向了对汤姆的描写。前31章的故事是相对完整的，所以本书选择了小说最精彩的前31章作为精读内容。从经典性方面来讲，这样的选择也是比较合适的。另外，本书也适合作为教材使用。考虑到大多数学校的教学周期，一个学期详细分析和学习31章内容也是比较合适的。

本书编写中，单俊负责全书第1至12章的批注、精华赏析、术语解说、阅读思考和第22章的精华赏析、阅读思考的撰写工作，以及设计了所有练习题的问答题部分；张锦红负责全书第13至21章的批注、精华赏析、术语解说、阅读思考的撰写工作，以及设计了所有练习题的写作题部分；熊焕力负责全书第23至31章的批注、精华赏析、术语解说、阅读思考和第21章部分批注的撰写工作，以及设计了所有练习题的口语题部分；余嘉负责设计了所有练习题的词汇题部分；王慧负责设计了所有练习题的翻译题部分。本书原著部分主要参照的是上海世界图书出版公司于2008年6月出版的版本。

未来我们还将制作与本书配套的慕课，并初步设计慕课每单元将由四部分构成：从经典阅读中提高口语表达能力，从经典阅读中学习翻译技巧，从经典阅读中学习文学鉴赏，从经典阅读中学习英语写作。从阅读经典走向鉴赏经典，从鉴赏经典走向语言的融合性产出。本书的出版是一次尝试，未来我们还有很长的路要走。

单　俊
2020年春于成都

CONTENTS

CHAPTER I

导读:哈克被好心的道格拉斯寡妇收养。寡妇想要教化哈克,寡妇的妹妹沃森小姐教哈克读书、认字,不过对哈克要求严格。各种规矩使哈克对这种体面的生活很难适应。晚上,哈克又听到了那个熟悉的声音,“咪呜”。

(1) YOU don't know about me without you have read a book by the name of *The Adventures of Tom Sawyer*[1]; but that ain't no matter. That book was made by Mr. Mark Twain, and he told the truth, mainly. There was things which he stretched[2], but mainly he told the truth. That is nothing. I never seen anybody but lied one time or another, without it was Aunt Polly, or the widow, or maybe Mary. Aunt Polly—Tom's Aunt Polly, she is—and Mary, and the Widow Douglas is all told about in that book, which is mostly a true book, with some stretchers, as I said before.

(2) Now the way that the book winds up[3] is this: Tom and me found the money that the robbers hid in the cave, and it made us rich. We got six thousand dollars apiece—all gold. It was an awful sight of money when it was piled up. Well, Judge Thatcher he took it and put it out at interest, and it fetched us a dollar a day apiece all the year round—more than a body could tell what to do with. The Widow Douglas she took me for her son, and allowed she would sivilize[4] me; but it was rough living in the house all the time, considering how dismal[5] regular and decent the widow was in all her ways; and so when I couldn't stand it no longer I lit out.[6] I got into my old rags and my sugar-hogshead again, and was free and satisfied. But Tom Sawyer he hunted me up and said he was going to start a band of

[1] *The Adventures of Tom Sawyer*:《汤姆·索亚历险记》,马克·吐温在1876年发表的长篇小说。

[2] **stretch** /stretʃ/ *v.* 牵强附会

[3] **wind up**: 完成;停止

[4] **sivilize** /ˈsɪvəlaɪz/ *v.* 教化;使文明

[5] **dismal** /ˈdɪzməl/ *adj.* 忧郁的;凄凉的;惨淡的

[6] 哈克过惯了无拘无束的日子,无法忍受规矩的生活。(lit out: 跑出去)

robbers, and I might join if I would go back to the widow and be respectable. So I went back.

(3) The widow she cried over me, and called me a poor lost lamb, and she called me a lot of other names, too, but she never meant no harm by it. She put me in them new clothes again, and I couldn't do nothing but sweat and sweat, and feel all cramped up[7]. Well, then, the old thing commenced again. The widow rung a bell for supper, and you had to come to time. When you got to the table you couldn't go right to eating, but you had to wait for the widow to tuck down her head and grumble[8] a little over the victuals[9], though there warn't really anything the matter with them,—that is, nothing only everything was cooked by itself. In a barrel of odds and ends it is different; things get mixed up, and the juice kind of swaps around, and the things go better.

(4) After supper she got out her book and learned me about Moses and the Bulrushers[10], and I was in a sweat to find out all about him; but by and by she let it out that Moses had been dead a considerable long time; so then I didn't care no more about him, because I don't take no stock in dead people.

(5) Pretty soon I wanted to smoke, and asked the widow to let me. But she wouldn't. She said it was a mean practice and wasn't clean, and I must try to not do it any more. That is just the way with some people. They get down on a thing when they don't know nothing about it. Here she was a-bothering about Moses, which was no kin[11] to her, and no use to anybody, being gone, you see, yet finding a power of fault with me for doing a thing that had some good in it. And she took snuff, too; of course that was all right, because she done it herself.

(6) Her sister, Miss Watson, a tolerable slim old maid, with goggles on, had just come to live with her, and took a set at me now with a spelling-book. She worked me middling hard for about an hour, and then the widow made her ease up. I couldn't stood it much longer. Then for an hour it was deadly dull, and I was fidgety[12]. Miss Watson would say, "Don't put your feet up there, Huckleberry;" and "Don't scrunch up[13] like that, Huckleberry—set up straight;" and pretty soon she would say,

[7] **cramped up**: 束手束脚
从这句话可看出，哈克不习惯穿新衣服。穿上新衣服让他感觉束手束脚，不停地出汗。

[8] **grumble** /ˈgrʌmbl/ *v.* 嘟囔；发牢骚

[9] **victuals** /ˈvɪtlz/ *n.* 食物
这段中哈克以为寡妇是不满意食物，才会在吃饭前嘟囔几句，其实寡妇是在做祷告。

[10] **Moses and the Bulrushers**: 《圣经》中说埃及王虐待以色列人，下令把以色列人所生的男孩都扔到河里淹死。国王的女儿发现了躺在纸莎草编织的篮筐里的婴儿摩西，就收养了他。后来摩西率领以色列人逃出埃及。道格拉斯寡妇把自己和古埃及国王的女儿相比，可是哈克没听懂，把纸莎草篮筐说成了"纸莎草帮"。

[11] **kin** /kɪn/ *n.* 亲属；亲戚

[12] **fidgety** /ˈfɪdʒɪti/ *adj.* 坐立不安的

[13] **scrunch up**: 蜷缩

"Don't gap and stretch like that, Huckleberry—why don't you try to behave?" Then she told me all about the bad place[14], and I said I wished I was there[15]. She got mad then, but I didn't mean no harm. All I wanted was to go somewheres; all I wanted was a change, I warn't particular. She said it was wicked to say what I said; said she wouldn't say it for the whole world; she was going to live so as to go to the good place. Well, I couldn't see no advantage in going where she was going, so I made up my mind I wouldn't try for it. But I never said so, because it would only make trouble, and wouldn't do no good.

(7) Now she had got a start, and she went on and told me all about the good place. She said all a body would have to do there was to go around all day long with a harp[16] and sing, forever and ever. So I didn't think much of it. But I never said so. I asked her if she reckoned Tom Sawyer would go there, and she said not by a considerable sight[17]. I was glad about that, because I wanted him and me to be together.[18]

(8) Miss Watson she kept pecking at me, and it got tiresome and lonesome. By and by they fetched the niggers in and had prayers, and then everybody was off to bed. I went up to my room with a piece of candle, and put it on the table. Then I set down in a chair by the window and tried to think of something cheerful, but it warn't no use. I felt so lonesome I most wished I was dead.[19] The stars were shining, and the leaves rustled in the woods ever so mournful; and I heard an owl, away off, who-whooing about somebody that was dead, and a whippowill and a dog crying about somebody that was going to die; and the wind was trying to whisper something to me, and I couldn't make out what it was, and so it made the cold shivers run over me.[20] Then away out in the woods I heard that kind of a sound that a ghost makes when it wants to tell about something that's on its mind and can't make itself understood, and so can't rest easy in its grave, and has to go about that way every night grieving. I got so down-hearted and scared I did wish I had some company. Pretty soon a spider went crawling up my shoulder, and I flipped it off and it lit in the candle; and before I could

[14] bad place: 此处指地狱

[15] 哈克告诉沃森小姐他想去地狱，这让沃森小姐很生气，其实他只是不想继续和沃森小姐待在一起，想换换环境。

[16] harp /hɑːp/ *n.* 竖琴

[17] not by a considerable sight: 看不到

[18] 听说汤姆可能也上不了天堂，这让哈克很高兴，因为他想和汤姆在一起玩。

[19] 心理描写。哈克对新的环境不适应，他觉得孤单。

[20] 天上的星星闪闪发亮，树林里的叶子沙沙直响，听起来总是那么凄凄惨惨；我听见远处一只猫头鹰在叫，莫不是有人要死了；还有一只夜莺和一头野狗在那里乱嚷嚷，想必是有人快要咽气了。微风想要跟我喃喃细语，可我听不清它在诉说些什么，反而使我冷得浑身直哆嗦。（潘庆舲　译）（此句话是由and连接的几个并列句，... that was dead... 和 ... that was going to die... 是两个定语从句。这句话寓情于景，哈克此时感到沮丧和害怕，所以在他看来，周围的景色也是死气沉沉的。）

budge[21] it was all shriveled up. I didn't need anybody to tell me that that was an awful bad sign and would fetch me some bad luck, so I was scared and most shook the clothes off of me. I got up and turned around in my tracks three times and crossed my breast every time; and then I tied up a little lock of my hair with a thread to keep witches away. But I hadn't no confidence. You do that when you've lost a horseshoe that you've found, instead of nailing it up over the door, but I hadn't ever heard anybody say it was any way to keep off bad luck when you'd killed a spider.

(9) I set down again, a-shaking all over, and got out my pipe for a smoke; for the house was all as still as death now, and so the widow wouldn't know. Well, after a long time I heard the clock away off in the town go boom—boom—boom—twelve licks; and all still again—stiller than ever. Pretty soon I heard a twig[22] snap down[23] in the dark amongst the trees—something was a-stirring. I set still and listened. Directly I could just barely hear a "me-yow! me-yow!" down there. That was good! Says I, "me-yow! me-yow!" as soft as I could, and then I put out the light and scrambled[24] out of the window on to the shed. Then I slipped down to the ground and crawled in among the trees, and, sure enough, there was Tom Sawyer waiting for me.

[21] budge /bʌdʒ/ v. 挪动

[22] twig /twɪg/ n. 细枝；嫩枝

[23] snap down:（咔嚓）断裂

[24] scramble /'skræmbl/ v. 攀爬

精华赏析

这一章塑造了三个人物：道格拉斯寡妇、沃森小姐和哈克。道格拉斯寡妇，她是一个很善良的人，同情哈克的遭遇，收养哈克后想要改造哈克，让他成为一个体面的人。她把哈克当自己的儿子看，看到妹妹对哈克要求过于严格时，也会帮哈克说话。在一定程度上，她能够体会哈克适应新环境的艰难。

沃森小姐，她是道格拉斯寡妇的妹妹，对待哈克的态度要更加严格、苛刻些。在哈克看来，沃森小姐总是挑刺、找茬。沃森小姐看哈克总是达不到自己的要求，就大讲特讲地狱的事情，想要吓唬哈克。不过哈克并不在意下地狱，因为那里不会再有沃森小姐的指责。

第一章中的哈克，我们看到了他无拘无束的天性，对于寡妇想要"教化"他这件事情，他能够体会到寡妇的良苦用心,可是天性使然,所谓规矩、体面的生活让他浑身不自在。寡妇提供的舒适生活,让哈克觉得孤单、沮丧,以至于晚上难以入眠。

这一章中最有趣的地方就是,道格拉斯寡妇、沃森小姐和哈克的对话常常是鸡同鸭讲,哈克根本搞不懂她们话里话外的意思。比如寡妇给哈克讲摩西的故事,《圣经》中说埃及王虐待以色列人,下令把以色列人所生的男孩,都扔到河里淹死。国王的女儿发现了躺在纸莎草编织的篮筐里的婴儿摩西,就收养了他。后来摩西率领以色列人逃出埃及。在这里道格拉斯寡妇把自己和古埃及国王的女儿相比。可是哈克根本没听懂,把纸莎草篮筐说成了"纸莎草帮"。当哈克知道摩西老早就死了,觉得根本没有必要管摩西的事情,因为他压根不看重死人。还有哈克在对付沃森小姐的严苛管教时,可谓是"你有你的张良计,我有我的过墙梯",读起来让人忍俊不禁。

在这一章中我们集中探讨一个基本话题:讲故事和叙述。翻看这本书我们可以发现这是哈克在讲一个关于自己和身边人的故事。我们常常被各种小说所吸引,因为好的小说讲的故事总是能引人入胜。我们也许听过这样的说法,人就是讲故事的动物。

"叙述是人类集群的、社会性的活动中的一个重要部分,这个活动可能是人性的根本意识的一个部分。"(赵毅衡,2013a:1)

为了说明叙述是人性根本意识的一部分,我们可以回忆一下自己的梦,在每晚的梦中我们就像是在看一个故事。人类的梦有很强的叙述性。梦叙述是叙述中比较特别的一类,梦中我们自己既是故事的观看者,又是故事的导演,还可能是故事的参与者。虽然自人类之初,梦就伴随着人类,但是想要研究清楚它,并不是那么容易。我们这里不必从学术角度过多地去探讨梦中的叙述者是谁,受述者又是谁等,但是我们却可以清楚地认识到"叙述"的确是人类"根本意识"的一部分。自打人类诞生之初,人类活动、发展就和"叙述"密不可分。所以说,人是讲故事的动物,人也是最擅长讲故事的动物。

叙述是人类把世界"看出一个名堂、说出一个意义"的方式,是人类生存的基本组织方式。(赵毅衡,2013b:1)

从人类的发展史来看,人类用叙述记录过去发生的事情。人类的历史正是通过讲故事的方式得以世代相传。比如中国的史家"二司马",司马迁和司马光,都是讲故事的高手。人类用叙述预见未来可能发生的事情,比如科学预言,科幻小说等。这里特别提一下十九世纪法国科幻小说家凡尔纳,他的作品有《海底两万里》《神秘岛》《地心游记》等。他通过严肃认真的科学研究,比如他研究过空气动力、飞行速度、太空中的失重等,把自己的幻想建立在科学基础上,再通过讲故事的方式付诸笔端。凡尔纳的才能在于,他实际上是在科学技术所容许的范围里,根据科学发展的规律与必然的趋势做出了种种在当时是奇妙无比的构想。而这些构想到了二十世纪几乎全都成了现实。另外,人类通过叙述的方式总结生产、生活中的各种经验、各种规律。古时候师傅带徒弟,用口头叙述的方式将生产技术传授给徒弟,后来这些技术被用文字的方式记录下来,但无论传播媒介怎么变化,都是在用叙述的方式总结人类的生存经验、生产经验和社会文化经验。如此看来人类历史的发展与叙述是密不可分的。

法国哲学家李奥塔（Lyotard,1984）甚至把人类知识分成两大部分：科学知识和叙述知识。

按照叙述的内容是真实的还是虚构的，我们可以把叙述分成两类：一类是虚构性叙述，一类是非虚构性叙述。这本小说《哈克贝利·费恩历险记》就是虚构性叙述。小说、电影、电视剧等都属于虚构性叙述；新闻报道、历史传记等属于非虚构性叙述。

伴随着媒介的发展，人类用来叙述的手段也越来越多，如言语、文字、音乐、姿势、图形、图像等。

叙述与我们的生活息息相关，随着时代的发展，叙述的手段越来越多，它一直伴随着人类社会的发展。试着让自己成为一个讲故事的高手吧，这种能力会给你的生活和工作带来不少便利。

阅读思考

1. 你认为“叙述”对人类重要吗？为什么？请列举出你的理由。

2. 你是一个讲故事的高手吗？你认为怎样才能讲好一个故事？

CHAPTER II

导读：哈克和汤姆趁着夜色逃出了寡妇的花园。汤姆想要戏弄黑人吉姆，把他的帽子摘下来挂在了一根树枝上。可这件事情被吉姆编成了一个神乎其神的故事，吸引了周围不少黑人专门赶过来听他讲故事。哈克、汤姆，还有一群孩子成立了强盗帮，定名为"汤姆·索亚帮"。

（1）WE went tiptoeing along a path amongst the trees back towards the end of the widow's garden, stooping down so as the branches wouldn't scrape our heads. When we was passing by the kitchen I fell over a root and made a noise. We scrouched down and laid still.[1] Miss Watson's big nigger, named Jim, was setting in the kitchen door; we could see him pretty clear, because there was a light behind him. He got up and stretched his neck out about a minute, listening. Then he says:

（2）"Who dah?"

（3）He listened some more; then he come tiptoeing down and stood right between us; we could a touched him, nearly. Well, likely it was minutes and minutes that there warn't a sound, and we all there so close together. There was a place on my ankle that got to itching[2], but I dasn't scratch[3] it; and then my ear begun to itch; and next my back, right between my shoulders. Seemed like I'd die if I couldn't scratch. Well, I've noticed that thing plenty of times since. If you are with the quality, or at a funeral, or trying to go to sleep when you ain't sleepy—if you are anywheres where it won't do for you to scratch, why you will itch all over in upwards of a thousand places. Pretty soon Jim says:

（4）"Say, who is you? Whar is you? Dog my cats ef I didn'

[1] 动作描写。描写两个孩子悄悄溜出花园时的动作，两个人小心翼翼，蹑手蹑脚，生怕弄出声响，可惜还是不小心绊了一跤，惊得两人赶紧蹲下身子，一动不动。（tiptoe /ˈtɪptəʊ/ v. 垫着脚尖走；stoop /stuːp/ v. 俯身；弯腰；scrape /skreɪp/ v. 刮；擦）

[2] itching /ˈɪtʃɪŋ/ v. 发痒

[3] scratch /skrætʃ/ v. 挠；搔

hear sumf'n. Well, I knows what I's gwyne to do: I's gwyne to set down here and listen tell I hears it agin."

(5) So he set down on the ground betwixt[4] me and Tom. He leaned his back up against a tree, and stretched his legs out till one of them most touched one of mine. My nose begun to itch. It itched till the tears come into my eyes. But I dasn't scratch. Then it begun to itch on the inside. Next I got to itching underneath. I didn't know how I was going to set still. This miserableness went on as much as six or seven minutes; but it seemed a sight longer than that. I was itching in eleven different places now. I reckoned I couldn't stand it more'n a minute longer, but I set my teeth hard and got ready to try. Just then Jim begun to breathe heavy; next he begun to snore[5]—and then I was pretty soon comfortable again.

(6) Tom he made a sign to me—kind of a little noise with his mouth—and we went creeping away on our hands and knees. When we was ten foot off Tom whispered to me, and wanted to tie Jim to the tree for fun[6]. But I said no; he might wake and make a dis-turbance[7], and then they'd find out I warn't in. Then Tom said he hadn't got candles enough, and he would slip in the kitchen and get some more. I didn't want him to try. I said Jim might wake up and come. But Tom wanted to resk it; so we slid in there and got three candles, and Tom laid five cents on the table for pay. Then we got out, and I was in a sweat to get away; but nothing would do Tom but he must crawl to where Jim was, on his hands and knees, and play something on him. I waited, and it seemed a good while, everything was so still and lonesome.

(7) As soon as Tom was back we cut along the path, around the garden fence, and by and by fetched up on the steep top of the hill the other side of the house. Tom said he slipped Jim's hat off of his head and hung it on a limb right over him, and Jim stirred a little, but he didn't wake. Afterwards Jim said the witches bewitched him and put him in a trance, and rode him all over the State, and then set him under the trees again, and hung his hat on a limb to show who done it.[8] And next time Jim told

[4] **betwixt** /bɪˈtwɪkst/ *prep.* 在……之间

[5] **snore** /snɔːr/ *v.* 打鼾

[6] 汤姆想要戏弄吉姆。

[7] **disturbance** /dɪˈstɜːrbəns/ *n.* 打扰；干扰

[8] 从此以后，吉姆常说那时他给妖怪迷住了。妖怪先是使他昏迷过去，接着骑在他背上走遍全州，最后才把他挪到那棵大树底下，再把他的帽子拴到树枝上，让他知道是谁开的玩笑。（吉姆把汤姆捉弄他的事情编成一个故事。吉姆是个想象力丰富的人。）（trance /trɑːns/ *n.* 昏睡状态）

it he said they rode him down to New Orleans; and, after that, every time he told it he spread it more and more, till by and by he said they rode him all over the world, and tired him most to death, and his back was all over saddle-boils. Jim was monstrous proud about it, and he got so he wouldn't hardly notice the other niggers. Niggers would come miles to hear Jim tell about it, and he was more looked up to than any nigger in that country.[9] Strange niggers would stand with their mouths open and look him all over, same as if he was a wonder. Niggers is always talking about witches in the dark by the kitchen fire; but whenever one was talking and letting on to know all about such things, Jim would happen in and say, "Hm! What you know 'bout witches?" and that nigger was corked up[10] and had to take a back seat. Jim always kept that five-center piece round his neck with a string, and said it was a charm the devil give to him with his own hands, and told him he could cure anybody with it and fetch witches whenever he wanted to just by saying something to it; but he never told what it was he said to it. Niggers would come from all around there and give Jim anything they had, just for a sight of that five-center piece; but they wouldn't touch it, because the devil had had his hands on it. Jim was most ruined for a servant, because he got stuck up on account of having seen the devil and been rode by witches.

(8) Well, when Tom and me got to the edge of the hilltop we looked away down into the village and could see three or four lights twinkling, where there was sick folks, maybe; and the stars over us was sparkling ever so fine; and down by the village was the river, a whole mile broad, and awful still and grand[11]. We went down the hill and found Jo Harper and Ben Rogers, and two or three more of the boys, hid in the old tanyard[12]. So we unhitched[13] a skiff[14] and pulled down the river two mile and a half, to the big scar on the hillside, and went ashore.

(9) We went to a clump of bushes, and Tom made everybody swear to keep the secret, and then showed them a hole in the hill, right in the thickest part of the bushes. Then we lit the candles, and crawled in on our hands and knees. We

[9] 吉姆对这件事感到很自豪，他觉得自己很了不起。许多黑人从好几英里以外赶来听吉姆的故事，他们很钦佩吉姆。这里可以看出吉姆在才智上优于其他黑奴，在心理地位上他也高于其他黑奴。

[10] cork up: 封堵；封锁

[11] grand /grænd/ *adj.* 壮丽的；宏伟的

[12] tanyard /'tænjɑːd/ *n.* 制革厂

[13] unhitch /ʌn'hɪtʃ/ *v.* 解开；卸掉

[14] skiff /skɪf/ *n.* 小艇

went about two hundred yards, and then the cave opened up. Tom poked about amongst the passages, and pretty soon ducked under a wall where you wouldn't a noticed that there was a hole. We went along a narrow place and got into a kind of room, all damp and sweaty and cold, and there we stopped. Tom says:

(10) "Now, we'll start this band of robbers and call it Tom Sawyer's Gang.[15] Everybody that wants to join has got to take an oath[16], and write his name in blood."

(11) Everybody was willing. So Tom got out a sheet of paper that he had wrote the oath on, and read it. It swore every boy to stick to the band, and never tell any of the secrets; and if anybody done anything to any boy in the band, whichever boy was ordered to kill that person and his family must do it, and he mustn't eat and he mustn't sleep till he had killed them and hacked a cross in their breasts, which was the sign of the band. And nobody that didn't belong to the band could use that mark, and if he did he must be sued[17]; and if he done it again he must be killed. And if anybody that belonged to the band told the secrets, he must have his throat cut, and then have his carcass[18] burnt up and the ashes scattered all around, and his name blotted off of the list with blood and never mentioned again by the gang, but have a curse put on it and be forgot forever.

(12) Everybody said it was a real beautiful oath, and asked Tom if he got it out of his own head. He said, some of it, but the rest was out of pirate-books and robber-books[19], and every gang that was high-toned had it.

(13) Some thought it would be good to kill the families of boys that told the secrets. Tom said it was a good idea, so he took a pencil and wrote it in. Then Ben Rogers says:

(14) "Here's Huck Finn, he hain't got no family; what you going to do 'bout him?"

(15) "Well, hain't he got a father?" says Tom Sawyer.

(16) "Yes, he's got a father, but you can't never find him these days. He used to lay drunk with the hogs in the tanyard, but he hain't been seen in these parts for a year or more."

(17) They talked it over, and they was going to rule

[15] 孩子们成立了强盗帮，定名为汤姆·索亚帮。

[16] oath /əʊθ/ *n.* 宣誓；誓言

[17] sue /suː/ *v.* 控告

[18] carcass /ˈkaːkəs/ *n.* 尸体

[19] 这里指的是英国文学名著《金银岛》《罗宾汉》等。汤姆爱看书，这里的誓言多半是他从书里抄来的。

me out[20], because they said every boy must have a family or somebody to kill, or else it wouldn't be fair and square for the others. Well, nobody could think of anything to do—everybody was stumped[21], and set still. I was most ready to cry; but all at once I thought of a way, and so I offered them Miss Watson—they could kill her. Everybody said:

(18) "Oh, she'll do. That's all right. Huck can come in."

(19) Then they all stuck a pin in their fingers to get blood to sign with, and I made my mark on the paper.

(20) "Now," says Ben Rogers, "what's the line of business of this Gang?"

(21) "Nothing only robbery and murder," Tom said.

(22) "But who are we going to rob?—houses, or cattle, or—"

(23) "Stuff! stealing cattle and such things ain't robbery; it's burglary[22]," says Tom Sawyer. "We ain't burglars. That ain't no sort of style. We are highwaymen. We stop stages and carriages on the road, with masks on, and kill the people and take their watches and money."

(24) "Must we always kill the people?"

(25) "Oh, certainly. It's best. Some authorities think different, but mostly it's considered best to kill them—except some that you bring to the cave here, and keep them till they're ransomed[23]."

(26) "Ransomed? What's that?"

(27) "I don't know. But that's what they do. I've seen it in books; and so of course that's what we've got to do."

(28) "But how can we do it if we don't know what it is?"

(29) "Why, blame it all, we've *got* to do it. Don't I tell you it's in the books? Do you want to go to doing different from what's in the books, and get things all muddled up?"

(30) "Oh, that's all very fine to *say*, Tom Sawyer, but how in the nation are these fellows going to be ransomed if we don't know how to do it to them?—that's the thing I want to get at. Now, what do you reckon it is?"

(31) "Well, I don't know. But per'aps if we keep them till

[20] **rule out**: 排除

[21] **stump** /stʌmp/ *v.* 难倒

[22] **burglary** /ˈbɜːgləri/ *n.* 入室偷盗罪

[23] **ransom** /ˈrænsəm/ *v.*(为某人)交付赎金

they're ransomed, it means that we keep them till they're dead."

(32) "Now, that's something LIKE. That'll answer. Why couldn't you said that before? We'll keep them till they're ransomed to death; and a bothersome lot they'll be, too—eating up everything, and always trying to get loose."

(33) "How you talk, Ben Rogers. How can they get loose when there's a guard over them, ready to shoot them down if they move a peg[24]?"

(34) "A guard! Well, that *is* good. So somebody's got to set up all night and never get any sleep, just so as to watch them. I think that's foolishness. Why can't a body take a club and ransom them as soon as they get here?"

(35) "Because it ain't in the books so—that's why. Now, Ben Rogers, do you want to do things regular, or don't you?—that's the idea. Don't you reckon that the people that made the books knows what's the correct thing to do? Do you reckon *you* can learn 'em anything? Not by a good deal. No, sir, we'll just go on and ransom them in the regular way."

(36) "All right. I don't mind; but I say it's a fool way, anyhow. Say, do we kill the women, too?"

(37) "Well, Ben Rogers, if I was as ignorant as you I wouldn't let on. Kill the women? No; nobody ever saw anything in the books like that. You fetch them to the cave, and you're always as polite as pie to them; and by and by they fall in love with you, and never want to go home any more."

(38) "Well, if that's the way I'm agreed, but I don't take no stock in it. Mighty soon we'll have the cave so cluttered up[25] with women, and fellows waiting to be ransomed, that there won't be no place for the robbers. But go ahead, I ain't got nothing to say."

(39) Little Tommy Barnes was asleep now, and when they waked him up he was scared, and cried, and said he wanted to go home to his ma, and didn't want to be a robber any more.

(40) So they all made fun of him, and called him cry-baby, and that made him mad, and he said he would go straight and tell all the secrets. But Tom give him five cents to keep quiet,

[24] move a peg: 跨出一条腿；走动

[25] clutter up: 挤满

and said we would all go home and meet next week, and rob somebody and kill some people.

(41) Ben Rogers said he couldn't get out much, only Sundays, and so he wanted to begin next Sunday; but all the boys said it would be wicked to do it on Sunday, and that settled the thing. They agreed to get together and fix a day as soon as they could, and then we elected Tom Sawyer first captain and Jo Harper second captain of the Gang, and so started home.

(42) I clumb up the shed and crept into my window just before day was breaking. My new clothes was all greased up and clayey, and I was dog-tired.[26]

[26] 我的新衣服沾满了油污和泥巴,我实在是累坏了。

精华赏析

上一章中我们研究了什么是"叙述",以及"叙述"对人类发展的重要性。这一章我们重点研究一下在叙述学中从"视点"到"叙述方位"的术语变化,以及这本小说所采用的叙述方位。

叙述角度问题是较早引起叙述批评家关注的一个话题。在二十世纪初关于这个话题的讨论异常热烈,最流行的术语为"视点"(point of view),美国批评家玻西·勒博克在他 1921 年出版的《小说技法》中提出了这个术语。后来的学者认为此术语不够准确,不少批评家都在寻找更为准确、合适的术语。

法国的让·布庸建议用"视界"(vision);美国新批评派的阿伦·推特建议用"观察点"(post of observation),另两位新批评派克利昂斯·布鲁克斯和罗伯特·潘·沃伦建议用"叙述焦点";法国结构主义者托多诺夫建议用"方位"(aspect);热奈特认为布鲁克斯和沃伦的术语"焦点"可用,而改之为"集焦"(focalization)。(赵毅衡,2013a:128)

学者也根据自己的研究给叙述角度做了不同分类。叙述角度分类在不断的研究中变得越来越多,越来越细。但是 1972 年热奈特明确提出了一个引起批评界反思的问题,他认为在各种叙述角度的分类中都混淆了一个概念,即把叙述者身份的各种形态与叙述角度范围的变化相混淆了。实则在叙述的过程中存在两方面的问题:一个是"谁在看",一个是"谁在说"。

这个问题不光是批评界以外的人难以厘清,在很长一段时间里,即使是批评界的专家可能也很难分清。马登(Madden)在他的著作中就曾这样写道:"作家控制材料,努力使其视角统一。他小心地不让人物知道他不可能知道的东西,同时也不让他的人物使用他不可能用的语汇。”（Madden，1980：112）我们来仔细分析一下这段话的错误在哪里。人物无法知道他不可能知道的事情，这是“谁在看”的问题，比如故事中在客厅中的客人是无法知道此时正在卧室中发生的事情，所以前半句没有问题；问题出现在后半句，“不让他的人物使用他不可能用的语汇”，这就不对了，故事的叙述语言是属于叙述者的，并不完全受人物的控制。后半句讨论的是“谁在说”的问题，小说的叙述语言始终属于叙述者。“叙述角度是事件被感知的具体方式，叙述者却是叙述信息的发送者。”（赵毅衡，2013a：130）

当然在不少小说中“谁在看”和“谁在说”这里的“谁”可能是重合的，但有时则不然。比如弗兰西斯·伯纳特的小说《秘密花园》中的主人公是一个九岁小女孩玛丽，她是一个粗鲁野蛮的孩子，从她六岁起，来教她的家庭教师被她一个个气走，差点她可能连字母都不认识。一来玛丽年纪小文化程度不高，二来她平常说话粗鲁无礼。小说中在看的那个人就是玛丽。她在见到迪肯时有这样一段文字：“当她离他更近一点儿的时候，她发现他身上散发出一种混合着欧石南花、青草和树叶的清新气息，仿佛他就是这些植物做成的。她非常喜欢这种气味。”（邱晓亮 译，2015：90）如果用玛丽的语言，应该是这样的“瞧他那乱蓬蓬的头发，一身的补丁，还有那滑稽的脸，哪跑来的野孩子，不过他身上的味道倒是挺好闻的，和花园里花花草草的味道闻起来差不多呢。”

小说中其实有两个人，一个是看的人，这是叙述角度的问题；一个人在说，就是叙述者。赵毅衡（2013c：74）在重新厘清这两者关系后提出了叙述方位的概念，“在叙述加工中，叙述者限制其特权，只讲他所选择的人物所能经验的范围。因此，这是叙述者与人物的联合行动，‘角心’人物提供经验，叙述者提供声音。二者合起来，构成‘叙述方位’的特殊叙述者——人物组合。”赵毅衡（2013a）认为叙述者和叙述角度的配合一共有八种形式，隐身叙述者四种，也就是第三人称叙述者，显身叙述者四种，也就是第一人称叙述者。分别是：隐身叙述者＋全知视角；隐身叙述者＋主要人物视角；隐身叙述者＋次要人物视角；隐身叙述者＋旁观者视角；显身叙述者＋主要人物视角，即“第一人称全知”；显身叙述者＋主要人物视角，即正常的“第一人称”小说；显身叙述者＋次要人物视角，显身叙述者＋绝对旁观人物视角。

《哈克贝利·费恩历险记》采用的是显身叙述者＋主要人物视角。根据上文中“叙述方位”的概念，首先，作者选择了角心人物，那么整个的故事只能从角心人物的角度，讲人物自己经验范围内的事情。《哈克贝利·费恩历险记》是第一人称小说，也就是显身叙述者。从小说中我们直接看到的就是“I”，他就是主人公哈克。哈克来讲这个故事，就只能讲他看到的、他听到的、他想到的、他感受到的。比如在第一章中道格拉斯寡妇晚饭后，搬出书来，给哈克大讲特讲摩西的故事，要是站在道格拉斯寡妇的角度，故事应该是这样的，“我呀，和古埃及国王的女儿一样善良，就像拯救那个要被淹死的摩西一样，我拯救了小哈克，我会用我的爱去改变这个野蛮生长的小男孩，让他洗心革面，焕然一新。瞧瞧我，是多么的善良，多么的无私啊！一个虔诚的基督徒就应该这样做。”可是故事是哈克来讲的，就完全是另一个模样了。在哈克的经验范围内，他是没法理解道格拉斯寡妇的真实用意的。哈克这样说道：我急巴巴要把摩西的身世弄个明白。但过了好久，她才说到摩西老早就死了，那时我就再也不管他摩西不摩西了，因为我压根儿不看重死人的。再比如，寡妇觉得哈克是“迷途的羔羊”，误入歧途，迷失方向，还觉得哈克身上有太多坏习惯，不规矩的地方，穿得破破烂烂，没人照顾甚是可怜。可哈克怎么看这些问题呢，他觉得穿上自己的破衣烂衫才自在、知足，这样那样的规矩让他难以理解，也很难受，甚至不管上天堂，还是下地狱，对哈克来说也是无关痛痒的事情。这些都是叙述者哈克的经验范围，只有他会这么想。

也有学者大力提倡降低小说家的叙述声音，让故事自己上演，增加小说的戏剧性，主张尽量采用小说人物的眼光，客观地展示处于人物观察下的现实，使事物在人物意识屏幕上得到最丰富的投射，以最经济的手段创造最大限度的戏剧张力。

弄清楚了小说中在看的那个人，角心人物，我们再来看看叙述者提供声音的问题。第一人称叙述者很自然地采用人物角度讲故事，马克·吐温在这本小说中已经很好地坚持了人物视角，甚至是在叙述语言上也尽量靠近哈克这个文化程度不高的十三四岁的小孩子。小说中有非常多不规则的用法，比如双重否定句不表示肯定意义，如第一章中 She put me in them new clothes again, and I **couldn't do nothing** but sweat and sweat, and feel all cramped up. 把形容词当副词使用，如 Whenever I got **uncommon tired**, I played hookey. 还有就是该用 be 动词的复数形式却用了单数，如第三章中 I judged I could see that **there was** two Providences. 正是小说这种独特的语言风格，使其最初在美国出版时被不少人批评，认为该小说极端粗俗。但是正是因为坚持了人物视角，那么这些俚俗语言、民间方言反倒成了最符合人物的叙述语言，因此也被更多的人所接受，批评家也逐渐意识到马克·吐温开创了一种新的文学风格。可是即使这样，我们还是能够在小说中找到叙述者控制语言、词汇使用的地方，与人物语言拉开距离的地方，比如在第九章中有一大段描写暴风雨的景色，“Directly it begun to rain, and it rained like all fury, too, and I never see the wind blow so. It was one of these regular summer storms. It would get so dark that it looked all blue-black outside, and lovely; and the rain would thrash along by so thick that the trees off a little ways looked dim and spider-webby; and here would come a blast of wind that would bend the trees down and turn up the pale under-side of the leaves; and then a perfect ripper of a gust would follow along and set the branches to tossing their arms as if they was just wild; and next, when it was just about the bluest and blackest—FST! it was as bright as glory, and you'd have a little glimpse of tree-tops a-plunging about away off yonder in the storm, hundreds of yards further than you could see before; dark as sin again in a second, and now you'd hear the thunder let go with an awful crash, and then go rumbling, grumbling, tumbling, down the sky towards the under side of the world, like rolling empty barrels down stairs—where it's long stairs and they bounce a good deal, you know.” 这段话对暴雨天的描绘细节饱满，生动形象，文中使用了各类修辞手法，明喻、隐喻、押韵、拟人等。这段话所达到的艺术水平就不会是哈克能做到的，调配语言、如何遣词造句的权利是掌握在叙述者手里的。

术语解说

叙述方位：在叙述加工中，叙述者限制其特权，只讲他所选择的人物所能经验的范围。因此，这是叙述者与人物的联合行动，“角心”人物提供经验，叙述者提供声音。二者合起来，构成“叙述方位”的特殊叙述者——人物组合。

阅读思考

1. 在你读过的小说中还见过其他类型的“叙述方位”吗？请举例说明。
2. 你认为《哈克贝利·费恩历险记》为什么选择了哈克作为角心人物？

CHAPTER III

导读:哈克对沃森小姐和寡妇道格拉斯的说教产生怀疑,他发现她们两个人的上帝并不相同。沃森小姐叮嘱哈克天天做祷告,说不管想要什么全都能得到。而寡妇却说人们从祷告中得到的只是"精神礼物"。哈克决定还是相信寡妇的说法,跟着她的上帝走。人们都说哈克的父亲淹死了,哈克不相信,可是也不希望父亲再回来。他们的"海盗"事业发展得不太顺利。

(1) WELL, I got a good going-over in the morning from old Miss Watson on account of my clothes; but the widow she didn't scold, but only cleaned off the grease and clay, and looked so sorry that I thought I would behave awhile[1] if I could. Then Miss Watson she took me in the closet and prayed, but nothing come of it. She told me to pray every day, and whatever I asked for I would get it.[2] But it warn't so. I tried it. Once I got a fish-line, but no hooks. It warn't any good to me without hooks. I tried for the hooks three or four times, but somehow I couldn't make it work. By and by, one day, I asked Miss Watson to try for me, but she said I was a fool. She never told me why, and I couldn't make it out no way.

(2) I set down one time back in the woods, and had a long think about it. I says to myself, if a body can get anything they pray for, why don't Deacon Winn get back the money he lost on pork? Why can't the widow get back her silver snuffbox[3] that was stole? Why can't Miss Watson fat up? No, says I to myself, there ain't nothing in it. I went and told the widow about it, and she said the thing a body could get by praying for it was "spiritual gifts."[4] This was too many for me, but she told me what she meant—I must help other people, and do everything I could

[1] awhile /ə'waɪl/ *adv.* 暂时;片刻

[2] 沃森小姐告诉哈克要每天祈祷,那么想要什么就能得到什么。

[3] snuffbox /'snʌfbɒks/ *n.* 鼻烟盒

[4] 寡妇告诉哈克祈祷只能得到"精神礼物"。

for other people, and look out for them all the time, and never think about myself. This was including Miss Watson, as I took it. I went out in the woods and turned it over in my mind a long time, but I couldn't see no advantage about it—except for the other people; so at last I reckoned I wouldn't worry about it any more, but just let it go. Sometimes the widow would take me one side and talk about Providence in a way to make a body's mouth water[5]; but maybe next day Miss Watson would take hold and knock it all down again. I judged I could see that there was two Providences, and a poor chap would stand considerable show with the widow's Providence, but if Miss Watson's got him there warn't no help for him any more. I thought it all out, and reckoned I would belong to the widow's if he wanted me, though I couldn't make out how he was a-going to be any better off then than what he was before, seeing I was so ignorant, and so kind of low-down and ornery[6].

(3) Pap he hadn't been seen for more than a year, and that was comfortable for me; I didn't want to see him no more. He used to always whale[7] me when he was sober and could get his hands on me; though I used to take to the woods most of the time when he was around. Well, about this time he was found in the river drownded, about twelve mile above town, so people said. They judged it was him, anyway; said this drownded man was just his size, and was ragged[8], and had uncommon long hair, which was all like pap; but they couldn't make nothing out of the face, because it had been in the water so long it warn't much like a face at all. They said he was floating on his back in the water. They took him and buried him on the bank. But I warn't comfortable long, because I happened to think of something. I knowed mighty well that a drownded man don't float on his back, but on his face. So I knowed, then, that this warn't pap, but a woman dressed up in a man's clothes. So I was uncomfortable again. I judged the old man would turn up again by and by, though I wished he wouldn't.

(4) We played robber now and then about a month, and then I resigned. All the boys did. We hadn't robbed nobody,

[5]《圣经·旧约全书·约珥书》第3章第18节里这样写道："In that day the mountains will drip new wine, and the hills will flow with milk; all the ravines of Judah will run with water."（到那日，大山要滴甜酒，小山要流奶子，犹大溪河都有水流。）

[6] ornery /ˈɔːnəri/ *adj.* 脾气不好的

[7] whale /weɪl/ *v.* 打

[8] ragged /ˈrægɪd/ *adj.* 衣衫褴褛的

hadn't killed any people, but only just pretended. We used to hop out[9] of the woods and go charging down on hog-drivers[10] and women in carts taking garden stuff to market, but we never hived[11] any of them. Tom Sawyer called the hogs "ingots," and he called the turnips[12] and stuff "julery," and we would go to the cave and powwow over what we had done, and how many people we had killed and marked. But I couldn't see no profit in it. One time Tom sent a boy to run about town with a blazing stick, which he called a slogan (which was the sign for the Gang to get together), and then he said he had got secret news by his spies that next day a whole parcel of Spanish merchants and rich A-rabs was going to camp in Cave Hollow with two hundred elephants, and six hundred camels, and over a thousand "sumter" mules, all loaded down with di'monds, and they didn't have only a guard of four hundred soldiers, and so we would lay in ambuscade, as he called it, and kill the lot and scoop the things.[13] He said we must slick up our swords and guns, and get ready. He never could go after even a turnip-cart but he must have the swords and guns all scoured[14] up for it, though they was only lath[15] and broomsticks, and you might scour at them till you rotted, and then they warn't worth a mouthful of ashes more than what they was before. I didn't believe we could lick such a crowd of Spaniards and A-rabs, but I wanted to see the camels and elephants, so I was on hand next day, Saturday, in the ambuscade; and when we got the word we rushed out of the woods and down the hill. But there warn't no Spaniards and A-rabs, and there warn't no camels nor no elephants. It warn't anything but a Sunday-school picnic, and only a primer-class at that. We busted it up, and chased the children up the hollow; but we never got anything but some doughnuts[16] and jam, though Ben Rogers got a rag doll, and Jo Harper got a hymn-book[17] and a tract[18]; and then the teacher charged in, and made us drop everything and cut. I didn't see no di'monds, and I told Tom Sawyer so. He said there was loads of them there, anyway; and he said there was A-rabs there, too, and elephants and things. I said, why couldn't we see them, then? He said if I warn't so

9 **hop out**: 跳出来

10 **hog-driver**: 放猪倌

11 **hive** /haɪv/ *v.* 从团体中分出,这里是指把其中一个人抓起来

12 **turnip** /ˈtɜːnɪp/ *n.* 芜菁;萝卜

13 有一回,汤姆派一个孩子举着熊熊燃烧的火棍,在城里头到处转悠——他管这火棍叫作"广而告之",这个是强盗帮集合的信号——随后,他说自己接到探子送来的密报,转天有大队人马的西班牙商人和阿拉伯富豪,将在霍洛洞里扎营住宿,跟他们一块随行的有两百头大象、六百匹骆驼、一千匹"拖"(驮)骡,满驮满载都是钻石,可他们总共也只有四百名卫兵。所以嘛,我们不妨打埋伏——用他的话儿说——包管杀上一大批,把所有的东西都抢过来。(潘庆舲 译)(ambuscade: *n.* 埋伏;scoop /skuːp/ *v.* 挖空;拿起;捡起)

14 **scour** /ˈskaʊə(r)/ *v.* 擦亮

15 **lath** /lɑːθ/ *n.* 木板条

16 **doughnut** /ˈdəʊnʌt/ *n.* 炸面圈;圈饼

17 **hymn-book**: 赞美诗集

18 **tract** /trækt/ *n.* 小册子

ignorant, but had read a book called *Don Quixote*[19], I would know without asking. He said it was all done by enchantment[20]. He said there was hundreds of soldiers there, and elephants and treasure, and so on, but we had enemies which he called magicians; and they had turned the whole thing into an infant Sunday-school, just out of spite[21]. I said, all right; then the thing for us to do was to go for the magicians. Tom Sawyer said I was a numskull[22].

(5) "Why," says he, "a magician could call up a lot of genies[23], and they would hash you up[24] like nothing before you could say Jack Robinson. They are as tall as a tree and as big around as a church.[25]"

(6) "Well," I says, "s'pose we got some genies to help US—can't we lick[26] the other crowd then?"

(7) "How you going to get them?"

(8) "I don't know. How do *they* get them?"

(9) "Why, they rub an old tin lamp or an iron ring, and then the genies come tearing in, with the thunder and lightning a-ripping around and the smoke a-rolling, and everything they're told to do they up and do it[27]. They don't think nothing of pulling a shot-tower up by the roots, and belting[28] a Sunday-school superintendent[29] over the head with it—or any other man."

(10) "Who makes them tear around so?"

(11) "Why, whoever rubs the lamp or the ring. They belong to whoever rubs the lamp or the ring, and they've got to do whatever he says. If he tells them to build a palace forty miles long out of di'monds, and fill it full of chewing-gum, or whatever you want, and fetch an emperor's daughter from China for you to marry, they've got to do it—and they've got to do it before sun-up next morning, too. And more: they've got to waltz[30] that palace around over the country wherever you want it, you understand."

(12) "Well," says I, "I think they are a pack of flat-heads for not keeping the palace themselves 'stead of fooling them away like that. And what's more—if I was one of them I would see a man in Jericho before I would drop my business and come

[19] **Don Quixote**:《堂吉诃德》，西班牙作家塞万提斯的代表作。和其他孩子比较起来，汤姆读过不少书，这是其中的一本。

[20] **enchantment** /ɪnˈtʃɑːntmənt/ *n.* 着魔

[21] **just out of spite**：出于怨恨；出于泄愤

[22] **numskull** /ˈnʌmskʌl/ *n.* 白痴；傻瓜

[23] **genies** /ˈdʒiːniz/ *n.*（阿拉伯故事中，尤指瓶子或灯里的）精灵

[24] **hash up**: 切细

[25] 明喻（simile）。妖怪像树一样高，像教堂一样大。

[26] **lick** /lɪk/ *v.* 击败

[27] 源自《天方夜谭》中的《阿拉丁神灯》

[28] **belt** /belt/ *v.* 猛击；狠打

[29] **superintendent** /ˌsuːpərɪnˈtendənt/ *n.* 监督人

[30] **waltz** /wɔːls/ *v.* 轻而易举地举起；大摇大摆地走

to him for the rubbing of an old tin lamp."

(13) "How you talk, Huck Finn. Why, you'd *have* to come when he rubbed it, whether you wanted to or not."

(14) "What! and I as high as a tree and as big as a church? All right, then; I *would* come; but I lay I'd make that man climb the highest tree there was in the country."

(15) "Shucks, it ain't no use to talk to you, Huck Finn. You don't seem to know anything, somehow—perfect saphead[31]."

(16) I thought all this over for two or three days, and then I reckoned I would see if there was anything in it. I got an old tin lamp and an iron ring, and went out in the woods and rubbed and rubbed till I sweat like an Injun, calculating to build a palace and sell it; but it warn't no use, none of the genies come.[32] So then I judged that all that stuff was only just one of Tom Sawyer's lies. I reckoned he believed in the A-rabs and the elephants, but as for me I think different. It had all the marks of a Sunday-school.

[31] saphead *n.* 笨蛋

[32] 为了验证汤姆说的话，哈克找了一盏旧的锡铁皮灯，跑到林子里，擦了一遍又一遍，看会不会有妖怪从灯里出来。哈克是一个行动派、实践派。

精华赏析

哈克发现沃森小姐和寡妇对上帝有不同的解释，这让哈克很困惑。沃森小姐告诉哈克要天天祷告，那么不管要什么都能得到。而寡妇却说从祷告中得到的只是"精神礼物"。寡妇告诉哈克要帮助别人，始终关心照顾他们，不要计较自己的得失。在哈克看来，如果相信寡妇的上帝，那么穷小子也是有希望的。哈克最终选择跟着寡妇的上帝走，我们可以看到哈克本质上是善良的，他希望成为一个善良的人，也愿意去帮助别人。在后文中哈克主动去帮助逃奴吉姆，追随了心中的上帝，践行了他奉行的善良。

在这一章中，哈克、汤姆还有一群伙伴在一起玩强盗的游戏。汤姆显然是一个想象力丰富的孩子，他总是有很多点子。汤姆告诉大家会有商人带着很多财宝经过，可是哈克说他什么也没看见。汤姆告诉哈克，他没有看见阿拉伯人、大象、金银财宝，是因为这一切都被施了魔法。汤姆提到了《堂吉诃德》这本书，还给哈克讲了《阿拉丁神灯》的故事。汤姆丰富的想象力和满脑子的鬼主意全来自他读过的各种书籍。

汤姆告诉哈克不断摩擦铁皮灯，就会在电闪雷鸣之下从灯里钻出一个巨大的妖怪，它可以帮主人实现任何愿望。哈克不相信，他觉得妖怪这么神通广大为什么要听命于它的主人。不过为了验证汤姆的话，哈克思考了两三天，决定亲自试验一下。他找来一个旧的锡铁皮灯,使劲儿地摩擦,看会不会有妖怪出来,他要让妖怪帮他变出一座宫殿来。可是哈克辛苦地摩擦,直到汗流浃背,最终还是一无所获。哈克是一个实践派,他不轻易相信汤姆说的话,而要用实践去检验它。

我们继续来讲和叙述有关的问题。在叙述学中我们有一个概念叫"隐含作者",这一章中我们重点探讨一下"作者"和"隐含作者"的区别。

隐含作者是从文本分析中能够归纳推理出来的作者或者说人格,并不是我们认为的马克·吐温这个真实的人。从叙述学角度来看,我们从来不探讨和分析作者本人,因为作者的生平简历仅从文本中是无法获知的。在漫长的历史长河中,我们对一些作品的作者所知甚少,比如《荷马史诗》据传是古希腊的盲诗人荷马创作的,荷马究竟是何许人也,有怎样的经历,是什么样的性格,我们知道的很少。再者,还有一些作品如《水浒传》是历代改写编辑者的集体创作,其作者很难定位到一个人身上。这些都为我们研究作者带来了很大困难。

所以为了方便分析,叙述学提出了"隐含作者"这个概念。"隐含作者"是通过文本分析,可触可感的那个人,也就是我们前面说的从文本中归纳推理出来的人格。"隐含作者"的人格在文本中是清晰可见的,因为通过对文本的分析,我们可以得出"隐含作者"对待人和事的态度和观点。

让我们给"隐含作者"一个更准确的定义,"与叙述分析有关的所谓作者,是从叙述中归纳、推断出来的一个人格,这个人格代表了一系列社会文化形态、个人心理以及文学观念的价值,叙述分析的作者就是这些道德的、习俗的、心理的、审美的价值与观念之集合。整个作品就靠这个集合作为意识之源。"(赵毅衡,2013a:11)

为了证明作者和隐含作者不是同一个人,我们来看一个例子,比如曹操的诗歌《观沧海》:"东临碣石,以观沧海。水何澹澹,山岛竦峙。树木丛生,百草丰茂。秋风萧瑟,洪波涌起。日月之行,若出其中。星汉灿烂,若出其里。幸甚至哉,歌以咏志。"诗中描绘的都是雄伟壮丽的景色,表达了诗人的雄心壮志和宽广的胸怀。这些都是从诗歌中我们归纳分析出的人格。诗中看到的这个人是一个心胸宽广的人。他是曹操本人吗?可能不是,曹操有着多疑、凶狠的一面。《三国志·魏书·武帝纪》中记载曹操曾说"宁我负人,毋人负我"。曹操在逃亡的路上遇到吕伯奢,此人好心请曹操到家中休息,可是曹操只是听到磨刀声音,就误杀了自己父亲结义兄弟吕伯奢一家八口。好不残忍!

我们再从另一个角度来证实作者和隐含作者是不一样的。同一个作者可能在不同的作品中展示出不同的人格。换句话说,不同作品可以看到不同的隐含作者,实际上这些作品却是出自同一个作者。比如白居易的讽喻诗《卖炭翁》:"卖炭翁,伐薪烧炭南山中。满面尘灰烟火色,两鬓苍苍十指黑。卖炭得钱何所营?身上衣裳口中食。可怜身上衣正单,心忧炭贱愿天寒。夜来城外一尺雪,晓驾炭车辗冰辙。牛困人饥日已高,市南门外泥中歇。翩翩两骑来是谁?黄衣使者白衫儿。手把文书口称敕,回车叱牛牵向北。一车炭,千余斤,宫使驱将惜不得。半匹红绡一丈绫,系向牛头充炭直。"诗中悲伤地描绘了卖炭翁辛苦、贫困、艰辛的生活,批判了官家强取豪夺的残暴与罪恶。诗中的隐含作者针砭时弊,同情底层劳动人民,抨击鞭挞统治者的罪恶行径。这里的隐含作者一身浩然正气,是个敢为人先,为民请愿的真丈夫！而白居易的闲适诗则完全不同，比如这首《大林寺桃花》：“人间四月芳菲尽，山寺桃花始盛开。长恨春归无觅处，不知转入此中来。”诗中描写的春就像一个调皮的小孩子，在和人捉迷藏。本以为春已逝去，没想到躲到了山上的寺院里。从诗中我们看到的隐含作者平淡自然，快活悠闲，富有生活情趣。

术语解说

隐含作者：与叙述分析有关的所谓作者，是从叙述中归纳、推断出来的一个人格，这个人格代表了一系列社会文化形态、个人心理以及文学观念的价值，叙述分析的作者就是这些道德的、习俗的、心理的、审美的价值与观念之集合。整个作品就靠这个集合作为意识之源。

阅读思考

1. 结合你读过的文学作品，谈谈你对隐含作者和作者的理解。
2. 《哈克贝利·费恩历险记》中的隐含作者有什么样的人格？

CHAPTER IV

导读：哈克对学习不感兴趣。一天早上哈克在吃早餐的时候，把盐瓶子碰翻了，触了霉头。哈克在路上发现了奇怪的踪迹，于是跑到撒切尔法官家里，要把存在法官那的所有钱全都送给法官。哈克又去找吉姆帮自己占卜。

(1) WELL, three or four months run along, and it was well into the winter now. I had been to school most all the time and could spell and read and write just a little, and could say the multiplication table[1] up to six times seven is thirty-five, and I don't reckon I could ever get any further than that if I was to live forever. I don't take no stock[2] in mathematics, anyway.

(2) At first I hated the school, but by and by I got so I could stand it. Whenever I got uncommon tired I played hookey[3], and the hiding I got next day done me good and cheered me up. So the longer I went to school the easier it got to be. I was getting sort of used to the widow's ways, too, and they warn't so raspy on me. Living in a house and sleeping in a bed pulled on me pretty tight mostly, but before the cold weather I used to slide out and sleep in the woods sometimes, and so that was a rest to me. I liked the old ways best, but I was getting so I liked the new ones, too, a little bit.[4] The widow said I was coming along slow but sure, and doing very satisfactory. She said she warn't ashamed of me.

(3) One morning I happened to turn over the salt-cellar at breakfast[5]. I reached for some of it as quick as I could to throw over my left shoulder and keep off the bad luck, but Miss Watson was in ahead of me, and crossed me off. She says, "Take your hands away, Huckleberry; what a mess you are always making!"

[1] multiplication table: 乘法表

[2] take no stock: 对某事没有信心

[3] play hookey: 逃学

[4] 从这里我们可以看出哈克虽然还是怀念曾经无拘无束的日子，但是也开始慢慢去适应新生活。

[5] 古代盐是特别稀有、贵重之物，是保存易腐烂食品的物质之一。罗马帝国统治时期，盐也用于支付士兵的薪水。正因为盐如此昂贵，打翻盐瓶自然被认为是不好的行为。这里哈克打翻了盐瓶子，觉得会触霉头。

The widow put in a good word for me, but that warn't going to keep off the bad luck, I knowed that well enough. I started out, after breakfast, feeling worried and shaky, and wondering where it was going to fall on me, and what it was going to be. There is ways to keep off some kinds of bad luck, but this wasn't one of them kind; so I never tried to do anything, but just poked along low-spirited and on the watch-out.

(4) I went down to the front garden and clumb over the stile where you go through the high board fence. There was an inch of new snow on the ground, and I seen somebody's tracks. They had come up from the quarry and stood around the stile a while, and then went on around the garden fence. It was funny they hadn't come in, after standing around[6] so. I couldn't make it out. It was very curious, somehow. I was going to follow around, but I stooped down to look at the tracks first. I didn't notice anything at first, but next I did. There was a cross in the left boot-heel made with big nails, to keep off the devil.

[6] 这句话中的standing为现在分词,其逻辑主语是they。

(5) I was up in a second and shinning down the hill. I looked over my shoulder every now and then, but I didn't see nobody. I was at Judge Thatcher's as quick as I could get there. He said:

(6) "Why, my boy, you are all out of breath[7]. Did you come for your interest?"

[7] out of breath: 上气不接下气

(7) "No, sir," I says; "is there some for me?"

(8) "Oh, yes, a half-yearly is in last night—over a hundred and fifty dollars. Quite a fortune for you. You had better let me invest it along with your six thousand, because if you take it you'll spend it."

(9) "No, sir," I says, "I don't want to spend it. I don't want it at all—nor the six thousand, nuther. I want you to take it; I want to give it to you—the six thousand and all."[8]

[8] 哈克发现了奇怪的踪迹,所以要把所有钱都送给法官。后文我们会明白哈克为什么要这么做。

(10) He looked surprised. He couldn't seem to make it out. He says:

(11) "Why, what can you mean, my boy?"

(12) I says, "Don't you ask me no questions about it, please. You'll take it—won't you?"

(13) He says:

(14) "Well, I'm puzzled. Is something the matter?"

(15) "Please take it," says I, "and don't ask me nothing—then I won't have to tell no lies."

(16) He studied a while, and then he says:

(17) "Oho-o! I think I see. You want to *sell* all your property to me—not give it. That's the correct idea."

(18) Then he wrote something on a paper and read it over, and says:

(19) "There; you see it says 'for a consideration.' That means I have bought it of you and paid you for it. Here's a dollar for you. Now you sign it."

(20) So I signed it, and left.

(21) Miss Watson's nigger, Jim, had a hair-ball as big as your fist, which had been took out of the fourth stomach of an ox, and he used to do magic with it.[9] He said there was a spirit inside of it, and it knowed everything. So I went to him that night and told him pap was here again, for I found his tracks in the snow.[10] What I wanted to know was, what he was going to do, and was he going to stay? Jim got out his hair-ball and said something over it, and then he held it up and dropped it on the floor. It fell pretty solid, and only rolled about an inch. Jim tried it again, and then another time, and it acted just the same. Jim got down on his knees, and put his ear against it and listened. But it warn't no use; he said it wouldn't talk. He said sometimes it wouldn't talk without money. I told him I had an old slick counterfeit[11] quarter that warn't no good because the brass showed through the silver a little, and it wouldn't pass nohow, even if the brass didn't show, because it was so slick it felt greasy, and so that would tell on it every time. (I reckoned I wouldn't say nothing about the dollar I got from the judge.) I said it was pretty bad money, but maybe the hair-ball would take it, because maybe it wouldn't know the difference. Jim smelt it and bit it and rubbed it, and said he would manage so the hair-ball would think it was good[12]. He said he would split open a raw Irish potato and stick the quarter in between and keep it

[9] 吉姆有一个像拳头那样大的毛团，他常用它变戏法。用毛团占卜的风俗，来自非洲的伏都教，那是西非的一种民间宗教，现仍流行于海地和其他加勒比海诸岛的黑人中。

[10] 这里我们知道了哈克在雪地里发现奇怪踪迹，就立刻变得紧张不安的原因。因为哈克觉得可能是自己的爸爸回来了。哈克找吉姆占卜，是想知道他爸爸这次回来是想干什么。

[11] **counterfeit** /ˈkaʊntəfɪt/ *adj.* 伪造的；仿造的

[12] 拟人 (personification)

there all night, and next morning you couldn't see no brass, and it wouldn't feel greasy[13] no more, and so anybody in town would take it in a minute, let alone a hair-ball. Well, I knowed a potato would do that before, but I had forgot it.

(22) Jim put the quarter under the hair-ball, and got down and listened again. This time he said the hair-ball was all right. He said it would tell my whole fortune if I wanted it to. I says, go on. So the hair-ball talked to Jim, and Jim told it to me. He says:

(23) "Yo' ole father doan' know yit what he's a-gwyne to do.[14] Sometimes he spec he'll go 'way, en den agin he spec he'll stay. De bes' way is to res' easy en let de ole man take his own way. Dey's two angels hoverin' roun' 'bout him. One uv 'em is white en shiny, en t'other one is black. De white one gits him to go right a little while, den de black one sail in en bust it all up. A body can't tell yit which one gwyne to fetch him at de las'. But you is all right. You gwyne to have considable trouble in yo' life, en considable joy. Sometimes you gwyne to git hurt, en sometimes you gwyne to git sick; but every time you's gwyne to git well agin. Dey's two gals flyin' 'bout you in yo' life. One uv 'em's light en t'other one is dark. One is rich en t'other is po'. You's gwyne to marry de po' one fust en de rich one by en by. You wants to keep 'way fum de water as much as you kin, en don't run no resk, 'kase it's down in de bills dat you's gwyne to git hung."

(24) When I lit my candle and went up to my room that night there sat pap—his own self![15]

13 **greasy** /ˈgriːsi/ *adj.* 油腻的；油污的

14 吉姆使用的是黑人土话。黑人土话无论是在语音、语法还是词汇使用上都很不规范。这和他们受教育程度低下有很大关系。小说中大量使用各类方言，展示了不同人物的不同特点，这是小说的一个重要语言特色。这里的第一句话实际上应该是这样的，"Your old father doesn't know yet what he is going to do."

15 一直让哈克惴惴不安的事情终于发生了。哈克的爸爸回来了，验证了之前会触霉头的预测。

精华赏析

这一章中，从一大早打翻盐瓶子，哈克就一直有种不祥的预感。哈克一直很忧虑，当他发现雪地里的奇怪踪迹，他的这种担心变得更加强烈。于是哈克跑到法官那里要把所有放在法官那的钱全部送给法官。法官刚好从中敲竹杠。后来我们知道了哈克的不祥预感是觉得自己的爸爸可能回来了。哈克把钱送给法官是因为他知道自己的爸爸回来后肯定会问自己要钱。后来哈克还跑去找吉姆帮自己占卜,想知道他爸爸这次回来是什么原因。

在这一章中,我们会觉得吉姆的话不太好懂,因为他使用的是黑人土话。黑人土话中语音、词汇、语法的使用都很不规范。这本小说中,马克·吐温把大量的方言、口语变成了文学语言,他的这种大胆尝试成就了自己独到的艺术特色。

马克·吐温在小说开篇之前的Explanatory中这样写道:"IN this book a number of dialects are used, to wit: the Missouri negro dialect; the extremest form of the backwoods South Western dialect; the ordinary 'Pike County' dialect; and four modified varieties of this last. The shadings have not been done in a haphazard fashion, or by guesswork; but painstakingly, and with the trustworthy guidance and support of personal familiarity with these several forms of speech. I make this explanation for the reason that without it many readers would suppose that all these characters were trying to talk alike and not succeeding."

这部小说里使用了好几种方言:密苏里州的黑人方言;西部边远地区极端俚俗的方言;派克郡的普通方言;还有最末这一种方言的四种变体。这些方言色彩上有细微差别,不是偶尔随意,或凭猜测揣度造成的,而是煞费苦心,以作者个人熟悉这几种专门语言作为可信的指靠所致。

一方面,方言的使用使小说富有生活气息。读到这些地地道道的方言土语,好像吉姆就站在我们眼前。喜欢看电影的人会发现其实不少电影为了追求真实感、幽默感、生活气息和乡土气息,也会使用各种方言对白。比如《十八洞村》《被光抓走的人》等。

另一方面,方言的使用也会使人物特色鲜明。无须作者作任何的解释和说明,我们就可以想象到吉姆的生活境遇。不规范的发音、语法是因为吉姆的受教育程度很低。黑人的生活环境完全可以想象出来了。

再次,马克·吐温把各类方言放进自己的小说中,也使小说有了不同特色。传统的小说,因为其文学作品的身份,一般都要使用标准的书面语以区别于日常生活中的口语,马克·吐温在这本小说中却另辟蹊径,这无疑是一种大胆的尝试。

最后,马克·吐温也在自己的小说中记录了美国地方语言的历史,留下了各类方言曾经存在过的证据。

说到方言,中国也有很多方言。我国现代汉语方言大致可以分为七大方言区:北方方言、吴方言、湘方言、闽方言、粤方言、赣方言、客家方言。现代汉语各方言之间的差异表现在语音、词汇、语法各个方面,其中语音方面尤为突出。我国不仅地域广阔,历史悠久,就连方言也是种类繁多,除了我们说到的七大方言区,每个方言区还有次方言。有些方言差异大到相互之间无法交流的程度,比如北方方言区的人就听不懂闽方言,或是客家方言。这些方言成为了不同民族的身份象征。中国有56个民族,每个民族有自己的方言,自己的服装,自己的传统习俗等。而各个民族和谐相处,共同发展,使我国呈现出了丰富多彩的文化风貌。

阅读思考

1. 你知道自己是属于哪个方言区吗?
2. 你看得懂本章中吉姆说的话吗?请翻译本章中吉姆所说的话。

CHAPTER V

导读：哈克父亲回来后听说儿子去上学，能认字读书，大为光火，说哈克摆架子。他是听说儿子得了一大笔钱才回来的，逼着哈克交出钱。法官和寡妇想让哈克和他的父亲脱离关系，可是新任的法官不了解情况，觉得不能让父子分离。新法官想帮助哈克的父亲洗心革面，重新做人，可是一切都是徒劳。

(1) I *had* shut the door to. Then I turned around. and there he was. I used to be scared of him all the time, he tanned[1] me so much. I reckoned I was scared now, too; but in a minute I see I was mistaken—that is, after the first jolt[2], as you may say, when my breath sort of hitched, he being so unexpected; but right away after I see I warn't scared of him worth bothering about.

(2) He was most fifty, and he looked it. His hair was long and tangled and greasy, and hung down, and you could see his eyes shining through like he was behind vines. It was all black, no gray; so was his long, mixed-up whiskers. There warn't no color in his face, where his face showed; it was white; not like another man's white, but a white to make a body sick, a white to make a body's flesh crawl—a tree-toad white, a fish-belly white. As for his clothes—just rags, that was all. He had one ankle resting on t'other knee; the boot on that foot was busted, and two of his toes stuck through, and he worked them now and then. His hat was laying on the floor—an old black slouch with the top caved in, like a lid.[3]

(3) I stood a-looking at him; he set there a-looking at me, with his chair tilted back a little. I set the candle down. I noticed the window was up; so he had climb in by the shed[4]. He kept a-looking me all over. By and by he says:

[1] **tan** /tæn/ *v.* 晒黑；鞣(革)；硝(皮) [have/tan sb's hide (old-fashioned, informal or humorous) 严惩某人]

[2] **jolt** /dʒəʊlt/ *n.* 摇晃；颠簸；震动

[3] 外貌描写。这段话中我们看到哈克父亲头发油腻，眼神鬼祟，面色苍白，衣服破烂不堪，鞋子开裂等。我们可以推测出哈克父亲的生活处境不是很好，生活贫穷，非常邋遢。因为长期酗酒，可能他的身体状况也不是很好。这段话的外貌描写抓住了人物特点。

[4] **shed** /ʃed/ *n.* 棚屋；简易房

(4) "Starchy clothes[5]—very. You think you're a good deal of a big-bug, *don't* you?"

(5) "Maybe I am, maybe I ain't," I says.

(6) "Don't you give me none o' your lip," says he. "You've put on considerable many frills[6] since I been away. I'll take you down a peg[7] before I get done with you. You're educated, too, they say—can read and write. You think you're better'n your father, now, don't you, because he can't? I'll take it out of you. Who told you you might meddle with[8] such hifalut'n foolishness, hey?—who told you you could?"

(7) "The widow. She told me."

(8) "The widow, hey?—and who told the widow she could put in her shovel about a thing that ain't none of her business?"

(9) "Nobody never told her."

(10) "Well, I'll learn her how to meddle. And looky here—you drop that school, you hear? I'll learn people to bring up a boy to put on airs[9] over his own father and let on to be better'n what *he* is. You lemme catch you fooling around that school again, you hear? Your mother couldn't read, and she couldn't write, nuther, before she died. None of the family couldn't before *They* died. I can't; and here you're a-swelling yourself up[10] like this. I ain't the man to stand it—you hear? Say, lemme hear you read."

(11) I took up a book and begun something about General Washington and the wars. When I'd read about a half a minute, he fetched the book a whack[11] with his hand and knocked it across the house. He says:

(12) "It's so. You can do it. I had my doubts when you told me. Now looky here; you stop that putting on frills. I won't have it. I'll lay for you, my smarty; and if I catch you about that school I'll tan you good. First you know you'll get religion, too. I never see such a son."

(13) He took up a little blue and yaller[12] picture of some cows and a boy, and says:

(14) "What's this?"

(15) "It's something they give me for learning my lessons

[5] starchy clothes: 上过浆的衣服

[6] put on frills: 装腔作势;摆架子

[7] take down a peg: 挫挫锐气

[8] meddle with: 瞎弄;干预

[9] put on airs: 摆架子;装腔作势

[10] swell up: 充满能力;神气活现

[11] whack /wæk/ *n.* 重击

[12] yaller /ˈjælə/ *adj.* 黄色的

good."

(16) He tore it up, and says:

(17) "I'll give you something better—I'll give you a cow-hide[13]."

(18) He set there a-mumbling and a-growling[14] a minute, and then he says:

(19) "*Ain't* you a sweet-scented dandy, though? A bed; and bedclothes; and a look'n'-glass; and a piece of carpet on the floor—and your own father got to sleep with the hogs in the tanyard. I never see such a son. I bet I'll take some o' these frills out o' you before I'm done with you. Why, there ain't no end to your airs—they say you're rich. Hey?—how's that?"

(20) "They lie—that's how."

(21) "Looky here—mind how you talk to me; I'm a-standing about all I can stand now—so don't gimme no sass. I've been in town two days, and I hain't heard nothing but about you bein' rich. I heard about it away down the river, too. That's why I come. You git me that money to-morrow—I want it.[15]"

(22) "I hain't got no money."

(23) "It's a lie. Judge Thatcher's got it. You git it. I want it."

(24) "I hain't got no money, I tell you. You ask Judge Thatcher; he'll tell you the same."

(25) "All right. I'll ask him; and I'll make him pungle[16], too, or I'll know the reason why. Say, how much you got in your pocket? I want it."

(26) "I hain't got only a dollar, and I want that to—"

(27) "It don't make no difference what you want it for—you just shell it out[17]."

(28) He took it and bit it to see if it was good, and then he said he was going down town to get some whisky; said he hadn't had a drink all day. When he had got out on the shed he put his head in again, and cussed[18] me for putting on frills and trying to be better than him; and when I reckoned he was gone he came back and put his head in again, and told me to mind about that school, because he was going to lay for me and lick me if I

[13] cowhide /ˈkaʊhaɪd/ *n.* 牛皮鞭

[14] 这里使用了两个象声词：a-mumbling 形容粗重的喘气；a-growling 嘟囔声，对事物不满意时所发出的声音。

[15] 哈克的父亲说出了自己回来的真实目的，他是听说儿子发了大财，回来要钱的。

[16] pungle /ˈpʌŋgl/ *v.* 付钱

[17] shell out: 为……花费一大笔钱

[18] cuss /kʌs/ *v.* 诅咒；咒骂

didn't drop that.

(29) Next day he was drunk, and he went to Judge Thatcher's and bullyragged[19] him, and tried to make him give up the money; but he couldn't, and then he swore he'd make the law force him.

(30) The judge and the widow went to law to get the court to take me away from him and let one of them be my guardian; but it was a new judge that had just come, and he didn't know the old man; so he said courts mustn't interfere and separate families if they could help it; said he'd druther not take a child away from its father. So Judge Thatcher and the widow had to quit on the business.

(31) That pleased the old man till he couldn't rest. He said he'd cowhide me till I was black and blue if I didn't raise some money for him. I borrowed three dollars from Judge Thatcher, and pap took it and got drunk, and went a-blowing around and cussing and whooping and carrying on; and he kept it up all over town, with a tin pan, till most midnight;[20] then they jailed him, and next day they had him before court, and jailed him again for a week. But *he* said he was satisfied; said he was boss of his son, and he'd make it warm for HIM.

(32) When he got out the new judge said he was a-going to make a man of him. So he took him to his own house, and dressed him up clean and nice, and had him to breakfast and dinner and supper with the family, and was just old pie to him, so to speak. And after supper he talked to him about temperance and such things till the old man cried, and said he'd been a fool, and fooled away his life; but now he was a-going to turn over a new leaf[21] and be a man nobody wouldn't be ashamed of, and he hoped the judge would help him and not look down on him. The judge said he could hug him for them words; so he cried, and his wife she cried again; pap said he'd been a man that had always been misunderstood before, and the judge said he believed it. The old man said that what a man wanted that was down was sympathy, and the judge said it was so; so they cried again. And when it was bedtime the old man rose up and held out his hand,

[19] bullyrag /'bʊlɪræg/ *v.* 威吓；欺凌

[20] 描写哈克父亲喝醉酒后的情形。"老爸拿了钱去买酒，喝得醉醺醺的，就到处乱砍乱骂，乱吵乱闹；他手里还敲着铁皮锅，就这么闹了全镇，一直到深更半夜。"（潘庆舲 译）

[21] turn over a new leaf：重新开始；洗心革面；改过自新

and says:

(33) "Look at it, gentlemen and ladies all; take a-hold of it; shake it. There's a hand that was the hand of a hog; but it ain't so no more; it's the hand of a man that's started in on a new life, and'll die before he'll go back. You mark them words—don't forget I said them. It's a clean hand now; shake it—don't be afeard."

(34) So they shook it, one after the other, all around, and cried. The judge's wife she kissed it. Then the old man he signed a pledge—made his mark. The judge said it was the holiest time on record, or something like that. Then they tucked the old man into a beautiful room, which was the spare room, and in the night some time he got powerful thirsty and clumb out on to the porch-roof and slid down a stanchion and traded his new coat for a jug of forty-rod, and clumb back again and had a good old time; and towards daylight he crawled out again, drunk as a fiddler[22], and rolled off the porch and broke his left arm in two places, and was most froze to death when somebody found him after sun-up. And when they come to look at that spare room they had to take soundings before they could navigate it.[23]

(35) The judge he felt kind of sore. He said he reckoned a body could reform the old man with a shotgun, maybe, but he didn't know no other way.[24]

[22] drunk as a fiddler:酩酊大醉,这里使用了明喻(simile)。

[23] 这句话使用了夸张(hyperbole)和隐喻(metaphor)。这里是说人们走进房间,在确定航线之前要先探测一下。暗指房间里被吐得狼狈不堪。

[24] 法官被眼前的情景气坏了。他说除了拿枪毙了这老头,怕再也没有其他方法了。

精华赏析

这一章中我们讨论一下如何塑造人物。本章生动地塑造了哈克父亲的形象,给人留下了深刻的印象。

塑造人物时,一般我们先描写人物的外貌,使人物可视化。在描写人物外貌时,我们一定要抓住人物的特征,区别于其他人的特征。比如,我们这样描述一个人的外貌,"她留着长长的头发,大大的眼睛,高高的鼻梁……",这样毫无特点的描写,没有人知道我们写的是谁。我们来看看马克·吐温是如何描写哈克父亲的。他抓住了哈克父亲的几个重要特征:油腻的头发,又长又乱的络腮胡子,衣服破烂,脚上的靴子早已开裂,露出了两个脚趾头,头上的帽顶早已经塌下去。这一连串的描写说明他生活困顿。一方面是因为贫穷的生活让他呈现出这样一副状态;而另一方面他自己也是整日游手好闲,生活才变得更加邋遢。再者,作者还强调了他惨白的脸色,"There warn't no color in his face, where his face showed; it was white; not like another man's white, but a white to make a body sick, a white to make a body's flesh crawl—a tree-toad white, a fish-belly white."(一望而知他面无血色,很白,但并不是像别人那种白,他是一种惨白色,看上去让人恶心,浑身起鸡皮疙瘩——是一种既像雨蛙,又像鱼肚皮的白色。)为什么要强调哈克父亲面无血色,脸色惨白呢?我们可以猜测出哈克父亲的身体状况不是很好,后面我们会知道他嗜酒如命,没有规律的生活才会让他看起来很不健康。外貌描写需要饱满的细节,而这些细节一定是要能反映人物特征的细节。

其次,就是人物的语言描写。哈克父亲使用的是不规范的方言,"Don't you give me none o' your lip," says he. "You've put on considerable many frills since I been away. I'll take you down a peg before I get done with you."我们随便找一句就会发现,哈克父亲使用的语言,语音上不规范,语法上也不规范,而且常用一些俚语。这说明他是一个下层人民,没接受过什么教育。在他与哈克的对话中,我们还发现两个问题,其一他反对哈克读书,说自己没读过书,哈克的母亲也没读过书,哈克现在能读书了,神气活现的样子让他很受不了。他警告哈克要是再去学校就会狠狠地揍他。他反对自己的儿子接受教育,一来是他可能觉得读书无用,家里祖祖辈辈的人都没有读过书,也没怎么样;二来我们也明显地看出他对自己儿子的未来一点也不关心,儿子能不能通过读书和学习将来过上更体面的生活完全不是他关心的问题;再者,看到儿子现在比自己强,能读书写字,穿着体面的衣服,他反而心生不满。另一个问题就是他为什么要回来找哈克。这也是通过他和哈克的对话我们才知道的,原来是听说哈克发了一大笔财,他才回来找儿子讨要钱财。在语言描写中,哈克父亲的形象更加清晰了,他是一个完全不关心自己孩子,毫无责任感,冷血无情的父亲。

再次,人物的动作描写在这一章中也很生动。"I borrowed three dollars from Judge Thatcher, and pap took it and got drunk, and went a-blowing around and cussing and whooping and carrying on; and he kept it up all over town, with a tin pan, till most midnight."比如他醉酒后的这一串动作描写,就把他发酒疯的样子写得绘声绘色。再比如,"He took it and bit it to see if it was good, and then he said he was going down town to get some whisky; said he hadn't had a drink all day. When he had got out on the shed he put his head in again, and cussed me for putting on frills and trying to be better than him; and when I reckoned he was gone he come back and put his head in again, and told me to mind about that school, because he was going to lay for me and lick me if I didn't drop that."这一段话,哈克父亲接过哈克给他的钱,先是咬了一下确认钱是真是假,小人物的典型动作跃然纸上;再者他出门爬到了棚屋顶上,也是他习以为常的动作,翻墙爬窗就是他一贯的行径;还有就是几次探头回来警告哈克的动作,这些都使整个描写变得细节饱满。我们在描写人物的时候不是简单地给人物下个定义,比如他行为鬼祟,行为放荡等,而是要用细节去说明他是如何行为鬼祟,如何行事放荡的。这一章给了我们很好的范例,用细节描写支撑起人物来。

最后，作者还叙述了一个典型事件。哈克父亲向新法官保证一定洗心革面，重新做人，又是握手，又是拥抱，当众发誓，哭得眼泪汪汪，很有仪式感的一阵表演之后，当晚就用新外套换了酒喝，把新法官家的漂亮房间吐得一塌糊涂。前后的对照，夸张的描述，使得故事很具有幽默感。

阅读思考

1. 根据本章内容，总结哈克父亲的性格特征。

2. 请写一段话描写一个人物，注意抓住这个人物的特征。

CHAPTER VI

导读：为了从哈克那里拿到钱，哈克的父亲把哈克带到森林中的一个小木屋里，把哈克囚禁了起来，每日毒打哈克。哈克忍无可忍，计划逃跑。在这一章的最后，哈克的父亲发起酒疯来，把哈克吓得不轻。

(1) WELL, pretty soon the old man was up and around again, and then he went for Judge Thatcher in the courts to make him give up that money, and he went for me, too, for not stopping school. He catched me a couple of times and thrashed[1] me, but I went to school just the same, and dodged[2] him or outrun[3] him most of the time. I didn't want to go to school much before, but I reckoned I'd go now to spite pap. That law trial was a slow business—appeared like they warn't ever going to get started on it; so every now and then I'd borrow two or three dollars off of the judge for him, to keep from getting a cowhiding. Every time he got money he got drunk; and every time he got drunk he raised Cain[4] around town; and every time he raised Cain he got jailed.[5] He was just suited—this kind of thing was right in his line.

(2) He got to hanging around the widow's too much and so she told him at last that if he didn't quit using around there she would make trouble for him. Well, *wasn't* he mad? He said he would show who was Huck Finn's boss. So he watched out for me one day in the spring, and catched me, and took me up the river about three mile in a skiff, and crossed over to the Illinois[6] shore where it was woody and there warn't no houses but an old log hut in a place where the timber was so thick you couldn't find it if you didn't know where it was.

[1] thrash /θræʃ/ *v.* 抽打；连续击打

[2] dodge /dɒdʒ/ *v.* 闪开；躲开；避开

[3] outrun /ˌaʊtˈrʌn/ *v.* 跑得比……快（远）

[4] raise Cain: 引起骚乱；闹事

[5] 反复（anadiplosis），强调这样的事情周而复始地发生。每次他拿到钱就会喝醉；每次他喝醉就会满镇子的惹事；而每次他惹了事就会被抓起来。

[6] Illinois: 伊利诺伊州，是一个位于美国中西部的州。其州府是位于该州南部的斯普林菲尔德（Springfield）。

（3）He kept me with him all the time, and I never got a chance to run off. We lived in that old cabin, and he always locked the door and put the key under his head, nights. He had a gun which he had stole, I reckon, and we fished and hunted, and that was what we lived on. Every little while he locked me in and went down to the store, three miles, to the ferry, and traded fish and game for whisky, and fetched it home and got drunk and had a good time, and licked me. The widow she found out where I was by and by, and she sent a man over to try to get hold of me; but pap drove him off with the gun, and it warn't long after that till I was used to being where I was, and liked it—all but the cowhide part.[7]

（4）It was kind of lazy and jolly[8], laying off comfortable all day, smoking and fishing, and no books nor study.[9] Two months or more run along, and my clothes got to be all rags and dirt, and I didn't see how I'd ever got to like it so well at the widow's, where you had to wash, and eat on a plate, and comb up, and go to bed and get up regular, and be forever bothering over a book, and have old Miss Watson pecking at you all the time. I didn't want to go back no more. I had stopped cussing, because the widow didn't like it; but now I took to it again because pap hadn't no objections. It was pretty good times up in the woods there, take it all around.

（5）But by and by pap got too handy with his hick'ry, and I couldn't stand it. I was all over welts[10]. He got to going away so much, too, and locking me in. Once he locked me in and was gone three days. It was dreadful lonesome. I judged he had got drowned, and I wasn't ever going to get out any more. I was scared. I made up my mind I would fix up some way to leave there. I had tried to get out of that cabin many a time, but I couldn't find no way. There warn't a window to it big enough for a dog to get through. I couldn't get up the chimbly; it was too narrow. The door was thick, solid oak slabs[11]. Pap was pretty careful not to leave a knife or anything in the cabin when he was away; I reckon I had hunted the place over as much as a hundred times; well, I was most all the time at it, because it

[7] 这里哈克写到自己遭受毒打，语气显得很轻松。他说自己已经习惯了这里的生活，而且是喜欢，除了挨皮鞭这类事之外。

[8] **jolly** /ˈdʒɒli/ *adj.* 愉快的

[9] 整天游手好闲，抽抽烟，钓钓鱼，不用读书，不动脑筋——这就是地地道道的好逸恶劳。（潘庆舲 译）这段话中哈克说明了自己喜欢现在这种生活的原因。

[10] **welt** /welt/ *n.* 伤痕；红肿

[11] **solid oak slabs**：坚硬牢固的橡木板

was about the only way to put in the time. But this time I found something at last; I found an old rusty wood-saw[12] without any handle; it was laid in between a rafter[13] and the clapboards of the roof. I greased it up[14] and went to work. There was an old horse-blanket nailed against the logs at the far end of the cabin behind the table, to keep the wind from blowing through the chinks[15] and putting the candle out. I got under the table and raised the blanket, and went to work to saw a section of the big bottom log out—big enough to let me through. Well, it was a good long job, but I was getting towards the end of it when I heard pap's gun in the woods. I got rid of the signs of my work, and dropped the blanket and hid my saw, and pretty soon pap come in.

12 rusty wood-saw: 生锈的锯子

13 rafter /ˈrɑːftə(r)/ *n.* 椽子

14 grease up: 加润滑油

15 chink /tʃɪŋk/ *n.* 裂口;缝隙

(6) Pap warn't in a good humor—so he was his natural self. He said he was down town, and everything was going wrong. His lawyer said he reckoned he would win his lawsuit and get the money if they ever got started on the trial; but then there was ways to put it off a long time, and Judge Thatcher knowed how to do it. And he said people allowed there'd be another trial to get me away from him and give me to the widow for my guardian, and they guessed it would win this time. This shook me up[16] considerable, because I didn't want to go back to the widow's any more and be so cramped up[17] and sivilized, as they called it. Then the old man got to cussing, and cussed everything and everybody he could think of, and then cussed them all over again to make sure he hadn't skipped any, and after that he polished off with a kind of a general cuss all round, including a considerable parcel of people which he didn't know the names of, and so called them what's-his-name when he got to them, and went right along with his cussing.

16 shake up: 使受惊

17 cramped up: 局促的

(7) He said he would like to see the widow get me. He said he would watch out, and if they tried to come any such game on him he knowed of a place six or seven mile off to stow me in, where they might hunt till they dropped and they couldn't find me. That made me pretty uneasy again, but only for a minute; I reckoned I wouldn't stay on hand till he got that chance.

(8) The old man made me go to the skiff and fetch the

things he had got. There was a fifty-pound sack of corn meal, and a side of bacon, ammunition[18], and a four-gallon jug of whisky, and an old book and two newspapers for wadding, besides some tow. I toted[19] up a load, and went back and set down on the bow of the skiff to rest. I thought it all over, and I reckoned I would walk off with the gun and some lines, and take to the woods when I run away. I guessed I wouldn't stay in one place, but just tramp[20] right across the country, mostly night times, and hunt and fish to keep alive, and so get so far away that the old man nor the widow couldn't ever find me any more[21]. I judged I would saw out and leave that night if pap got drunk enough, and I reckoned he would. I got so full of it I didn't notice how long I was staying till the old man hollered and asked me whether I was asleep or drownded.

(9) I got the things all up to the cabin, and then it was about dark. While I was cooking supper the old man took a swig[22] or two and got sort of warmed up, and went to ripping again. He had been drunk over in town, and laid in the gutter[23] all night, and he was a sight to look at. A body would a thought he was Adam—he was just all mud.[24] Whenever his liquor begun to work he most always went for the govment, this time he says:

(10) "Call this a govment! why, just look at it and see what it's like.[25] Here's the law a-standing ready to take a man's son away from him—a man's own son, which he had had all the trouble and all the anxiety and all the expense of raising. Yes, just as that man has got that son raised at last, and ready to go to work and begin to do suthin' for HIM and give him a rest, the law up and goes for him. And they call *that* govment! That ain't all, nuther. The law backs that old Judge Thatcher up and helps him to keep me out o' my property. Here's what the law does: The law takes a man worth six thousand dollars and up'ards, and jams him into an old trap of a cabin like this, and lets him go round in clothes that ain't fitten for a hog. They call that govment! A man can't get his rights in a govment like this. Sometimes I've a mighty notion to just leave the country for good and all. Yes, and I *told* 'em so; I told old Thatcher so to his

[18] **ammunition** /ˌæmjuˈnɪʃn/ *n.* 弹药

[19] **tote** /təʊt/ *v.* 携带；搬运

[20] **tramp** /træmp/ *v.*（尤指长时间地）重步行走

[21] 我想我不会一直待在一个地方，我要徒步穿越整个国家，多半是在夜里赶路，我还要打猎、钓鱼维持生计。我要逃得远远的，让老爸和寡妇再也找不到我。

[22] **swig** /swɪɡ/ *n.* 痛饮；大喝

[23] **gutter** /ˈɡʌtə(r)/ *n.* 路旁排水沟；阴沟

[24] 隐喻（metaphor）。这里是说人们觉得哈克的父亲是亚当，因为他浑身上下都是泥巴，而亚当就是上帝用泥土造出来的。

[25] 哈克的父亲常常要抱怨政府。这一段话中他主要在抱怨法律要抢走他的儿子，政府还要把一个本来价值六千多块金币的老头给抓起来。

face. Lots of 'em heard me, and can tell what I said. Says I, for two cents I'd leave the blamed country and never come a-near it agin. Them's the very words. I says look at my hat—if you call it a hat—but the lid raises up and the rest of it goes down till it's below my chin, and then it ain't rightly a hat at all, but more like my head was shoved up through a jint o' stove-pipe. Look at it, says I—such a hat for me to wear—one of the wealthiest men in this town if I could git my rights.

(11) "Oh, yes, this is a wonderful govment, wonderful. Why, looky here. There was a free nigger there from Ohio[26]—a mulatter[27], most as white as a white man. He had the whitest shirt on you ever see, too, and the shiniest hat; and there ain't a man in that town that's got as fine clothes as what he had; and he had a gold watch and chain, and a silver-headed cane—the awfulest old gray-headed nabob in the State. And what do you think? They said he was a p'fessor in a college, and could talk all kinds of languages, and knowed everything. And that ain't the wust. They said he could VOTE when he was at home. Well, that let me out. Thinks I, what is the country a-coming to? It was 'lection day, and I was just about to go and vote myself if I warn't too drunk to get there; but when they told me there was a State in this country where they'd let that nigger vote, I drawed out. I says I'll never vote agin. Them's the very words I said; they all heard me; and the country may rot for all me—I'll never vote agin as long as I live. And to see the cool way of that nigger—why, he wouldn't a give me the road if I hadn't shoved him out o' the way. I says to the people, why ain't this nigger put up at auction and sold?—that's what I want to know. And what do you reckon they said? Why, they said he couldn't be sold till he'd been in the State six months, and he hadn't been there that long yet. There, now—that's a specimen. They call that a govment that can't sell a free nigger till he's been in the State six months. Here's a govment that calls itself a govment, and lets on to be a govment, and thinks it is a govment, and yet's got to set stock-still for six whole months before it can take a hold of a prowling, thieving, infernal, white-shirted free nigger, and—"[28]

[26] Ohio: 俄亥俄州，位于美国东北部，当时那里已经废除了蓄奴制。

[27] mulatter: 穆拉托。专指黑人与白人的混血儿，黑人与高加索人混血的后裔。

[28] 这是一个自命为政府的政府，装扮得像个政府，自以为是个政府，可还得纹丝不动地干等六个月，才能抓住一个到处流窜、贼头狗脑、穷凶极恶、穿白衬衫的自由黑人，而且——（潘庆舲　译）（prowling /'praʊlɪŋ/ *adj.* 图谋不轨的；infernal /ɪn'fɜːnl/ *adj.* 极讨厌的；可恶的）

(12) Pap was agoing on so he never noticed where his old limber[29] legs was taking him to, so he went head over heels over the tub of salt pork and barked both shins, and the rest of his speech was all the hottest kind of language—mostly hove at the nigger and the govment, though he give the tub some, too, all along, here and there. He hopped around the cabin considerable, first on one leg and then on the other, holding first one shin[30] and then the other one, and at last he let out with his left foot all of a sudden and fetched the tub a rattling kick. But it warn't good judgment, because that was the boot that had a couple of his toes leaking out of the front end of it; so now he raised a howl that fairly made a body's hair raise, and down he went in the dirt, and rolled there, and held his toes; and the cussing he done then laid over anything he had ever done previous.[31] He said so his own self afterwards. He had heard old Sowberry Hagan in his best days, and he said it laid over him, too; but I reckon that was sort of piling it on, maybe.

(13) After supper pap took the jug, and said he had enough whisky there for two drunks and one delirium tremens[32]. That was always his word. I judged he would be blind drunk in about an hour, and then I would steal the key, or saw myself out, one or t'other. He drank and drank, and tumbled down on his blankets by and by; but luck didn't run my way. He didn't go sound asleep, but was uneasy. He groaned[33] and moaned[34] and thrashed[35] around this way and that for a long time. At last I got so sleepy I couldn't keep my eyes open all I could do, and so before I knowed what I was about I was sound asleep, and the candle burning.

(14) I don't know how long I was asleep, but all of a sudden there was an awful scream and I was up.[36] There was pap looking wild, and skipping around every which way and yelling about snakes. He said they was crawling up his legs; and then he would give a jump and scream, and say one had bit him on the cheek—but I couldn't see no snakes. He started and run round and round the cabin, hollering "Take him off! take him off! he's biting me on the neck!" I never see a man look so wild in the

[29] limber /ˈlɪmbə(r)/ *adj.* 敏捷的

[30] shin /ʃɪn/ *n.* 颈;颈部

[31] 不过这一招并不高明,因为他脚上穿的靴子,头上已裂开,露出两个脚趾头。因此,他先是怒吼了一阵,简直令人发指,接着,他就干脆躺倒在地,捂住脚趾头在污泥里乱打滚。那时他骂人的话,简直把他早先骂人的话全都盖过去了。(潘庆舲 译)

[32] delirium tremens:(因酒精中毒引起的)震颤性谵妄

[33] groan /grəʊn/ *v.* 呻吟

[34] moan /məʊn/ *v.* 呻吟;抱怨

[35] thrash /θræʃ/ *v.* 连续击打;激烈扭动;翻来覆去

[36] 这一段话以及下文描写哈克父亲发酒疯。几段话中都详细描写了他发酒疯时的动作和语言,特别是动作描写,抓住了这种状态下的人物特点,描写得非常细致。

eyes. Pretty soon he was all fagged out[37], and fell down panting; then he rolled over and over wonderful fast, kicking things every which way, and striking and grabbing at the air with his hands, and screaming and saying there was devils a-hold of him. He wore out by and by, and laid still a while, moaning. Then he laid stiller, and didn't make a sound. I could hear the owls and the wolves away off in the woods, and it seemed terrible still. He was laying over by the corner. By and by he raised up part way and listened, with his head to one side. He says, very low:

(15) "Tramp—tramp—tramp; that's the dead; tramp—tramp—tramp; they're coming after me; but I won't go. Oh, they're here! don't touch me—don't! hands off—they're cold; let go. Oh, let a poor devil alone!"

(16) Then he went down on all fours and crawled off, begging them to let him alone, and he rolled himself up in his blanket and wallowed[38] in under the old pine table, still a-begging; and then he went to crying. I could hear him through the blanket.

(17) By and by he rolled out and jumped up on his feet looking wild, and he see me and went for me. He chased me round and round the place with a clasp-knife, calling me the Angel of Death, and saying he would kill me, and then I couldn't come for him no more. I begged, and told him I was only Huck; but he laughed SUCH a screechy laugh, and roared and cussed, and kept on chasing me up. Once when I turned short and dodged under his arm he made a grab and got me by the jacket between my shoulders, and I thought I was gone; but I slid out of the jacket quick as lightning,[39] and saved myself. Pretty soon he was all tired out, and dropped down with his back against the door, and said he would rest a minute and then kill me[40]. He put his knife under him, and said he would sleep and get strong, and then he would see who was who.

(18) So he dozed off pretty soon. By and by I got the old split-bottom chair and clumb up as easy as I could, not to make any noise, and got down the gun. I slipped the ramrod down it to make sure it was loaded, then I laid it across the turnip barrel,

[37] **fagged out**: 筋疲力尽;累得要死

[38] **wallow** /'wɒləʊ/ *v.* 打滚;翻滚

[39] 明喻(simile)。我像闪电一样,以迅雷不及掩耳之势从夹克衫里窜了出来。

[40] 哈克的父亲发酒疯,差点杀了哈克,这让哈克感到后怕。

pointing towards pap, and set down behind it to wait for him to stir. And how slow and still the time did drag along.[41]

[41] 感叹句加强调句。感叹并强调时间过得很慢,此时哈克面对随时都会发起疯来的父亲,和他待在一起简直是度日如年。

精华赏析

这一章中哈克和自己的父亲在一起短暂地生活了一段时间。我们看到哈克父亲对这个儿子是不管不顾,比如他怕哈克逃跑,就把他锁在树林深处的一个小屋子里,自己却老是往外跑。有一次可能是喝醉闹事,三天三夜没回来,他完全不关心被独自锁在屋子里的儿子的安危。他常常毒打儿子,哈克身上经常是伤痕累累。有一次喝醉发酒疯,居然拿着小刀满屋子追哈克,差点杀了哈克。这些都坚定了哈克逃离父亲掌控的决心。

这一章从第十段一直到结尾,在一个特殊场景下重点描写了哈克父亲的语言和动作。哈克父亲喝醉后说话常常是大喊大闹、骂骂咧咧,作者用了不少词语表现哈克父亲这种状态下的语言特征,比如 raise a howl, cuss, groan, moan, an awful scream, holler, call, roar, yell 等。还有就是哈克父亲醉酒时踢打翻滚的动作,比如 roll, tumble down, thrash, crawl up, give a jump, run round and round, fall down panting, kick, strike and grab at the air, wallow, chase round and round, drop down 等。这些不断变化的词语,生动地再现了哈克父亲酒醉发疯时的样子。

在这一章中我们探讨一下如何让语言变得丰富起来。在语言上有两个轴:一个是组合轴,一个是聚合轴。组合轴是连接关系,聚合轴是替换关系。为什么有些作品中的描写生动多姿、富有变化,而有些作品中的描写则单调乏味呢?我们用一个简单的例子来说明这两个轴在文学作品描写中所起到的作用吧。

我们走进两间装修好的房子里,是不是一眼就能辨别出哪家房子的主人更富裕呢?大家一定觉得这是件很容易判断的事情。那么我们是如何判断出来的呢?我们会发现大家在装修的时候都会铺地板、刷墙、装好灯饰、摆上家具,其实在房子装修的时候这种组合关系是相似的。但是如果主人更富裕,他在选地板的时候,可以用瓷砖,可以用复合木地板,也可以用实木地板,而这些选择就是聚合关系,也就是同一位置上的替换关系。

放在语言上,组合关系保证语言在连接上的正确性。英语中的五种基本句型结构——SV, SVO, SVOO, SVOC, SVP——都是组合关系。但是只有组合关系,只保证组合关系上的正确性,文章不一定会写得生动多彩。如果我们在描写哈克父亲大喊大闹时一直用一个词,如 roar,那么读者读起来肯定觉得枯燥乏味。所以想让语言变得丰富多彩,还要考虑语言上的聚合关系。聚合轴有宽窄问题。聚合轴越宽,表示我们在同一个位置上的选择就越多。回到装修房子的问题上,更富裕的主人在地板或刷墙材料的选择上当然会有更多选择,这就是为什么我们一走进不同房子就能辨别出哪家房子的主人更富裕。所以说,聚合轴会在组合轴上留下深深的投影,聚合轴决定文本的风格。

无论是学习英语还是中文,老师会经常指导我们总结一些同义词或同义表达方法,其目的就是扩大聚合轴。比如表示“不明确的,模糊的,模棱两可的”的单词有 ambiguous, implicit, vague, obscure, indefinite, unclear;表示“包含”的单词和词组有 include, involve, comprehend, inclusive of, embrace, embody, comprise, contain, encompass。在平时的学习中注意积累这样的同义词、同义表达方法,我们就会像那个富裕的主人一样,在写作的时候驾轻就熟、挥洒自如。

“聚合是文本建构的方式,一旦文本形成,就退入幕后,因此是隐藏的;组合就是文本的构成方式,因此组合是显示的。可以说,聚合是组合的背景,组合是聚合的投影。”(赵毅衡,2016:158)

在这一章中我们看到了马克·吐温为什么会成为一位经典的作家,而《哈克贝利·费恩历险记》会成为经典小说。本章中的两处描写,一是哈克父亲醉酒后的吵闹,一是醉酒后的翻滚踢打,其背后的聚合轴都很宽,所以我们才看到了一段生动形象、变幻多姿的描写,看到作者马克·吐温在遣词造句上是多么地游刃有余。

术语解说

组合轴:雅柯布森提出,组合轴可以称为“结合轴”(axis of combination),功能是邻接黏合。之后的符号学家索绪尔改称其为组合轴(syntagmatic)。

聚合轴:雅柯布森提出,聚合轴可称为“选择轴”(axis of selection),功能是比较与选择。之后的符号学家索绪尔改称其为聚合轴(paradigmatic)。

阅读思考

1. 你能举出一些生活中体现双轴关系的例子吗?
2. 设置一个场景,描写一个人物的一系列动作。

EXERCISE I

I. Oral presentation.

1. 请复述哈克贝利·费恩和小伙伴们在山洞中时发生的事情。

   要求：

   （1）请使用以下关键词（key words）：

   wear, Tom Sawyer's Gang, a sheet of paper, book, nothing but, robbery and murder, ransom, as polite as a pie, cry-baby

   （2）请注意交代清楚各要素（5w + h：who, when, where, what, why, how）。

2. 假设你是二十一世纪的大学一年级新生 Huckleberry，在开学时遇到同学 Tom，你们彼此打招呼并介绍自己的朋友 Jim 给对方认识。

   （1）请在打招呼时参考使用以下句型：

   It's been quite a while.

   How's everything?

   Fancy meeting you here.

   How goes it?

   How's life?

   How's it going?

   （2）请在相互介绍时参考使用以下句型：

   Please let me introduce you to my friend.

   May I introduce（present）…?

   Would you like to introduce…?

II. Choose the correct words to complete the sentences.

1. The project wasted a ____ amount of time and money.

   A.considerable　　B. considerate　　C. considering　　D. considered

2. Miss Watson always asked Huck to _____ well.

   A.perform　　B. eat　　C. sleep　　D. behave

3. He had to _____ as he came through the door.

   A.bend　　B. duck　　C. push　　D. rush

4. She heard the baby ____ in the next room.

   A.creeping　　C. stirring　　C. jumping　　D. shaking

5. I _____ that I am going to get that job.

A.reckon B. say C. ask D. regard

6. Jack became increasingly _____ throughout the interview.

A.quite B. fidgety C. dangerous D. shy

7. He had no right to _____ in her affairs.

A.join B. participate C. meddle D. control

8. Sorry, I've _____ some paint off the car.

A.cut B. spilled C. pulled D. scraped

9. We _____ our bags and suitcases to the airport.

A.moved B. placed C. toted D. pushed

10. The seat _____ forward, when you press this lever.

A.shakes B. tilts C. passes D. leaves

III. Fill in the blanks with suitable prepositions or adverbs.

1. Huck couldn't stand the life in the widow's house and lit _____.
2. Tom didn't take stock ____ what you had told him before.
3. We claim an allowance of $230 ____ account ____ the quality of this shipment.
4. Whether he acted _________ spite or necessity, the effect has been the same.
5. When it topples it will have to fall _____ one side or the other.

IV. Answer the following questions.

Questions on the content

1. How did Huck feel when he lived with the Widow Douglas?
2. After Tom slipped Jim's hat off his head and hung it on limb right over him, what did Jim think about it? And what did Jim say after it?
3. Did Huck believe Tom who said "they rub an old tin lamp or iron ring, and then the genies come tearing in, with the thunder and lightning a-ripping around and the smoke a-rolling, and everything they're told to do they up and do it." ? What did Huck do?
4. How did the widow think about the function of praying? How do you understand "spiritual gift" ?
5. Did Huck believe that this drownded man was his dad? And why?
6. Why did Huck feel worried and shaky in Chapter IV? Why did Huck tell Judge Thatcher he didn't want his money at all?
7. What did Huck's father look like? When Huck's father knew his son could read, what did he do?
8. How did Huck's father make comments on a free nigger from Ohio? What could you get from his words?

Questions on the structure and style

1. Why does the author choose Huck to tell this story?
2. From Chapter I to VI, what does the writer focus chiefly on—developing character, action or plot?
3. How does the author build up and sustain the suspense in Chapter IV?
4. Why does the author use so many ungrammatical sentences in this novel? Illustrate your answer with examples.
5. Can you identify words in Chapter V that reveal Huck's father's personality?

V. Complele the following translation with four-character expressions.

1. I judged he would **be blind drunk** in about an hour, and then I would steal the key, or saw myself out, one or t'other. (Chapter VI)
   我心里估摸,大约个把钟头以后,他就会喝得________,那时我就把钥匙偷走,或是锯个大窟窿逃出去,反正怎么都行。
2. It was kind of **lazy and jolly**, **laying off comfortable** all day, smoking and fishing, and no books nor study. (Chapter VI)
   整天________,抽抽烟,钓钓鱼,不用读书,不动脑筋——这就是地地道道的__________。
3. Here's a govment that calls itself a govment, and let on to be a govment, and thinks it is a govment, and yet's got to **set stock-still** for six whole months before it can take a hold of a **prowling, thieving, infernal**, white-shirted nigger… (Chapter VI)
   得了,这是一个自命为政府的政府,装扮得像个政府,自以为是个政府,可还得__________地坐着,足足满了六个月,才去踅摸一个____________、____________、____________、穿白衬衫的自由黑人……
4. Jim was most ruined for a servant, because he **got stuck up** on account of having seen the devil and been rode by witches. (Chapter II)
   这么一来,吉姆可真给毁了,哪儿还像个佣人呢。因为他跟魔鬼见过面,还驮着妖怪走天下,自然而然他就____________起来了。
5. And after supper he talked to him about **temperance** and such things till the old man cried, and said he'd been a fool, and fooled away his life; but now he was a-going to **turn over a new leaf** and **be a man** nobody wouldn't **be ashamed of**, and he hoped the judge would help him and not look down on him. (Chapter V)
   晚餐以后,法官给他大讲有关____________等大道理,使这老头听后直落眼泪,说自己一直是个傻瓜蛋,把一辈子的光阴都给浪掷了;可是,今日里他要____________,____________,再也不____________了。
6. The judge gave him some, and that evening he got drunk, and **was around till after midnight**

with a couple of **mighty hard-looking** strangers, and then went off with them. (Chapter XI)
法官给了他一些钱,当天晚上他就喝醉了酒,______________ 还跟两个 ______________ 的陌生人 ______________,后来竟跟他们一块儿远走了。

7. It was pretty ornery preaching—all about brotherly love, and such-like tiresomeness; but everybody said it was a good sermon, and they all talked it over going home, and had such a powerful lot to say about **faith** and **good works** and **free grace** and **preforeordestination**, and **I don't know what all**, that it did seem to me to be one of the roughest Sundays I had run across yet. (Chapter XVIII)
那天的布道可真是太差劲了——净说兄弟般的友爱,以及诸如此类的无聊话;可是,不管是谁全都说布道好;他们在回家路上胡扯,还说是什么 ______________,______________,______________,______________ 等,______________ 的一大套,我可不知道还有什么其他名堂;反正像那样糟得令人反感的一个礼拜天,我好像从来都没碰上过呢。

8. "Dern your skin, ain't the company good enough for you?" says the baldhead, pretty **pert** and **uppish**. (Chapter XIX)
"你这该死的家伙,跟我们一块儿厮混,对你还不是够好的吗?"那个秃顶 ______________、______________ 地说。

9. "... I am the lineal descendant of that infant—I am the rightful Duke of Bridgewater; and **here am I**, **forlorn**, torn from my **high estate**, **hunted of men**, despised by the cold world, **ragged**, **worn**, heart-broken, and degraded to the companionship of felons on a raft!" (Chapter XIX)
"……我本人就是那位幼小的公爵的直系后代——我本人就是合法的布里奇沃特公爵。可是如今我流落在这里,______________,______________,我的 ______________ 都被抢走了,这些姑且不谈;这个冷酷的世道还瞧不起我,弄得我 ______________,______________,______________,怪 ______________ 的,跟你们这帮子哥们儿一块厮混在木筏上!"

10. "... Yes, gentlemen, you see before you, in blue jeans and misery, the **wanderin'**, **exiled**, **trampled-on** and **sufferin'** rightful King of France." (Chapter XIX)
"……是的,诸位先生,不妨睁开眼睛看看,在你们眼前的这个身穿蓝色斜纹布裤子的穷鬼,原来就是那 ______________、______________、______________、______________、合法的法兰西国王。"

VI. Specific words.

Compared with general words, specific words help to make writing clear, concrete, exact, vivid and striking. Distinguish the underlined specific words and phrases in the following sentences and try to use them in your English writing.

1. Tom poked about amongst the passages and pretty soon ducked under a wall where you

wouldn't a noticed that there was a hole.

2. As soon as Tom was back we <u>cut along</u> the path, around the garden fence, and by and by fetched up on the steep top of the hill the other side of the house.
3. We went <u>tip-toeing</u> along a path amongst the trees back towards the end of the widow's garden, stooping down so as the branches wouldn't scrape our heads.
4. What are you <u>prowling around</u> here this time of night?
5. Tom he made a sign to me—kind of a little noise with his mouth—and we went <u>creeping</u> away on our hands and knees.
6. Then Tom said he hadn't got candles enough, and he would <u>slip in</u> the kitchen and get some more.
7. Then we got out, and I was in a sweat to <u>get away</u>; but nothing would do Tom but he must <u>crawl</u> to where Jim was, on his hands and knees, and play something on him.
8. I <u>slunk along</u> another piece further, then listened again; and so on, and so on.

CHAPTER VII

导读:哈克找到了逃跑的机会。因为大河涨水,从上游漂来的木筏让哈克心生一计。哈克藏匿好木筏,为出逃做各种准备。他伪装了强盗抢东西,把自己杀死的假象,成功逃出了他父亲的掌控。

(1)"GIT up! What you 'bout?"

(2) I opened my eyes and looked around, trying to make out where I was. It was after sun-up, and I had been sound asleep. Pap was standing over me looking sour and sick, too. He says:

(3)"What you doin' with this gun?"

(4) I judged he didn't know nothing about what he had been doing, so I says:

(5)"Somebody tried to get in, so I was laying for him."

(6)"Why didn't you roust[1] me out?"

(7)"Well, I tried to, but I couldn't; I couldn't budge[2] you."

(8)"Well, all right. Don't stand there palavering[3] all day, but out with you and see if there's a fish on the lines for breakfast. I'll be along in a minute."

(9) He unlocked the door, and I cleared out up the river-bank. I noticed some pieces of limbs and such things floating down, and a sprinkling[4] of bark[5]; so I knowed the river had begun to rise.[6] I reckoned I would have great times now if I was over at the town. The June rise used to be always luck for me; because as soon as that rise begins here comes cordwood floating down, and pieces of log rafts—sometimes a dozen logs together; so all you have to do is to catch them and sell them to the wood-yards and the sawmill.[7]

[1] roust /raʊst/ v. 打扰;扰乱

[2] budge /bʌdʒ/ v.(使)轻微移动;挪动

[3] palaver /pəˈlɑːvə(r)/ n. 废话;空话

[4] sprinkling /ˈsprɪŋklɪŋ/ n. 少量

[5] bark /bɑːk/ n. 树皮

[6] 哈克发现一些树的主枝,还有一些树皮从上游漂来,得知大河涨水了。

[7] 六月里,大河一涨水,我的好运气就来了,因为涨水后会有成捆要出售的木材从上游漂下来,可能还会有木筏,有时还能碰上十几根大原木。你所要做的就是把这些东西打捞上来,然后卖给木材厂和锯木厂就行了。

(10) I went along up the bank with one eye out for pap and t'other one out for what the rise might fetch along. Well, all at once here comes a canoe; just a beauty, too, about thirteen or fourteen foot long, riding high like a duck[8]. I shot head-first off of the bank like a frog, clothes and all on[9], and struck out for the canoe. I just expected there'd be somebody laying down in it, because people often done that to fool folks, and when a chap[10] had pulled a skiff out most to it they'd raise up and laugh at him. But it warn't so this time. It was a drift-canoe sure enough, and I clumb in and paddled her ashore. Thinks I, the old man will be glad when he sees this—she's worth ten dollars. But when I got to shore pap wasn't in sight yet, and as I was running her into a little creek[11] like a gully[12], all hung over with vines and willows, I struck another idea: I judged I'd hide her good, and then, 'stead of taking to the woods when I run off, I'd go down the river about fifty mile and camp in one place for good, and not have such a rough time tramping on foot.

(11) It was pretty close to the shanty[13], and I thought I heard the old man coming all the time; but I got her hid; and then I out and looked around a bunch of willows, and there was the old man down the path a piece just drawing a bead on a bird with his gun. So he hadn't seen anything.

(12) When he got along I was hard at it taking up a "trot" line[14]. He abused me a little for being so slow; but I told him I fell in the river, and that was what made me so long. I knowed he would see I was wet, and then he would be asking questions. We got five catfish off the lines and went home.

(13) While we laid off after breakfast to sleep up, both of us being about wore out[15], I got to thinking that if I could fix up some way to keep pap and the widow from trying to follow me, it would be a certainer thing than trusting to luck to get far enough off before they missed me; you see, all kinds of things might happen. Well, I didn't see no way for a while, but by and by pap raised up a minute to drink another barrel of water, and he says:

(14) "Another time a man comes a-prowling round here

[8] 明喻(simile)。哈克发现木筏像一只鸭子一样。

[9] 这里说明哈克很急切，看见木筏连衣服都没脱，就跳进水中去抓木筏。

[10] chap /tʃæp/ *n.* 伙计

[11] creek /kriːk/ *n.* 小溪

[12] gully /ˈɡʌli/ *n.* 溪谷

[13] shanty /ˈʃænti/ *n.* 棚屋；简陋小屋

[14] "trot" line: 滚钓线。两头固定在两岸，线上连着另外几条上了鱼饵的线。

[15] wear out: 精疲力竭

you roust me out, you hear? That man warn't here for no good. I'd a shot him. Next time you roust me out, you hear?"

(15) Then he dropped down and went to sleep again; but what he had been saying give me the very idea I wanted.[16] I says to myself, I can fix it now so nobody won't think of following me.

[16] 哈克父亲说下次再有坏人来一定要叫醒他。这话提醒了哈克,他心生一计。

(16) About twelve o'clock we turned out and went along up the bank. The river was coming up pretty fast, and lots of driftwood going by on the rise. By and by along comes part of a log raft — nine logs fast together. We went out with the skiff and towed[17] it ashore. Then we had dinner. Anybody but pap would a waited and seen the day through, so as to catch more stuff; but that warn't pap's style.[18] Nine logs was enough for one time; he must shove right over to town and sell. So he locked me in and took the skiff, and started off towing the raft about half-past three. I judged he wouldn't come back that night. I waited till I reckoned he had got a good start; then I out with my saw, and went to work on that log again. Before he was t'other side of the river I was out of the hole; him and his raft was just a speck on the water away off yonder.

[17] **tow** /təʊ/ *v.* (用绳索)拖,拉,牵引,拽

[18] 除了老爸,其他人会等上一整天,希望能从河里捡到更多有用的东西,可这不是老爸的风格。这里说明哈克的父亲非常懒惰,连从河里直接捡东西卖了赚钱这种事情都不愿意一直做。一次捞了九根原木就觉得够了。

(17) I took the sack of corn meal and took it to where the canoe was hid, and shoved the vines and branches apart and put it in; then I done the same with the side of bacon; then the whisky-jug. I took all the coffee and sugar there was, and all the ammunition; I took the wadding; I took the bucket and gourd[19]; I took a dipper and a tin cup, and my old saw and two blankets, and the skillet and the coffee-pot. I took fish-lines and matches and other things — everything that was worth a cent. I cleaned out the place. I wanted an axe, but there wasn't any, only the one out at the woodpile, and I knowed why I was going to leave that. I fetched out the gun, and now I was done.

[19] **gourd** /gʊəd/ *n.* 葫芦(晾干后常做容器)

(18) I had wore the ground a good deal crawling out of the hole and dragging out so many things. So I fixed that as good as I could from the outside by scattering dust on the place, which covered up the smoothness and the sawdust[20]. Then I fixed the piece of log back into its place, and put two rocks under it and

[20] **sawdust** /ˈsɔːdʌst/ *n.* 锯末
这句话中用到了非限制性定语从句。

one against it to hold it there, for it was bent up at that place and didn't quite touch ground. If you stood four or five foot away and didn't know it was sawed, you wouldn't never notice it; and besides, this was the back of the cabin, and it warn't likely anybody would go fooling around there.

(19) It was all grass clear to the canoe, so I hadn't left a track. I followed around to see. I stood on the bank and looked out over the river. All safe. So I took the gun and went up a piece into the woods, and was hunting around for some birds when I see a wild pig; hogs soon went wild in them bottoms after they had got away from the prairie[21] farms. I shot this fellow and took him into camp.

[21] **prairie** /ˈpreəri/ *n.* 大草原

(20) I took the axe and smashed in the door. I beat it and hacked it considerable a-doing it. I fetched the pig in, and took him back nearly to the table and hacked into his throat with the axe, and laid him down on the ground to bleed; I say ground because it was ground—hard packed, and no boards. Well, next I took an old sack and put a lot of big rocks in it—all I could drag—and I started it from the pig, and dragged it to the door and through the woods down to the river and dumped it in, and down it sunk, out of sight. You could easy see that something had been dragged over the ground. I did wish Tom Sawyer was there;[22] I knowed he would take an interest in this kind of business, and throw in the fancy touches. Nobody could spread himself like Tom Sawyer in such a thing as that.

[22] 这句话是强调句。此时哈克对自己的整个计划和实施很满意,所以希望汤姆·索亚在场。汤姆肯定对这事很感兴趣,还能让这件事情锦上添花。

(21) Well, last I pulled out some of my hair, and blooded the axe good, and stuck it on the back side, and slung the axe in the corner. Then I took up the pig and held him to my breast with my jacket (so he couldn't drip) till I got a good piece below the house and then dumped him into the river. Now I thought of something else. So I went and got the bag of meal and my old saw out of the canoe, and fetched them to the house. I took the bag to where it used to stand, and ripped[23] a hole in the bottom of it with the saw, for there warn't no knives and forks on the place—pap done everything with his clasp-knife about the cooking. Then I carried the sack about a hundred yards

[23] **rip** /rɪp/ *v.* 撕破;裂开

across the grass and through the willows east of the house, to a shallow lake that was five mile wide and full of rushes—and ducks too, you might say, in the season. There was a slough[21] or a creek leading out of it on the other side that went miles away, I don't know where, but it didn't go to the river. The meal sifted out[25] and made a little track all the way to the lake. I dropped pap's whetstone[26] there too, so as to look like it had been done by accident. Then I tied up the rip in the meal sack with a string, so it wouldn't leak no more, and took it and my saw to the canoe again.

[21] slough /slʌt/ *n.* 沼泽

[25] sift out: 持续不断地筛出来

[26] whetstone /ˈwetstəʊn/ *n.* 磨刀石

(22) It was about dark now; so I dropped the canoe down the river under some willows that hung over the bank, and waited for the moon to rise. I made fast to a willow; then I took a bite to eat, and by and by laid down in the canoe to smoke a pipe and lay out a plan. I says to myself, they'll follow the track of that sackful of rocks to the shore and then drag the river for me. And they'll follow that meal track to the lake and go browsing[27] down the creek that leads out of it to find the robbers that killed me and took the things. They won't ever hunt the river for anything but my dead carcass. They'll soon get tired of that, and won't bother no more about me. All right; I can stop anywhere I want to. Jackson's Island is good enough for me; I know that island pretty well, and nobody ever comes there. And then I can paddle over to town, nights, and slink[28] around and pick up things I want. Jackson's Island's the place.

[27] browse /braʊz/ *v.* 浏览;搜寻信息

[28] slink /slɪŋk/ *v.* 悄悄移动

(23) I was pretty tired, and the first thing I knowed I was asleep. When I woke up I didn't know where I was for a minute. I set up and looked around, a little scared.[29] Then I remembered. The river looked miles and miles across. The moon was so bright I could a counted the drift logs that went a-slipping along, black and still, hundreds of yards out from shore. Everything was dead quiet, and it looked late, and *smelt* late[30]. You know what I mean—I don't know the words to put it in.

[29] 心理描写。突然醒来,哈克没反应过来自己身处何地,所以感到有点害怕。

[30] 通感(synesthesia)。闻起来也知道已经很晚了。

(24) I took a good gap and a stretch, and was just going to unhitch and start when I heard a sound away over the water. I listened. Pretty soon I made it out. It was that dull kind of a

regular sound that comes from oars working in rowlocks when it's a still night.[31] I peeped out through the willow branches, and there it was —a skiff, away across the water. I couldn't tell how many was in it. It kept a-coming, and when it was abreast of me I see there warn't but one man in it. Thinks I, maybe it's pap, though I warn't expecting him. He dropped below me with the current, and by and by he came a-swinging up shore in the easy water, and he went by so close I could a reached out the gun and touched him. Well, it *was* pap, sure enough—and sober, too, by the way he laid his oars.

[31] 这句话中用了两个that，其中第二个that引导的是定语从句。最后还有一个when引导的时间状语从句。寂静的夜里传来一阵有规律的声音，原来是夜晚摇桨时所发出的声音。

（25）I didn't lose no time. The next minute I was a-spinning down stream soft but quick in the shade of the bank. I made two mile and a half, and then struck out a quarter of a mile or more towards the middle of the river, because pretty soon I would be passing the ferry landing, and people might see me and hail me. I got out amongst the driftwood, and then laid down in the bottom of the canoe and let her float. I laid there, and had a good rest and a smoke out of my pipe, looking away into the sky; not a cloud in it. The sky looks ever so deep when you lay down on your back in the moonshine; I never knowed it before.[32] And how far a body can hear on the water such nights! I heard people talking at the ferry landing.[33] I heard what they said, too—every word of it. One man said it was getting towards the long days and the short nights now. The other one said *this* warn't one of the short ones, he reckoned—and then they laughed, and he said it over again, and they laughed again; then they waked up another fellow and told him, and laughed, but he didn't laugh; he ripped out something brisk, and said let him alone. The first fellow said he 'lowed to tell it to his old woman—she would think it was pretty good; but he said that warn't nothing to some things he had said in his time. I heard one man say it was nearly three o'clock, and he hoped daylight wouldn't wait more than about a week longer. After that the talk got further and further away, and I couldn't make out the words any more; but I could hear the mumble, and now and then a laugh, too, but it seemed a long ways off.

[32] 当我躺在船上，望着星光灿烂的天空，才发现夜晚的天空这么深邃，我以前从来没注意到。

[33] 因为夜晚安静，声音可以传得很远。哈克听到了一群人的闲聊。

(26) I was away below the ferry now. I rose up, and there was Jackson's Island,[34] about two mile and a half down stream, heavy timbered and standing up out of the middle of the river, big and dark and solid, like a steamboat without any lights. There warn't any signs of the bar at the head — it was all under water now.

[34]哈克到达了杰克逊岛。这是哈克选择的藏身之地。

(27) It didn't take me long to get there. I shot past the head at a ripping rate, the current was so swift, and then I got into the dead water and landed on the side towards the Illinois shore.[35] I run the canoe into a deep dent in the bank that I knowed about; I had to part the willow branches to get in; and when I made fast nobody could a seen the canoe from the outside.

[35]我健步如飞地穿过岛的顶端——那里水流湍急——随后来到一处死水那里，并在毗邻伊利诺伊州这边上了岸。(潘庆舲 译)

(28) I went up and set down on a log at the head of the island, and looked out on the big river and the black driftwood and away over to the town, three mile away, where there was three or four lights twinkling.[36] A monstrous big lumber-raft was about a mile up stream, coming along down, with a lantern in the middle of it. I watched it come creeping down, and when it was most abreast of where I stood I heard a man say, "Stern oars, there! heave her head to stabboard!" I heard that just as plain as if the man was by my side.

[36]我坐在岛顶端的一根原木上，望着这条大河，河面上是黑色的、漂浮着的木头，三英里外就是镇子，那里有三四处灯火在闪烁。

(29) There was a little gray in the sky now; so I stepped into the woods, and laid down for a nap before breakfast.

精华赏析

在这一章中，我们讨论一下小说中的情节，以及情节中的冲突。

小说中的几个基本要素包括人物(character)、场景(setting)、情节(plot)、主题(theme)、结构(structure)、风格(style)等。在前面的章节中我们谈到过人物塑造。在这一章中我们重点来探讨一下情节。

简单说来，情节就是一系列的事件。在情节的发展中会出现各种类型的冲突，而在主人公逐步解决冲突的过程中，情节也就随之发展。

小说中的冲突我们又可以大致分为两类：内部冲突和外部冲突。内部冲突一般是人物内心的自我冲突,常常以内心描写的形式展现出来。外部冲突可以再分为两类:一类是人物和人物之间的冲突,一类是人物和自然环境之间的冲突。

人物和人物之间的冲突正是这一章的主要冲突,也就是哈克和哈克父亲之间的冲突。他们之间的冲突原因,在表层是虐待与摆脱虐待的冲突。哈克父亲整日毒打哈克发泄出气,而哈克自然不想再忍受父亲这样的虐待。在深层是控制与摆脱控制的冲突。因为哈克父亲想要完全控制哈克,让哈克听自己的话,所以把哈克带到了一个隐蔽的小屋,而哈克则想要逃离父亲的掌控。哈克的父亲想在身体和精神上都能够完完全全地控制自己的儿子。我们可以回忆下在第五章中,为什么哈克父亲听说儿子能读书认字,会那么生气,因为他意识到儿子一旦在某些方面超越自己,他就失去了对儿子的控制权。正是因为哈克和父亲之间的冲突,才会推动后面情节的发展,哈克精心策划了自己的逃跑计划。试想一下,要是没有这个关键的冲突,情节肯定是没法推进的。假使哈克父亲关心、爱护自己的儿子,父子俩生活快乐和谐,哈克为什么要逃跑呢?

我们再来看看人物和自然环境之间的冲突,在灾难或极限运动相关的电影中,人物和自然环境之间的冲突就会成为文本的主要冲突,比如《2012》,再比如《攀登者》。

我们以 2019 年的国庆大片《攀登者》为例,来看看文本中各类冲突的交融。优秀的作品都是各种冲突的交错和融合。《攀登者》中有人物和人物之间的冲突,比如方五洲和曲松林之间,因为第一次登山方五洲为了救曲松林丢了相机,使第一次成功登顶珠穆朗玛峰没能得到国际认可,方五洲和曲松林之间有了矛盾和冲突。除此之外,还有各种人物和人物之间的冲突,比如方五洲和徐缨之间,李国梁和黑牡丹之间,等等。其实一般长篇经典小说之间的人物冲突都是错综复杂的,绝不是单一的矛盾。比如中国古代长篇小说的经典之作《红楼梦》里面的人物众多,人物之间的冲突也就相当复杂,光要理清这本小说中的人物关系就要花上不少时间。再回到《攀登者》这部电影,除了人物和人物之间的冲突以外,推动情节发展的主线是人类首次挑战从北坡登上珠穆朗玛峰,这里有一个最重要的冲突就是人物和自然环境之间的冲突。可想而知,以人类可以忍受的极限去挑战极寒天气、高海拔缺氧、随时可能发生的雪崩、十几级的大风等,都是人类和自然环境之间的巨大冲突。中国人以最大的决心和勇气去挑战自然并获成功才是这部电影中最震撼人心的部分。

说到人物内心的自我冲突,在这本小说的第十六章中有几段关于哈克内心冲突的描写就是典型的自我冲突。吉姆说自己马上要获得自由了,哈克反倒心烦意乱,坐立不安起来。哈克很自责,他不仅没有告发吉姆,还帮助他逃跑,如今吉姆不仅要让自己获得自由,还打算偷回自己的妻子和孩子,哈克觉得吉姆是得寸进尺。哈克还觉得很对不起沃森小姐,沃森小姐教自己读书认字,不遗余力地教自己做人,他怎么能眼看着沃森小姐的黑奴从自己眼前逃跑,居然一句话不说。可是另外一方面,吉姆认为哈克是他最好的朋友,说一辈子也不会忘记哈克的恩情,这让哈克犹豫彷徨。按照当时的法律帮助黑奴逃跑是不对的,可听从自己的内心,帮助好朋友吉姆获得自由又无可厚非。这种内心的冲突和挣扎让哈克如坐针毡。

另外,在情节推进的过程中还会存在一个冲突解决又出现新的冲突的现象。主人公不断遇到新问题,不断解决问题。有些长篇小说读起来扣人心悬就是由于各种冲突迭起,有种一波未平一波又起的感觉。哈克接下来还会遇到什么新问题,他又该如何解决呢?让我们拭目以待。

阅读思考

1. 你最喜欢的一本书是什么?为什么喜欢它呢?请给出自己的理由并将它推荐给朋友们。

2. 分析这本书中的各种类型的冲突,以及主人公是如何解决这些冲突来推进情节发展的。

CHAPTER VIII

导读：独自在杰克逊岛上生活的哈克很惬意。镇上的人们觉得哈克已经死了，在河上找寻他的尸体。过了几天，哈克发现岛上还有其他人，这让哈克大吃一惊。后来他发现黑人吉姆也来到了岛上。二人都讲述了自己的经历。原来吉姆是担心沃森小姐把自己卖掉，才冒险逃跑的。

(1) THE sun was up so high when I waked that I judged it was after eight o'clock. I laid there in the grass and the cool shade thinking about things, and feeling rested and ruther comfortable and satisfied. I could see the sun out at one or two holes, but mostly it was big trees all about, and gloomy in there amongst them. There was freckled places on the ground where the light sifted down through the leaves, and the freckled places swapped about a little, showing there was a little breeze up there.[1] A couple of squirrels set on a limb and jabbered[2] at me very friendly.

(2) I was powerful lazy and comfortable—didn't want to get up and cook breakfast. Well, I was dozing off again when I thinks I hears a deep sound of "boom!" away up the river. I rouses up, and rests on my elbow and listens; pretty soon I hears it again. I hopped up, and went and looked out at a hole in the leaves, and I see a bunch of smoke laying on the water a long ways up—about abreast the ferry. And there was the ferryboat full of people floating along down. I knowed what was the matter now.[3] "Boom!" I see the white smoke squirt[4] out of the ferryboat's side. You see, they was firing cannon over the water, trying to make my carcass come to the top.

(3) I was pretty hungry, but it warn't going to do for me to

[1] 阳光从树叶之间洒落下来，地面上就有斑斑驳驳的光影，那些光影稍微移动了一下，说明一阵微风刚从上空吹过。（潘庆舲 译）

[2] jabber /ˈdʒæbə(r)/ v. 急促(或激动)而含混不清地说

[3] 哈克立刻明白了大家在河上放炮，找寻他的尸体。

[4] squirt /skwɜːt/ v. 喷射；喷

start a fire, because they might see the smoke. So I set there and watched the cannon-smoke and listened to the boom. The river was a mile wide there, and it always looks pretty on a summer morning—so I was having a good enough time seeing them hunt for my remainders if I only had a bite to eat. Well, then I happened to think how they always put quicksilver[5] in loaves of bread and float them off, because they always go right to the drownded carcass and stop there.[6] So, says I, I'll keep a lookout, and if any of them's floating around after me I'll give them a show. I changed to the Illinois edge of the island to see what luck I could have, and I warn't disappointed. A big double loaf come along, and I most got it with a long stick, but my foot slipped and she floated out further. Of course I was where the current set in the closest to the shore—I knowed enough for that. But by and by along comes another one, and this time I won. I took out the plug and shook out the little dab of quicksilver, and set my teeth in. It was "baker's bread" —what the quality eat; none of your low-down corn-pone.

5 quicksilver /ˈkwɪksɪlvə(r)/ n. 汞，水银

6 我突然想到，他们常常给面包里放上水银，让面包在水里漂浮。面包总会朝溺水者漂去，并且停在他们面前。

(4) I got a good place amongst the leaves, and set there on a log, munching[7] the bread and watching[8] the ferry-boat, and very well satisfied. And then something struck me. I says, now I reckon the widow or the parson or somebody prayed that this bread would find me, and here it has gone and done it. So there ain't no doubt but there is something in that thing—that is, there's something in it when a body like the widow or the parson prays, but it don't work for me, and I reckon it don't work for only just the right kind.

7 munch /mʌntʃ/ v. 大声咀嚼；用力咀嚼

8 munching 和 watching 是两个现在分词，逻辑主语都是 I。

(5) I lit a pipe and had a good long smoke, and went on watching. The ferryboat was floating with the current, and I allowed I'd have a chance to see who was aboard when she come along, because she would come in close, where the bread did. When she'd got pretty well along down towards me, I put out my pipe and went to where I fished out the bread, and laid down behind a log on the bank in a little open place. Where the log forked[9] I could peep through.

9 fork /fɔːk/ v. 分岔

(6) By and by she come along, and she drifted in so close

that they could a run out a plank[10] and walked ashore. Most everybody was on the boat. Pap, and Judge Thatcher, and Bessie Thatcher, and Jo Harper, and Tom Sawyer, and his old Aunt Polly, and Sid and Mary, and plenty more. Everybody was talking about the murder, but the captain broke in and says:

(7) "Look sharp, now; the current sets in the closest here, and maybe he's washed ashore and got tangled amongst the brush at the water's edge. I hope so, anyway."

(8) I didn't hope so. They all crowded up and leaned over the rails, nearly in my face, and kept still, watching with all their might. I could see them first-rate, but they couldn't see me. Then the captain sung out:

(9) "Stand away!" and the cannon let off such a blast right before me that it made me deef with the noise and pretty near blind with the smoke, and I judged I was gone.[11] If they'd a had some bullets in, I reckon they'd a got the corpse they was after. Well, I see I warn't hurt, thanks to goodness. The boat floated on and went out of sight around the shoulder of the island. I could hear the booming now and then, further and further off, and by and by, after an hour, I didn't hear it no more. The island was three mile long. I judged they had got to the foot, and was giving it up. But they didn't yet a while. They turned around the foot of the island and started up the channel on the Missouri[12] side, under steam, and booming once in a while as they went. I crossed over to that side and watched them. When they got abreast the head of the island they quit shooting and dropped over to the Missouri shore and went home to the town.

(10) I knowed I was all right now. Nobody else would come a-hunting after me. I got my traps out of the canoe and made me a nice camp in the thick woods. I made a kind of a tent out of my blankets to put my things under so the rain couldn't get at them. I catched a catfish and haggled him open with my saw, and towards sundown I started my camp fire and had supper. Then I set out a line to catch some fish for breakfast.

(11) When it was dark I set by my camp fire smoking, and feeling pretty well satisfied; but by and by it got sort of lone-

[10] plank /plæŋk/ *n.* 木板；板条

[11] 就在我眼前，大炮发出爆炸声。我的耳朵差点被这震耳欲聋的声音震聋，大炮的烟差点把我眼睛熏瞎。我以为我已经死了。

[12] Missouri /mɪˈzʊri/ 密苏里（美国州名）

some,[13] and so I went and set on the bank and listened to the current swashing along, and counted the stars and drift logs and rafts that come down, and then went to bed; there ain't no better way to put in time when you are lonesome; you can't stay so, you soon get over it.

[13] 心理描写。开始哈克觉得挺满足的,但很快又觉得孤单起来。

(12) And so for three days and nights. No difference—just the same thing. But the next day I went exploring around down through the island. I was boss of it; it all belonged to me, so to say, and I wanted to know all about it; but mainly I wanted to put in the time. I found plenty strawberries, ripe[14] and prime[15]; and green summer grapes, and green razberries; and the green blackberries was just beginning to show. They would all come handy by and by, I judged.

[14] ripe /raɪp/ *adj.* 成熟的

[15] prime /praɪm/ *adj.* 优质的;上乘的

(13) Well, I went fooling along in the deep woods till I judged I warn't far from the foot of the island. I had my gun along, but I hadn't shot nothing; it was for protection; thought I would kill some game nigh[16] home. About this time I mighty near stepped on a good-sized snake, and it went sliding off through the grass and flowers, and I after it, trying to get a shot at it. I clipped along, and all of a sudden I bounded right on to the ashes of a camp fire that was still smoking.

[16] nigh /naɪ/ *adv.* 几乎;差不多;靠近

(14) My heart jumped up amongst my lungs.[17] I never waited for to look further, but uncocked my gun and went sneaking back on my tiptoes as fast as ever I could. Every now and then I stopped a second amongst the thick leaves and listened, but my breath come so hard I couldn't hear nothing else. I slunk[18] along another piece further, then listened again; and so on, and so on. If I see a stump, I took it for a man; if I trod on a stick and broke it, it made me feel like a person had cut one of my breaths in two and I only got half, and the short half, too.

[17] 夸张(hyperbole)。哈克发现了还在冒烟的灰烬,被吓得不轻。心脏都要从胸腔里蹦出来了。

[18] slink /slɪŋk/ *v.* 躲躲闪闪地走

(15) When I got to camp I warn't feeling very brash[19], there warn't much sand in my craw; but I says, this ain't no time to be fooling around. So I got all my traps into my canoe again so as to have them out of sight, and I put out the fire and scattered the ashes around to look like an old last year's camp, and then

[19] brash /bræʃ/ *adj.* 自以为是的

clumb a tree.

(16) I reckon I was up in the tree two hours; but I didn't see nothing, I didn't hear nothing—I only *thought* I heard and seen as much as a thousand things. Well, I couldn't stay up there forever; so at last I got down, but I kept in the thick woods and on the lookout all the time. All I could get to eat was berries and what was left over from breakfast.

(17) By the time it was night I was pretty hungry. So when it was good and dark I slid out from shore before moonrise and paddled over to the Illinois bank—about a quarter of a mile. I went out in the woods and cooked a supper, and I had about made up my mind I would stay there all night when I hear a *plunkety-plunk*[20], *plunkety-plunk*, and says to myself, horses coming; and next I hear people's voices. I got everything into the canoe as quick as I could, and then went creeping through the woods to see what I could find out. I hadn't got far when I hear a man say:

(18) "We better camp here if we can find a good place; the horses is about beat out. Let's look around."

(19) I didn't wait, but shoved out and paddled away easy. I tied up in the old place, and reckoned I would sleep in the canoe.

(20) I didn't sleep much.[21] I couldn't, somehow, for thinking. And every time I waked up I thought somebody had me by the neck. So the sleep didn't do me no good. By and by I says to myself, I can't live this way; I'm a-going to find out who it is that's here on the island with me; I'll find it out or bust[22]. Well, I felt better right off.

(21) So I took my paddle and slid out from shore just a step or two, and then let the canoe drop along down amongst the shadows. The moon was shining, and outside of the shadows it made it most as light as day. I poked along well on to an hour, everything still as rocks and sound asleep. Well, by this time I was most down to the foot of the island. A little ripply, cool breeze begun to blow, and that was as good as saying the night was about done. I give her a turn with the paddle and brung her nose to shore; then I got my gun and slipped out and into the

[20] plunkety-plunk: 拟声词，模拟马蹄的声音。

[21] 发现岛上还有别人，这让哈克寝食难安。最终哈克决定去弄个水落石出。

[22] bust /bʌst/ v. 打破；突击搜查

edge of the woods. I sat down there on a log, and looked out through the leaves. I see the moon go off watch, and the darkness begin to blanket the river.[23] But in a little while I see a pale streak over the treetops, and knowed the day was coming. So I took my gun and slipped off towards where I had run across that camp fire, stopping every minute or two to listen. But I hadn't no luck somehow; I couldn't seem to find the place. But by and by, sure enough, I catched a glimpse of fire away through the trees. I went for it, cautious and slow. By and by I was close enough to have a look, and there laid a man on the ground. It most give me the fantods[24]. He had a blanket around his head, and his head was nearly in the fire. I set there behind a clump of bushes in about six foot of him, and kept my eyes on him steady. It was getting gray daylight now. Pretty soon he gapped and stretched himself and hove off the blanket, and it was Miss Watson's Jim! I bet I was glad to see him. I says:

(22) "Hello, Jim!" and skipped out.

(23) He bounced up[25] and stared at me wild. Then he drops down on his knees, and puts his hands together and says:

(24) "Doan' hurt me—don't! I hain't ever done no harm to a ghos'. I alwuz liked dead people, en done all I could for 'em.[26] You go en git in de river agin, whah you b'longs, en doan' do nuffn to Ole Jim, 'at 'uz awluz yo' fren'."

(25) Well, I warn't long making him understand I warn't dead. I was ever so glad to see Jim. I warn't lonesome now. I told him I warn't afraid of HIM telling the people where I was. I talked along, but he only set there and looked at me; never said nothing. Then I says:

(26) "It's good daylight. Le's get breakfast. Make up your camp fire good."

(27) "What's de use er makin' up de camp fire to cook strawbries en sich truck? But you got a gun, hain't you? Den we kin git sumfn better den strawbries."

(28) "Strawberries and such truck," I says. "Is that what you live on?"

(29) "I couldn' git nuffn else," he says.

[23] 我看见月亮已经消逝，黑暗开始笼罩河面。

[24] fantod /ˈfænˌtɒd/ *n.* 烦躁；坐立不安；惊恐

[25] bounce up: 弹跳起来

[26] 吉姆使用的是黑人土语。在阅读的时候可以根据发音进行猜测。以这一段的第一句话为例：Don't hurt me—don't! I haven't ever done no harm to a ghost. I always liked dead people, and done all I could for them.

(30) "Why, how long you been on the island, Jim?"

(31) "I come heah de night arter you's killed."

(32) "What, all that time?"

(33) "Yes—indeedy."

(34) "And ain't you had nothing but that kind of rubbage to eat?"

(35) "No, sah—nuffn else."

(36) "Well, you must be most starved, ain't you?"

(37) "I reck'n I could eat a hoss. I think I could. How long you ben on de islan'?"

(38) "Since the night I got killed."

(39) "No! W'y, what has you lived on? But you got a gun. Oh, yes, you got a gun. Dat's good. Now you kill sumfn en I'll make up de fire.[27]"

(40) So we went over to where the canoe was, and while he built a fire in a grassy open place amongst the trees, I fetched meal and bacon and coffee, and coffee-pot and frying-pan, and sugar and tin cups, and the nigger was set back considerable, because he reckoned it was all done with witchcraft. I catched a good big catfish, too, and Jim cleaned him with his knife, and fried him.

(41) When breakfast was ready we lolled[28] on the grass and eat it smoking hot. Jim laid it in with all his might, for he was most about starved. Then when we had got pretty well stuffed, we laid off and lazied. By and by Jim says:

(42) "But looky here, Huck, who wuz it dat'uz killed in dat shanty ef it warn't you?"

(43) Then I told him the whole thing, and he said it was smart. He said Tom Sawyer couldn't get up no better plan than what I had. Then I says:

(44) "How do you come to be here, Jim, and how'd you get here?"

(45) He looked pretty uneasy, and didn't say nothing for a minute. Then he says:

(46) "Maybe I better not tell."

(47) "Why, Jim?"

[27] 这部分是哈克询问吉姆。吉姆一直以草莓为食，已经饿坏了。吉姆告诉哈克，他在听说哈克被人杀死的那个晚上就来到了岛上。吉姆看到哈克有枪，让他去打点野味来，他生火，一起美餐一顿。

[28] loll /lɒl/ *v.* 懒洋洋地躺着

(48) "Well, dey's reasons. But you wouldn' tell on me ef I uz to tell you, would you, Huck?"

(49) "Blamed if I would, Jim."

(50) "Well, I b'lieve you, Huck. I—I RUN OFF."

(51) "Jim!"

(52) "But mind, you said you wouldn' tell—you know you said you wouldn' tell, Huck." [29]

(53) "Well, I did. I said I wouldn't, and I'll stick to it. Honest *injun*, I will. People would call me a low-down Abolitionist and despise me for keeping mum—but that don't make no difference. I ain't a-going to tell, and I ain't a-going back there, anyways. So, now, le's know all about it."

(54) "Well, you see, it 'uz dis way.[30] Ole missus—dat's Miss Watson—she pecks on me all de time, en treats me pooty rough, but she awluz said she wouldn' sell me down to Orleans[31]. But I noticed dey wuz a nigger trader roun' de place considable lately, en I begin to git oneasy. Well, one night I creeps to de do' pooty late, en de do' warn't quite shet, en I hear old missus tell de widder she gwyne to sell me down to Orleans, but she didn' want to, but she could git eight hund'd dollars for me, en it 'uz sich a big stack o' money she couldn' resis'. De widder she try to git her to say she wouldn' do it, but I never waited to hear de res'. I lit out mighty quick, I tell you.

(55) "I tuck out en shin down de hill, en 'spec to steal a skift 'long de sho' som'ers 'bove de town, but dey wuz people a-stirring yit, so I hid in de ole tumble-down cooper-shop on de bank to wait for everybody to go 'way. Well, I wuz dah all night. Dey wuz somebody roun' all de time. 'Long 'bout six in de mawnin' skifts begin to go by, en 'bout eight er nine every skift dat went 'long wuz talkin' 'bout how yo' pap come over to de town en say you's killed. Dese las' skifts wuz full o' ladies en genlmen a-goin' over for to see de place. Sometimes dey'd pull up at de sho' en take a res' b'fo' dey started acrost, so by de talk I got to know all 'bout de killin'. I 'uz powerful sorry you's killed, Huck, but I ain't no mo' now.

(56) "I laid dah under de shavin's all day. I 'uz hungry, but

[29] 吉姆让哈克保证不会说出去，才告诉哈克自己逃跑的原因。

[30] 原来吉姆是觉得沃森小姐想要把他卖到奥尔良，于是才决定出逃的。

[31] Orleans /ɔːˈliənz/ 奥尔良，是当时美国南方黑奴买卖盛行的地区。

I warn't afeard; bekase I knowed ole missus en de widder wuz goin' to start to de camp-meet'n' right arter breakfas' en be gone all day, en dey knows I goes off wid de cattle 'bout daylight, so dey wouldn' 'spec to see me roun' de place, en so dey wouldn' miss me tell arter dark in de evenin'. De yuther servants wouldn' miss me, kase dey'd shin out en take holiday soon as de ole folks 'uz out'n de way.

(57) "Well, when it come dark I tuck out up de river road, en went 'bout two mile er more to whah dey warn't no houses. I'd made up my mine 'bout what I's agwyne to do. You see, ef I kep' on tryin' to git away afoot, de dogs 'ud track me; ef I stole a skift to cross over, dey'd miss dat skift, you see, en dey'd know 'bout whah I'd lan' on de yuther side, en whah to pick up my track. So I says, a raff is what I's arter; it doan' *make* no track.

(58) "I see a light a-comin' roun' de p'int bymeby, so I wade' in en shove' a log ahead o' me en swum more'n half way acrost de river, en got in 'mongst de drift-wood, en kep' my head down low, en kinder swum agin de current tell de raff come along. Den I swum to de stern uv it en tuck a-holt. It clouded up en 'uz pooty dark for a little while. So I clumb up en laid down on de planks. De men 'uz all 'way yonder in de middle, whah de lantern wuz. De river wuz a-risin', en dey wuz a good current; so I reck'n'd 'at by fo' in de mawnin' I'd be twenty-five mile down de river, en den I'd slip in jis b'fo' daylight en swim asho', en take to de woods on de Illinois side.

(59) "But I didn' have no luck. When we 'uz mos' down to de head er de islan' a man begin to come aft wid de lantern, I see it warn't no use fer to wait, so I slid overboard en struck out fer de islan'. Well, I had a notion I could lan' mos' anywhers, but I couldn't—bank too bluff. I 'uz mos' to de foot er de islan' b'fo' I found' a good place. I went into de woods en jedged I wouldn' fool wid raffs no mo', long as dey move de lantern roun' so. I had my pipe en a plug er dog-leg, en some matches in my cap, en dey warn't wet, so I 'uz all right[32]."

(60) "And so you ain't had no meat nor bread to eat all this time? Why didn't you get mud-turkles?"

[32] 从第55段到第59段，吉姆向哈克讲述了自己逃跑的全过程。

(61) "How you gwyne to git 'm? You can't slip up on um en grab um; en how's a body gwyne to hit um wid a rock? How could a body do it in de night? En I warn't gwyne to show myset on de bank in de daytime."

(62) "Well, that's so. You've had to keep in the woods all the time, of course. Did you hear 'em shooting the cannon?"

(63) "Oh, yes. I knowed dey was arter you. I see um go by heah—watched um thoo de bushes."

(64) Some young birds come along, flying a yard or two at a time and lighting. Jim said it was a sign it was going to rain. He said it was a sign when young chickens flew that way, and so he reckoned it was the same way when young birds done it. I was going to catch some of them, but Jim wouldn't let me. He said it was death.[33] He said his father laid mighty sick once, and some of them catched a bird, and his old granny said his father would die, and he did.

(65) And Jim said you mustn't count the things you are going to cook for dinner, because that would bring bad luck. The same if you shook the table-cloth after sundown.[34] And he said if a man owned a beehive[35] and that man died, the bees must be told about it before sun-up next morning, or else the bees would all weaken down and quit work and die. Jim said bees wouldn't sting idiots; but I didn't believe that, because I had tried them lots of times myself, and they wouldn't sting me.

(66) I had heard about some of these things before, but not all of them. Jim knowed all kinds of signs. He said he knowed most everything. I said it looked to me like all the signs was about bad luck, and so I asked him if there warn't any good-luck signs.[36] He says:

(67) "Mighty few—an' dey ain't no use to a body. What you want to know when good luck's a-comin' for? Want to keep it off?"[37] And he said: "Ef you's got hairy arms en a hairy breas', it's a sign dat you's agwyne to be rich. Well, dey's some use in a sign like dat, 'kase it's so fur ahead. You see, maybe you's got to be po' a long time fust, en so you might git discourage' en kill yo'sef 'f you didn' know by de sign dat you

[33] 吉姆很迷信。哈克想要抓鸟,吉姆不让,说抓鸟是要死人的。

[34] 吉姆还说,做饭的时候,千万不要数那些东西,你只要数一数,就会倒霉的。太阳落山以后,你要是抖桌布,也是要倒霉的。

[35] beehive /ˈbiːhaɪv/ *n.* 蜂窝

[36] 我问吉姆,好像所有迹象都是说会带来霉运,难道没有什么是好兆头吗?

[37] 在这里吉姆的回答很机智,他认为好兆头是不需要躲避开的,所以不需要特别关注。

gwyne to be rich bymeby."

(68) "Have you got hairy arms and a hairy breast, Jim?"

(69) "What's de use to ax dat question? Don't you see I has?"

(70) "Well, are you rich?"

(71) "No, but I ben rich wunst, and gwyne to be rich agin. Wunst I had foteen dollars, but I tuck to specalat'n', en got busted out."

(72) "What did you speculate in, Jim?"

(73) "Well, fust I tackled stock."

(74) "What kind of stock?"

(75) "Why, live stock—cattle, you know. I put ten dollars in a cow. But I ain' gwyne to resk no mo' money in stock. De cow up 'n' died on my han's."

(76) "So you lost the ten dollars." [38]

(77) "No, I didn't lose it all. I on'y los' 'bout nine of it. I sole de hide en taller for a dollar en ten cents."

(78) "You had five dollars and ten cents left. Did you speculate any more?"

(79) "Yes. You know that one-laigged nigger dat b'longs to old Misto Bradish? Well, he sot up a bank, en say anybody dat put in a dollar would git fo' dollars mo' at de en' er de year. Well, all de niggers went in, but dey didn't have much. I wuz de on'y one dat had much. So I stuck out for mo' dan fo' dollars, en I said 'f I didn' git it I'd start a bank mysef. Well, o' course dat nigger want' to keep me out er de business, bekase he says dey warn't business 'nough for two banks, so he say I could put in my five dollars en he pay me thirty-five at de en' er de year.

(80) "So I done it. Den I reck'n'd I'd inves' de thirty-five dollars right off en keep things a-movin'. Dey wuz a nigger name' Bob, dat had ketched a wood-flat, en his marster didn' know it; en I bought it off'n him en told him to take de thirty-five dollars when de en' er de year come; but somebody stole de wood-flat dat night, en nex day de one-laigged nigger say de bank's busted. So dey didn' none uv us git no money."

[38] 吉姆和哈克谈论了自己之前的一次投资经历。他花了十块钱去买了一头牛，结果牛死了，白白损失了九块钱。

(81) "What did you do with the ten cents, Jim?"

(82) "Well, I 'uz gwyne to spen' it, but I had a dream, en de dream tole me to give it to a nigger name' Balum[39]—Balum's Ass dey call him for short; he's one er dem chuckleheads, you know. But he's lucky, dey say, en I see I warn't lucky. De dream say let Balum inves' de ten cents en he'd make a raise for me. Well, Balum he tuck de money, en when he wuz in church he hear de preacher say dat whoever give to de po' len' to de Lord, en boun' to git his money back a hund'd times. So Balum he tuck en give de ten cents to de po', en laid low to see what wuz gwyne to come of it."

(83) "Well, what did come of it, Jim?"

(84) "Nuffn never come of it. I couldn' manage to k'leck dat money no way; en Balum he couldn'. I ain' gwyne to len' no mo' money 'dout I see de security. Boun' to git yo' money back a hund'd times, de preacher says! Ef I could git de ten *cents* back, I'd call it squah, en be glad er de chanst."

(85) "Well, it's all right anyway, Jim, long as you're going to be rich again some time or other."

(86) "Yes; en I's rich now, come to look at it. I owns mysef, en I's wuth eight hund'd dollars. I wisht I had de money, I wouldn' want no mo'."[40]

[39] Balum: 巴兰,《圣经·旧约全书》中的一位先知,他被派去诅咒以色列,在遭到自己所骑驴子的责备后,转而祝福了以色列人。

[40] "是的,我现在已经富了。看看,我现在属于我自己,我自己就值八百块钱。我希望我有这笔钱,其他再无所求。"
吉姆认为自由对他来说很重要,当他自己属于自己时,他就别无所求了。

精华赏析

在这一章中哈克和吉姆在岛上见面。大家可以分析下这两个人物有什么相似点。我们可以从很多角度提出自己的看法。这里我们从"原型"这个角度探讨一下两个人物之间的相似之处。

弗雷泽的代表作《金枝》采用文化人类学的方法对原型批评的产生起到了重要的作用。弗雷泽主要是发现和提出了作为原始民族思维和行动规则的"交感巫术"原则,他发现原始人类有这样一个共同信念:"人类与自然之间始终存在着某种交互感应的关系,人们可以通过各种象征性的活动把自我的情感、愿望与意志投射到自然中去,这样就可以达到对对象的控制目的。交感巫术具有两种基本形式,即'模仿巫术'和'染触巫术'。"(邱运华,2006:

113）心理学家荣格的“集体无意识”理论也对原型批评产生了重要影响。

荣格是弗洛伊德的学生，后来他们因为学术观点不同而分道扬镳。荣格主要反对老师弗洛伊德的“性”理论和“无意识”理论。弗洛伊德认为人类一切行为的内心源动力都来自性欲望（sexual desire），性欲是人类最本能的欲望。另外，弗洛伊德所说的无意识只包括“个体无意识”。荣格将无意识分成了两类：一类是“个体无意识”，一类是“集体无意识”。而“集体无意识”的内容主要是原型。

荣格（1987）认为“原型概念对集体无意识观点是不可缺少的，它指出了精神中各种确定形式的存在，这些形式无论在何时何地都普遍地存在着。在神话研究中它们被称为‘母题’”。荣格将原型分为了两类，形象的型式（types of figures）和情境的型式（types of situations）。

形象的型式是与人类形象相关的各种原型，如阴影、人格面具、阿尼玛、阿尼姆斯等。

情境的型式在文学艺术故事中很常见，如《圣安娜与圣母子》中的“双重母亲”“双重血统”的母题，再如《尤利西斯》中“英雄还乡”的母题。

加拿大学者弗莱也是原型批评的重要学者之一。弗莱在《批评的解剖》中认为原型就是“典型的即反复出现”的意象。在《布莱克的原型处理手法》中，他更加明确地认为“我把原型看作文学作品里的因素，它或是一个人物，一个意象，一个叙述定势，或是一种可以从范畴较大的同类描述中抽取出来的思想”。（邱运华，2006：13）

让我们回到最初提出的那个问题，从原型批评这个角度能否找到这一章中哈克和吉姆的相似点呢？

其一，哈克和吉姆有着相同的人物形象原型。他们都是低于一般人和环境的底层人民，也就是被奴役、受迫害的人物原型。哈克没有母亲，父亲不管儿子死活，整日毒打他。吉姆则是一个黑奴，没有自由，每日辛苦劳作，还要面临随时被主人变卖的可能性。

其二，这一章中我们看到了一个相同的故事原型，那就是“逃离”。这与上一点的人物原型有着密切关系。因为两个人物原型都是被奴役、被迫害的底层人民，所以为了获得自由他们同样选择了“逃离”。在这一章中我们也发现故事设计上有个很巧合的地方，二人是在同一天“逃离”，同一天来到了杰克逊岛上的。鲁迅的小说中也常常出现“逃离”的故事原型，比如《祝福》中的“我”就有一个“离开—归来—再离开”的过程。“我”的离开就是一种“逃离”。

其三，故事中的思想原型，那就是追求自由。哈克想要逃离父亲的掌控，但是又不想再次回到道格拉斯寡妇那里。因为无论是父亲把他锁在树林深处的小屋，还是寡妇让他穿上整洁的衣服，每天让他规规矩矩地吃饭、上学，都让哈克觉得没有自由。吉姆的失去自由就更显而易见了，黑奴可以被主人随意买卖。于是我们发现整本小说的思想原型就是二人冒险追求自由的故事。在中外众多小说中这样的思想原型反反复复地出现，比如巴金的“激流三部曲”中的觉慧就是封建大家族中追求自由的先锋人物，整本小说中一部分青年人与大家族对抗追求自由，甚至一些年轻人为此付出了生命的代价，比如鸣凤。

我们还发现从人物原型到故事原型，再到思想原型，这三者是紧密相连的。因为底层人民的人物原型设计,所以才会在故事情节发展中自然而然地不断促成他们的“逃离”。把人物放在这样的故事情节中是合情合理的。那么作者想用这样的故事去阐明一个什么道理呢?很显然,人物的“逃离”都有明确的目的性,追求自由,追求向往的生活。本章中吉姆说的最后一句话,此时看来极有深意,“我自己属于自己,其他再无所求!”

阅读思考

1. 讲讲你读过的书中关于“追求自由”的故事。
2. 你还能在书中找到哪些原型?哪些典型的意象?

CHAPTER IX

导读：在吉姆的建议下，哈克和吉姆一起把东西搬进了山洞里。正如吉姆所说，一场暴雨来袭。雨停后，岛上涨水，哈克和吉姆撑着木筏四处转悠，发现了一座飘来的木板房。他们在里面发现了一个死人。他们从木板房中搜罗了一些有用的东西，满载而归。

(1) I WANTED to go and look at a place right about the middle of the island that I'd found when I was exploring; so we started and soon got to it, because the island was only three miles long and a quarter of a mile wide.

(2) This place was a tolerable long, steep hill or ridge about forty foot high. We had a rough time getting to the top, the sides was so steep and the bushes so thick. We tramped and clumb around all over it, and by and by found a good big cavern in the rock, most up to the top on the side towards Illinois. The cavern was as big as two or three rooms bunched together[1], and Jim could stand up straight in it. It was cool in there. Jim was for putting our traps in there right away, but I said we didn't want to be climbing up and down there all the time.

(3) Jim said if we had the canoe hid in a good place, and had all the traps in the cavern, we could rush there if anybody was to come to the island, and they would never find us without dogs. And, besides, he said them little birds had said it was going to rain, and did I want the things to get wet?[2]

(4) So we went back and got the canoe, and paddled up abreast the cavern, and lugged[3] all the traps up there. Then we hunted up a place close by to hide the canoe in, amongst the thick willows. We took some fish off of the lines and set them

[1] bunch together:(使)集中；聚拢

[2] 吉姆说，要是我们把木筏好好藏起来，把所有的东西都搬进山洞里，这样有人来到岛上，我们就能跑去那躲起来。他们只要不带狗，肯定找不到我们。另外，那些鸟已经告诉我们要下雨了，难道你想让所有的东西都打湿吗？

[3] lug /lʌg/ v. 吃力地搬运；用力拖

again, and begun to get ready for dinner.

(5) The door of the cavern was big enough to roll a hogshead in, and on one side of the door the floor stuck out a little bit, and was flat and a good place to build a fire on. So we built it there and cooked dinner.

(6) We spread the blankets inside for a carpet, and eat our dinner in there. We put all the other things handy at the back of the cavern. Pretty soon it darkened up, and begun to thunder and lighten; so the birds was right about it. Directly it begun to rain, and it rained like all fury[4], too, and I never see the wind blow so. It was one of these regular summer storms. It would get so dark that it looked all blue-black outside, and lovely; and the rain would thrash[5] along by so thick that the trees off a little ways looked dim and spider-webby[6]; and here would come a blast of wind that would bend the trees down and turn up the pale under-side of the leaves; and then a perfect ripper of a gust would follow along and set the branches to tossing their arms as if they was just wild[7]; and next, when it was just about the bluest and blackest[8]—FST! it was as bright as glory, and you'd have a little glimpse of tree-tops a-plunging about away off yonder in the storm, hundreds of yards further than you could see before; dark as sin again in a second, and now you'd hear the thunder let go with an awful crash, and then go rumbling, grumbling, tumbling[9], down the sky towards the under side of the world, like rolling empty barrels down stairs[10]—where it's long stairs and they bounce a good deal, you know.

(7) "Jim, this is nice," I says. "I wouldn't want to be nowhere else but here. Pass me along another hunk of fish and some hot corn-bread."

(8) "Well, you wouldn't a ben here 'f it hadn't a ben for Jim.[11] You'd a ben down dah in de woods widout any dinner, en gittn' mos' drownded, too; dat you would, honey. Chickens knows when it's gwyne to rain, en so do de birds, chile."

(9) The river went on raising and raising for ten or twelve days, till at last it was over the banks. The water was three or four foot deep on the island in the low places and on the Illinois

[4] 拟人(personification)

[5] thrash /θræʃ/ v. 抽打;连续击打

[6] 隐喻(metaphor)

[7] 拟人(personification)

[8] 谐音(consonance)

[9] 这三个词都有两个音节,第一个音节重读,而且两个音节都押韵,这种情况是诗中的阴韵(feminine rhyme),也叫双韵(double rhyme)。

[10] 明喻(simile)

[11] 这一段中,吉姆夸耀自己,幸亏因为他的提醒,他们才能躲进山洞,不会在雨地里没吃没喝,还被淋成落汤鸡。吉姆的生活经验比哈克丰富。

bottom. On that side it was a good many miles wide, but on the Missouri side it was the same old distance across—a half a mile—because the Missouri shore was just a wall of high bluffs[12].

(10) Daytimes we paddled all over the island in the canoe, It was mighty cool and shady in the deep woods, even if the sun was blazing outside. We went winding in and out amongst the trees, and sometimes the vines hung so thick we had to back away and go some other way. Well, on every old broken-down tree you could see rabbits and snakes and such things; and when the island had been overflowed a day or two they got so tame,[13] on account of being hungry, that you could paddle right up and put your hand on them if you wanted to; but not the snakes and turtles—they would slide off in the water. The ridge our cavern was in was full of them. We could a had pets enough if we'd wanted them.

(11) One night we catched a little section of a lumber raft—nice pine planks. It was twelve foot wide and about fifteen or sixteen foot long, and the top stood above water six or seven inches—a solid, level floor. We could see saw-logs go by in the daylight sometimes, but we let them go; we didn't show ourselves in daylight.

(12) Another night when we was up at the head of the island, just before daylight, here comes a frame-house down, on the west side. She was a two-story, and tilted over considerable. We paddled out and got aboard—clumb in at an upstairs window. But it was too dark to see yet, so we made the canoe fast and set in her to wait for daylight.

(13) The light begun to come before we got to the foot of the island. Then we looked in at the window. We could make out a bed, and a table, and two old chairs, and lots of things around about on the floor, and there was clothes hanging against the wall. There was something laying on the floor in the far corner that looked like a man. So Jim says:

(14) "Hello, you!"

(15) But it didn't budge. So I hollered again, and then Jim

[12] bluff /blʌf/ *n.*（尤指海边或河边的）峭壁；陡岸

[13] 这里写了涨水后动物的变化。因为饥饿，动物都会变得温顺。这样的描写来自仔细的观察和丰富的生活体验。

says:

(16) "De man ain't asleep—he's dead. You hold still—I'll go en see."

(17) He went, and bent down and looked, and says:

(18) "It's a dead man. Yes, indeedy; naked, too. He's ben shot in de back. I reck'n he's ben dead two er three days. Come in, Huck, but doan' look at his face—it's too gashly." [14]

(19) I didn't look at him at all. Jim throwed some old rags over him, but he needn't done it; I didn't want to see him. There was heaps of old greasy cards scattered around over the floor, and old whisky bottles, and a couple of masks made out of black cloth; and all over the walls was the ignorantest kind of words and pictures made with charcoal. There was two old dirty calico dresses, and a sun-bonnet, and some women's underclothes hanging against the wall, and some men's clothing, too.[15] We put the lot into the canoe—it might come good. There was a boy's old speckled straw hat on the floor; I took that, too. And there was a bottle that had had milk in it, and it had a rag stopper for a baby to suck. We would a took the bottle, but it was broke. There was a seedy old chest, and an old hair trunk with the hinges broke. They stood open, but there warn't nothing left in them that was any account. The way things was scattered about we reckoned the people left in a hurry, and warn't fixed so as to carry off most of their stuff.

(20) We got an old tin lantern, and a butcher-knife without any handle, and a bran-new Barlow knife worth two bits in any store, and a lot of tallow[16] candles, and a tin candlestick[17], and a gourd, and a tin cup, and a ratty old bedquilt off the bed, and a reticule[18] with needles and pins and beeswax[19] and buttons and thread and all such truck in it, and a hatchet[20] and some nails, and a fishline as thick as my little finger with some monstrous hooks on it, and a roll of buckskin[21], and a leather dog-collar, and a horseshoe, and some vials of medicine that didn't have no label on them; and just as we was leaving I found a tolerable good curry-comb, and Jim he found a ratty[22] old fiddle-bow, and a wooden leg. The straps was broke off of it, but, barring that, it

[14] "是个死人。他没穿衣服，背后中了一枪。我猜想他可能已经死了两三天了。进来，哈克，但是不要看他的脸——太吓人了。"

[15] 地上东一堆，西一簇，都是油汪汪的旧纸牌，好几个盛威士忌的旧瓶子，还有两个黑布做的假面具；四壁都是用木炭乱涂的最无聊的字和画。两件肮脏的印花棉布旧褂子，一顶遮太阳的女帽，加上好几件女人内衣，全都挂在墙上；此外还有好些男人的衣服。（潘庆舲 译）

[16] **tallow** /ˈtæləʊ/ *n.*（用以制造蜡烛、肥皂等）动物油脂

[17] **candlestick** /ˈkændlstɪk/ *n.* 蜡烛台

[18] **reticule** /ˈretɪkjuːl/ *n.*（女用）收口手提包

[19] **beeswax** /ˈbiːzwæks/ *n.* 黄蜡

[20] **hatchet** /ˈhætʃɪt/ *n.* 短柄小斧

[21] **buckskin** /ˈbʌkskɪn/ *n.* 鹿皮

[22] **ratty** /ˈræti/ *adj.* 糟糕的；状况差的

was a good enough leg, though it was too long for me and not long enough for Jim, and we couldn't find the other one, though we hunted all around.

(21) And so, take it all around, we made a good haul[23]. When we was ready to shove off we was a quarter of a mile below the island, and it was pretty broad day; so I made Jim lay down in the canoe and cover up with the quilt,[24] because if he set up people could tell he was a nigger a good ways off. I paddled over to the Illinois shore, and drifted down most a half a mile doing it. I crept up the dead water under the bank, and hadn't no accidents and didn't see nobody. We got home all safe.

[23] make a good haul: 满载而归；干得不错

[24] 天已大亮，为了保护吉姆不被别人发现，哈克让他躺在木筏上，还用被子盖住了他。

精华赏析

在这一章中我们学习一下角色—背景理论（Figure-Ground Theory）。角色—背景理论是1915年丹麦心理学家鲁宾首先提出的，是以突显原则为基础的一种理论。"角色"指某一认知概念和感知中突出的部分，即注意的焦点；"背景"则是为突出角色而衬托的部分。角色和背景是无法同时被感知到的，这就是所谓的角色背景分离（figure / ground segregation）的观点。（Ungerer，1996）

下面的图形中，上面是鸟，下面是鱼。注意看一下鱼和鸟相交的那一行，也就是最中间那一行，如果以黑色为背景，我们看到的是鱼；如果以白色为背景，我们看到的是鸟。在这一行中鱼和鸟不能同时被看到，看到什么取决于我们以什么为背景。

后来的格式塔心理学家将其用于对知觉的研究,他们认为人的知觉场始终被分为角色和背景两部分。角色部分更容易被知觉者所注意,背景部分则是细节比较模糊、不容易引起注意。(刘世生,2006)

我们以这本小说为例,小说主要讲的是哈克和吉姆撑着木筏,沿密西西比河顺流而下,这一路他们的经历。因此,小说中的"角色"应该是人物的活动和行为,其中对哈克这个人物的塑造是小说中最重要的部分。这一章的前五段"角色"依然是人物的活动。这五段主要是说哈克和吉姆爬到山顶,发现了很大一个山洞。吉姆建议把所有东西都搬进山洞,一来万一有人来了很难发现他们;二来也快下雨了,避免所有东西被淋湿。哈克起初觉得整天上上下下爬山洞很麻烦,后来还是听从了吉姆的建议。景色、环境描写在前五段中是"背景",如"This place was a tolerable long, steep hill or ridge about forty foot high""The cavern was as big as two or three rooms bunched together"等。

首先,我们要知道所有人物的活动都会在特定的环境、场景中进行。想要突出人物的形象,展现人物的行为活动,就一定要把人物置于特定的环境、场景中。虽然在不少情况下,环境、场景的描写是"背景",没有"角色"描写那么引人注目,却是必不可少的。甚至我们可以这样认为,在特定的"背景"中才能展现出有特色的"角色"。比如老舍的《骆驼祥子》在一开始用了大段笔墨详详细细地介绍了北平洋车夫的几派:有自己的车,年轻力壮,腿脚灵便的算是一派;拉着八成新的车,年纪稍大,跑得不是那么好的算作另一派;还有一派,车破,年纪在四十岁以上或者二十岁以下,因为他们跑得慢,所以要多走路少要钱;最惨的一派是半路失去了活命的营生,失了业,到了卖无可卖,当无可当的情况下才开始拉车,即使在车夫这个行当里也是最没地位的。有了这些详细的"背景"描写,我们再看小说中的"角色"——祥子,对这个人物形象也就更容易理解了。老舍先生这样写道:"有了这点简单的分析,我们再说祥子的地位,就像说——我们希望——一盘机器上的某种钉子那么准确了。祥子,在与'骆驼'这个外号发生关系以前,是个比较有自由的洋车夫,这就是说,他是属于年轻力壮,而且自己有车的那一类:自己的车,自己的生活,都在自己手里,高等车夫。这可绝不是件容易的事。一年,二年,至少有三四年;一滴汗,两滴汗,不知道多少万滴汗,才挣出那辆车。从风里雨里的咬牙,从饭里茶里的自苦,才赚出那辆车。"老舍先生自己就言明了"背景"和"角色"的关系,有了前面"背景"的分析,再说"角色"祥子的情况,就非常准确了。此时祥子的形象清晰可见,真真切切。祥子是一个吃苦耐劳的人,用自己的汗水和付出挣来了属于自己的一辆车,虽然拉车的生活依然辛苦,但是在车夫这个大群体里,他算是比较体面的高等车夫。此时的祥子有自己的车,有自己的生活,在一定程度上是有自由的。我们常常说要在典型环境中去塑造典型人物,也是同样的道理。

我们再回到哈克身上。这一章的前五段"角色"是哈克和吉姆的活动,"背景"是山洞周围的环境描写。从第六段开始到第十段,"角色"和"背景"的位置被调换了,"角色"是对暴雨天气的描写和小岛涨水后的景色描写,哈克和吉姆的活动被放置在了"背景"的位置。特别是第六段对暴雨天的描绘细节饱满,生动形象。这段被置于"角色"位置的环境描写是值得我们学习的优秀范文。文中使用了各类修辞手法,明喻、隐喻、押韵、拟人等。还有就是在描写景色的时候，为了能更好地再现场景，我们可以尽量调动多种感官去感受，比如文中的描写除了运用视觉以外，还成功地使用了听觉这一感官去再现那场暴风雨。"… and now you'd hear the thunder let go with an awful crash, and then go rumbling, grumbling, tumbling, down the sky towards the under side of the world, like rolling empty barrels down stairs—where it's long stairs and they bounce a good deal, you know." 用了一个明喻，把雷声比作好几个空木桶，顺着长长的楼梯，活蹦乱跳地往下滚。雨大风急，电闪雷鸣的场景就好像在我们眼前一般。

术语解说

角色—背景理论（Figure-Ground Theory）：角色—背景理论是 1915 年丹麦心理学家鲁宾首先提出的，是以突显原则为基础的一种理论。"角色" 指某一认知概念和感知中突出的部分，即注意的焦点，"背景" 则是为突出角色而衬托的部分。

阅读思考

1. 仿照本章中的第六段，描写一处景色或一个场景。
2. 运用 "角色—背景理论" 分析你读过的小说、诗歌等中的一个片段。

CHAPTER X

导读：哈克的恶作剧，把死蛇放在吉姆的毯子下面，使吉姆被这条死蛇的配偶咬了，哈克很后悔，也相信了吉姆之前说的触摸蛇皮会遭厄运。时间长了，哈克和吉姆觉得日子过得太闷，太乏味，于是哈克装扮成女孩的模样回到镇上去打探消息。

(1) AFTER breakfast I wanted to talk about the dead man and guess out how he come to be killed, but Jim didn't want to. He said it would fetch bad luck;[1] and besides, he said, he might come and ha'nt us; he said a man that warn't buried was more likely to go a-ha'nting around than one that was planted and comfortable. That sounded pretty reasonable, so I didn't say no more; but I couldn't keep from studying over it and wishing I knowed who shot the man, and what they done it for.

(2) We rummaged[2] the clothes we'd got, and found eight dollars in silver sewed up in the lining of an old blanket overcoat. Jim said he reckoned the people in that house stole the coat, because if they'd a knowed the money was there they wouldn't a left it. I said I reckoned they killed him, too; but Jim didn't want to talk about that. I says:

(3) "Now you think it's bad luck; but what did you say when I fetched in the snake-skin that I found on the top of the ridge day before yesterday?[3] You said it was the worst bad luck in the world to touch a snake-skin with my hands. Well, here's your bad luck! We've raked[4] in all this truck and eight dollars besides. I wish we could have some bad luck like this every day, Jim."

(4) "Never you mind, honey, never you mind. Don't you git too peart. It's a-comin'. Mind I tell you, it's a-comin'."

(5) It did come, too. It was a Tuesday that we had that talk.

[1] 吉姆不愿意谈论之前的那个死人，觉得这样会招来厄运。

[2] **rummage** /ˈrʌmɪdʒ/ *v.* 翻寻；乱翻；搜寻

[3] 这是一个反问句，哈克并不相信吉姆说的触摸蛇皮会遭厄运的说法。在这句话中 what 引导问句；when 引导的是时间状语从句；that 引导定语从句，其先行词是 snake-skin。

[4] **rake** /reɪk/ *v.* 搜寻

Well, after dinner Friday we was laying around in the grass at the upper end of the ridge, and got out of tobacco. I went to the cavern to get some, and found a rattlesnake in there. I killed him, and curled him up on the foot of Jim's blanket, ever so natural, thinking there'd be some fun when Jim found him there. Well, by night I forgot all about the snake, and when Jim flung himself down[5] on the blanket while I struck a light the snake's mate was there, and bit him.

(6) He jumped up yelling, and the first thing the light showed was the varmint[6] curled up and ready for another spring. I laid him out in a second with a stick, and Jim grabbed pap's whisky-jug and begun to pour it down.

(7) He was barefooted, and the snake bit him right on the heel. That all comes of my being such a fool as to not remember that wherever you leave a dead snake its mate always comes there and curls around it. Jim told me to chop off[7] the snake's head and throw it away, and then skin the body and roast[8] a piece of it. I done it, and he eat it and said it would help cure him. He made me take off the rattles and tie them around his wrist, too. He said that that would help. Then I slid out quiet and throwed the snakes clear away amongst the bushes; for I warn't going to let Jim find out it was all my fault, not if I could help it.

(8) Jim sucked and sucked at the jug, and now and then he got out of his head and pitched around[9] and yelled; but every time he come to himself he went to sucking at the jug again. His foot swelled up pretty big, and so did his leg; but by and by the drunk begun to come, and so I judged he was all right; but I'd druther been bit with a snake than pap's whisky.

(9) Jim was laid up for four days and nights. Then the swelling was all gone and he was around again. I made up my mind I wouldn't ever take a-holt of a snake-skin again with my hands, now that I see what had come of it.[10] Jim said he reckoned I would believe him next time. And he said that handling a snake-skin was such awful bad luck that maybe we hadn't got to the end of it yet. He said he druther see the new moon over his left shoulder as much as a thousand times than

[5] fling down: 躺下;迅速卧倒

[6] varmint /ˈvɑːmɪnt/ *n.* 恶棍;惹事生非的人
这里指的是响尾蛇。

[7] chop off: 砍掉;剪下

[8] roast /rəʊst/ *v.* 烘;烤

[9] pitch around: 左摇右晃

[10] 我下定决心,绝不再摸蛇皮一下,我明白这前因后果是怎么回事。(哈克认为吉姆被蛇咬,是他不听吉姆的劝告,用手摸蛇皮带来的厄运。)

take up a snake-skin in his hand. Well, I was getting to feel that way myself, though I've always reckoned that looking at the new moon over your left shoulder is one of the carelessest and foolishest things a body can do. Old Hank Bunker done it once, and bragged about[11] it; and in less than two years he got drunk and fell off of the shot-tower, and spread himself out so that he was just a kind of a layer,[12] as you may say; and they slid him edgeways between two barn doors for a coffin, and buried him so, so they say, but I didn't see it. Pap told me. But anyway it all come of looking at the moon that way, like a fool.

(10) Well, the days went along, and the river went down between its banks again; and about the first thing we done was to bait[13] one of the big hooks with a skinned rabbit and set it and catch a catfish that was as big as a man, being six foot two inches long, and weighed over two hundred pounds. We couldn't handle him, of course; he would a flung us into Illinois. We just set there and watched him rip and tear around till he drownded. We found a brass button in his stomach and a round ball, and lots of rubbage. We split the ball open with the hatchet, and there was a spool[14] in it. Jim said he'd had it there a long time, to coat it over so and make a ball of it. It was as big a fish as was ever catched in the Mississippi, I reckon. Jim said he hadn't ever seen a bigger one. He would a been worth a good deal over at the village. They peddle out such a fish as that by the pound in the market-house there; everybody buys some of him; his meat's as white as snow[15] and makes a good fry.

(11) Next morning I said it was getting slow and dull, and I wanted to get a stirring up[16] some way. I said I reckoned I would slip over the river and find out what was going on. Jim liked that notion; but he said I must go in the dark and look sharp. Then he studied it over and said, couldn't I put on some of them old things and dress up like a girl? That was a good notion, too. So we shortened up one of the calico[17] gowns, and I turned up my trouser-legs to my knees and got into it. Jim hitched it behind with the hooks, and it was a fair fit. I put on the sun-bonnet and tied it under my chin, and then for a body to look in and see

[11] brag out: 吹嘘；炫耀

[12] 这句话使用了夸张（hyperbole）和隐喻（metaphor）。

[13] bait /beɪt/ v. 在（鱼钩上）放诱饵

[14] spool /spuːl/ n. 线轴

[15] 明喻（simile）

[16] stirring up: 激动人心的事

[17] calico /ˈkælɪkəʊ/ n. 厚棉布；印花平布

my face was like looking down a joint of stove-pipe[18]. Jim said nobody would know me, even in the daytime, hardly. I practiced around all day to get the hang of the things, and by and by I could do pretty well in them, only Jim said I didn't walk like a girl; and he said I must quit pulling up my gown to get at my britches-pocket[19]. I took notice, and done better.

(12) I started up the Illinois shore in the canoe just after dark.

(13) I started across to the town from a little below the ferry-landing, and the drift of the current fetched me in at the bottom of the town. I tied up and started along the bank. There was a light burning in a little shanty that hadn't been lived in for a long time, and I wondered who had took up quarters there. I slipped up and peeped in at the window. There was a woman about forty year old in there knitting by a candle that was on a pine table. I didn't know her face; she was a stranger, for you couldn't start a face in that town that I didn't know.[20] Now this was lucky, because I was weakening; I was getting afraid I had come; people might know my voice and find me out. But if this woman had been in such a little town two days she could tell me all I wanted to know; so I knocked at the door, and made up my mind I wouldn't forget I was a girl.

[18] stove-pipe: *n.* 烟囱管

[19] britches-pocket:裤子口袋

[20] 这句话中使用了双重否定。哈克确定这个女人是外来人，因为他对镇子上的人很熟悉，没有他不认识的。

精华赏析

在这一章中我们来探讨一下词类与文体的关系。“在日常语言中，各种词类都有不同的功能，其出现都有一定的频率。爱里伽德曾经研究出美国英语中各种词类的平均使用频率。”（刘世生，2006:99）一些词类使用过多或者过少，相应的文体效果也会有所不同。爱里伽德认为名词的平均使用频率为27%，动词的平均使用频率为12.1%，形容词的平均使用频率为7.4%。

基于拉丁语法的传统，英语中一般把词分成九个词类：名词、动词、形容词、副词、介词、连词、冠词、感叹词以及限定词。这九个词类我们又可以划分成两类：一是开放类词，一是封闭类词。动词、形容词、副词、感叹词属于开放类词。开放类词的特点是随着时代的发展，这类词会不断扩大，不断有新词产生。介词、代词、连词、冠词和限定词属于封闭类词。封闭类词数量相对稳定，受时代、环境影响不大。

以本章的第十一段为例,这段话的总词汇量为214个,共使用各类动词49个,动词所占比率为22.9%,远远超过了爱里伽德给出的动词平均使用比率12.1%。其中描写哈克动作行为的动词有15个。这一段中哈克先告诉吉姆,他觉得这样的日子很无聊,想要找点刺激。哈克提出了一个想法,他想要回到岸上去,看看究竟发生了什么,吉姆支持哈克的想法。接下来就是在吉姆的帮助下,哈克为回到镇子上做各种准备。他们"截断了一件棉布褂子",哈克"把裤腿捋到膝盖上","穿上褂子",吉姆"用钓钩在背后把褂子钩住",哈克"戴上遮太阳的女帽","在下巴下面系上带子",哈克"练习了一整天","没多久就装扮得很到家了"。这一系列的动词使用详细描述了他们准备的细节,动感很强。

我们发现像这样动词占主体性位置的段落在小说中还很多,比如前面章节中描写哈克和汤姆半夜溜出寡妇家的院子,后面章节中描写哈克登上触礁轮船等。为什么小说中不少文段的动词使用频率会偏高呢?我们来分析一下这个问题。

首先,小说的角心人物是一个孩子——哈克,从哈克本身的特征来看,他就是一个天性好动,具有冒险精神、实践精神的孩子,他对世界的感知和认识是通过自己的行动。比如在第三章中我们提到过的,为了验证汤姆说的是不是真的,哈克是这样做的"I got an old tin lamp and an iron ring, and went out in the woods and rubbed and rubbed till I sweat like an Injun, calculating to build a palace and sell it; but it warn't no use, none of the genies come."这句话中,各类动词也有10个,所占比率为22.2%。这里一连串的动作描写,生动地刻画了哈克天真可爱的一面。我们仔细观察一下周围的孩子,会发现孩子们都具有一个相同的特征,好像他们永远也停不下来,随时都在不停地做各种动作,摸、抓、咬、舔、爬……这就是孩子认识世界的第一步。抓住了他们的动作特征,就抓住了孩子的本质。所以说,抓住哈克的动作特征,能够更好、更直接地体现这个人物的基本特征。

其次,哈克还有另外一个特点就是受教育程度低,没什么文化知识。如形容词性文体的文字大多是描写性的文体。以哈克有限的知识和文化水平来说,他不太能文采飞扬,极尽修饰之能事地去描写一个事物、一个场景。如果大量使用丰富多彩的形容词,与哈克的身份和能力不相符。小说更多地还是想让哈克去讲这个故事,用哈克的眼睛去看这个世界,用简单朴实的语言去展示密西西比河的人情风貌。不过话又说回来,小说中有没有形容词占主导的段落呢?当然是有的。这就是我们在前面章节中说到的"叙述方位"的问题了,角心人物提供经验,叙述者提供声音。小说中优美的风景描写是叙述者的语言,哈克提供的是经验和感受。

阅读思考

1. 找一段名词性文体的文字,并分析其特征。
2. 找一段形容词性文体的文字,并分析其特征。

CHAPTER XI

导读：哈克装扮成女孩上岸打探消息，遇到一位妇女热情地和哈克话家常。这个女人提到了哈克“被杀事件”。后来在相处中，她发现哈克是个男孩子。

(1) "*come* in," says the woman, and I did. She says:

(2) "Take a cheer."

(3) I done it. She looked me all over with her little shiny eyes, and says:

(4) "What might your name be?"

(5) "Sarah Williams."

(6) "Where 'bouts do you live? In this neighborhood?'"

(7) "No'm. In Hookerville, seven mile below. I've walked all the way and I'm all tired out."

(8) "Hungry, too, I reckon. I'll find you something." [1]

(9) "No'm, I ain't hungry. I was so hungry I had to stop two miles below here at a farm; so I ain't hungry no more. It's what makes me so late. My mother's down sick, and out of money and everything, and I come to tell my uncle Abner Moore. He lives at the upper end of the town, she says. I hain't ever been here before. Do you know him?"

(10) "No; but I don't know everybody yet. I haven't lived here quite two weeks. [2] It's a considerable ways to the upper end of the town. You better stay here all night. Take off your bonnet."

(11) "No," I says; "I'll rest a while, I reckon, and go on. I ain't afeared of the dark."

(12) She said she wouldn't let me go by myself, but her husband would be in by and by, maybe in a hour and a half, and

[1] 这个女人问哈克是不是饿了，打算给哈克找点儿吃的。

[2] 正如上一章哈克所判断的，这个女人的确是个外来人。她住在这儿还不满两个星期。

she'd send him along with me.[3] Then she got to talking about her husband, and about her relations up the river, and her relations down the river, and about how much better off they used to was, and how they didn't know but they'd made a mistake coming to our town, instead of letting well alone—and so on and so on, till I was afeard I had made a mistake coming to her to find out what was going on in the town;[4] but by and by she dropped on to pap and the murder, and then I was pretty willing to let her clatter right along. She told about me and Tom Sawyer finding the six thousand dollars (only she got it ten) and all about pap and what a hard lot he was, and what a hard lot I was, and at last she got down to where I was murdered. I says:

(13) "Who done it? We've heard considerable about these goings on down in Hookerville, but we don't know who 'twas that killed Huck Finn."

(14) "Well, I reckon there's a right smart chance of people *here* that'd like to know who killed him. Some think old Finn done it himself."

(15) "No—is that so?"

(16) "Most everybody thought it at first. He'll never know how nigh he come to getting lynched[5]. But before night they changed around and judged it was done by a runaway nigger named Jim.[6]"

(17) "Why *he*—"

(18) I stopped. I reckoned I better keep still. She run on, and never noticed I had put in at all:

(19) "The nigger run off the very night Huck Finn was killed. So there's a reward out for him—three hundred dollars. And there's a reward out for old Finn, too—two hundred dollars. You see, he come to town the morning after the murder, and told about it, and was out with 'em on the ferryboat hunt, and right away after he up and left. Before night they wanted to lynch him, but he was gone, you see. Well, next day they found out the nigger was gone; they found out he hadn't ben seen sence ten o'clock the night the murder was done. So then they put it on him, you see; and while they was full of it, next day, back comes

[3] 她说她不会让我独自一个人赶夜路的，她的丈夫再有一个半小时左右就回来了。到时她让她丈夫送我。

[4] 这个女人絮絮叨叨说了好多家事，让哈克觉得找她来打探消息可能是个错误的决定。

[5] lynch /lɪntʃ/ *v.* 用私刑处死

[6] 起初大家觉得是哈克的父亲杀死了哈克，后来又觉得是逃奴吉姆干的。

old Finn, and went boo-hooing to Judge Thatcher to get money to hunt for the nigger all over Illinois with. The judge gave him some, and that evening he got drunk, and was around till after midnight with a couple of mighty hard-looking strangers, and then went off with them. Well, he hain't come back sence, and they ain't looking for him back till this thing blows over a little, for people thinks now that he killed his boy and fixed things so folks would think robbers done it, and then he'd get Huck's money without having to bother a long time with a lawsuit. People do say he warn't any too good to do it. Oh, he's sly, I reckon. If he don't come back for a year he'll be all right. You can't prove anything on him, you know; everything will be quieted down then, and he'll walk in Huck's money as easy as nothing."

(20) "Yes, I reckon so, 'm. I don't see nothing in the way of it. Has everybody guit thinking the nigger done it?"

(21) "Oh, no, not everybody. A good many thinks he done it. But they'll get the nigger pretty soon now, and maybe they can scare it out of him."

(22) "Why, are they after him yet?"

(23) "Well, you're innocent, ain't you! Does three hundred dollars lay around every day for people to pick up? Some folks think the nigger ain't far from here. I'm one of them—but I hain't talked it around. A few days ago I was talking with an old couple that lives next door in the log shanty, and they happened to say hardly anybody ever goes to that island over yonder that they call Jackson's Island. Don't anybody live there? says I. No, nobody, says they. I didn't say any more, but I done some thinking. I was pretty near certain I'd seen smoke over there,[7] about the head of the island, a day or two before that, so I says to myself, like as not that nigger's hiding over there; anyway, says I, it's worth the trouble to give the place a hunt. I hain't seen any smoke sence, so I reckon maybe he's gone, if it was him; but husband's going over to see—him and another man. He was gone up the river; but he got back today, and I told him as soon as he got here two hours ago."

[7] 这个女人曾经看见岛上有过烟火，觉得逃奴吉姆可能藏在岛上。她还打算让她丈夫去岛上搜寻一下。因为抓住吉姆可以获得三百块钱的奖金。

(24) I had got so uneasy I couldn't set still.[8] I had to do something with my hands; so I took up a needle off of the table and went to threading it. My hands shook, and I was making a bad job of it. When the woman stopped talking I looked up, and she was looking at me pretty curious and smiling a little. I put down the needle and thread, and let on to be interested—and I was, too—and says:

[8] 这个女人发现了哈克和吉姆的藏身之所，这让哈克烦躁不安，坐立不宁。

(25) "Three hundred dollars is a power of money. I wish my mother could get it. Is your husband going over there to-night?"

(26) "Oh, yes. He went up-town with the man I was telling you of, to get a boat and see if they could borrow another gun. They'll go over after midnight."

(27) "Couldn't they see better if they was to wait till daytime?"

(28) "Yes. And couldn't the nigger see better, too? After midnight he'll likely be asleep, and they can slip around through the woods and hunt up his camp fire all the better for the dark, if he's got one."

(29) "I didn't think of that."

(30) The woman kept looking at me pretty curious, and I didn't feel a bit comfortable. Pretty soon she says:

(31) "What did you say your name was, honey?"

(32) "M—Mary Williams."[9]

[9] 女人第一次问哈克的时候，他说自己叫 Sarah Williams。

(33) Somehow it didn't seem to me that I said it was Mary before, so I didn't look up—seemed to me I said it was Sarah; so I felt sort of cornered, and was afeared maybe I was looking it, too. I wished the woman would say something more; the longer she set still the uneasier I was. But now she says:

(34) "Honey, I thought you said it was Sarah when you first come in?"

(35) "Oh, yes'm, I did. Sarah Mary Williams. Sarah's my first name. Some calls me Sarah, some calls me Mary."

(36) "Oh, that's the way of it?"

(37) "Yes'm."

(38) I was feeling better then, but I wished I was out of

there, anyway. I couldn't look up yet.

(39) Well, the woman fell to talking about how hard times was, and how poor they had to live, and how the rats was as free as if they owned the place, and so forth and so on, and then I got easy again.[10] She was right about the rats. You'd see one stick his nose out of a hole in the corner every little while. She said she had to have things handy to throw at them when she was alone, or they wouldn't give her no peace. She showed me a bar of lead twisted up into a knot, and said she was a good shot with it generly, but she'd wrenched[11] her arm a day or two ago, and didn't know whether she could throw true now. But she watched for a chance, and directly banged away at a rat; but she missed him wide, and said "Ouch!" it hurt her arm so. Then she told me to try for the next one. I wanted to be getting away before the old man got back, but of course I didn't let on. I got the thing, and the first rat that showed his nose I let drive, and if he'd a stayed where he was he'd a been a tolerable sick rat. She said that was first-rate, and she reckoned I would hive the next one. She went and got the lump of lead and fetched it back, and brought along a hank of yarn[12] which she wanted me to help her with. I held up my two hands and she put the hank over them, and went on talking about her and her husband's matters. But she broke off to say:

[10] 排比句（parallel sentence）。描写女人家的生活艰难、贫穷。

[11] wrench /rentʃ/ *v.* 扭伤

[12] a hank of yarn: 一绞毛线

(40) "Keep your eye on the rats. You better have the lead in your lap, handy."

(41) So she dropped the lump into my lap just at that moment, and I clapped my legs together on it and she went on talking. But only about a minute. Then she took off the hank and looked me straight in the face, and very pleasant, and says:

(42) "Come, now, what's your real name?"

(43) "Wh—what, mum?"

(44) "What's your real name? Is it Bill, or Tom, or Bob?—or what is it?"

(45) I reckon I shook like a leaf, and I didn't know hardly what to do. But I says:

(46) "Please to don't poke fun at a poor girl like me, mum.

If I'm in the way here, I'll—"

(47) "No, you won't. Set down and stay where you are. I ain't going to hurt you, and I ain't going to tell on you, nuther. You just tell me your secret, and trust me. I'll keep it; and, what's more, I'll help you. So'll my old man if you want him to. You see, you're a runaway 'prentice, that's all. It ain't anything. There ain't no harm in it. You've been treated bad, and you made up your mind to cut. Bless you, child, I wouldn't tell on you. Tell me all about it now, that's a good boy."

(48) So I said it wouldn't be no use to try to play it any longer, and I would just make a clean breast and tell her everything, but she musn't go back on her promise. Then I told her my father and mother was dead, and the law had bound me out to a mean old farmer in the country thirty mile back from the river, and he treated me so bad I couldn't stand it no longer; he went away to be gone a couple of days, and so I took my chance and stole some of his daughter's old clothes and cleared out, and I had been three nights coming the thirty miles.[13] I traveled nights, and hid daytimes and slept, and the bag of bread and meat I carried from home lasted me all the way, and I had a-plenty. I said I believed my uncle Abner Moore would take care of me, and so that was why I struck out for this town of Goshen.

(49) "Goshen, child? This ain't Goshen. This is St. Petersburg. Goshen's ten mile further up the river. Who told you this was Goshen?"

(50) "Why, a man I met at daybreak this morning, just as I was going to turn into the woods for my regular sleep. He told me when the roads forked I must take the right hand, and five mile would fetch me to Goshen."

(51) "He was drunk, I reckon. He told you just exactly wrong."

(52) "Well, he did act like he was drunk, but it ain't no matter now. I got to be moving along. I'll fetch Goshen before daylight."

(53) "Hold on a minute. I'll put you up a snack to eat. You

[13] 于是我告诉她,我父母双亡,被卖给了一个刻薄的农民,他就住在离河三十英里的乡下。他待我很不好,我实在忍无可忍,趁他要出去两三天,就偷了他女儿的旧衣服跑了。我用了三个晚上走了三十英里。

might want it."

(54) So she put me up a snack, and says:

(55) "Say, when a cow's laying down, which end of her gets up first? Answer up prompt now—don't stop to study over it. Which end gets up first?"

(56) "The hind end, mum."

(57) "Well, then, a horse?"

(58) "The for'rard end, mum."

(59) "Which side of a tree does the moss grow on?"

(60) "North side."

(61) "If fifteen cows is browsing on a hillside, how many of them eats with their heads pointed the same direction?"

(62) "The whole fifteen, mum."

(63) "Well, I reckon you HAVE lived in the country.[14] I thought maybe you was trying to hocus[15] me again. What's your real name, now?"

(64) "George Peters, mum."

(65) "Well, try to remember it, George. Don't forget and tell me it's Elexander before you go, and then get out by saying it's George Elexander when I catch you. And don't go about women in that old calico. You do a girl tolerable poor, but you might fool men, maybe. Bless you, child, when you set out to thread a needle don't hold the thread still and fetch the needle up to it; hold the needle still and poke the thread at it; that's the way a woman most always does, but a man always does t'other way. And when you throw at a rat or anything, hitch yourself up a tiptoe and fetch your hand up over your head as awkward as you can, and miss your rat about six or seven foot. Throw stiff-armed from the shoulder, like there was a pivot[16] there for it to turn on, like a girl; not from the wrist and elbow, with your arm out to one side, like a boy. And, mind you, when a girl tries to catch anything in her lap she throws her knees apart; she don't clap them together, the way you did when you catched the lump of lead. Why, I spotted you for a boy when you was threading the needle; and I contrived the other things just to make certain.[17] Now trot along to your uncle, Sarah Mary Williams

[14] 女人连续问了好几个问题来测试哈克，看他是不是又在撒谎。

[15] hocus: *v.* 欺骗

[16] pivot /ˈpɪvət/ *n.* 支点；中心；枢轴

[17] 其实你穿针的时候，我已经发现你是个男孩。只是为了进一步确认，我又观察了一番。

George Elexander Peters, and if you get into trouble you send word to Mrs. Judith Loftus, which is me, and I'll do what I can to get you out of it.[19] Keep the river road all the way, and next time you tramp take shoes and socks with you. The river road's a rocky one, and your feet'll be in a condition when you get to Goshen, I reckon."

(66) I went up the bank about fifty yards, and then I doubled on my tracks and slipped back to where my canoe was, a good piece below the house. I jumped in, and was off in a hurry. I went up-stream far enough to make the head of the island, and then started across. I took off the sun-bonnet, for I didn't want no blinders[19] on then. When I was about the middle I heard the clock begin to strike, so I stops and listens; the sound come faint over the water but clear—eleven. When I struck the head of the island I never waited to blow, though I was most winded, but I shoved right into the timber where my old camp used to be, and started a good fire there on a high and dry spot.

(67) Then I jumped in the canoe and dug out for our place, a mile and a half below, as hard as I could go. I landed, and slopped through the timber and up the ridge and into the cavern. There Jim laid, sound asleep on the ground. I roused him out and says:

(68) "Git up and hump yourself, Jim! There ain't a minute to lose. They're after us!"

(69) Jim never asked no questions, he never said a word; but the way he worked for the next half an hour showed about how he was scared. By that time everything we had in the world was on our raft, and she was ready to be shoved out from the willow[20] cove where she was hid. We put out the camp fire at the cavern the first thing, and didn't show a candle outside after that.

(70) I took the canoe out from the shore a little piece, and took a look; but if there was a boat around I couldn't see it, for stars and shadows ain't good to see by. Then we got out the raft and slipped along down in the shade, past the foot of the island dead still—never saying a word[21].

[19] 女人关照哈克，要是遇到什么麻烦一定告诉她。她会设法帮助他的。

[19] blinder /ˈblaɪndə(r)/ *n.* 眼罩

[20] willow /ˈwɪləʊ/ *n.* 柳树

[21] 吉姆和哈克都处在一种惊慌不安的状态，两人一句话都没说。

精华赏析

在这一章中我们介绍一下女性主义文学批评。女性主义是伴随着西方的妇女解放运动而兴起的。特别是在二十世纪六十年代，西方第二次女权运动的高涨直接引发了女权主义文学批评。

女性主义的理论先驱有英国的弗吉尼亚·伍尔夫和法国的西蒙·波伏娃。

弗吉尼亚·伍尔夫的《一间自己的屋子》是女性主义批评的奠基之作。伍尔夫（1989:2）指出："一个女人如果要想写小说一定要有钱，还要有一间自己的屋子。"伍尔夫认为女性在文学界的地位不如男性，主要是因为经济上不独立。因经济上受困，女性没法得到良好的教育，因此缺乏文学创作的知识、文化积累。因经济上受困，女性在生活上依附男性，被限制在家里负责家庭琐事、照顾孩子这些事情，所以也就没有了独立的空间和自由支配的时间。伍尔夫提出了著名的"双性同体"思想，她认为每个人都同时被两种力量支配着，一个是男性力量，一个是女性力量，男性阳刚果敢，女性温柔细腻。伍尔夫认为没有纯粹的男人和女人，"双性同体"才是理想的人格，双性和谐才是理想的文学创作境界。

法国的西蒙·波伏娃在她《第二性》中认为男人把女人变成了"他者"。也就是说，男人是社会中的主要者，女人是次要者，是"他者"。在《第二性》的第十章中，波伏娃分析了五位作家笔下的女人神话。"在蒙特朗的作品中，男人是超人，女人只是作为一个低下的参照物来证明男人的高尚；劳伦斯的作品虽然在性爱关系上肯定了男性与女性的完美结合，但男人永远是引导者，女人只是被引导者；克劳代笔下的女人更接近上帝，但她们只是用来拯救男人的工具；布勒东虽然将女人视为诗，极尽赞美之能事，但仍将女人作为另一性来看待；司汤达的作品用更加人性化的眼光来看待妇女，但妇女仍被视为依附男性的另一性别。"（邱运华，2006:218）

后来肖瓦尔特研究了大量女性作家的作品，她认为女性和男性的创作有着很大差异，因此女性文学有自己独特的属性，然而女性的写作传统一直是被男权文化人为地压制和埋没了。在她全面研究了英国女性小说家的作品之后，提出了著名的女性文学"三个阶段"的学说。女性文学三段论是肖瓦尔特对女性主义批评理论框架的构建，也是对女权主义批评的重要理论贡献。肖瓦尔特把出现女性作家采用男性化笔名的流行做法的十九世纪四十年代至乔治·艾略特去世的1880年划为第一阶段，称之为"女性"阶段，这一阶段为较长时期的对主流传统流行模式的模仿以及对其艺术标准和社会角色观点的内化；把1880年至妇女取得选举权的1920年划为第二阶段，称之为"女权"阶段，这一阶段是对这些标准和价值观的抗议以及对少数派权利和价值观的倡导，也包括对自主权的要求；把自1920年至今划为第三阶段，称之为"女人"阶段，在这一阶段里女性的自我意识在二十世纪六十年代又取得了新的进展，这一阶段是自我发现阶段，是摆脱了对对立面的依赖之后向内在的转化，是对身份的寻找。

在男性笔下,女性具有一些共同的刻板形象。我们来看看《哈克贝利·费恩历险记》中的女性形象是什么样的。

一、女性皆为次要角色。这本小说中出现了不少女性形象,如道格拉斯寡妇、沃森小姐、朱迪·洛芙德斯太太、夏洛蒂小姐、索非亚小姐、玛丽·珍妮、苏珊、乔安娜等,无一例外都是次要角色。在小说中她们都是为衬托男性角色而出现的不重要的角色,这与女性的“他者”地位甚为符合。

二、刻板、不知变通的女性形象。以道格拉斯寡妇和沃森小姐为例,这两个女性都是因循守旧、正经古板的形象。这种女性形象区别于男性形象哈克和吉姆。两位男性形象都有敢于冲破传统规范的勇气和行动,都在努力追求新的生活,都认为自由重于一切。道格拉斯寡妇和妹妹沃森小姐则是每天按时按点吃饭、睡觉、做祷告,生活规规矩矩,一成不变,这一点很让哈克受不了,所以哈克宁愿去流浪也不愿再回到道格拉斯寡妇身边。哈克的生活随时都可能来点儿刺激和冒险,比如下一章中哈克就要到触礁的轮船上来一番历险。

三、阴郁、缺乏生气的女性形象。在小说的第十七章中描写了这样一位女性。他是格伦基福特家一位已故的女儿,名叫哀美琳·格伦基福特。从她生前的画作和诗作来看,这个孩子小小年纪却缺乏生气,她的生活笼罩在一片死气沉沉的氛围中。她画的女人穿着黑裙子,戴着黑帽子、黑面纱,穿着黑鞋子,右肘依偎着一块墓碑。在她的画中处处可以嗅到死亡的气息。这个女孩生前还喜欢写诗,可是她写的诗都是悼亡诗,也直接与死亡相关。这样的女性形象与活泼、充满生气的哈克形成了巨大的反差。哈克的生命中处处充满阳光,虽然生活贫穷,但哈克总能用自己的方法找点儿乐子,让日子快活起来。

四、单纯、头脑简单的女性形象。比如小说第二十五章中玛丽·简、苏珊、乔安娜三姐妹都是善良而有教养的女性形象。哈克、“国王”和“公爵”三个人原本骗了女孩儿们的钱,可是三姐妹却待哈克很好,尽量让哈克像在自己家里一样无拘无束,还把哈克当朋友。虽是善良,但也显得头脑简单,对“国王”和“公爵”导演的这场骗钱的戏没有丝毫警觉。“国王”只是呼呼啦啦一通胡扯,假装痛哭流涕一番,玛丽·简就把父亲临终时留下的那封信交给了“国王”。信中明确说了留下了些什么财产,以及金币藏在了什么地方。遇到这样的女孩儿,这意外之财得来也真是全不费工夫。这与哈克的鬼精灵形象也形成了对比和反差,哈克后来想办法帮三姐妹拿回了金币,藏在了彼得的棺材里。

这一章中朱迪·洛芙德斯太太是一个什么样的形象呢?大家不妨自己分析一下。

阅读思考

1. 分析这一章中朱迪·洛芙德斯太太的形象。
2. 朱迪·洛芙德斯太太是怎么发现哈克是个男孩儿的?

CHAPTER XII

导读：在这一章中哈克和吉姆继续顺流而下，他们在途中看到了一艘触礁的小轮船。哈克很好奇。虽然吉姆反对，但是哈克还是决定登船一探究竟。原来，在这艘船上还有三个人。

（1）IT must a been close on to one o'clock when we got below the island at last, and the raft did seem to go mighty slow. If a boat was to come along we was going to take to the canoe and break for the Illinois shore; and it was well a boat didn't come, for we hadn't ever thought to put the gun in the canoe, or a fishing-line, or anything to eat. We was in ruther too much of a sweat to think of so many things. It warn't good judgment to put *everything* on the raft.

（2）If the men went to the island I just expect they found the camp fire I built, and watched it all night for Jim to come. Anyways, they stayed away from us, and if my building the fire never fooled them it warn't no fault of mine. I played it as low down on them as I could.

（3）When the first streak of day began to show we tied up to a towhead in a big bend on the Illinois side, and hacked off cottonwood branches with the hatchet, and covered up the raft with them so she looked like there had been a cave-in in the bank there. A tow-head is a sandbar that has cottonwoods on it as thick as harrow-teeth.[1]

（4）We had mountains on the Missouri shore and heavy timber on the Illinois side, and the channel was down the Missouri shore at that place, so we warn't afraid of anybody running across us. We laid there all day, and watched the rafts

[1] 天边刚露出第一道曙光的时候，我就在毗邻伊利诺伊州一侧大河湾里某个沙洲把木筏拴在岸边，用斧头砍下很多三角叶杨枝条，覆盖在木筏上，看过去岸上这块地方好像凹下去了。沙洲是一片拦门沙，上面长满了一丛丛三角叶杨，茂密得赛过耙齿一样。（潘庆舲 译）

and steamboats spin[2] down the Missouri shore, and up-bound steamboats fight the big river in the middle. I told Jim all about the time I had jabbering with that woman; and Jim said she was a smart one, and if she was to start after us herself she wouldn't set down and watch a camp fire—no, sir, she'd fetch a dog. Well, then, I said, why couldn't she tell her husband to fetch a dog? Jim said he bet she did think of it by the time the men was ready to start, and he believed they must a gone up-town to get a dog and so they lost all that time, or else we wouldn't be here on a towhead sixteen or seventeen mile below the village—no, indeedy, we would be in that same old town again. So I said I didn't care what was the reason they didn't get us as long as they didn't.

(5) When it was beginning to come on dark we poked our heads out[3] of the cottonwood thicket, and looked up and down and across; nothing in sight; so Jim took up some of the top planks of the raft and built a snug[4] wigwam[5] to get under in blazing weather and rainy, and to keep the things dry. Jim made a floor for the wigwam, and raised it a foot or more above the level of the raft, so now the blankets and all the traps was out of reach of steamboat waves. Right in the middle of the wigwam we made a layer of dirt about five or six inches deep with a frame around it for to hold it to its place; this was to build a fire on in sloppy weather or chilly[6]; the wigwam would keep it from being seen. We made an extra steering-oar, too, because one of the others might get broke on a snag or something. We fixed up a short forked stick to hang the old lantern on, because we must always light the lantern whenever we see a steamboat coming down-stream, to keep from getting run over; but we wouldn't have to light it for up-stream boats unless we see we was in what they call a "crossing"; for the river was pretty high yet, very low banks being still a little under water; so up-bound boats didn't always run the channel, but hunted easy water.

(6) This second night we run between seven and eight hours, with a current that was making over four mile an hour. We catched fish and talked, and we took a swim now and then

[2] spin /spɪn/ *v.* (使)快速旋转

[3] poke our heads out: 探出头来

[4] sug /snʌg/ *adj.* 温暖舒适的

[5] wigwam /ˈwɪgwæm/ *n.* 棚屋

[6] chilly /ˈtʃɪli/ *adj.* 寒冷的；阴冷的

to keep off sleepiness. It was kind of solemn, drifting down the big, still river, laying on our backs looking up at the stars, and we didn't ever feel like talking loud, and it warn't often that we laughed—only a little kind of a low chuckle.[7] We had mighty good weather as a general thing, and nothing ever happened to us at all—that night, nor the next, nor the next.

(7) Every night we passed towns, some of them away up on black hillsides, nothing but just a shiny bed of lights; not a house could you see. The fifth night we passed St. Louis[8], and it was like the whole world lit up[9]. In St. Petersburg they used to say there was twenty or thirty thousand people in St. Louis, but I never believed it till I see that wonderful spread of lights at two o'clock that still night. There warn't a sound there; everybody was asleep.

(8) Every night now I used to slip ashore towards ten o'clock at some little village, and buy ten or fifteen cents' worth of meal or bacon or other stuff to eat; and sometimes I lifted a chicken that warn't roosting[10] comfortable, and took him along. Pap always said, take a chicken when you get a chance, because if you don't want him yourself you can easy find somebody that does, and a good deed ain't ever forgot.[11] I never see pap when he didn't want the chicken himself, but that is what he used to say, anyway.

(9) Mornings before daylight I slipped into cornfields and borrowed a watermelon, or a mushmelon, or a punkin, or some new corn, or things of that kind. Pap always said it warn't no harm to borrow things[12] if you was meaning to pay them back some time; but the widow said it warn't anything but a soft name for stealing, and no decent body would do it. Jim said he reckoned the widow was partly right and pap was partly right; so the best way would be for us to pick out two or three things from the list and say we wouldn't borrow them any more[13]—then he reckoned it wouldn't be no harm to borrow the others. So we talked it over all one night, drifting along down the river, trying to make up our minds whether to drop the watermelons, or the cantelopes[14], or the mushmelons, or what. But towards

[7] 第二天夜里，我们走了七八个小时，这时的水速每小时我们大概能走出四英里。我们抓鱼、聊天，有时直接跳进河里游个泳赶走疲倦。在静谧的大河上顺流而下，我们躺在船上看星星是件很庄重的事情。我们很少大声说话，也不大声笑，只是偶尔低声轻笑一下。

[8] St. Louis：圣路易斯，美国密苏里州最大的城市，位于密西西比河畔，由此进入了美国中西部。

[9] 好像整个世界都被点亮了。这里形容灯火辉煌。圣路易斯人口密集，很繁华。

[10] roost /ruːst/ *v.* 栖息

[11] 老爸说，如果有机会就顺手牵羊抓走一只鸡，你要是不这样做，别人也会这样做，你做的好事不会被忘记的。哈克的父亲经常干些偷鸡摸狗的事情，还给自己找了合适的理由。

[12] 委婉语（euphemism）。明明是偷，却说成借。

[13] 哈克的父亲把顺手牵羊偷东西叫作“借”，寡妇说这就是偷。这让哈克和吉姆有些迷茫，觉得二人说的都有些道理，于是他们决定挑出两三件东西，并保证以后再也不“借”了。

[14] cantelope /ˈkæntəluːp/ *n.* 甜瓜；哈密瓜

daylight we got it all settled satisfactory, and concluded to drop crabapples[15] and p'simmons. We warn't feeling just right before that, but it was all comfortable now. I was glad the way it come out, too, because crabapples ain't ever good, and the p'simmons wouldn't be ripe for two or three months yet.

(10) We shot a water-fowl now and then that got up too early in the morning or didn't go to bed early enough in the evening. Take it all round, we lived pretty high.

(11) The fifth night below St. Louis we had a big storm after midnight, with a power of thunder and lightning, and the rain poured down in a solid sheet. We stayed in the wigwam and let the raft take care of itself. When the lightning glared out[16] we could see a big straight river ahead, and high, rocky bluffs on both sides. By and by says I, "Hel-Lo, Jim, looky yonder!" It was a steamboat that had killed herself on a rock.[17] We was drifting straight down for her. The lightning showed her very distinct. She was leaning over, with part of her upper deck above water, and you could see every little chimbly-guy clean and clear, and a chair by the big bell, with an old slouch hat hanging on the back of it, when the flashes come.

(12) Well, it being away in the night and stormy, and all so mysterious-like, I felt just the way any other boy would a felt when I see that wreck laying there so mournful and lonesome in the middle of the river. I wanted to get aboard of her and slink[18] around a little, and see what there was there. So I says:

(13) "Le's land on her, Jim."

(14) But Jim was dead against it at first. He says:

(15) "I doan' want to go fool'n 'long er no wrack. We's doin' blame' well, en we better let blame' well alone, as de good book says. Like as not dey's a watchman on dat wrack."

(16) "Watchman your grandmother," I says; "there ain't nothing to watch but the texas and the pilot-house; and do you reckon anybody's going to resk his life for a texas and a pilot-house such a night as this, when it's likely to break up and wash off down the river any minute?" Jim couldn't say nothing to that, so he didn't try. "And besides," I says, "we might borrow

[15] crabapple /ˈkræbˌæpəl/ *n.* 海棠；野苹果

[16] glare out: 发出刺眼的光

[17] 那是一条触礁后沉没的小轮船。

[18] slink /slɪŋk/ *v.* 偷偷摸摸地走；躲躲闪闪地走

something worth having out of the captain's stateroom. Seegars, I bet you—and cost five cents apiece, solid cash. Steamboat captains is always rich, and get sixty dollars a month, and *they* don't care a cent what a thing costs, you know, long as they want it. Stick a candle in your pocket; I can't rest, Jim, till we give her a rummaging. Do you reckon Tom Sawyer would ever go by this thing? Not for pie, he wouldn't. He'd call it an adventure—that's what he'd call it; and he'd land on that wreck if it was his last act. And wouldn't he throw style into it?—wouldn't he spread himself, nor nothing? Why, you'd think it was Christopher C'lumbus[19] discovering Kingdom-Come. I wish Tom Sawyer *was* here."

(17) Jim he grumbled a little, but give in. He said we mustn't talk any more than we could help, and then talk mighty low. The lightning showed us the wreck again just in time, and we fetched the stabboard derrick[20], and made fast there.

(18) The deck was high out here. We went sneaking down the slope of it to labboard, in the dark, towards the texas, feeling our way slow with our feet, and spreading our hands out to fend off the guys, for it was so dark we couldn't see no sign of them. Pretty soon we struck the forward end of the skylight, and clumb on to it; and the next step fetched us in front of the captain's door, which was open, and by Jimminy, away down through the texas-hall we see a light! and all in the same second we seem to hear low voices in yonder!

(19) Jim whispered and said he was feeling powerful sick, and told me to come along. I says, all right, and was going to start for the raft; but just then I heard a voice wail out and say:

(20) "Oh, please don't, boys; I swear I won't ever tell!"

(21) Another voice said, pretty loud:

(22) "It's a lie, Jim Turner. You've acted this way before. You always want more'n your share of the truck, and you've always got it, too, because you've swore 't if you didn't you'd tell. But this time you've said it jest one time too many. You're the meanest, treacherousest hound in this country."

(23) By this time Jim was gone for the raft. I was just

[19] **Christopher C'lumbus**: 克里斯托弗·哥伦布，意大利探险家、殖民者、航海家，大航海时代的主要人物之一，出生于中世纪的热那亚共和国(今意大利西北部)。

[20] **derrick** /ˈderɪk/ *n.* (尤指船上的)吊杆式起重机

a-biling with curiosity; and I says to myself, Tom Sawyer wouldn't back out now, and so I won't either; I'm a-going to see what's going on here. So I dropped on my hands and knees in the little passage, and crept aft in the dark till there warn't but one stateroom betwixt me and the cross-hall of the texas. Then in there I see a man stretched on the floor and tied hand and foot, and two men standing over him, and one of them had a dim lantern in his hand, and the other one had a pistol.[21] This one kept pointing the pistol at the man's head on the floor, and saying:

(24) "I'd *like* to! And I orter, too—a mean skunk!"

(25) The man on the floor would shrivel[22] up and say, "Oh, please don't, Bill; I hain't ever goin' to tell."

(26) And every time he said that the man with the lantern would laugh and say:

(27) "Deed you *ain't*! You never said no truer thing 'n that, you bet you." And once he said: "Hear him beg! and yit if we hadn't got the best of him and tied him he'd a killed us both. And what *for*? Jist for noth'n. Jist because we stood on our *rights*—that's what for. But I lay you ain't a-goin' to threaten nobody any more, Jim Turner. Put UP that pistol, Bill."

(28) Bill says:

(29) "I don't want to, Jake Packard. I'm for killin' him—and didn't he kill old Hatfield jist the same way—and don't he deserve it?"

(30) "But I don't *want* him killed, and I've got my reasons for it."

(31) "Bless yo' heart for them words, Jake Packard! I'll never forgit you long's I live!" says the man on the floor, sort of blubbering[23].

(32) Packard didn't take no notice of that, but hung up his lantern on a nail and started towards where I was there in the dark, and motioned Bill to come. I crawfished as fast as I could about two yards, but the boat slanted[24] so that I couldn't make very good time; so to keep from getting run over and catched I crawled into a stateroom on the upper side. The man came a-pawing along in the dark, and when Packard got to my

[21] 在那里我看见一个人手脚都被捆住，直挺挺地躺在地板上，另外两个人站在他旁边，其中一个人手里提着灯，灯光很暗，另一个人手里拿着枪。

[22] shrivel /'ʃrɪvl/ v.（使）枯萎；干枯

[23] blubber /'blʌbə(r)/ v. 大声哭

[24] slant /slɑːnt/ v.（使）倾斜；歪斜

stateroom, he says:

(33) "Here—come in here."

(34) And in he come, and Bill after him. But before they got in I was up in the upper berth[25], cornered, and sorry I come. Then they stood there, with their hands on the ledge of the berth, and talked. I couldn't see them, but I could tell where they was by the whisky they'd been having. I was glad I didn't drink whisky; but it wouldn't made much difference anyway, because most of the time they couldn't a tree'd me because I didn't breathe. I was too scared. And, besides, a body *couldn't* breathe[26] and hear such talk. They talked low and earnest. Bill wanted to kill Turner. He says:

(35) "He's said he'll tell, and he will. If we was to give both our shares to him *now* it wouldn't make no difference after the row and the way we've served him. Shore's you're born, he'll turn State's evidence; now you hear *me*. I'm for putting him out of his troubles."

(36) "So'm I," says Packard, very quiet.

(37) "Blame it, I'd sorter begun to think you wasn't. Well, then, that's all right. Le's go and do it."

(38) "Hold on a minute; I hain't had my say yit. You listen to me. Shooting's good, but there's quieter ways if the thing's *got* to be done. But what I say is this: it ain't good sense to go court'n around after a halter if you can git at what you're up to in some way that's jist as good and at the same time don't bring you into no resks. Ain't that so?"

(39) "You bet it is. But how you goin' to manage it this time?"

(40) "Well, my idea is this: we'll rustle around and gather up whatever pickins we've overlooked in the state-rooms, and shove for shore and hide the truck. Then we'll wait. Now I say it ain't a-goin' to be more'n two hours befo' this wrack breaks up and washes off down the river. See? He'll be drownded, and won't have nobody to blame for it but his own self. I reckon that's a considerble sight better 'n killin' of him. I'm unfavorable to killin' a man as long as you can git aroun' it; it ain't good

[25] berth /bɜːθ/ *n.* (船或火车等)卧铺;铺位

[26] 提喻(synecdoche)。这里的 a body 指的是 a person。

sense, it ain't good morals. Ain't I right?"

(41) "Yes, I reck'n you are. But s'pose she *don't* break up and wash off?"

(42) "Well, we can wait the two hours anyway and see, can't we?"

(43) "All right, then; come along."

(44) So they started, and I lit out, all in a cold sweat, and scrambled[27] forward. It was dark as pitch there; but I said, in a kind of a coarse whisper, "Jim !" and he answered up, right at my elbow, with a sort of a moan, and I says:

[27] scramble /'skræmbl/ *v.* (迅速而吃力地)爬;攀登

(45) "Quick, Jim, it ain't no time for fooling around and moaning; there's a gang of murderers in yonder, and if we don't hunt up their boat and set her drifting down the river so these fellows can't get away from the wreck there's one of 'em going to be in a bad fix[28]. But if we find their boat we can put *all* of 'em in a bad fix—for the sheriff 'll get 'em. Quick—hurry! I'll hunt the labboard side, you hunt the stabboard. You start at the raft, and —"

[28] in a bad fix: 陷入困境

(46) "Oh, my lordy, lordy! RAF'? Dey ain' no raf' no mo'; she done broke loose en gone I—en here we is!"

精华赏析

在这一章中我们来探讨一下社会学批评。孔子说"诗,可以兴,可以观,可以群,可以怨"(《论语·阳货》)。诗可以"兴",就是说诗可以感发意志。诗可以"观",是指通过别人所做之诗,可以观得其志。"兴"和"观"都是说文学作品的基本功能,也是针对个体的功能,抒发情感、宣泄积郁、表达志向。诗可以"群",是说"群居而切磋"。"独学而无友,孤陋而寡闻",所以需要大家在一起交流切磋,以达成社会和谐。诗可以"怨",是指对社会不满,则赋诗以怨。"群"和"怨"是文学作品的社会功能,观国家之兴替,考社会之得失,用文学作品反映社会现实,针砭时弊,引导道德规范。比如杜甫就在《自京赴奉先县咏怀五百字》中写过"朱门酒肉臭,路有冻死骨"的句子。白居易的《秦中吟》十首和《新乐府》五十首对社会现实的关注,对当权者的抨击更是有目共睹。从这里我们可以看到文学与社会、时代是密不可分的。如果文学只是一家之言,一己之情不免显得小家子气了。只有融入历史、社会的洪流中,文学作品才能彰显出它的大气魄。

社会学批评作为一种批评理论，开始于十九世纪的法国。随着大革命风潮的平息，法国不少知识分子开始关注文学的社会性内容，这既是对现实的逃避，也是通过对文学作品的分析达成对现实热情的一种虚拟性实现。

最早的社会批评家有斯达尔夫人。她的批评理论主要有两个方面。一个是自然环境对文学形态的影响，她根据自然环境的不同，把当时的欧洲文学分为南方文学和北方文学。斯达尔夫人的另一个观点是将文学与广义上的社会制度相联系，考察文学与社会制度的互动关系，她曾说道："我的本旨在于考察宗教、风尚和法律对文学的影响以及文学对宗教、风尚和法律的影响。"（1986:145）

另一位社会批评理论家是泰纳，他提出了著名文学艺术的"三要素"。泰纳(1994)认为文学艺术是人类所建立的道德形态之一，而"有助于产生这个基本的道德状态的，是三个不同的根源——'种族''环境'和'时代'"。

在社会批评理论中，环境是文学作品中的一个关键因素。

第一，自然环境，包括气候、地理等因素。这本小说的故事发生在密西西比河沿途，这里的自然环境为一条奔流不息的大河，河两岸有茂密的树林，河里水产资源丰富，有着清新的空气，满天的繁星。这样美好的环境容易激起人强烈的感情。所以小说的整体气质是充满阳光、充满激情的历险故事。美好的环境滋养出来的主人公哈克是一个无忧无虑、乐观、善良的孩子。自然环境不仅影响小说的形态和气质，还影响社会的形态。比如大河文明就不同于海洋文明。四大文明古国，中国、古巴比伦、古埃及、古印度都是大河文明[分别是黄河流域、两河流域(底格里斯河和幼发拉底河)、尼罗河流域、恒河流域]的代表。因为都有一条适合灌溉的大河，所以这些地区发展了农耕文明。农耕文明使大河流域周边的人们可以自给自足，依靠大河建立聚居地，发展城市，最终形成高度集权的国家。这里的人们的性格特质也是自足平和的。然而海洋文明则不同，海洋周围不适合发展农业，只能依靠海上贸易交换所需物品，因此不利于形成高度集权的国家，而是形成了一个个独立的城邦，比如地中海文明。另外大海与大河相比，大海是神秘莫测的，是看不到边际的，因此这里的人们充满了冒险精神，有着天马行空的想象力，在古希腊神话中我们可见一斑。

第二，社会环境，包括政治制度、经济发展程度、民俗等因素。在这本小说的背景时代，废奴运动已经在进行中了，在第六章中提到的俄亥俄州已经废除了蓄奴制。在小说中哈克和父亲对蓄奴制有着不同的态度。之前的第六章中我们已经知道哈克的父亲反对废除蓄奴制，他不能接受一个黑人和白人的混血儿居然可以穿着光鲜得体地走在大街上，更不能理解这样的人还是一个大学教授，会说好几个国家的语言。哈克的父亲不愿意和这样的人一起参加选举。而哈克却能平等地对待黑奴吉姆，甚至把他当作朋友，一路上保护、帮助吉姆。不过在当时的政治环境下，要不要帮助吉姆获得自由，哈克还是经过了一番思想斗争。这与小说设置的社会环境相当符合。在小说的第十六章中有一段哈克的心理描写："They went off and I got aboard the raft, feeling bad and low, because I knowed very well I had done wrong, and I see it warn't no use for me to try to learn to do right; a body that don't get *started* right when he's little ain't got no show—when the pinch comes there ain't nothing to back him up and keep him to his work, and so he gets beat. Then I thought a minute, and says to myself, hold on; s'pose you'd a done right and give Jim up, would you felt better than what you do now? No, says I, I'd feel bad — I'd feel just the same way I do now. Well, then, says I, what's the use you learning to do right when it's troublesome to do right and ain't no trouble to do wrong, and the wages is just the same? I was stuck. I couldn't answer that. So I reckoned I wouldn't bother no more about it, but after this always do whichever come handiest at the time." 根据美国当时的法律,白人帮助黑奴逃跑是违法的,所以哈克才会陷入要不要帮助吉姆的矛盾中。最后哈克选择听从自己的内心,帮助吉姆摆脱追捕逃奴的白人。小说从哈克这个孩子的角度讽刺了当时不公正的社会道德和法律,连孩子都能想明白的道理,大人却不明白。

如果《哈克贝利·费恩历险记》只是简简单单写一个孩子的历险故事,它是不可能被奉为经典的。有美国评论家这样说过:只要我们这个星球上依然存在着贫困、仇恨、种族主义、溺爱儿童、兽行、暴力、伪善、压迫、苦工,以及奴役——不言而喻,人们还得一遍又一遍地仔细捧读《哈克贝利·费恩历险记》。这本小说"涉及南北战争以后美国社会、种族、宗教、风俗、历史、传统、女权的各个方面"。一个孩子的历险故事其实海纳百川,包罗万象,我们甚至可以把这本小说看成当时美国社会的百科全书。

所以说,"文学归根结底是一种社会现象,在整个社会系统中,各部分之间、构成因素之间存在着密不可分的有机联系,因此,在批评中忽略了艺术文本生成的社会环境将无法对其进行充分的阐释"。(邱运华,2006:18)

阅读思考

1. 选择一本你读过的小说,分析一下环境因素在小说中起到的作用。

2. "真正的艺术必然是道德的,是本能冲动转化为文化形态的高级形式。"你同意这种说法吗?为什么?

EXERCISE Ⅱ

I. Oral presentation.

1. 本书中法官撒切尔将哈克的父亲告上法庭，要求解除两人父子关系，成为哈克的监护人。请模拟法庭辩论环节。

   参考词汇：adjourn, appeal, accused, bail, sustain, overrule, civil action, contempt of court, affidavit, convict, sentence, jury…

2. 在本书第十一章中，哈克伪装成女孩子出门打探消息，遇到一位四十岁左右的妇女，两人聊了起来。请按照现代社交礼仪扩充并适当演绎这部分谈话。

   （1）开启谈话的参考句型：

   Excuse me, is anybody…?

   Nice day, isn't it?

   Horrible weather we're having.

   Sorry, I couldn't help overhearing—did you mention something about…?

   （2）结束谈话的参考句型：

   I'd better go.

   See you later.

   So long.

II. Choose the correct words to complete the sentences.

1. She pushed at the door but it wouldn't ______.

   A. budge B. break C. change D. bend

2. He was ______ at her through his fingers.

   A. staring B. glaring C. peeping D. watching

3. A voice ______ us from the other side of the street.

   A. heard B. hailed C. bailed D. wailed

4. Can't we ______ places? I can't see the screen.

   A. move B. change C. swap D. swing

5. It would be good to have a pencil and paper ______.

   A. hand B. convenient C. soon D. handy

6. She was ______ around in her bag for her keys.

   A. rummaging B. running C. damaging D. beginning

7. The inhabitants have to walk a mile to ______ water.

A. bring B. reach C. fetch D. save

8. John was trying to ______ into the house by the back door.

A. slink B. slide C. glide D. fling

9. The leaves on the plant had ______ up from lack of water.

A. fallen B. dropped C. shriveled D. gone

10. The report ______ careful consideration.

A. must B. has C. takes D. deserves

III. Fill in the blanks with suitable prepositions or adverbs.

1. He came _____ himself after a week in the hospital.
2. My mother is right ______ my marriage problem.
3. It is possible to make ______ something in those caves, but not very much.
4. "He was a lawyer before that," Mary Ann put _____.
5. If they get ______ trouble, there are plenty of people who will help them out.

IV. Answer the following questions.

Questions on the content

1. What did Huck prepare for his escape in Chapter VII?
2. How did Huck feel when he found the ashes of a camp fire that was still smoking in Chapter VIII?
3. Why did Jim run away?
4. Why did Jim suggest that they should have the canoe hidden in a good place, and have all the traps in the cavern in Chapter IX?
5. In Chapter X, when the snake's mate bit Jim, what did Huck do?
6. Did Huck find out what was going on in the town from the woman in Chapter XI? What happened after Huck was "killed" ?
7. Did the woman find out Huck was a boy? If so, how did she find out?
8. Why did Huck decide to get aboard that wreck in Chapter XII? What did Huck find there?

Questions on the structure and style

1. Identify the figures of speech in this sentence "Everything was dead quiet, and it looked late, and smelt late." (Chapter VII)
2. What was Huck's major impression of the river? What symbols did the author use from Chapter VII to Chapter XII?
3. Paragraph 6 in Chapter IX describe a summer storm. Comment on the techniques the author uses in describing this summer storm. What effect is achieved by these techniques?

4. What is the plot of the story in Chapter XI? Sum up the plot briefly in your own words.
5. How does the author show Jim's social status through his speech and manners?

V. Translate the following sentences into Chinese, paying attention to the conversion of the bold words.

1. He jumped up yelling, and the first thing the light showed was the varmint curled up and ready for another **spring.** (Chapter X)
2. But Tom Sawyer he hunted me up and said he was going to start a band of robbers, and I might join if I would go back to the widow and be **respectable.** (Chapter I)
3. This **miserableness** went on as much as six or seven minutes; but it seemed a sight longer than that. (Chapter II)
4. Him and his horse both went home pretty **leaky** and **crippled,** but the Grangerfords had to be fetched home—and one of 'em was dead, and another died the next day. (Chapter XVIII)
5. … and now you'd hear the thunder let go with an **awful** crash, and then go rumbling, grumbling, tumbling down the sky towards the under side of the world, like rolling empty barrels downstairs—where it's long stairs and they **bounce a good deal**, you know. (Chapter IX)
6. He was **a-reeling across** the street towards me, bare-headed, with a friend on both sides of him a-holt of his arms and hurrying him along. (Chapter XXI)
7. Jim laid it in **with all his might**, for he was most about starved. Then when we had got pretty well stuffed, we laid off and **lazied**. (Chapter VIII)
8. And afterwards we would watch the **lonesomeness** of the river, and kind of **lazy** along, and by and by lazy off to sleep. (Chapter XIX)
9. I was sorry to hear Jim say that, it was such a lowering of him. My conscience got to stirring me up hotter than ever, until at last I says to it, "Let up on me—it ain't too late yet—I'll **paddle** ashore at the first light and tell." (Chapter XVI)
10. The pitifulest thing out is a mob; that's what an army is—a mob; they don't fight with courage that's born in them, but with courage that's borrowed from their mass, and from their officers. But a mob without any man at the head of it is **beneath pitifulness**. (Chapter XXII)

VI. Sentence variety.

Sentence variety can be achieved through many means. First study how sentence varieties have been achieved and then rewrite the sentences as required to achieve variety.

A. embedding:

It was mighty cool and shady in the deep woods, even if the sun was blazing outside.

So I fixed that as good as I could from the outside by scattering dust on the place, which covered up the smoothness and the sawdust.

B. conjoining:

After breakfast I wanted to talk about the dead man and guess out how he come to be killed, but Jim didn't want to.

C. passive voice:

A little smoke couldn't be noticed, now, so we would take some fish off of the lines and cook up a hot breakfast.

D. parenthesis:

I didn't sleep much. I couldn't, somehow, for thinking.

E. participial phrase:

So I took my gun and slipped off towards where I had run across that camp fire, stopping every minute or two to listen.

F. inversion:

By and by I was close enough to have a look, and there laid a man on the ground.

G. nominalization in the position of subject:

The June rise used to be always luck for me; because as soon as that rise begins, here comes cordwood floating down.

Rewrite the following sentences as required to achieve sentence variety.

1. The factory affects the residents nearby seriously. It emits toxic gases and makes deafening noise. (embedding)
2. Most young people have received formal education in university. There they acquire abundant knowledge and skills. (embedding)
3. Some people think the Internet only has positive impacts. Other people think it also has negative influence on our lives. (conjoining)
4. We cannot deny the obvious benefits of computer skills for young children. (passive voice)
5. When functioning well, universities should offer both theoretical knowledge as well as professional training. (parenthesis)
6. When people come across difficulties, they often choose to give them up, but perseverance regularly helps them succeed in the last. (participial phrase)
7. The young man with an umbrella under his arm stood by the window. (inversion)
8. If people only apply book knowledge, they will not get good results. (nominalization in the position of subject)

CHAPTER XIII

导读：哈克和吉姆在密西西比河上的探险还在继续，哈克目睹了一艘即将沉没的轮船上的谋杀阴谋。生死攸关的当口，哈克和吉姆乘坐的木筏子又被水冲走了……机智的哈克和忠厚的老吉姆能躲过这一遭劫难吗？

(1) WELL, I catched my breath and most fainted. Shut up on a wreck with such a gang as that! But it warn't no time to be sentimentering[1]. We'd *got* to find that boat now—had to have it for ourselves. So we went a-quaking and shaking down the stabboard side, and slow work it was, too —seemed a week before we got to the stern.[2] No sign of a boat. Jim said he didn't believe he could go any further—so scared he hadn't hardly any strength left, he said. But I said, come on, if we get left on this wreck we are in a fix[3], sure. So on we prowled[4] again. We struck for the stern of the texas[5], and found it, and then scrabbled along forwards on the skylight, hanging on from shutter to shutter, for the edge of the skylight was in the water. When we got pretty close to the cross-hall door there was the skiff[6], sure enough! I could just barely see her. I felt ever so thankful. In another second I would a been aboard of her, but just then the door opened. One of the men stuck his head out only about a couple of foot from me, and I thought I was gone; but he jerked it in again, and says:

(2) "Heave that blame lantern out o' sight, Bill!"

(3) He flung a bag of something into the boat, and then got in himself and set down. It was Packard. Then Bill *he* come out and got in. Packard says, in a low voice:

(4) "All ready—shove off[7]!"

[1] **sentimenter** 即 sentiment 的口语变体，此处哈克误用作动词，意为"伤感；感慨"。

[2] 我们浑身哆嗦着顺着右舷走过去。走得很慢，好像花了整整一个星期才摸到了船尾。这里的 stabboard 应为 starboard，船的右舷。

[3] **to be in a fix**: 陷入困境

[4] **prowl** /praʊl/ *v.* 潜行

[5] **the texas**: 指轮船上的最高甲板舱，是船上最大的舱房，驾驶室就在它的前面或者上面。在该书成书的年代，德克萨斯州是美国最大的州，因此作者以此称呼船上最大的舱房。

[6] **skiff** /skɪf/ *n.* 小划艇；小帆船

[7] **shove off**: 撑船离开

(5) I couldn't hardly hang on to the shutters, I was so weak. But Bill says:

(6) "Hold on—'d you go through him?"

(7) "No. Didn't you?"

(8) "No. So he's got his share o' the cash yet."

(9) "Well, then, come along; no use to take truck and leave money."

(10) "Say, won't he suspicion[8] what we're up to?"

(11) "Maybe he won't. But we got to have it anyway. Come along."

(12) So they got out and went in.

(13) The door slammed to because it was on the careened[9] side; and in a half second I was in the boat, and Jim come tumbling after me. I out with my knife and cut the rope, and away we went!

(14) We didn't touch an oar, and we didn't speak nor whisper, nor hardly even breathe. We went gliding swift along, dead silent, past the tip of the paddle-box, and past the stern; then in a second or two more we was a hundred yards below the wreck, and the darkness soaked her up, every last sign of her, and we was safe, and knowed it.

(15) When we was three or four hundred yards down-stream we see the lantern show like a little spark at the texas door for a second, and we knowed by that that the rascals[10] had missed their boat, and was beginning to understand that they was in just as much trouble now as Jim Turner was.

(16) Then Jim manned[11] the oars, and we took out after our raft. Now was the first time that I begun to worry about the men—I reckon I hadn't had time to before. I begun to think how dreadful it was, even for murderers, to be in such a fix. I says to myself, there ain't no telling but I might come to be a murderer myself yet, and then how would I like it? So says I to Jim:

(17) "The first light we see we'll land a hundred yards below it or above it, in a place where it's a good hiding-place for you and the skiff, and then I'll go and fix up some kind of a yarn[12], and get somebody to go for that gang and get them out of

[8] suspicion: 此处误用作动词。

[9] careen /kə'riːn/ v. (船)倾斜

[10] rascal /'rɑːskl/ n. 无赖;坏蛋;淘气鬼

[11] man /mæn/ v. 操纵(机器等)

[12] yarn /jɑːn/ n. 编造的故事;胡诌

their scrape, so they can be hung when their time comes."

(18) But that idea was a failure; for pretty soon it begun to storm again, and this time worse than ever. The rain poured down, and never a light showed; everybody in bed, I reckon. We boomed along down the river, watching for lights and watching for our raft. After a long time the rain let up[13], but the clouds stayed, and the lightning kept whimpering[14], and by and by a flash showed us a black thing ahead, floating, and we made for it.

(19) It was the raft, and mighty glad was we to get aboard of it again. We seen a light now away down to the right, on shore. So I said I would go for it. The skiff was half full of plunder[15] which that gang had stole there on the wreck. We hustled it on to the raft in a pile, and I told Jim to float along down, and show a light when he judged he had gone about two mile, and keep it burning till I come; then I manned my oars and shoved for the light. As I got down towards it three or four more showed—up on a hillside. It was a village. I closed in above the shore light, and laid on my oars and floated. As I went by I see it was a lantern hanging on the jackstaff[16] of a double-hull ferryboat[17]. I skimmed around for the watchman, a-wondering whereabouts he slept; and by and by I found him roosting on the bitts forward, with his head down between his knees. I gave his shoulder two or three little shoves, and begun to cry.

(20) He stirred up in a kind of a startlish[18] way; but when he see it was only me he took a good gap[19] and stretch, and then he says:

(21) "Hello, what's up? Don't cry, bub. What's the trouble?"

(22) I says:

(23) "Pap, and mam, and sis, and—"

(24) Then I broke down. He says:

(25) "Oh, dang it now, *don't* take on so; we all has to have our troubles, and this 'n 'll come out all right. What's the matter with 'em?"

(26) "They're—they're—are you the watchman of the

[13] let up：减弱；缓和；停止

[14] 此处使用了拟人（personification）的修辞手法。（whimper /ˈwɪmpə(r)/ *v.* 抽泣；呜咽）

[15] plunder /ˈplʌndə(r)/ *n.* 赃赃

[16] jackstaff /ˈdʒækstɑːf/ *n.* 船首旗杆

[17] double-hull ferryboat：双壳渡轮

[18] startlish /ˈstɑːtlɪʃ/ *adj.* 受惊的；易受惊吓的

[19] take a gap：打哈欠

boat?"

(27) "Yes," he says, kind of pretty-well-satisfied like. "I'm the captain and the owner and the mate[20] and the pilot and watchman and head deck-hand; and sometimes I'm the freight[21] and passengers. I ain't as rich as old Jim Hornback, and I can't be so blame' generous and good to Tom, Dick, and Harry as what he is, and slam around money the way he does; but I've told him a many a time 't I wouldn't trade places with him; for, says I, a sailor's life's the life for me, and I'm derned[22] if I'D live two mile out o' town, where there ain't nothing ever goin' on, not for all his spondulicks[23] and as much more on top of it. Says I—"

(28) I broke in and says:

(29) "They're in an awful peck of[24] trouble, and—"

(30) "*Who* is?"

(31) "Why, pap and mam and sis and Miss Hooker; and if you'd take your ferryboat and go up there—"

(32) "Up where? Where are they?"

(33) "On the wreck."

(34) "What wreck?"

(35) "Why, there ain't but one."

(36) "What, you don't mean the *Walter Scott*[25]?"

(37) "Yes."

(38) "Good land! what are they doin' *there*, for gracious sakes?"

(39) "Well, they didn't go there a-purpose."

(40) "I bet they didn't! Why, great goodness, there ain't no chance for 'em if they don't git off mighty quick! Why, how in the nation did they ever git into such a scrape[26]?"

(41) "Easy enough. Miss Hooker was a-visiting up there to the town—"

(42) "Yes, Booth's Landing—go on."

(43) She was a-visiting there at Booth's Landing, and just in the edge of the evening she started over with her nigger woman in the horse-ferry to stay all night at her friend's house, Miss What-you-may-call-her I disremember her name—and

[20] 即 first mate，大副

[21] freight /freɪt/ *n.* 货物

[22] 即 darned，可恶的；该死的

[23] spondulicks /spɒnˈduːlɪks/ *n.* 金钱；钞票（幽默的说法）

[24] a peck of: 大量；许多

[25] Walter Scott: 英国著名历史小说家和诗人，英国浪漫主义文学的代表人物。马克·吐温以此命名这艘即将沉没的轮船，无疑有嘲弄之意，讽刺司各特的思想和作品如同沉船，日渐没落。

[26] scrape /skreɪp/ *n.*（自己造成的）窘境；困境

they lost their steering-oar, and swung around and went a-floating down, stern first, about two mile, and saddle-baggsed on the wreck, and the ferryman and the nigger woman and the horses was all lost, but Miss Hooker she made a grab and got aboard the wreck. Well, about an hour after dark we come along down in our trading-scow, and it was so dark we didn't notice the wreck till we was right on it; and so *we* saddle-baggsed; but all of us was saved but Bill Whipple—and oh, he *was* the best cretur[27]!—I most wish 't it had been me, I do."

(44) "My George! It's the beatenest thing I ever struck. And *then* what did you all do?"

(45) "Well, we hollered and took on, but it's so wide there we couldn't make nobody hear. So pap said somebody got to get ashore and get help somehow. I was the only one that could swim, so I made a dash for it, and Miss Hooker she said if I didn't strike help sooner, come here and hunt up her uncle, and he'd fix the thing. I made the land about a mile below, and been fooling along[28] ever since, trying to get people to do something, but they said, 'What, in such a night and such a current? There ain't no sense in it; go for the steam ferry.' Now if you'll go and—"

(46) "By Jackson, I'd *like* to, and, blame it, I don't know but I will; but who in the dingnation's[29] a-going to *pay* for it? Do you reckon your pap—"

(47) "Why *that*'s all right. Miss Hooker she tole me, *particular*, that her uncle Hornback—"

(48) "Great guns! is *he* her uncle? Looky here, you break for that light over yonder-way, and turn out west when you git there, and about a quarter of a mile out you'll come to the tavern[30]; tell 'em to dart you out to Jim Hornback's, and he'll foot the bill[31]. And don't you fool around any, because he'll want to know the news. Tell him I'll have his niece all safe before he can get to town. Hump yourself, now; I'm a-going up around the corner here to roust[32] out my engineer."

(49) I struck for the light, but as soon as he turned the corner I went back and got into my skiff and bailed her out[33], and

27 即 creature

28 fool along:(美俚)游荡;磨蹭;不务正业

29 即 damnation's

30 tavern /ˈtævən/ *n.* 酒馆;小旅店

31 foot the bill: 支付账单

32 roust /raʊst/ *v.* 唤醒

33 bail out:(美俚)(往外)舀水;帮助摆脱困境

then pulled up shore in the easy water about six hundred yards, and tucked myself in among some woodboats; for I couldn't rest easy till I could see the ferryboat start. But take it all around, I was feeling ruther comfortable on accounts of taking all this trouble for that gang, for not many would a done it. I wished the widow knowed about it. I judged she would be proud of me for helping these rapscallions[34], because rapscallions and dead beats[35] is the kind the widow and good people takes the most interest in.

(50) Well, before long here comes the wreck, dim and dusky, sliding along down! A kind of cold shiver went through me, and then I struck out for her. She was very deep, and I see in a minute there warn't much chance for anybody being alive in her. I pulled all around her and hollered a little, but there wasn't any answer; all dead still. I felt a little bit heavy-hearted about the gang, but not much, for I reckoned if they could stand it I could.[36]

(51) Then here comes the ferryboat; so I shoved for the middle of the river on a long down-stream slant; and when I judged I was out of eye-reach I laid on my oars, and looked back and see her go and smell around the wreck for Miss Hooker's remainders, because the captain would know her uncle Hornback would want them; and then pretty soon the ferryboat give it up and went for the shore, and I laid into my work and went a-booming down the river.

(52) It did seem a powerful long time before Jim's light showed up; and when it did show it looked like it was a thousand mile off. By the time I got there the sky was beginning to get a little gray in the east; so we struck for an island, and hid the raft, and sunk the skiff, and turned in and slept like dead people.

[34] **rapscallion** /ræpˈskæljən/ *n.* 无赖；流氓；恶棍

[35] **dead beats**: 懒人；赖债人；游手好闲的人

[36] 我为了那伙强盗心里感到不好受，但也不是十分难受，因为我觉得如果他们能狠得下心去，我也能狠得下心。

精华赏析

目前国内英语专业的学习者被推荐阅读的英美名著，除了近期作家的现代主义、后现代主义作品外，绝大多数可以划分为两个流派：浪漫主义和现实主义。在文学艺术创作中，现实主义和浪漫主义是并驾齐驱的两大思潮。在课堂学习和课外阅读的过程中，很多学生总会有种种困惑和不解：为什么美国作家霍桑的《红字》是浪漫主义文学，而狄更斯的《雾都孤儿》或者夏洛蒂·勃朗特的《简·爱》又是现实主义文学了呢？浪漫主义文学和现实主义文学的本质区别是什么？

要理解浪漫主义和现实主义的区别，首先我们要有一个基本的认知，就是艺术领域的"浪漫"并不是一般人理解的那种风花雪月、花前月下，也不一定就是细腻抒情、诗情画意。相反，它或许是穷困潦倒的郁郁寡欢，也许是金戈铁马的血雨腥风。浪漫主义是一种创作方法，要辨别浪漫主义，应关注的是其核心精神，而不应纠结于其语言形式和情节内容。

其一，浪漫主义是一种充满激情的艺术表现形式，带有强烈的主观色彩，抒发强烈的个人感情，注重个人的主观感受和体验，主观性是浪漫主义思潮最突出的本质特征。浪漫主义思潮本来就起源于对启蒙运动所提倡的理性主义的对抗，对于浪漫主义者来说，文学是内心情感的表露，文学创作是对幻想的满足。他们眼中的世界不是真实的社会生活，他们关注的是"美丽的理想"，这就是席勒说的，"试图用美丽的理想去代替那不足的真实"。雪莱的《西风颂》是浪漫主义的巅峰之作，诗人把桀骜不羁、气势磅礴的"西风"视为摧枯拉朽的革命力量的象征，诗的字里行间透露出诗人如火的激情，读来令人热血沸腾。诗人看似歌唱西风摧毁一切的力量，实则是对人类生活场景作理想化描写，表达的是作者对摧毁旧世界的革命风暴和即将到来的自由生活的无限向往。而现实主义则是写实的，一切创作基于对真实的社会生活的再现，是对伪善、罪恶的社会现实和人性的无情揭露和尖锐批判。狄更斯的《雾都孤儿》通过塑造一个孤儿凄苦的身世和悲惨遭遇，如实刻画了十九世纪伦敦社会种种丑恶和黑暗现实。通过文学作品还原真实的社会生活，这是现实主义写作的基本表现形式。

其二，正是由于浪漫主义强烈的理想化色彩，浪漫主义文学在表现手法上往往借助夸张的手段、瑰丽的语言，使作品呈现非凡的想象力，这是浪漫主义文学的重要特征。由于浪漫主义文学强调远离现实生活描写，因此不用拘泥于社会生活的真实性，可以全凭想象天马行空地进行创作。与雪莱同时代的英国"湖畔派"诗人柯勒律治的《忽必烈汗》以充满韵律的语言描写了壮丽奇幻的梦中场景：富丽堂皇的东方宫殿、深不可测的神河、不见天日的大海、绚烂明媚的花园、月下哭泣的美妇、抚琴而歌的阿比西尼亚姑娘……诗人借助奔放不羁的超凡想象力，把一个个奇诡的场景组合成充满浓郁异国情调的梦幻场景。而现实主义作家则忠实于生活，对现实中的社会场景进行细致描写、真实再现，以此揭露隐藏在琐碎的社会生活背后的社会和人性的本质，这一点我们在上面已经提过。

其三，浪漫主义作家在素材的选择上也有异于现实主义作家，这主要表现在三个方面。第一，浪漫主义作家热衷于描写自然风光，抒发对大自然的热爱，主张回归自然。浪漫主义思潮的发展历程中，其作品充满了对物质文明的鄙夷，对丑陋现实的厌恶，对工业文明的恐惧。作家们通过对朴素纯净的大自然的讴歌，衬托出对城市生活的无比憎恶。浪漫主义对自然风光的迷恋带着宗教般的虔诚，他们把大自然看作充满神秘力量的存在，蕴藏着无穷的道德法则和精神法则，而人类应该视自然为师。第二，浪漫主义作家格外青睐历史题材，重视民间文学的收集整理，以借古讽今，反衬现实。司各特取材于古代民间故事和苏格兰、英格兰历史的小说为他赢得了"欧洲历史小说之父"的美誉。怀旧、伤逝成为许多浪漫主义文学作品的基本格调，其忧郁、感伤的情绪让人迷恋。第三，浪漫主义作家对超自然和哥特风格的话题情有独钟，目的还是逃避现实。霍桑擅长运用象征手法和宗教因素探索隐藏在人类内心的罪与罚，赫尔曼·梅尔维尔在 *Moby Dick* 中讲述了人类和未知大自然的神秘力量的较量……浪漫主义文学传统中充斥着神话故事、民间传奇、鬼怪幽灵等怪力乱神的内容。由于对神秘主义的推崇，浪漫主义作家沉迷于对异国风光和习俗的描写，作品充满浓郁的异国风情，令人着迷。这恰恰与现实主义文学传统格格不入，因为现实主义文学往往取材于现实生活，提倡通过对真实生活的描写探索人与社会的关系，反映时代特征。

最后，浪漫主义文学在人物的塑造上也与现实主义文学大相径庭。浪漫主义重视个人的价值和力量，爱默生说："世界将其自身缩小成为一滴露水。"美国超验主义认为人可以通过直觉的力量超越感觉、理性以及直接经验而认识真理。受这种精神的鼓舞，浪漫主义文学醉心于塑造带有理想主义色彩的非凡人物形象，这些人物一般具有超出普通人的禀赋和力量。通过主人公跌宕起伏、离奇怪诞的经历，刻画其异乎寻常且具有隐喻色彩的人物性格。例如英国浪漫主义文学杰出的代表人物拜伦擅长刻画"拜伦式英雄"，这些"奥德修斯"式的人物个性鲜明，才能出众，具有震撼心灵的力量。而现实主义文学注重典型环境里的典型人物，我们将在下一章重点分析这一点。

有了以上的比较，我们就不难理解为什么现实主义文学大师马克·吐温对英国浪漫主义小说家沃尔特·司各特进行冷嘲热讽了。在另一部反映密西西比河生活的作品 *Life on the Mississippi* 中，马克·吐温对司各特和他那套"中古时代的玩意儿"进行了无情抨击，指出司各特以浮夸的语言和空虚感伤的浪漫情调，像魔术一样，"凭着一个人的力量，阻挡了进步的浪潮，并且还使它倒流：他使人们嗜好梦境和幻影；嗜好腐朽和粗野的宗教仪式，嗜好腐朽和退化的行政制度；嗜好一个毫无头脑、毫无价值的，早已消灭的社会里的种种死气沉沉和空虚无聊的生活，以及虚假的浮华、虚假的排场和虚假的豪侠行为"。（马敬福　译，2005：19）

术语解说

美国超验主义：兴起于十九世纪三十年代美国新英格兰地区的一场文学和哲学思潮，代表人是拉尔夫·沃尔多·爱默生和亨利·大卫·梭罗。其核心观点是认为人能超越感觉和理性而直接认识真理，人类世界只是宇宙的一个缩影。超验主义者强调精神或者超灵的重要性；尊重人的个性及独立；认为自然是上帝的象征，外部世界是精神世界的体现。超验主义是美国浪漫主义发展到高峰时期的产物，对十九世纪的美国影响巨大。

拜伦式英雄：十九世纪英国浪漫主义诗人拜伦在其作品中塑造的一系列个人主义反叛者的形象，带有拜伦的个性气质特征。他们的共同特征是高傲、倔强、叛逆、忧郁、孤独、悲观。他们虽然才华出众，但往往脱离群众，我行我素，始终找不到正确的出路。例如，《恰尔德·哈洛尔德游记》中的哈洛尔德，《曼弗雷德》中的主人公曼弗雷德等。

阅读思考

1. 韦勒克指出，浪漫主义“就诗歌观来说是想象，就世界观来说是自然，就诗体风格来说是象征与神话”。如何理解这句话？

2. 就你所读过的一本浪漫主义作家的小说，分析浪漫主义因素在该小说中的体现。

CHAPTER XIV

导读:在刚刚经历的劫难中,哈克和吉姆不仅得以脱身,还从强盗那里发了一笔横财。二人在岸边的林子里逍遥地躺了整整一个下午,谈天说地,颇有兴致。可是,哈克很快就没了和吉姆聊天的兴趣,抱怨说"根本没法跟一个黑人讲理"。俩人聊了什么让哈克如此丧气?

(1) BY and by, when we got up, we turned over the truck the gang had stole off of the wreck, and found boots, and blankets, and clothes, and all sorts of other things, and a lot of books, and a spyglass, and three boxes of seegars[1]. We hadn't ever been this rich before in neither of our lives. The seegars was prime. We laid off all the afternoon in the woods talking, and me reading the books, and having a general good time. I told Jim all about what happened inside the wreck and at the ferryboat, and I said these kinds of things was adventures; but he said he didn't want no more adventures. He said that when I went in the texas and he crawled back to get on the raft and found her gone he nearly died, because he judged it was all up with *him* anyway it could be fixed; for if he didn't get saved he would get drownded; and if he did get saved, whoever saved him would send him back home so as to get the reward, and then Miss Watson would sell him South, sure. Well, he was right; he was most always right; he had an uncommon level head for a nigger.

[1] 即 cigars

(2) I read considerable to Jim about kings and dukes and earls and such, and how gaudy they dressed, and how much style they put on, and called each other your majesty, and your grace, and your lordship, and so on, 'stead of mister; and Jim's eyes bugged out, and he was interested. He says:

(3) "I didn' know dey was so many un um. I hain't hearn 'bout none un um, skasely, but ole King Sollermun, onless you counts dem kings dat's in a pack er k'yards. How much do a king git?" [2]

(4) "Get?" I says; "why, they get a thousand dollars a month if they want it; they can have just as much as they want; everything belongs to them."

(5) "*Ain'* dat gay? En what dey got to do, Huck?"

(6) "*They* don't do nothing! Why, how you talk! They just set around."

(7) "No; is dat so?"

(8) "Of course it is. They just set around—except, maybe, when there's a war; then they go to the war. But other times they just lazy around; or go hawking[3]—just hawking and sp—Sh!—d' you hear a noise?"

(9) We skipped out and looked; but it warn't nothing but the flutter of a steamboat's wheel away down, coming around the point; so we come back.

(10) "Yes," says I, "and other times, when things is dull, they fuss with the parlyment[4]; and if everybody don't go just so he whacks their heads off[5]. But mostly they hang round the harem."

(11) "Roun' de which?"

(12) "Harem."

(13) "What's de harem?"

(14) "The place where he keeps his wives. Don't you know about the harem? Solomon had one; he had about a million wives." [6]

(15) "Why, yes, dat's so; I—I'd done forgot it. A harem's a bo'd'n-house[7], I reck'n. Mos' likely dey has rackety[8] times in de nussery[9]. En I reck'n de wives quarrels considable; en dat 'crease de racket. Yit dey say Sollermun de wises' man dat ever live'. I doan' take no stock in dat. Bekase why: would a wise man want to live in de mids' er sich a blim-blammin' all de time?[10] No—'deed he wouldn't. A wise man 'ud take en buil' a biler-factry; en den he could shet *down* de biler-factry when he want to res'." [11]

(16) "Well, but he *was* the wisest man, anyway; because

[2] 我不知道有这么多贵人哩。除了一个所罗门老国王,我还没听说过别的国王呐,除非你把扑克牌上的国王也算上。国王挣多少钱呢?

[3] 这里意为"架鹰打猎"。

[4] parlyment: 应为parliament。此处指英王查理一世干涉国会事务。

[5] whack off: (美俚)砍掉。

[6] 这是夸张的说法,根据《旧约·列王纪上》,所罗门有妃七百,都是公主;还有嫔三百。

[7] 即boarding-house

[8] rackety /'rækəti/ *adj.* 吵闹;喧嚷

[9] 即nursery

[10] 我才不信那一套。因为什么呢:一个聪明人怎么会整天住在那样乱糟糟的地方?

[11] 一个聪明人会建一座锅炉厂,想歇歇的话就关掉它。biler-factry即boiler-factory。

the widow she told me so, her own self."

(17) "I doan k'yer what de widder say, he *warn't* no wise man nuther. He had some er de dad-fetchedes' ways I ever see. Does you know 'bout dat chile dat he 'uz gwyne to chop in two?"[12]

(18) "Yes, the widow told me all about it."

(19) "*Well*, den! Warn' dat de beatenes' notion in de worl'? You jes' take en look at it a minute. Dah's de stump, dah—dat's one er de women; heah's you—dat's de yuther one; I's Sollermun; en dish yer dollar bill's de chile. Bofe un you claims it. What does I do? Does I shin aroun' mongs' de neighbors en fine out which un you de bill *do* b'long to, en han' it over to de right one, all safe en soun', de way dat anybody dat had any gumption would?[13] No; I take en whack de bill in *two*, en give half un it to you, en de yuther half to de yuther woman. Dat's de way Sollermun was gwyne to do wid de chile. Now I want to ast you: what's de use er dat half a bill?—can't buy noth'n wid it. En what use is a half a chile? I wouldn' give a dern for a million un um.[14]"

(20) "But hang it, Jim, you've clean missed the point—blame it, you've missed it a thousand mile."

(21) "Who? Me? Go 'long. Doan' talk to me 'bout yo' pints[15]. I reck'n I knows sense when I sees it; en dey ain' no sense in sich doin's as dat.[16] De 'spute[17] warn't 'bout a half a chile, de 'spute was 'bout a whole chile; en de man dat think he kin settle a 'spute 'bout a whole chile wid a half a chile doan' know enough to come in out'n de rain.[18] Doan' talk to me 'bout Sollermun, Huck, I knows him by de back.[19]"

(22) "But I tell you you don't get the point."

(23) "Blame de point! I reck'n I knows what I knows. En mine you, de *real* pint is down furder—it's down deeper. It lays in de way Sollermun was raised. You take a man dat's got on'y one or two chillen; is dat man gwyne to be waseful[20] o' chillen? No, he ain't; he can't 'ford it. *He* know how to value 'em. But you take a man dat's got 'bout five million chillen runnin' roun' de house, en it's diffunt[21]. *He* as soon chop a chile in two as a cat. Dey's plenty mo'. A chile er two, mo' er less, warn't no con-

12 他可干过不少荒唐事儿。你知道他打算把一个孩子劈成两半的故事吧。(这里是说所罗门智断亲子案的故事,详见《旧约·列王纪上》第三章。)(chile 即 child;gwyne 即 going)

13 这还不是世界上最坏的主意吗?你把这件事拿过来看看。那里有段树桩——权当它是一个女人;你在这里——当你是另一个女人;我算是所罗门;这一块钱的钞票就当它是个孩子。你俩都说这钱是你们的,我该咋办?难道不是应该找街坊四邻去打听打听,找出这张票子到底是谁的,原封不动给人还回去吗?凡是有点脑筋的人恐怕都会这样做吧?

14 给我一百万个我也不要。

15 即上文的 points

16 我认为凡是我看得透的就是有道理的。那样的做法根本没一点道理。

17 即 dispute

18 他拿半个孩子去解决一整个孩子的争端,跟那种下了雨都不知道进屋躲躲的傻瓜一个样。

19 我早把他看透了。

20 应为 wasteful

21 应为 difficult

sekens to Sollermun, dad fatch him![22]"

(24) I never see such a nigger. If he got a notion in his head once, there warn't no getting it out again. He was the most down on Solomon of any nigger I ever see. So I went to talking about other kings, and let Solomon slide. I told about Louis Sixteenth[23] that got his head cut off in France long time ago; and about his little boy the dolphin[24], that would a been a king, but they took and shut him up in jail, and some say he died there.

(25) "Po' little chap."

(26) "But some says he got out and got away, and come to America."[25]

(27) "Dat's good! But he'll be pooty lonesome—dey ain' no kings here, is dey, Huck?"

(28) "No."

(29) "Den he cain't git no situation. What he gwyne to do?"

(30) "Well, I don't know. Some of them gets on the police, and some of them learns people how to talk French."

(31) "Why, Huck, doan' de French people talk de same way we does?"

(32) "*No*, Jim; you couldn't understand a word they said—not a single word."

(33) "Well, now, I be ding-busted! How do dat come?"

(34) "I don't know; but it's so. I got some of their jabber[26] out of a book. S'pose a man was to come to you and say *Polly-voo-franzy*[27]—what would you think?"

(35) "I wouldn' think nuff'n[28]; I'd take en bust him over de head—dat is, if he warn't white. I wouldn't 'low no nigger to call me dat."

(36) "Shucks, it ain't calling you anything. It's only saying, do you know how to talk French?"

(37) "Well, den, why couldn't he *say* it?"

(38) "Why, he *is* a-saying it. That's a Frenchman's *way* of saying it."

(39) "Well, it's a blame ridicklous way, en I doan' want to hear no mo' 'bout it. Dey ain' no sense in it."

(40) "Looky here, Jim; does a cat talk like we do?"

[22] 一个孩子或者两个孩子,多也好少也好,对所罗门来说都没有关系,他真是个混账东西!(consekens 应为 consequence)

[23] 路易十六:法兰西波旁王朝复辟前的最后一位国王(1774—1792 年在位),于 1793 年在法国大革命中被处死。

[24] the dolphin(海豚),是法国王位继承人的称号,也是法国皇太子的符号象征。

[25] 路易十六的儿子,年仅十岁的路易十七于 1795 年死于狱中,死前饱受精神及肉体的折磨。出于对他可怜遭遇的同情,坊间有传闻说他被调包,真人越狱逃亡国外。

[26] jabber /ˈdʒæbə(r)/ *n.* 叽里咕噜;含混不清的话

[27] Polly-voo-franzy: 即 Parlez vous Francais(法语),你会说法语吗?

[28] 即 nothing

(41) "No, a cat don't."

(42) "Well, does a cow?"

(43) "No, a cow don't, nuther."

(44) "Does a cat talk like a cow, or a cow talk like a cat?"

(45) "No, dey don't."

(46) "It's natural and right for 'em to talk different from each other, ain't it?"

(47) "Course."

(48) "And ain't it natural and right for a cat and a cow to talk different from *us*?"

(49) "Why, mos' sholy it is."

(50) "Well, then, why ain't it natural and right for a *Frenchman* to talk different from us? You answer me that."

(51) "Is a cat a man, Huck?"

(52) "No."

(53) "Well, den, dey ain't no sense in a cat talkin' like a man. Is a cow a man?—er is a cow a cat?"

(54) "No, she ain't either of them."

(55) "Well, den, she ain't got no business to talk like either one er the yuther of 'em. Is a Frenchman a man?"

(56) "Yes."

(57) "*Well*, den! Dad blame it, why doan' he *talk* like a man? You answer me *dat*!"

(58) I see it warn't no use wasting words—you can't learn a nigger to argue. So I quit.

精华赏析

从上一章对浪漫主义和现实主义的差异的介绍不难看出,《哈克贝利·费恩历险记》是一部带有浓郁现实主义风格的作品。事实上,作者马克·吐温不仅是美国现实主义文学的杰出代表,也是世界著名的现实主义小说大师。

西方现实主义运动源于十九世纪三十年代,随着资本主义制度在西欧各国确立,各种社会问题和社会矛盾也日益突出,一种崇尚客观真实地反映社会现实生活的文学思潮应运而生。下面我们以本书为例,简要概述现实主义文学在创作手法上的特点。

第一,写实性。和浪漫主义文学丰富的想象、大胆的夸张以及强烈的抒情不同,细致观察、真实再现社会现实生活,是现实主义文学的核心理念。马克·吐温通过生活在美国南部密西西比河畔的一个少年——哈克的叙述,不仅展现了密西西比河沿岸秀美壮丽的风光,更生动地描写了十九世纪美国密西西比河沿岸百姓真实的生活习俗、生活场景,向读者展示了一幅美国社会的人生百态图。另外,根据马克·吐温在卷首的说明,作品中使用了大量密苏里州的黑人土语、西南边远地区极端俚俗的方言、派克县的普通方言及其四种变体。这些方言土语的使用,令人身临其境,不仅为故事增加了浓郁的本土气息,如实再现了沿岸本土居民的真实生活,还生动刻画了一大批栩栩如生的人物形象。

第二,批判性。现实主义思潮本身就起源于对资本主义鼓吹的"自由、平等、博爱"的精神童话的批判,鼓励对自然及社会生活作如实的摹写,以揭露社会的种种弊端以及人类的种种苦难。因此,现实主义文学体现出对社会现实的批判性认知。在这个故事里,虽然是以哈克这一少年的视角讲述故事,使用的也是幽默诙谐的语言,但读者在会心一笑的同时,也强烈体会到作者对罪恶的蓄奴制、虚伪贪婪的畸形道德观、腐朽荒唐的上流社会生活、伪善愚昧的宗教的辛辣嘲讽和无情控诉。马克·吐温更是借助小哈克的嘴,表示自己不愿做虚伪的"文明人",为此宁愿下地狱,体现出作者对所谓的"文明社会"无比的厌恶与不屑。

第三,典型性格。现实主义的意思是,除细节的真实外,还要真实地再现典型环境中的典型人物。所谓典型,人们比较一致的看法是个性与共性的统一。典型人物既有鲜明的个性特征,又具备当时社会历史背景下人民大众的一般特征。马克·吐温在《哈克贝利·费恩历险记》中塑造了一群栩栩如生、个性十足但又极具代表性、普遍性的人物。这些人物分布在十九世纪的美国一个南方小镇的社会各阶层,既有教会的忠诚信徒、地方法官、封建家族、上流社会的孩子,又有处于社会底层的酒鬼、流浪汉、骗子、黑奴,个性鲜明,令人印象深刻,但这些人物都是当时的社会背景下美国南方社会的一个缩影,反映了特定历史环境下的社会百态,体现了强烈的时代特征。

以上现实主义文学的特征和创作主张,对后世的文学创作影响深远。我们在学习这些伟大的现实主义作品时,应把握这些鲜明而突出的特征,这样才能加深我们对作品的理解。

阅读思考

1. 现实主义文学对人性的关注和浪漫主义文学有何区别?

2. 找出现实主义文学批判性在《哈克贝利·费恩历险记》中的体现。

CHAPTER XV

导读：哈克和吉姆撑着木筏顺流而下，自由州自在快活的生活指日可待。这天晚上，大雾弥漫，夜幕中的密西西比河笼罩在茫茫白雾之中，两人由此失散。可是，当哈克终于设法找到吉姆乘坐的木筏，两位老友再次会面时，吉姆却被惹恼了。淘气的哈克又捣了什么鬼？

(1) WE judged that three nights more would fetch us to Cairo[1], at the bottom of Illinois, where the Ohio River comes in, and that was what we was after. We would sell the raft and get on a steamboat and go way up the Ohio amongst the free States, and then be out of trouble.[2]

(2) Well, the second night a fog begun to come on, and we made for a towhead[3] to tie to, for it wouldn't do to try to run in a fog; but when I paddled ahead in the canoe, with the line to make fast, there warn't anything but little saplings to tie to. I passed the line around one of them right on the edge of the cut bank, but there was a stiff current, and the raft come booming down so lively she tore it out by the roots and away she went. I see the fog closing down, and it made me so sick and scared I couldn't budge for most a half a minute it seemed to me—and then there warn't no raft in sight; you couldn't see twenty yards. I jumped into the canoe and run back to the stern, and grabbed the paddle and set her back a stroke. But she didn't come. I was in such a hurry I hadn't untied her. I got up and tried to untie her, but I was so excited my hands shook so I couldn't hardly do anything with them.

(3) As soon as I got started I took out after the raft, hot and heavy, right down the towhead. That was all right as far as

[1] Cairo：这里指伊利诺伊州南端的城镇开罗，位于密西西比河和其水量最大的支流俄亥俄河交汇的三角地带。

[2] 哈克和吉姆打算漂流到开罗，再乘轮渡沿俄亥俄河北上到北方自由州。

[3] towhead /ˈtəʊhed/ *n.* 河中的浅滩；沙洲

it went, but the towhead warn't sixty yards long, and the minute I flew by the foot of it I shot out into the solid white fog, and hadn't no more idea which way I was going than a dead man.

(4) Thinks I, it won't do to paddle; first I know I'll run into the bank or a towhead or something; I got to set still and float, and yet it's mighty fidgety[4] business to have to hold your hands still at such a time. I whooped and listened. Away down there somewheres I hears a small whoop, and up comes my spirits. I went tearing after it, listening sharp to hear it again. The next time it come I see I warn't heading for it, but heading away to the right of it. And the next time I was heading away to the left of it—and not gaining on it much either, for I was flying around, this way and that and t'other, but it was going straight ahead all the time.

(5) I did wish the fool would think to beat a tin pan, and beat it all the time, but he never did, and it was the still places between the whoops that was making the trouble for me.[5] Well, I fought along, and directly I hears the whoop *behind* me. I was tangled good now. That was somebody else's whoop, or else I was turned around.

(6) I throwed the paddle down. I heard the whoop again; it was behind me yet, but in a different place; it kept coming, and kept changing its place, and I kept answering, till by and by it was in front of me again, and I knowed the current had swung the canoe's head down-stream, and I was all right if that was Jim and not some other raftsman hollering. I couldn't tell nothing about voices in a fog, for nothing don't look natural nor sound natural in a fog.

(7) The whooping went on, and in about a minute I come a-booming down on a cut bank with smoky ghosts of big trees on it, and the current throwed me off to the left and shot by, amongst a lot of snags[6] that fairly roared, the currrent was tearing by them so swift.

(8) In another second or two it was solid white and still again. I set perfectly still then, listening to my heart thump, and I reckon I didn't draw a breath while it thumped a hundred.[7]

[4] fidgety /ˈfidʒiti/ *adj.* 烦躁的；坐立不安的

[5] 前后两次喊叫的间隙，我听不到一点儿声音，这可真叫人心烦的。

[6] 此处指暗藏在河水中的残枝断木。

[7] 上文"鬼影一般的树木"和此处"心跳了100下都没吸一口气"的说话方式符合哈克叙述的视角，完全是小孩子的语言风格，读来令人不觉会心一笑。（thump /θʌmp/ *v.* 怦怦地跳）

(9) I just give up then. I knowed what the matter was. That cut bank was an island, and Jim had gone down t'other side of it. It warn't no towhead that you could float by in ten minutes. It had the big timber of a regular island; it might be five or six miles long and more than half a mile wide.

(10) I kept quiet, with my ears cocked, about fifteen minutes, I reckon. I was floating along, of course, four or five miles an hour; but you don't ever think of that. No, you feel like you are laying dead still on the water; and if a little glimpse of a snag slips by you don't think to yourself how fast *you're* going, but you catch your breath and think, my! how that snag's tearing along.[8] If you think it ain't dismal[9] and lonesome out in a fog that way by yourself in the night, you try it once—you'll see.

(11) Next, for about a half an hour, I whoops now and then; at last I hears the answer a long ways off, and tries to follow it, but I couldn't do it, and directly I judged I'd got into a nest of towheads, for I had little dim glimpses of them on both sides of me—sometimes just a narrow channel between, and some that I couldn't see I knowed was there because I'd hear the wash of the current against the old dead brush and trash that hung over the banks. Well, I warn't long loosing the whoops down amongst the towheads; and I only tried to chase them a little while, anyway, because it was worse than chasing a Jack-o'-lantern[10]. You never knowed a sound dodge[11] around so, and swap[12] places so quick and so much.

(12) I had to claw away from the bank pretty lively four or five times, to keep from knocking the islands out of the river; and so I judged the raft must be butting[13] into the bank every now and then, or else it would get further ahead and clear out of hearing—it was floating a little faster than what I was.

(13) Well, I seemed to be in the open river again by and by, but I couldn't hear no sign of a whoop nowheres. I reckoned Jim had fetched up on a snag, maybe, and it was all up with him. I was good and tired, so I laid down in the canoe and said I wouldn't bother no more. I didn't want to go to sleep, of course; but I was so sleepy I couldn't help it; so I thought I would take

[8] 这种感受来自作者丰富的水上生活经验。在水上航行,失去了参照物,即使自己在快速前进,也很容易认为自己是静止的。

[9] dismal /ˈdɪzməl/ *adj.* 凄凉的;惨淡的

[10] Jack-o'-lantern:杰克灯,即万圣节的南瓜灯,源自爱尔兰民间传说。此处指哈克在重重沙洲的包围之下,追踪若隐若现的呼叫声,比追踪游魂鬼火还难。

[11] dodge /dɒdʒ/ *v.* 躲开;躲避

[12] swap /swɒp/ *v.* 替换;调换

[13] butt /bʌt/ *v.* 用头顶撞

jest[14] one little cat-nap.

(14) But I reckon it was more than a cat-nap, for when I waked up the stars was shining bright, the fog was all gone, and I was spinning down a big bend stern first.[15] First I didn't know where I was; I thought I was dreaming; and when things began to come back to me they seemed to come up dim out of last week.

(15) It was a monstrous big river here, with the tallest and the thickest kind of timber on both banks; just a solid wall, as well as I could see by the stars. I looked away down-stream, and seen a black speck on the water. I took after it; but when I got to it it warn't nothing but a couple of sawlogs[16] made fast together. Then I see another speck, and chased that; then another, and this time I was right. It was the raft.

(16) When I got to it Jim was setting there with his head down between his knees, asleep, with his right arm hanging over the steering-oar[17]. The other oar was smashed off, and the raft was littered up with leaves and branches and dirt. So she'd had a rough time.[18]

(17) I made fast and laid down under Jim's nose on the raft, and began to gap, and stretch my fists out against Jim, and says:

(18) "Hello, Jim, have I been asleep? Why didn't you stir me up?"

(19) "Goodness gracious, is dat you, Huck? En you ain' dead—you ain' drownded—you's back agin? It's too good for true, honey, it's too good for true. Lemme look at you chile, lemme feel o' you. No, you ain' dead! you's back agin, 'live en soun', jis de same ole Huck—de same ole Huck, thanks to goodness!"

(20) "What's the matter with you, Jim? You been a-drinking?"

(21) "Drinkin'? Has I ben a-drinkin'? Has I had a chance to be a-drinkin'?"

(22) "Well, then, what makes you talk so wild[19]?"

(23) "How does I talk wild?"

[14] 即 just

[15] 船尾向前，沿着一个大河湾，随着水流向下飘。(spin /spɪn/ v. 急转弯；快速旋转)

[16] sawlog /ˈsɔːlɒg/ n. 锯材原木

[17] 熟悉并掌握 with 复合结构的用法。

[18] 看来这木筏也刚刚经历了一场劫难。这里 she 指的是失而复得的木筏。

[19] talk wild: 胡言乱语

(24) "*How*? Why, hain't you been talking about my coming back, and all that stuff, as if I'd been gone away?"

(25) "Huck—Huck Finn, you look me in de eye; look me in de eye. *Hain't* you ben gone away?"

(26) "Gone away? Why, what in the nation do you mean? I hain't been gone anywheres. Where would I go to?"

(27) "Well, looky here, boss, dey's sumf'n[20] wrong, dey is. Is I *me*, or who *is* I? Is I heah, or whah *is* I? Now dat's what I wants to know."

(28) "Well, I think you're here, plain enough, but I think you're a tangle-headed old fool, Jim."

(29) "I is, is I? Well, you answer me dis: Didn't you tote out de line in de canoe fer to make fas' to de tow-head?"[21]

(30) "No, I didn't. What tow-head? I hain't see no tow-head."

(31) "You hain't seen no towhead? Looky here, didn't de line pull loose en de raf' go a-hummin' down de river, en leave you en de canoe behine in de fog?"

(32) "What fog?"

(33) "Why, *de* fog!—de fog dat's been aroun' all night. En didn't you whoop, en didn't I whoop, tell we got mix' up in de islands en one un us got los' en t'other one was jis' as good as los', 'kase he didn' know whah he wuz? En didn't I bust up agin a lot er dem islands en have a turrible time en mos' git drownded? Now ain' dat so, boss—ain't it so? You answer me dat."

(34) "Well, this is too many for me, Jim. I hain't seen no fog, nor no islands, nor no troubles, nor nothing. I been setting here talking with you all night till you went to sleep about ten minutes ago, and I reckon I done the same. You couldn't a got drunk in that time, so of course you've been dreaming."

(35) "Dad fetch it, how is I gwyne to dream all dat in ten minutes?"

(36) "Well, hang it all[22], you did dream it, because there didn't any of it happen."

(37) "But, Huck, it's all jis' as plain to me as—"

[20] 即 something

[21] 你不是坐着独木船，拿着绳子，要把木筏拴在沙洲上吗？（tote /təʊt/ *v.* 携带；手提；搬运）

[22] hang it all：（俚）该死！

（38）"It don't make no difference how plain it is; there ain't nothing in it. I know, because I've been here all the time."

（39）Jim didn't say nothing for about five minutes, but set there studying over it. Then he says:

（40）"Well, den, I reck'n I did dream it, Huck; but dog my cats[23] ef it ain't de powerfullest dream I ever see. En I hain't ever had no dream b'fo' dat's tired me like dis one."

[23] dog my cats: 美国南部俚语，表示惊讶的语气。

（41）"Oh, well, that's all right, because a dream does tire a body like everything sometimes. But this one was a staving[24] dream; tell me all about it, Jim."

[24] staving: (俚)特好的；特大的

（42）So Jim went to work and told me the whole thing right through, just as it happened, only he painted it up considerable[25]. Then he said he must start in and "'terpret"[26] it, because it was sent for a warning. He said the first towhead stood for a man that would try to do us some good, but the current was another man that would get us away from him. The whoops was warnings that would come to us every now and then, and if we didn't try hard to make out to understand them they'd just take us into bad luck, 'stead of keeping us out of it. The lot of towheads was troubles we was going to get into with quarrelsome people and all kinds of mean folks, but if we minded our business and didn't talk back and aggravate them, we would pull through and get out of the fog and into the big clear river, which was the free States, and wouldn't have no more trouble.[27]

[25] 添油加醋地描述

[26] 即 interpret

[27] 本段中，吉姆这一充满奇思异想的"解梦"，朴素地阐释了人与自然的关系，同时与第四章吉姆替人算命的情节遥相呼应。传统批判主义分析方法认为这反映了吉姆的愚昧无知，但这又何尝不是一个处于社会底层的黑奴的生活经验和生存智慧的体现呢。

（43）It had clouded up pretty dark just after I got on to the raft, but it was clearing up again now.

（44）"Oh, well, that's all interpreted well enough as far as it goes, Jim," I says; "but what does *these* things stand for?"

（45）It was the leaves and rubbish on the raft and the smashed oar. You could see them first-rate now.

（46）Jim looked at the trash, and then looked at me, and back at the trash again. He had got the dream fixed so strong in his head that he couldn't seem to shake it loose and get the facts back into its place again right away. But when he did get the thing straightened around he looked at me steady without ever smiling, and says:

(47) "What do dey stan' for? I'se gwyne to tell you. When I got all wore out wid work, en wid de callin' for you, en went to sleep, my heart wuz mos' broke bekase you wuz los', en I didn' k'yer no' mo' what become er me en de raf'. En when I wake up en fine you back agin, all safe en soun', de tears come, en I could a got down on my knees en kiss yo' foot, I's so thankful. En all you wuz thinkin' 'bout wuz how you could make a fool uv ole Jim wid a lie. Dat truck dah is *trash*; en trash is what people is dat puts dirt on de head er dey fren's en makes 'em ashamed." [28]

(48) Then he got up slow and walked to the wigwam, and went in there without saying anything but that. But that was enough. It made me feel so mean I could almost kissed *his* foot to get him to take it back.

(49) It was fifteen minutes before I could work myself up to go and humble myself to a nigger; but I done it, and I warn't ever sorry for it afterwards, neither. I didn't do him no more mean tricks, and I wouldn't done that one if I'd a knowed it would make him feel that way.[29]

[28] 这段话反映了吉姆金子般高尚的品质，表现了他淳朴的天性，说得哈克无地自容，读来不禁令人肃然起敬。

[29] 这段话反映出哈克天性淳良，至少在他的认知里，奴隶的身份并不影响他判断一个人的善良。

精华赏析

对于小说创作来说，人物刻画成功与否至关重要。一个好的故事，都会有一个或者多个令人印象深刻的人物形象。随着时间的流逝，其情节或许会在读者的脑海里变得印象淡薄，但其塑造的人物形象却能鲜活地留存在读者心中。《献给艾米丽的玫瑰》中阴郁、有怪癖、病态的艾米丽，《奥赛罗》中多疑善妒、轻信盲从的奥赛罗，《堂吉诃德》中沉溺于幻想、荒唐可笑的堂吉诃德……这些人物栩栩如生，经久不衰，成为散落在世界文学宝库里的一颗颗璀璨明珠，深受各国文学爱好者的喜爱。

英国著名小说家和批评家 E.M. 福斯特（2016）将小说人物分为"扁平人物"（flat character）和"圆形人物"（round character）两大类型。所谓扁平人物，是指性格比较单一的人物，因此容易辨识和记忆。作者着重塑造其某一种特定性格，使该特点得以突出和强调，所以也被称为"类型人物"或者"漫画人物"。福斯特认为，扁平人物"其最纯粹的形式是基于某种单一观念或品质塑造而成的；当其中包括的要素超过一种时，我们得到的就是一条趋向圆形的弧线了”。中国文学中不乏这样的扁平人物，如《三国演义》中分别代表义、勇、智的关羽、张飞、诸葛亮，他们性格和才能中的某一特质被纯粹地放大而突显，读者对其人物形象的认知始终如一，直至故事结束，并且历经时代的变迁而不改。

而“圆形人物”，指的是文学作品中具有复杂、多变性格的人物，他们变化莫测，随着故事情节的发展和环境的变化展现出不一样，甚至前后截然相反的性格差异。读者对他们的认知，需要不断地进行调整，正所谓坏人不会坏到底，好人不会好到底。如莎士比亚笔下的哈姆雷特，便是典型的圆形人物。他原本是一个富于理想、品格高尚且多才多艺的王子，未来大有作为的国王，但面对父亲枉死的亡魂，目睹国家如人间地狱般的黑暗，直视亲友的叛离，他开始变得优柔寡断，忧郁而多疑，其性格呈现出多面性，如立体几何，充满层次感和空间感，读者对其人物形象的认知也在不断变化。

正如扁平人物不全是次要人物，圆形人物也不是主要人物的同义词。但在文学创作中，优秀的作家往往更青睐于圆形人物的塑造，这是因为圆形人物有复杂多变的性格，细腻丰富的内心世界，因此人物更具立体感和艺术感，对作家来说更具挑战性。就本故事而言，哈克就是一个典型的圆形人物。在故事的开始，哈克给读者的印象，是一个与文明社会中某些刻板、虚伪的道德规范格格不入的少年。他崇尚自由，富有正义感，具有叛逆精神，所以在遇到逃跑的黑奴吉姆时，他义无反顾地选择掩护他、帮助他，更是把吉姆当成朋友看待。与一味索取吉姆劳动力，为了一个好价钱，动辄就想卖掉吉姆的沃森小姐相比，马克·吐温赋予了哈克，一个白人孩子，更多人性中善良的美德。而在本章中，哈克为了寻找被水流冲走的木筏，在浓雾与激流中划着小船，镇定自若，终于安然而归。在西方的文学传统中，这样的情节带有强烈的古典英雄主义色彩，哈克被这种英雄主义情结所鼓舞，白人的优越感占了上风，去捉弄为他担惊受怕得“心都要碎了”的老吉姆。这里，哈克戏弄吉姆的情节表现出他人性中“向恶”的一面。但难能可贵的是，面对吉姆的指责，哈克认识到了自己的错误，真诚悔悟，恨不得用嘴去亲吉姆的脚来安慰他，其人物形象也得以升华。随着故事情节的发展，哈克的人物形象，将呈现出更加复杂多变的性格，读者如同在密林中寻宝，一定会有更多惊喜的发现。

那么，你如何看待吉姆这一人物形象呢？两人的密西西比河之旅仍在继续，精彩的故事还在发生，让我们在后面的探险之旅中去挖掘更多关于人物塑造的秘密吧。

阅读思考

1. 扁平人物和圆形人物的区别是什么？

2. 分析吉姆的人物性格，他是扁平人物还是圆形人物？

CHAPTER XVI

导读：离自由州越来越近，吉姆难掩激动的心情。然而，常言说人生不如意十之八九，吉姆早已在那场惊心动魄的大雾中错过了心心念念的目的地。二人正为此发愁呢，倒霉的事儿接二连三来凑热闹。先是独木舟丢了，随后一条轰隆隆开过来的大船直接撞碎了两个人乘坐的木筏。情急之下跳水逃生的哈克再次探出头的时候，发现吉姆不见了……

（1）WE slept most all day, and started out at night, a little ways behind a monstrous long raft that was as long going by as a procession.[1] She had four long sweeps[2] at each end, so we judged she carried as many as thirty men, likely. She had five big wigwams aboard, wide apart, and an open camp fire in the middle, and a tall flag-pole at each end. There was a power of style about her.[3] It *amounted* to something being a raftsman on such a craft as that.[4]

（2）We went drifting down into a big bend, and the night clouded up and got hot. The river was very wide, and was walled with solid timber on both sides; you couldn't see a break in it hardly ever, or a light.[5] We talked about Cairo, and wondered whether we would know it when we got to it. I said likely we wouldn't, because I had heard say there warn't but about a dozen houses there, and if they didn't happen to have them lit up, how was we going to know we was passing a town? Jim said if the two big rivers joined together there, that would show. But I said maybe we might think we was passing the foot of an island and coming into the same old river again. That disturbed Jim—and me too. So the question was, what to do? I said, paddle ashore the first time a light showed, and tell them pap was behind,

[1] 在我们前面不远处漂着一排长得出奇的木筏，长得像游行队伍一样。

[2] 木桨

[3] 这木筏的气派老大了。

[4] 在这样的筏子上当个船夫，那才够得上人物呢。

[5] 透不出一丝光亮。

coming along with a trading-scow, and was a green hand at the business, and wanted to know how far it was to Cairo. Jim thought it was a good idea, so we took a smoke on it and waited.

(3) There warn't nothing to do now but to look out sharp for the town, and not pass it without seeing it. He said he'd be mighty sure to see it, because he'd be a free man the minute he seen it, but if he missed it he'd be in a slave country again and no more show for freedom. Every little while he jumps up and says:

(4) "Dah she is?"

(5) But it warn't. It was Jack-o'-lanterns, or lightning bugs; so he set down again, and went to watching, same as before. Jim said it made him all over trembly and feverish to be so close to freedom. Well, I can tell you it made me all over trembly and feverish, too, to hear him, because I begun to get it through my head that he *was* most free—and who was to blame for it? Why, *me*. I couldn't get that out of my conscience, no how nor no way. It got to troubling me so I couldn't rest; I couldn't stay still in one place. It hadn't ever come home to me before, what this thing was that I was doing. But now it did; and it stayed with me, and scorched me more and more. I tried to make out to myself that I warn't to blame, because I didn't run Jim off from his rightful owner; but it warn't no use, conscience up and says, every time, "But you knowed he was running for his freedom, and you could a paddled ashore and told somebody." That was so—I couldn't get around that noway. That was where it pinched. Conscience says to me, "What had poor Miss Watson done to you that you could see her nigger go off right under your eyes and never say one single word? What did that poor old woman do to you that you could treat her so mean? Why, she tried to learn you your book, she tried to learn you your manners, she tried to be good to you every way she knowed how. *That's* what she done."

(6) I got to feeling so mean and so miserable I most wished I was dead. I fidgeted[6] up and down the raft, abusing myself to myself, and Jim was fidgeting up and down past me. We neither

[6] **fidget** /ˈfɪdʒɪt/ *v.* 坐立不安

of us could keep still. Every time he danced around and says, "Dah's Cairo!" it went through me like a shot, and I thought if it *was* Cairo I reckoned I would die of miserableness.

(7) Jim talked out loud all the time while I was talking to myself. He was saying how the first thing he would do when he got to a free State he would go to saving up money and never spend a single cent, and when he got enough he would buy his wife, which was owned on a farm close to where Miss Watson lived; and then they would both work to buy the two children, and if their master wouldn't sell them, they'd get an Ab'litionist[7] to go and steal them.

(8) It most froze me to hear such talk. He wouldn't ever dared to talk such talk in his life before. Just see what a difference it made in him the minute he judged he was about free. It was according to the old saying, "Give a nigger an inch and he'll take an ell[8]." Thinks I, this is what comes of my not thinking. Here was this nigger, which I had as good as helped to run away, coming right out flat-footed[9] and saying he would steal his children—children that belonged to a man I didn't even know; a man that hadn't ever done me no harm.

(9) I was sorry to hear Jim say that, it was such a lowering of him. My conscience got to stirring me up hotter than ever, until at last I says to it, "Let up on me—it ain't too late yet—I'll paddle ashore at the first light and tell." I felt easy and happy and light as a feather right off. All my troubles was gone. I went to looking out sharp for a light, and sort of singing to myself. By and by one showed.[10] Jim sings out:

(10) "We's safe, Huck, we's safe! Jump up and crack yo' heels[11]! Dat's de good ole Cairo at las', I jis knows it!"

(11) I says:

(12) "I'll take the canoe and go and see, Jim. It mightn't be, you know."

(13) He jumped and got the canoe ready, and put his old coat in the bottom for me to set on, and give me the paddle; and as I shoved off, he says:

(14) "Pooty soon I'll be a-shout'n' for joy, en I'll say, it's

[7] 即 abolitionist，废奴主义者。

[8] ell /el/ *n.* 旧时长度单位，等于 45 英寸。

[9] flat-footed:（不顾及他人感受）直截了当地

[10] 以上几段真实描述了在哈克的内心中，两种感情在激烈交锋。一方面哈克同情吉姆，希望帮助他逃到自由州；另一方面又深感自责，觉得自己的行为是不对的，有愧于自己的"良知"。

[11] 应该是"kick up your heels"，美国俚语，意为"好好轻松一番，尽情享受一下"。

all on accounts o' Huck; I's a free man, en I couldn't ever ben free ef it hadn' ben for Huck; Huck done it. Jim won't ever forgit you, Huck; you's de bes' fren' Jim's ever had; en you's de *only* fren' ole Jim's got now."

(15) I was paddling off, all in a sweat to tell on him[12]; but when he says this, it seemed to kind of take the tuck all out of me[13]. I went along slow then, and I warn't right down certain whether I was glad I started or whether I warn't. When I was fifty yards off, Jim says:

(16) "Dah you goes, de ole true Huck; de on'y white genlman dat ever kep' his promise to ole Jim."

(17) Well, I just felt sick. But I says, I *got* to do it—I can't get *out* of it. Right then along comes a skiff with two men in it with guns, and they stopped and I stopped. One of them says:

(18) "What's that yonder?"

(19) "A piece of a raft," I says.

(20) "Do you belong on it?"

(21) "Yes, sir."

(22) "Any men on it?"

(23) "Only one, sir."

(24) "Well, there's five niggers run off to-night up yonder, above the head of the bend. Is your man white or black?"

(25) I didn't answer up prompt. I tried to, but the words wouldn't come. I tried for a second or two to brace up[14] and out with it, but I warn't man enough—hadn't the spunk[15] of a rabbit. I see I was weakening; so I just give up trying, and up and says:

(26) "He's white."[16]

(27) "I reckon we'll go and see for ourselves."

(28) "I wish you would," says I, "because it's pap that's there, and maybe you'd help me tow the raft ashore where the light is. He's sick—and so is mam and Mary Ann."

(29) "Oh, the devil! we're in a hurry, boy. But I s'pose we've got to. Come, buckle to your paddle[17], and let's get along."

(30) I buckled to my paddle and they laid to their oars. When we had made a stroke or two, I says:

12 **tell on sb**: 告发;检举

13 **take the tuck out of sb**: (美俚)使某人丧失斗志;使某人不敢狂妄。哈克本来急着上岸告发吉姆,却被吉姆一席话打动,打消了去告发他的念头。

14 **brace up**: 打起精神;振作起来

15 **spunk** /spʌŋk/ *n.* 勇气;胆量

16 作者在描述哈克的内心矛盾中,反复强调帮助吉姆逃到自由州是"违反良知"。我们阅读时应考虑到当时的社会背景。教会和白人的"良知"就是蓄奴制。这句话说明哈克战胜了这种"良知",这是哈克的"成长之旅"中重要的转折点。

17 用尽全力划你的桨。(buckle to: 认真干;努力做)

(31) "Pap'll be mighty much obleeged[18] to you, I can tell you. Everybody goes away when I want them to help me tow the raft ashore, and I can't do it by myself."

(32) "Well, that's infernal[19] mean. Odd, too. Say, boy, what's the matter with your father?"

(33) "It's the—a—the—well, it ain't anything much."

(34) They stopped pulling. It warn't but a mighty little ways to the raft now. One says:

(35) "Boy, that's a lie. What IS the matter with your pap? Answer up square now, and it'll be the better for you."

(36) "I will, sir, I will, honest—but don't leave us, please. It's the—the—Gentlemen, if you'll only pull ahead, and let me heave you the headline, you won't have to come a-near the raft—please do."

(37) "Set her back, John, set her back!" says one. They backed water. "Keep away, boy—keep to looard[20]. Confound it[21], I just expect the wind has blowed it to us. Your pap's got the small-pox, and you know it precious well. Why didn't you come out and say so? Do you want to spread it all over?"

(38) "Well," says I, a-blubbering[22], "I've told everybody before, and they just went away and left us."

(39) "Poor devil, there's something in that.[23] We are right down sorry for you, but we—well, hang it, we don't want the small-pox, you see. Look here, I'll tell you what to do. Don't you try to land by yourself, or you'll smash everything to pieces. You float along down about twenty miles, and you'll come to a town on the left-hand side of the river. It will be long after sun-up then, and when you ask for help you tell them your folks are all down with chills and fever. Don't be a fool again, and let people guess what is the matter. Now we're trying to do you a kindness; so you just put twenty miles between us, that's a good boy. It wouldn't do any good to land yonder where the light is—it's only a wood-yard. Say, I reckon your father's poor, and I'm bound to say he's in pretty hard luck. Here, I'll put a twenty-dollar gold piece on this board, and you get it when it floats by. I feel mighty mean to leave you; but my kingdom! it won't do to

[18] 即 obliged

[19] infernal /ɪn'fɜːnl/ *adj.* 可恨的；坏透的；地狱的；阴间的

[20] 即 leeward/'liːwəd/ *adj.* 背风的；在下风方向的

[21] confound it:（旧）讨厌；该死（用于表达愤怒、烦恼）

[22] blubber /'blʌbə(r)/ *v.* 大声哭；哭诉

[23] 可怜的小鬼，说得也有几分道理。

fool with small-pox, don't you see?"

(40) "Hold on, Parker," says the other man, "here's a twenty to put on the board for me. Good-bye, boy; you do as Mr. Parker told you, and you'll be all right."

(41) "That's so, my boy—good-bye, good-bye. If you see any runaway niggers you get help and nab them, and you can make some money by it."

(42) "Good-bye, sir," says I; "I won't let no runaway niggers get by me if I can help it."

(43) They went off and I got aboard the raft, feeling bad and low, because I knowed very well I had done wrong, and I see it warn't no use for me to try to learn to do right; a body that don't get *started* right when he's little ain't got no show—when the pinch comes there ain't nothing to back him up and keep him to his work, and so he gets beat.[24] Then I thought a minute, and says to myself, hold on; s'pose you'd a done right and give Jim up, would you felt better than what you do now? No, says I, I'd feel bad—I'd feel just the same way I do now. Well, then, says I, what's the use you learning to do right when it's troublesome to do right and ain't no trouble to do wrong, and the wages is just the same?[25] I was stuck. I couldn't answer that. So I reckoned I wouldn't bother no more about it, but after this always do whichever come handiest at the time.

[24] 一个人要是小时候一开始就不学好，以后也难有作为——危急关头，没有什么能支撑他坚持到底，于是只能败下阵来。

[25] 做正确的事，给自己惹麻烦；做错事，反而啥事没有。做对做错付出的代价反正都一样，那费劲去学做正确的事又有什么用呢？

(44) I went into the wigwam; Jim warn't there. I looked all around; he warn't anywhere. I says:

(45) "Jim!"

(46) "Here I is, Huck. Is dey out o' sight yit? Don't talk loud."

(47) He was in the river under the stern oar, with just his nose out. I told him they were out of sight, so he come aboard. He says:

(48) "I was a-listenin' to all de talk, en I slips into de river en was gwyne to shove for sho' if dey come aboard. Den I was gwyne to swim to de raf' agin when dey was gone. But lawsy, how you did fool 'em, Huck! Dat *wuz* de smartes' dodge! I tell you, chile, I'spec it save' ole Jim—ole Jim ain't going to forgit

you for dat, honey."

(49) Then we talked about the money. It was a pretty good raise—twenty dollars apiece. Jim said we could take deck passage on a steamboat now, and the money would last us as far as we wanted to go in the free States. He said twenty mile more warn't far for the raft to go, but he wished we was already there.

(50) Towards daybreak we tied up, and Jim was mighty particular about hiding the raft good. Then he worked all day fixing things in bundles, and getting all ready to quit rafting.

(51) That night about ten we hove in sight of the lights of a town away down in a left-hand bend.

(52) I went off in the canoe to ask about it. Pretty soon I found a man out in the river with a skiff, setting a trot-line. I ranged up and says:

(53) "Mister, is that town Cairo?"

(54) "Cairo? no. You must be a blame' fool."

(55) "What town is it, mister?"

(56) "If you want to know, go and find out. If you stay here botherin' around me for about a half a minute longer you'll get something you won't want."

(57) I paddled to the raft. Jim was awful disappointed, but I said never mind, Cairo would be the next place, I reckoned.

(58) We passed another town before daylight, and I was going out again; but it was high ground, so I didn't go. No high ground about Cairo, Jim said. I had forgot it. We laid up for the day on a towhead tolerable close to the left-hand bank. I begun to suspicion something. So did Jim. I says:

(59) "Maybe we went by Cairo in the fog that night."

(60) He says:

(61) "Doan' le's talk about it, Huck. Po' niggers can't have no luck. I awluz 'spected dat rattlesnake-skin warn't done wid its work."

(62) "I wish I'd never seen that snake-skin, Jim—I do wish I'd never laid eyes on it."

(63) "It ain't yo' fault, Huck; you didn' know. Don't you blame yo'self 'bout it."

(64) When it was daylight, here was the clear Ohio water inshore, sure enough, and outside was the old regular Muddy! So it was all up with Cairo.[26]

(65) We talked it all over. It wouldn't do to take to the shore; we couldn't take the raft up the stream, of course. There warn't no way but to wait for dark, and start back in the canoe and take the chances. So we slept all day amongst the cottonwood thicket, so as to be fresh for the work, and when we went back to the raft about dark the canoe was gone!

(66) We didn't say a word for a good while. There warn't anything to say. We both knowed well enough it was some more work of the rattlesnake-skin; so what was the use to talk about it? It would only look like we was finding fault, and that would be bound to fetch more bad luck —and keep on fetching it, too, till we knowed enough to keep still.

(67) By and by we talked about what we better do, and found there warn't no way but just to go along down with the raft till we got a chance to buy a canoe to go back in. We warn't going to borrow it when there warn't anybody around, the way pap would do, for that might set people after us.[27]

(68) So we shoved out after dark on the raft.

(69) Anybody that don't believe yet that it's foolishness to handle a snake-skin, after all that that snake-skin done for us, will believe it now if they read on and see what more it done for us.

(70) The place to buy canoes is off of rafts laying up at shore. But we didn't see no rafts laying up; so we went along during three hours and more. Well, the night got gray and ruther thick, which is the next meanest thing to fog. You can't tell the shape of the river, and you can't see no distance. It got to be very late and still, and then along comes a steamboat up the river. We lit the lantern, and judged she would see it. Up-stream boats didn't generly come close to us; they go out and follow the bars and hunt for easy water under the reefs; but nights like this they bull right up the channel against the whole river.

(71) We could hear her pounding along, but we didn't see

[26] 俄亥俄河河水较清，密西西比河河水浑浊。哈克和吉姆看到内河水清，外侧浑浊，明白他们已经错过了位于两河交汇处的开罗了。

[27] 像爸爸那样去“借”一艘独木舟，暗指像爸爸那样“顺手牵羊”。

her good till she was close. She aimed right for us. Often they do that and try to see how close they can come without touching; sometimes the wheel bites off a sweep, and then the pilot sticks his head out and laughs, and thinks he's mighty smart. Well, here she comes, and we said she was going to try and shave us;[28] but she didn't seem to be sheering off a bit. She was a big one, and she was coming in a hurry, too, looking like a black cloud with rows of glow-worms around it; but all of a sudden she bulged out, big and scary, with a long row of wide-open furnace doors shining like red-hot teeth, and her monstrous bows and guards hanging right over us. There was a yell at us, and a jingling of bells to stop the engines, a powwow of cussing[29], and whistling of steam—and as Jim went overboard on one side and I on the other, she come smashing straight through the raft.

[28] 哈克以为这艘大船径直朝他们开来,又是水手的恶作剧,故意贴着他们的木筏子开过去,像是给木筏子剃胡子。

[29] cuss /kʌs/ *v.* 诅咒;咒骂

(72) I dived—and I aimed to find the bottom, too, for a thirty-foot wheel had got to go over me, and I wanted it to have plenty of room. I could always stay under water a minute; this time I reckon I stayed under a minute and a half. Then I bounced for the top in a hurry, for I was nearly busting. I popped out to my armpits and blowed the water out of my nose, and puffed a bit. Of course there was a booming current; and of course that boat started her engines again ten seconds after she stopped them, for they never cared much for raftsmen; so now she was churning along up[30] the river, out of sight in the thick weather, though I could hear her.

[30] churn up: 搅动;翻起

(73) I sung out for Jim about a dozen times, but I didn't get any answer; so I grabbed a plank that touched me while I was "treading water," and struck out for shore, shoving it ahead of me. But I made out to see that the drift of the current was towards the left-hand shore, which meant that I was in a crossing; so I changed off and went that way.

(74) It was one of these long, slanting, two-mile crossings; so I was a good long time in getting over. I made a safe landing, and clumb up the bank. I couldn't see but a little ways, but I went poking along[31] over rough ground for a quarter of a mile or more, and then I run across a big old-fashioned double log-

[31] poke along: 缓慢行走

house before I noticed it. I was going to rush by and get away, but a lot of dogs jumped out and went to howling and barking at me, and I knowed better than to move another peg[32].

[32] move a peg: 迈出一条腿；迈步走

精华赏析

哈克和吉姆乘着木筏沿密西西比河一路南下，惊心动魄的旅程中充满刺激，更充满对自由的向往和期待。吉姆满心欢喜，一心憧憬着未来自由幸福的生活：努力攒钱，赎回妻子，救回孩子……但另一头，哈克的心情却是一言难尽。

1492年，哥伦布率领的船队在美洲登陆。"新大陆"的发现，对于蠢蠢欲动的欧洲殖民者来说，无疑是一个巨大的机会——辽阔的美洲大陆为他们提供了广阔的土地。随后，大批欧洲殖民者蜂拥而至，纷纷在美洲建立了殖民据点。他们在肥沃富饶的美洲大陆上开采矿藏、开辟种植园，因此需要大量的劳动力。但由于美洲的原著居民印第安人遭到了欧洲殖民者疯狂的屠杀和驱赶，人口急剧减少，对于这些种植园主来说，补充大量廉价劳动力迫在眉睫。欧洲的奴隶贩子们从中发现"商机"，从事起黑奴贸易的罪恶勾当。他们贩卖身强力壮的非洲黑人到美洲，换取殖民地生产的蔗糖、咖啡、棉花等原料后，返回欧洲。自十六世纪初至十九世纪，罪恶的"黑三角"贸易历时400年，给非洲大陆造成了极其深重的灾难，也为西方殖民者带来了巨大的财富。

随着美洲殖民者种植园面积越来越大，从非洲运来的黑奴也越来越多。美国独立之前，13个英属殖民地的黑奴总数已达50万，约占殖民地人口的1/7。美国独立之后，南方诸州普遍实行黑人奴隶制。随着南方种植园经济的迅速发展，奴隶制已渗透到美国南方各州社会生活的方方面面。作为奴隶主的种植园主们，在获得巨大财富的同时，也通过奴隶制获取了极高的政治地位，他们是无论如何也不愿放弃奴隶制这棵摇钱树的。例如在著名的斯科特诉桑福德案中，美国联邦最高法院以黑奴不属于《美国宪法》中所指的公民，而是主人的私有财产判决，从而驳回黑人奴隶斯科特要求恢复自由的诉求。蓄奴制受美国法律的保护，这极大助长了奴隶主们的气焰。

奴隶是私有财产，像牲畜一样可以自由买卖，这种观念在蓄奴的南方各州根深蒂固。马克·吐温的故乡密苏里州在1821年加入联邦时，成为一个蓄奴州。白人阶层享受特权，黑奴没有公民权，更不可能主宰自己和家人的命运。在当时的社会背景下，自觉维护奴隶制是所有白人的基本"良知"。所以，本章中当哈克意识到吉姆即将开始"自由"的生活，内心难免有不安，有公然违背特权阶层"良知"的愧疚感。哈克内心世界的矛盾和斗争，是当时社会生活的真实写照，如实地刻画了一个与社会规范格格不入的白人少年纯真无瑕、有血有肉的生动形象。

术语解说

“黑三角”贸易：指始于十六世纪历时400年的奴隶贸易。欧洲奴隶贩子从本国出发，在非洲用一些廉价物品与当地的黑人猎奴贩子交易获得黑奴，然后横渡大西洋，来到美洲换成糖、烟草和稻米等返回欧洲。在欧洲西部、非洲的几内亚湾附近、美洲西印度群岛之间，航线大致构成三角形状，故称作“黑三角”贸易。

斯科特诉桑福德案：美国最高法院于1857年判决的一个关于奴隶制的案件。该案的主角是一名叫德雷德·斯科特的黑人奴隶，因为他曾经随主人到过自由州，所以在主人死后他提起诉讼要求获得自由。案件在密苏里州最高法院和联邦法院被驳回后，斯科特上诉到美国最高法院，经过两次法庭辩论，最终9位大法官以7 ： 2的票数维持原判。该案的判决成为南北战争的关键起因之一。

阅读思考

1. 长达400年的黑奴贸易对美国的影响表现在哪些方面？

2. 阅读Harriet Beecher Stowe的小说《汤姆叔叔的小屋》，比较小说中汤姆叔叔和《哈克贝利·费恩历险记》中的黑奴吉姆在性格上的异同。

CHAPTER XVII

导读：与吉姆失散后，浑身湿透的哈克狼狈地爬上了岸，不知不觉邂逅了格伦基福特一家。在热情的格伦基福特家那宽敞气派、装饰别致的房子里，隐姓埋名的哈克暂时安顿了下来。他用好奇的目光打量着这个大房子里的每一个物件，观察着每一个人的行踪……

(1) IN about a minute somebody spoke out of a window without putting his head out, and says:

(2) "Be done, boys! Who's there?"

(3) I says:

(4) "It's me."

(5) "Who's me?"

(6) "George Jackson, sir."

(7) "What do you want?"

(8) "I don't want nothing, sir. I only want to go along by, but the dogs won't let me."

(9) "What are you prowling[1] around here this time of night for—hey?"

(10) "I warn't prowling around, sir, I fell overboard off of the steamboat."

(11) "Oh, you did, did you? Strike a light there, somebody. What did you say your name was?"

(12) "George Jackson, sir. I'm only a boy."

(13) "Look here, if you're telling the truth you needn't be afraid—nobody'll hurt you. But don't try to budge[2]; stand right where you are. Rouse out Bob and Tom, some of you, and fetch the guns. George Jackson, is there anybody with you?"

(14) "No, sir, nobody."

[1] prowl /praʊl/ v. 悄悄移动

[2] budge /bʌdʒ/ v. 稍微移动

(15) I heard the people stirring around in the house now, and see a light. The man sung out:

(16) "Snatch that light away, Betsy, you old fool—ain't you got any sense? Put it on the floor behind the front door. Bob, if you and Tom are ready, take your places."

(17) "All ready."

(18) "Now, George Jackson, do you know the Shepherdsons?"

(19) "No, sir; I never heard of them."

(20) "Well, that may be so, and it mayn't. Now, all ready. Step forward, George Jackson. And mind, don't you hurry—come mighty slow. If there's anybody with you, let him keep back—if he shows himself he'll be shot. Come along now. Come slow; push the door open yourself—just enough to squeeze in, d' you hear?"

(21) I didn't hurry; I couldn't if I'd a wanted to. I took one slow step at a time and there warn't a sound, only I thought I could hear my heart. The dogs were as still as the humans, but they followed a little behind me. When I got to the three log doorsteps I heard them unlocking and unbarring and unbolting. I put my hand on the door and pushed it a little and a little more till somebody said, "There, that's enough—put your head in." I done it, but I judged they would take it off.

(22) The candle was on the floor, and there they all was, looking at me, and me at them, for about a quarter of a minute: Three big men with guns pointed at me, which made me wince, I tell you; the oldest, gray and about sixty, the other two thirty or more—all of them fine and handsome—and the sweetest old gray-headed lady, and back of her two young women which I couldn't see right well. The old gentleman says:

(23) "There; I reckon it's all right. Come in."

(24) As soon as I was in the old gentleman he locked the door and barred it and bolted it, and told the young men to come in with their guns, and they all went in a big parlor that had a new rag carpet on the floor, and got together in a corner that was out of the range of the front windows[3]—there warn't none on the side. They held the candle, and took a good look at

[3] 指站在枪从前窗打不到的范围。

me, and all said, "Why, *he* ain't a Shepherdson—no, there ain't any Shepherdson about him." Then the old man said he hoped I wouldn't mind being searched for arms, because he didn't mean no harm by it—it was only to make sure. So he didn't pry into my pockets, but only felt outside with his hands, and said it was all right. He told me to make myself easy and at home, and tell all about myself; but the old lady says:

(25) "Why, bless you, Saul, the poor thing's as wet as he can be; and don't you reckon it may be he's hungry?"

(26) "True for you, Rachel—I forgot."

(27) So the old lady says:

(28) "Betsy" (this was a nigger woman), "you fly around and get him something to eat as quick as you can, poor thing; and one of you girls go and wake up Buck and tell him—oh, here he is himself. Buck, take this little stranger and get the wet clothes off from him and dress him up in some of yours that's dry."

(29) Buck looked about as old as me—thirteen or fourteen or along there, though he was a little bigger than me. He hadn't on anything but a shirt, and he was very frowzy[4]-headed. He came in gaping and digging one fist into his eyes[5], and he was dragging a gun along with the other one. He says:

(30) "Ain't they no Shepherdsons around?"

(31) They said, no, 'twas a false alarm.

(32) "Well," he says, "if they'd a ben some, I reckon I'd a got one."

(33) They all laughed, and Bob says:

(34) "Why, Buck, they might have scalped us all, you've been so slow in coming."[6]

(35) "Well, nobody come after me, and it ain't right I'm always kept down; I don't get no show."

(36) "Never mind, Buck, my boy," says the old man, "you'll have show enough, all in good time, don't you fret[7] about that. Go 'long with you now, and do as your mother told you."

(37) When we got up-stairs to his room he got me a coarse shirt and a roundabout and pants of his, and I put them on. While I was at it he asked me what my name was, but before I could

[4] frowzy /ˈfraʊzɪ/ *adj.* 不整洁的;邋遢的

[5] 打着哈欠,揉着眼睛

[6] 割头皮的风俗盛行于美洲印第安文化,尤其在哥伦布时代,北美的印第安部落常常割下敌人的头皮作为战利品,用于供奉祭祀,以彰显勇气和力量。

[7] fret /fret/ *v.* 烦恼;焦急

tell him he started to tell me about a bluejay[8] and a young rabbit he had catched in the woods day before yesterday, and he asked me where Moses was when the candle went out. I said I didn't know; I hadn't heard about it before, no way.

(38) "Well, guess," he says.

(39) "How'm I going to guess," says I, "when I never heard tell of it before?"

(40) "But you can guess, can't you? It's just as easy."

(41) "*Which* candle?" I says.

(42) "Why, any candle," he says.

(43) "I don't know where he was," says I; "where was he?"

(44) "Why, he was in the *dark*![9] That's where he was!"

(45) "Well, if you knowed where he was, what did you ask me for?"

(46) "Why, blame it, it's a riddle, don't you see? Say, how long are you going to stay here? You got to stay always. We can just have booming times—they don't have no school now. Do you own a dog? I've got a dog—and he'll go in the river and bring out chips that you throw in. Do you like to comb up Sundays, and all that kind of foolishness? You bet I don't, but ma she makes me. Confound these ole britches[10]! I reckon I'd better put 'em on, but I'd ruther not, it's so warm. Are you all ready? All right. Come along, old hoss."

(47) Cold corn-pone, cold corn-beef, butter and buttermilk—that is what they had for me down there, and there ain't nothing better that ever I've come across yet. Buck and his ma and all of them smoked cob pipes, except the nigger woman, which was gone, and the two young women. They all smoked and talked, and I eat and talked. The young women had quilts around them, and their hair down their backs. They all asked me questions, and I told them how pap and me and all the family was living on a little farm down at the bottom of Arkansaw, and my sister Mary Ann run off and got married and never was heard of no more, and Bill went to hunt them and he warn't heard of no more, and Tom and Mort died, and then there warn't nobody but just me and pap left, and he was just trimmed down to nothing,

[8] 冠蓝鸦(生活在北美的一种蓝色鸟)

[9] 这个叫巴克的男孩子跟哈克玩一种基于双关语的猜谜游戏。根据《出埃及记》第二章,摩西出生三个月后,其母把他放到一个抹了石漆和石油的纸莎草篮筐(an ark of bulrushes)里,然后搁在河边的芦荻中。这里,"ark"和"dark"谐音。

[10] britches /ˈbrɪtʃɪz/ *n.* 裤子

on account of his troubles; so when he died I took what there was left, because the farm didn't belong to us, and started up the river, deck passage, and fell overboard; and that was how I come to be here. So they said I could have a home there as long as I wanted it. Then it was most daylight and everybody went to bed, and I went to bed with Buck, and when I waked up in the morning, drat it all, I had forgot what my name was. So I laid there about an hour trying to think, and when Buck waked up I says:

(48) "Can you spell, Buck?"

(49) "Yes," he says.

(50) "I bet you can't spell my name," says I.

(51) "I bet you what you dare I can," says he.

(52) "All right," says I, "go ahead."

(53) "G-e-o-r-g-e J-a-x-o-n—there now," he says.[11]

(54) "Well," says I, "you done it, but I didn't think you could. It ain't no slouch of a name to spell—right off without studying."

(55) I set it down, private, because somebody might want *me* to spell it next, and so I wanted to be handy with[12] it and rattle it off[13] like I was used to it.

(56) It was a mighty nice family, and a mighty nice house, too. I hadn't seen no house out in the country before that was so nice and had so much style. It didn't have an iron latch on the front door, nor a wooden one with a buckskin string, but a brass knob to turn, the same as houses in town. There warn't no bed in the parlor, nor a sign of a bed; but heaps of parlors in towns has beds in them. There was a big fireplace that was bricked on the bottom, and the bricks was kept clean and red by pouring water on them and scrubbing them with another brick; sometimes they wash them over with red water-paint that they call Spanish-brown, same as they do in town. They had big brass dog-irons[14] that could hold up a saw-log. There was a clock on the middle of the mantel-piece[15], with a picture of a town painted on the bottom half of the glass front, and a round place in the middle of it for the sun, and you could see the pendulum[16] swinging behind it. It was beautiful to hear that clock tick; and sometimes when

[11] Buck拼错了哈克的名字，本章开头哈克给自己编的名字叫“George Jackson”。

[12] be handy with：善于；对……很在行

[13] rattle sth off：快速背出；不假思索地说出

[14] 一种放置烧壁炉的木柴用的铁架子，架子两头往往用狗的图像作装饰。

[15] mantel-piece /ˈmæntlpiːs/ *n.* 壁炉台

[16] pendulum /ˈpendjʊləm/ *n.* 钟摆

one of these peddlers had been along and scoured[17] her up and got her in good shape, she would start in and strike a hundred and fifty before she got tuckered[18] out. They wouldn't took any money for her.

(57) Well, there was a big outlandish[19] parrot on each side of the clock, made out of something like chalk, and painted up gaudy[20]. By one of the parrots was a cat made of crockery[21], and a crockery dog by the other; and when you pressed down on them they squeaked[22], but didn't open their mouths nor look different nor interested. They squeaked through underneath. There was a couple of big wild-turkey-wing fans spread out behind those things. On the table in the middle of the room was a kind of a lovely crockery basket that bad apples and oranges and peaches and grapes piled up in it, which was much redder and yellower and prettier than real ones is, but they warn't real because you could see where pieces had got chipped off and showed the white chalk, or whatever it was, underneath.[23]

(58) This table had a cover made out of beautiful oilcloth, with a red and blue spread-eagle painted on it, and a painted border all around. It come all the way from Philadelphia, they said. There was some books, too, piled up perfectly exact, on each corner of the table. One was a big family Bible full of pictures. One was *Pilgrim's Progress*[24], about a man that left his family, it didn't say why. I read considerable in it now and then. The statements was interesting, but tough. Another was *Friendship's Offering*, full of beautiful stuff and poetry; but I didn't read the poetry. Another was *Henry Clay's Speeches*[25], and another was *Dr. Gunn's Family Medicine*, which told you all about what to do if a body was sick or dead. There was a hymn book, and a lot of other books. And there was nice split-bottom chairs, and perfectly sound, too—not bagged down in the middle and busted, like an old basket.[26]

(59) They had pictures hung on the walls—mainly Washingtons and Lafayettes[27], and battles, and Highland Marys[28], and one called "Signing the Declaration." There was some that they called crayons, which one of the daughters which

[17] scour /ˈskaʊə(r)/ *v.* (用粗糙的东西)擦净;擦亮

[18] tucker /ˈtʌkə(r)/ *v.* 使疲倦

[19] outlandish /aʊtˈlændɪʃ/ *adj.* 怪异的;奇特的

[20] gaudy /ˈgɔːdɪ/ *adj.* 花哨的;俗艳的

[21] crockery /ˈkrɒkərɪ/ *n.* 陶器;瓦器

[22] squeak /skwiːk/ *v.* 发出短促尖声

[23] 可惜它们不是真的,因为你能看到,它们的表皮有些已经剥落下来,漏出里面的白灰之类的东西。(chip off: 碎裂;剥落)

[24] 英国作家约翰·班扬的宗教小说,以寓言和梦境的形式讲述了一个叫"基督徒"的人逃离故乡、前往天国的勇敢而艰难的朝圣之旅。

[25] 亨利·克莱是美国十九世纪著名的政治家与演说家。

[26] 还有几把薄木条做底的椅子,看起来都好好的,椅垫没有像旧篮子那样塌陷或者裂开。

[27] 指拉法耶特侯爵,法国将军,曾率军参加美国独立战争,帮助美军抗击英军。

[28] 指苏格兰著名农民诗人罗伯特·彭斯的恋人玛丽·坎贝尔,彭斯曾写诗纪念,称她为"高原玛丽"。

was dead made her own self when she was only fifteen years old. They was different from any pictures I ever see before—blacker, mostly, than is common. One was a woman in a slim black dress, belted small under the armpits, with bulges like a cabbage in the middle of the sleeves, and a large black scoop-shovel bonnet with a black veil, and white slim ankles crossed about with black tape, and very wee[29] black slippers, like a chisel[30], and she was leaning pensive[31] on a tombstone on her right elbow, under a weeping willow, and her other hand hanging down her side holding a white handkerchief and a reticule[32], and underneath the picture it said "Shall I Never See Thee More Alas." Another one was a young lady with her hair all combed up straight to the top of her head, and knotted there in front of a comb like a chair-back, and she was crying into a handkerchief and had a dead bird laying on its back in her other hand with its heels up, and underneath the picture it said "I Shall Never Hear Thy Sweet Chirrup More Alas." There was one where a young lady was at a window looking up at the moon, and tears running down her cheeks; and she had an open letter in one hand with black sealing wax showing on one edge of it, and she was mashing a locket with a chain to it against her mouth,[33] and underneath the picture it said "And Art Thou Gone Yes Thou Art Gone Alas." These was all nice pictures, I reckon, but I didn't somehow seem to take to them, because if ever I was down a little they always give me the fan-tods[34]. Everybody was sorry she died, because she had laid out a lot more of these pictures to do, and a body could see by what she had done what they had lost.[35] But I reckoned that with her disposition she was having a better time in the graveyard. She was at work on what they said was her greatest picture when she took sick, and every day and every night it was her prayer to be allowed to live till she got it done, but she never got the chance. It was a picture of a young woman in a long white gown, standing on the rail of a bridge all ready to jump off, with her hair all down her back, and looking up to the moon, with the tears running down her face, and she had two arms folded across her breast, and two arms stretched

[29] wee /wiː/ *adj.* 极小的

[30] chisel /ˈtʃɪzl/ *n.* 凿子

[31] pensive /ˈpensɪv/ *adj.* 沉思的；忧虑的

[32] reticule /ˈretɪkjuːl/ *n.*（女用）收口手提包

[33] 她用力亲吻着一个带着链子的盒式吊坠。（locket：一种里面可放照片或头发的项链坠。）

[34] fantod /ˈfæntɒd/ *n.* 烦躁不安

[35] 所有的人都为她的死感到可惜，因为她生前本打算画更多这样的画出来。而且，人们从她所完成的画作里可知她的离世是多大的损失。

out in front, and two more reaching up towards the moon—and the idea was to see which pair would look best, and then scratch out all the other arms; but, as I was saying, she died before she got her mind made up, and now they kept this picture over the head of the bed in her room, and every time her birthday come they hung flowers on it. Other times it was hid with a little curtain. The young woman in the picture had a kind of a nice sweet face, but there was so many arms it made her look too spidery, seemed to me.

(60) This young girl kept a scrap-book[36] when she was alive, and used to paste obituaries[37] and accidents and cases of patient suffering in it out of the *Presbyterian Observer*, and write poetry after them out of her own head. It was very good poetry. This is what she wrote about a boy by the name of Stephen Dowling Bots that fell down a well and was drownded:

(61) ODE TO STEPHEN DOWLING BOTS, DEC'D

(62) And did young Stephen sicken,
(63) And did young Stephen die?
(64) And did the sad hearts thicken,
(65) And did the mourners cry?

(66) No; such was not the fate of
(67) Young Stephen Dowling Bots;
(68) Though sad hearts round him thickened,
(69) 'Twas not from sickness' shots.
(70) No whooping-cough did rack his frame,
(71) Nor measles drear with spots;
(72) Not these impaired the sacred name
(73) Of Stephen Dowling Bots.

(74) Despised love struck not with woe
(75) That head of curly knots,
(76) Nor stomach troubles laid him low,
(77) Young Stephen Dowling Bots.

(78) Oh no. Then list with tearful eye,
(79) Whilst I his fate do tell.
(80) His soul did from this cold world fly
(81) By falling down a well.

(82) They got him out and emptied him;

[36] **scrap-book**: 粘贴簿;剪贴簿
[37] **obituary** /əˈbɪtʃuərɪ/ *n.* 讣告

(83) Alas it was too late;
(84) His spirit was gone for to sport aloft
(85) In the realms of the good and great.

(86) If Emmeline Grangerford could make poetry like that before she was fourteen, there ain't no telling what she could a done by and by. Buck said she could rattle off poetry like nothing.[38] She didn't ever have to stop to think. He said she would slap down a line, and if she couldn't find anything to rhyme with it would just scratch it out and slap down another one, and go ahead. She warn't particular; she could write about anything you choose to give her to write about just so it was sadful. Every time a man died, or a woman died, or a child died, she would be on hand with her "tribute" before he was cold. She called them tributes. The neighbors said it was the doctor first, then Emmeline, then the undertaker—the undertaker never got in ahead of Emmeline but once, and then she hung fire[39] on a rhyme for the dead person's name, which was Whistler. She warn't ever the same after that; she never complained, but she kinder pined away[40] and did not live long. Poor thing, many's the time I made myself go up to the little room that used to be hers and get out her poor old scrap-book and read in it when her pictures had been aggravating me and I had soured on[41] her a little. I liked all that family, dead ones and all, and warn't going to let anything come between us. Poor Emmeline made poetry about all the dead people when she was alive, and it didn't seem right that there warn't nobody to make some about her now she was gone; so I tried to sweat out a verse or two myself, but I couldn't seem to make it go somehow. They kept Emmeline's room trim and nice, and all the things fixed in it just the way she liked to have them when she was alive, and nobody ever slept there. The old lady took care of the room herself, though there was plenty of niggers, and she sewed there a good deal and read her Bible there mostly.

(87) Well, as I was saying about the parlor, there was beautiful curtains on the windows: white, with pictures painted on them of castles with vines all down the walls, and cattle

[38] 巴克说她作起诗来出口成章，毫不费力。

[39] hang fire: 犹豫不决；举棋不定

[40] pine away: 消瘦；憔悴

[41] sour on: (美俚)讨厌；憎恶

coming down to drink. There was a little old piano, too, that had tin pans in it, I reckon, and nothing was ever so lovely as to hear the young ladies sing "The Last Link is Broken" and play "The Battle of Prague" on it. The walls of all the rooms was plastered, and most had carpets on the floors, and the whole house was whitewashed on the outside.

(88) It was a double house, and the big open place betwixt[42] them was roofed and floored, and sometimes the table was set there in the middle of the day, and it was a cool, comfortable place. Nothing couldn't be better. And warn't the cooking good, and just bushels[43] of it too!

[42] betwixt /bɪˈtwɪkst/ *prep.* 在……之间

[43] bushel /ˈbʊʃl/ *n.* 大量;许多

精华赏析

在本章中,哈克暂别了他自由自在的河上生活,我们也可以从他一次次惊心动魄的探险经历中稍微缓口气儿,聊聊小说的主题:逃离、流浪、成长。

从古希腊、古罗马时期的《奥德修斯》《埃涅阿斯纪》,到中世纪的骑士文学如《高文爵士和绿衣骑士》之类,再到十八世纪《格列佛游记》《鲁滨逊漂流记》《汤姆·琼斯》等大批现实主义小说,以及浪漫主义诗坛长篇叙事诗如《恰尔德·哈洛尔德游记》《唐璜》等,以流浪为主题的流浪汉小说一直是欧洲文学的重要内容。马克·吐温的《汤姆·索亚历险记》和《哈克贝利·费恩历险记》,无疑继承了这个传统,并把流浪这一主题带到了一个更高的境界。

流浪主题受到欧美作家的青睐有其文化根源。不同于中国的农耕文明,欧洲文明起源于以爱琴文明为代表的海洋文明,临海而居的独特地理位置孕育了开放、发达的海上贸易,在大海上航行的海洋民族在与大海的不断斗争中练就了勇于探索的民族性格和民族精神。他们具有冒险精神,渴望去开疆扩土,寻求新的"理想国""新大陆"。哥伦布在1492年发现了美洲大陆,三十年后麦哲伦的船队完成人类首次环球航行。这些壮举令人欢欣鼓舞,也鼓励了一大批勇敢者去探险、流浪。那些探险归来的勇士们往往会成为万人敬仰的英雄,他们的旅途见闻也为人津津乐道。这一时期,文学创作出现大批描述此类探险历程及见闻的作品,极受追捧。例如在莎士比亚的悲剧《奥赛罗》的第一幕就提到,威尼斯公国元老的女儿苔丝狄蒙娜,一位温柔美丽的公侯之女,就是因为听了奥赛罗的种种惊险刺激的冒险经历,才不可自拔地爱上了奥赛罗,一个黑脸摩尔人。

1620年,一艘名叫"五月花号"的三桅盖伦帆船载着包括妇女和儿童在内的102名船员离开英国南安普顿港口。他们在北美成功登陆,并在新英格兰的普利茅斯镇建立了殖民地。他们之中有一部分是清教徒,为了躲避英国国教的迫害,他们选择移民北美大陆,开始新的生活。这些人被后来的美国人视为开拓美利坚的先驱。登上美洲大陆的清教徒们崇尚节俭、勤勉、节欲,他们笃信自己是“上帝的选民”,来到北美大陆是上帝的安排,在那里建设“山巅之城”(City on a Hill)是他们实现自我救赎的使命。这种积极的使命感和乐观主义精神融入了美国的民族性格,是“美国精神”的重要特征。所以,逃离—流浪—救赎,可以说是美利坚民族的成长历程。

毫无疑问,这种成长历程一定会在美国文学作品里留下深深的烙印。该书中,哈克为了逃避文明社会枯燥、无聊、虚伪的道德训教,逃离了安定的生活,选择流浪。他独立、乐观、机智,一个十三四岁的少年担负起了协助黑奴逃跑、对抗社会的使命,在惊心动魄的探险之旅中总能克服一次次困难,最终完成从纯真、叛逆到成熟、自信的蜕变。

哈克的成长之旅,体现了他内心世界自我认知的不断挣扎,充满对社会现实和人性的重新认识和思考。他并不是从故事一开始就是一个勇敢、机智、充满正义的少年,他选择顺河流浪、探险,只是想逃脱道格拉斯寡妇姐妹对他的道德训教和自己老爸厚颜无耻的钱财敲诈和纠缠,最初他也并不真正关心吉姆的命运。在木筏上漂流的日日夜夜里,哈克重新认识到吉姆淳朴善良的高尚品质。例如在小说第十五章中,在大雾中失散又重聚后,哈克不由捉弄起吉姆来。这一举动,在一定程度上反映了哈克作为白人的优越感,他并没有真正把吉姆放到与白人平等的地位上来。但吉姆的指责令哈克“恨不得去亲吻他的脚”,这算是哈克自我认知的首次冲突。这种冲突在第十六章达到了白热化,随着自由州越来越近,哈克内心的矛盾进一步升级,他经历着“良心”的拷问,甚至想上岸去告发吉姆,但又不忍心背叛与吉姆结成的真挚情谊。最终善良的天性战胜“良心”,在遇到猎奴人的时候,哈克机智应对,帮助吉姆成功逃脱。

哈克的成长,还源于他对社会现实种种丑恶荒唐现象的反思。从本章开始,小说会从新的视角对哈克的成长进行更深度的剖析,哈克对蓄奴制有了更深刻的反省,而小说的主题也会进一步升华。那就让我们继续跟随哈克的探险之旅,一起见证他的成长吧。

阅读思考

1. 清教主义思想对美国民族性格的形成有什么影响?

2. 查阅资料,探寻《哈克贝利·费恩历险记》流浪主题的文学渊源。

CHAPTER XVIII

导读:哈克在格伦基福特家平静的新生活并没有持续多久,一个周日的上午,全家骑马去附近的教堂做礼拜。回来之后,哈克发现家里年轻可爱的索菲亚小姐心神不定,还交代哈克去教堂里把自己遗忘的《圣经》取回来。没想到,哈克竟由此发现了索菲亚小姐的一个秘密,更没想到,这个秘密竟引发了两个家族之间的一场恶战……

(1) COL. GRANGERFORD was a gentleman, you see. He was a gentleman all over; and so was his family. He was well born, as the saying is, and that's worth as much in a man as it is in a horse,[1] so the Widow Douglas said, and nobody ever denied that she was of the first aristocracy in our town; and pap he always said it, too, though he warn't no more quality than a mudcat himself.[2] Col. Grangerford was very tall and very slim, and had a darkish-paly complexion, not a sign of red in it anywheres; he was clean shaved every morning all over his thin face, and he had the thinnest kind of lips, and the thinnest kind of nostrils, and a high nose, and heavy eyebrows, and the blackest kind of eyes, sunk so deep back that they seemed like they was looking out of caverns at you, as you may say. His forehead was high, and his hair was black and straight and hung to his shoulders. His hands was long and thin, and every day of his life he put on a clean shirt and a full suit from head to foot made out of linen so white it hurt your eyes to look at it; and on Sundays he wore a blue tail-coat with brass buttons on it. He carried a mahogany[3] cane with a silver head to it. There warn't no frivolishness[4] about him, not a bit, and he warn't ever loud. He was as kind as he could be—you could feel that, you know, and so you had confidence. Sometimes he smiled, and it was good to see; but

[1] 就像老话儿说的那样,人也好,马也好,出身最重要。

[2] 老爸也常常这样说,尽管他的出身不比鲶鱼好多少。(mudcat /ˈmʌdkæt/ 生活在污水中的鲶鱼)

[3] mahogany /məˈhɒɡənɪ/ *n.* 桃花心木;红木(木材呈红褐色)

[4] 即 frivolousness 轻浮;可笑

when he straightened himself up like a liberty-pole, and the lightning begun to flicker out from under his eyebrows, you wanted to climb a tree first, and find out what the matter was afterwards. He didn't ever have to tell anybody to mind their manners—everybody was always good-mannered where he was. Everybody loved to have him around, too; he was sunshine most always—I mean he made it seem like good weather. When he turned into a cloudbank it was awful dark for half a minute, and that was enough; there wouldn't nothing go wrong again for a week.

(2) When him and the old lady come down in the morning all the family got up out of their chairs and give them good-day, and didn't set down again till they had set down. Then Tom and Bob went to the sideboard where the decanter[5] was, and mixed a glass of bitters and handed it to him, and he held it in his hand and waited till Tom's and Bob's was mixed, and then they bowed and said, "Our duty to you, sir, and madam;" and *they* bowed the least bit in the world[6] and said thank you, and so they drank, all three, and Bob and Tom poured a spoonful of water on the sugar and the mite of whisky or apple brandy in the bottom of their tumblers, and give it to me and Buck, and we drank to the old people too.

(3) Bob was the oldest and Tom next—tall, beautiful men with very broad shoulders and brown faces, and long black hair and black eyes. They dressed in white linen from head to foot, like the old gentleman, and wore broad Panama hats[7].

(4) Then there was Miss Charlotte; she was twenty-five, and tall and proud and grand, but as good as she could be when she warn't stirred up; but when she was she had a look that would make you wilt in your tracks[8], like her father. She was beautiful.

(5) So was her sister, Miss Sophia, but it was a different kind. She was gentle and sweet like a dove, and she was only twenty.

(6) Each person had their own nigger to wait on them—Buck too. My nigger had a monstrous easy time, because I warn't used to having anybody do anything for me, but Buck's

[5] **decanter** /dɪˈkæntə(r)/ *n.* 玻璃酒瓶

[6] 稍微欠欠身

[7] 由一种叫作"托奎拉"的植物的纤维编织成的草帽,带有黑条纹或花饰,边沿上翘。原产于厄瓜多尔,巴拿马人多戴此帽。

[8] **in one's tracks**: 当场;立即

was on the jump[9] most of the time.

(7) This was all there was of the family now, but there used to be more—three sons; they got killed; and Emmeline that died.

(8) The old gentleman owned a lot of farms and over a hundred niggers. Sometimes a stack of people would come there, horseback, from ten or fifteen mile around, and stay five or six days, and have such junketings round about and on the river, and dances and picnics in the woods daytimes, and balls at the house nights. These people was mostly kinfolks of the family. The men brought their guns with them. It was a handsome lot of quality, I tell you.

(9) There was another clan of aristocracy around there—five or six families—mostly of the name of Shepherdson. They was as high-toned and well born and rich and grand as the tribe of Grangerfords. The Shepherdsons and Grangerfords used the same steam-boat landing, which was about two mile above our house; so sometimes when I went up there with a lot of our folks I used to see a lot of the Shepherdsons there on their fine horses.

(10) One day Buck and me was away out in the woods hunting, and heard a horse coming. We was crossing the road. Buck says:

(11) "Quick! Jump for the woods!"

(12) We done it, and then peeped down the woods through the leaves. Pretty soon a splendid young man come galloping[10] down the road, setting his horse easy and looking like a soldier. He had his gun across his pommel[11]. I had seen him before. It was young Harney Shepherdson. I heard Buck's gun go off at my ear, and Harney's hat tumbled off from his head. He grabbed his gun and rode straight to the place where we was hid. But we didn't wait. We started through the woods on a run. The woods warn't thick, so I looked over my shoulder to dodge the bullet, and twice I seen Harney cover Buck with his gun; and then he rode away the way he come—to get his hat, I reckon, but I couldn't see. We never stopped running till we got home. The old gentleman's eyes blazed a minute—'twas pleasure, mainly, I

[9] **on the jump**: 东奔西跑；非常忙碌

[10] **gallop** /ˈgæləp/ *v.*（马）疾驰；飞奔

[11] **pommel** /ˈpɒml/ *n.*（马鞍的）鞍头

judged—then his face sort of smoothed down, and he says, kind of gentle:

(13) "I don't like that shooting from behind a bush. Why didn't you step into the road, my boy?"

(14) "The Shepherdsons don't, father. They always take advantage."

(15) Miss Charlotte she held her head up like a queen while Buck was telling his tale, and her nostrils spread and her eyes snapped. The two young men looked dark, but never said nothing. Miss Sophia she turned pale, but the color come back when she found the man warn't hurt.

(16) Soon as I could get Buck down by the corn-cribs under the trees by ourselves, I says:

(17) "Did you want to kill him, Buck?"

(18) "Well, I bet I did."

(19) "What did he do to you?"

(20) "Him? He never done nothing to me."

(21) "Well, then, what did you want to kill him for?"

(22) "Why, nothing—only it's on account of the feud[12]."

(23) "What's a feud?"

(24) "Why, where was you raised? Don't you know what a feud is?"

(25) "Never heard of it before—tell me about it."

(26) "Well," says Buck, "a feud is this way: A man has a quarrel with another man, and kills him; then that other man's brother kills *him*; then the other brothers, on both sides, goes for one another; then the *cousins* chip in—and by and by everybody's killed off, and there ain't no more feud. But it's kind of slow, and takes a long time."

(27) "Has this one been going on long, Buck?"

(28) "Well, I should *reckon*! It started thirty year ago, or som'ers along there. There was trouble 'bout something, and then a lawsuit to settle it; and the suit went agin one of the men, and so he up and shot the man that won the suit—which he would naturally do, of course. Anybody would."

(29) "What was the trouble about, Buck?—land?"

[12] **feud** /fjuːd/ *n.* 长期不和；世仇

(30) "I reckon maybe—I don't know."

(31) "Well, who done the shooting? Was it a Grangerford or a Shepherdson?"

(32) "Laws, how do I know? It was so long ago."

(33) "Don't anybody know?"

(34) "Oh, yes, pa knows, I reckon, and some of the other old people; but they don't know now what the row[13] was about in the first place."

(35) "Has there been many killed, Buck?"

(36) "Yes; right smart chance of[14] funerals. But they don't always kill. Pa's got a few buckshot[15] in him; but he don't mind it 'cuz he don't weigh much, anyway. Bob's been carved up some with a bowie[16], and Tom's been hurt once or twice."

(37) "Has anybody been killed this year, Buck?"

(38) "Yes; we got one and they got one. 'Bout three months ago my cousin Bud, fourteen year old, was riding through the woods on t'other side of the river, and didn't have no weapon with him, which was blame' foolishness, and in a lonesome place he hears a horse a-coming behind him, and sees old Baldy Shepherdson a-linkin' after him with his gun in his hand and his white hair a-flying in the wind; and 'stead of jumping off and taking to the brush, Bud 'lowed he could outrun him; so they had it, nip and tuck[17], for five mile or more, the old man a-gaining all the time; so at last Bud seen it warn't any use, so he stopped and faced around so as to have the bullet holes in front, you know, and the old man he rode up and shot him down. But he didn't git much chance to enjoy his luck, for inside of a week our folks laid *him* out."

(39) "I reckon that old man was a coward, Buck."

(40) "I reckon he *warn't* a coward. Not by a blame' sight[18]. There ain't a coward amongst them Shepherdsons—not a one. And there ain't no cowards amongst the Grangerfords either. Why, that old man kep' up his end in a fight one day for half an hour against three Grangerfords, and come out winner. They was all a-horseback; he lit off of his horse and got behind a little woodpile, and kep' his horse before him to stop the bullets; but

[13] row /rəʊ/ *n.* 纠纷；争吵

[14] a smart chance of:（美俚）大量的；许多的

[15] buckshot /ˈbʌkʃɒt/ *n.* 铅弹

[16] bowie /ˈbəʊɪ/ *n.* 一种猎刀

[17] nip and tuck: 势均力敌；不相上下

[18] 肯定不会

the Grangerfords stayed on their horses and capered[19] around the old man, and peppered away at him[20], and he peppered away at them. Him and his horse both went home pretty leaky[21] and crippled, but the Grangerfords had to be *fetched* home—and one of 'em was dead, and another died the next day. No, sir; if a body's out hunting for cowards he don't want to fool away[22] any time amongst them Shepherdsons, becuz they don't breed any of that *kind*."

（41）Next Sunday we all went to church, about three mile, everybody a-horseback. The men took their guns along, so did Buck, and kept them between their knees or stood them handy against the wall. The Shepherdsons done the same. It was pretty ornery[23] preaching—all about brotherly love, and such-like tiresomeness; but everybody said it was a good sermon, and they all talked it over going home, and had such a powerful lot to say about faith and good works and free grace and preforeordestination[24], and I don't know what all, that it did seem to me to be one of the roughest Sundays I had run across yet.

（42）About an hour after dinner everybody was dozing around, some in their chairs and some in their rooms, and it got to be pretty dull. Buck and a dog was stretched out on the grass in the sun sound asleep. I went up to our room, and judged I would take a nap myself. I found that sweet Miss Sophia standing in her door, which was next to ours, and she took me in her room and shut the door very soft, and asked me if I liked her, and I said I did; and she asked me if I would do something for her and not tell anybody, and I said I would. Then she said she'd forgot her Testament, and left it in the seat at church between two other books, and would I slip out quiet and go there and fetch it to her, and not say nothing to nobody. I said I would. So I slid out and slipped off up the road, and there warn't anybody at the church, except maybe a hog or two, for there warn't any lock on the door, and hogs likes a puncheon floor[25] in summer-time because it's cool. If you notice, most folks don't go to church only when they've got to; but a hog is different.

（43）Says I to myself, something's up; it ain't natural for a

[19] caper /ˈkeɪpə(r)/ *v.* 蹦蹦跳跳；跑来跑去

[20]（戏谑）（像撒胡椒一样）不停地射击

[21] 此处意为“流血的”

[22] fool away：浪费；虚度

[23] ornery /ˈɔːnərɪ/ *adj.* 下等的；低劣的；故意刁难的

[24] 为马克·吐温造的词，由predestination（预定论）和foreordination（命中注定）合成，都是长老会的主要教义。

[25] 由一面刨平的圆木铺成的地板，平的一面朝上。

girl to be in such a sweat about a Testament. So I give it a shake, and out drops a little piece of paper with "*Half-past two*" wrote on it with a pencil. I ransacked[26] it, but couldn't find anything else. I couldn't make anything out of that, so I put the paper in the book again, and when I got home and upstairs there was Miss Sophia in her door waiting for me. She pulled me in and shut the door; then she looked in the Testament till she found the paper, and as soon as she read it she looked glad; and before a body could think she grabbed me and give me a squeeze, and said I was the best boy in the world, and not to tell anybody. She was mighty red in the face for a minute, and her eyes lighted up, and it made her powerful pretty. I was a good deal astonished, but when I got my breath I asked her what the paper was about, and she asked me if I had read it, and I said no, and she asked me if I could read writing, and I told her "no, only coarse-hand," [27] and then she said the paper warn't anything but a book-mark to keep her place, and I might go and play now.

(44) I went off down to the river, studying over this thing, and pretty soon I noticed that my nigger was following along behind. When we was out of sight of the house he looked back and around a second, and then comes a-running, and says:

(45) "Mars Jawge, if you'll come down into de swamp I'll show you a whole stack o'[28] water-moccasins[29]."

(46) Thinks I, that's mighty curious; he said that yesterday. He oughter know a body don't love water-moccasins enough to go around hunting for them. What is he up to, anyway? So I says:

(47) "All right; trot[30] ahead."

(48) I followed a half a mile; then he struck out over the swamp, and waded[31] ankle deep as much as another half-mile. We come to a little flat piece of land which was dry and very thick with trees and bushes and vines, and he says:

(49) "You shove right in dah jist a few steps, Mars Jawge; dah's whah dey is. I's seed 'm befo'; I don't k'yer to see 'em no mo'."

(50) Then he slopped[32] right along and went away, and pretty soon the trees hid him. I poked into[33] the place a-ways and come to a little open patch as big as a bedroom all hung around

[26] ransack /ˈrænsæk/ v. 彻底搜索

[27] 她问我认不认识手写的字，我告诉她，"不认识，只认识印刷的字。"（writing 指手写体；coarse-hand 指印刷体）

[28] a stack of: 一堆

[29] 水生噬鱼蝮蛇（生长在美国东南部的一种有毒水蛇）

[30] trot /trɒt/ v. 疾走；小跑

[31] wade /weɪd/ v. 蹚（水）

[32] 踏着泥浆走

[33] 推开灌木、枝叶，探着身子走进

with vines, and found a man laying there asleep—and, by jings, it was my old Jim!

(51) I waked him up, and I reckoned it was going to be a grand surprise to him to see me again, but it warn't. He nearly cried he was so glad, but he warn't surprised. Said he swum along behind me that night, and heard me yell every time, but dasn't answer, because he didn't want nobody to pick *him* up and take him into slavery again. Says he:

(52) "I got hurt a little, en couldn't swim fas', so I wuz a considable ways behine you towards de las'; when you landed I reck'ned I could ketch up wid you on de lan' 'dout havin' to shout at you, but when I see dat house I begin to go slow. I 'uz off too fur to hear what dey say to you—I wuz 'fraid o' de dogs; but when it 'uz all quiet agin I knowed you's in de house, so I struck out for de woods to wait for day. Early in de mawnin' some er de niggers come along, gwyne to de fields, en dey tuk me en showed me dis place, whah de dogs can't track me on accounts o' de water, en dey brings me truck to eat every night, en tells me how you's a-gitt'n along."

(53) "Why didn't you tell my Jack to fetch me here sooner, Jim?"

(54) "Well, 'twarn't no use to 'sturb you, Huck, tell we could do sumfn—but we's all right now. I ben a-buyin' pots en pans en vittles[34], as I got a chanst, en a-patchin' up de raf' nights when—"

(55) "*What* raft, Jim?"

(56) "Our ole raf'."

(57) "You mean to say our old raft warn't smashed all to flinders[35]?"

(58) "No, she warn't. She was tore up a good deal—one en' of her was; but dey warn't no great harm done, on'y our traps was mos' all los'. Ef we hadn' dive' so deep en swum so fur under water, en de night hadn' ben so dark, en we warn't so sk'yerd, en ben sich punkin-heads, as de sayin' is, we'd a seed de raf'. But it's jis' as well we didn't, 'kase now she's all fixed up agin mos' as good as new, en we's got a new lot o' stuff, in de place o' what 'uz los'."

[34] vittle /'vɪtl/ *n.* (美)食物

[35] flinders /'flɪndəz/ *n.* 碎片

(59) "Why, how did you get hold of the raft again, Jim—did you catch her?"

(60) "How I gwyne to ketch her en I out in de woods? No; some er de niggers foun' her ketched on a snag along heah in de ben', en dey hid her in a crick 'mongst de willows, en dey wuz so much jawin' 'bout which un 'um she b'long to de mos' dat I come to heah 'bout it pooty[36] soon, so I ups en settles de trouble by tellin' 'um she don't b'long to none uv um, but to you en me; en I ast 'm if dey gwyne to grab a young white genlman's propaty[37], en git a hid'n for it? Den I gin 'm ten cents apiece, en dey 'uz mighty well satisfied, en wisht some mo' raf's 'ud come along en make 'm rich agin. Dey's mighty good to me, dese niggers is, en whatever I wants 'm to do fur me I doan' have to ast 'm twice, honey. Dat Jack's a good nigger, en pooty smart."

[36] 即 pretty

[37] 即 property

(61) "Yes, he is. He ain't ever told me you was here; told me to come, and he'd show me a lot of water-moccasins. If anything happens *he* ain't mixed up in it. He can say he never seen us together, and it 'll be the truth."

(62) I don't want to talk much about the next day. I reckon I'll cut it pretty short. I waked up about dawn, and was a-going to turn over and go to sleep again when I noticed how still it was—didn't seem to be anybody stirring. That warn't usual. Next I noticed that Buck was up and gone. Well, I gets up, a-wondering, and goes down stairs—nobody around; everything as still as a mouse. Just the same outside. Thinks I, what does it mean? Down by the wood-pile I comes across my Jack, and says:

(63) "What's it all about?"

(64) Says he:

(65) "Don't you know, Mars Jawge?"

(66) "No," says I, "I don't."

(67) "Well, den, Miss Sophia's run off! 'deed she has. She run off in de night some time—nobody don't know jis' when; run off to get married to dat young Harney Shepherdson, you know—leastways, so dey 'spec. De fambly foun' it out 'bout half an hour ago—maybe a little mo'—en' I *tell* you dey warn't no time los'. Sich another hurryin' up guns en hosses *you* never see! De

women folks has gone for to stir up de relations, en ole Mars Saul en de boys tuck dey guns en rode up de river road for to try to ketch dat young man en kill him 'fo' he kin git acrost de river wid Miss Sophia. I reck'n dey's gwyne to be mighty rough times."

(68) "Buck went off 'thout waking me up."

(69) "Well, I reck'n he *did*! Dey warn't gwyne to mix you up in it. Mars Buck he loaded up his gun en 'lowed he's gwyne to fetch home a Shepherdson or bust. Well, dey'll be plenty un 'm dah, I reck'n, en you bet you he'll fetch one ef he gits a chanst."

(70) I took up the river road as hard as I could put. By and by I begin to hear guns a good ways off. When I came in sight of the log store and the woodpile where the steamboats lands I worked along under the trees and brush till I got to a good place, and then I clumb up into the forks of a cottonwood that was out of reach,[38] and watched. There was a wood-rank four foot high a little ways in front of the tree, and first I was going to hide behind that; but maybe it was luckier I didn't.

(71) There was four or five men cavorting[39] around on their horses in the open place before the log store, cussing and yelling, and trying to get at a couple of young chaps that was behind the wood-rank alongside of the steamboat landing; but they couldn't come it. Every time one of them showed himself on the river side of the woodpile he got shot at. The two boys was squatting back to back behind the pile, so they could watch both ways.

(72) By and by the men stopped cavorting around and yelling. They started riding towards the store; then up gets one of the boys, draws a steady bead[40] over the wood-rank, and drops one of them out of his saddle. All the men jumped off of their horses and grabbed the hurt one and started to carry him to the store; and that minute the two boys started on the run. They got half way to the tree I was in before the men noticed. Then the men see them, and jumped on their horses and took out after them. They gained on[41] the boys, but it didn't do no good, the boys had too good a start; they got to the woodpile that was in front of my tree, and slipped in behind it, and so they had the

[38] 我爬上一棵棉白杨的树杈，那里在子弹的射程之外

[39] cavort /kə'vɔːt/ v. 欢跃；跳跃

[40] draw a bead: 瞄准

[41] gain on: 逼近；超过

bulge on the men[42] again. One of the boys was Buck, and the other was a slim young chap about nineteen years old.

(73) The men ripped around awhile, and then rode away. As soon as they was out of sight I sung out to Buck and told him. He didn't know what to make of my voice coming out of the tree at first. He was awful surprised. He told me to watch out sharp and let him know when the men come in sight again; said they was up to some devilment[43] or other—wouldn't be gone long. I wished I was out of that tree, but I dasn't come down. Buck begun to cry and rip, and 'lowed that him and his cousin Joe (that was the other young chap) would make up for this day yet. He said his father and his two brothers was killed, and two or three of the enemy. Said the Shepherdsons laid for them in ambush[44]. Buck said his father and brothers ought to waited for their relations—the Shepherdsons was too strong for them. I asked him what was become of young Harney and Miss Sophia. He said the'd got across the river and was safe. I was glad of that; but the way Buck did take on because he didn't manage to kill Harney that day he shot at him—I hain't ever heard anything like it.

(74) All of a sudden, bang! bang! bang! goes three or four guns—the men had slipped around through the woods and come in from behind without their horses! The boys jumped for the river—both of them hurt—and as they swum down the current the men run along the bank shooting at them and singing out, "Kill them, kill them!" It made me so sick I most fell out of the tree. I ain't a-going to tell *all* that happened—it would make me sick again if I was to do that. I wished I hadn't ever come ashore that night to see such things. I ain't ever going to get shut of them —lots of times I dream about them.

(75) I stayed in the tree till it begun to get dark, afraid to come down. Sometimes I heard guns away off in the woods; and twice I seen little gangs of men gallop past the log store with guns; so I reckoned the trouble was still a-going on. I was mighty downhearted; so I made up my mind I wouldn't ever go anear that house again, because I reckoned I was to blame,

[42] have the bulge on sb: 占某人上风;对某人占优势

[43] devilment /ˈdevəlmənt/ *n.* 恶行;恶作剧

[44] ambush /ˈæmbʊʃ/ *n.* 伏击;埋伏

somehow. I judged that that piece of paper meant that Miss Sophia was to meet Harney somewheres at half-past two and run off; and I judged I ought to told her father about that paper and the curious way she acted, and then maybe he would a locked her up, and this awful mess wouldn't ever happened.

(76) When I got down out of the tree I crept along down the river bank a piece, and found the two bodies laying in the edge of the water, and tugged[45] at them till I got them ashore; then I covered up their faces, and got away as quick as I could. I cried a little when I was covering up Buck's face, for he was mighty good to me.

[45] tug /tʌg/ v. (用力)拉;拖;拽

(77) It was just dark now. I never went near the house, but struck through the woods and made for the swamp. Jim warn't on his island, so I tramped off in a hurry for the crick, and crowded through the willows, red-hot[46] to jump aboard and get out of that awful country. The raft was gone! My souls, but I was scared! I couldn't get my breath for most a minute. Then I raised a yell. A voice not twenty-five foot from me says:

[46] red-hot: 激烈的;强烈的

(78) "Good lan'! is dat you, honey? Doan' make no noise."

(79) It was Jim's voice—nothing ever sounded so good before. I run along the bank a piece and got aboard, and Jim he grabbed me and hugged me, he was so glad to see me. He says:

(80) "Laws bless you, chile, I 'uz right down sho' you's dead agin. Jack's been heah; he say he reck'n you's ben shot, kase you didn' come home no mo'; so I's jes' dis minute a startin' de raf' down towards de mouf er de crick, so's to be all ready for to shove out en leave soon as Jack comes agin en tells me for certain you *is* dead. Lawsy, I's mighty glad to git you back again, honey."

(81) I says:

(82) "All right—that's mighty good; they won't find me, and they'll think I've been killed, and floated down the river—there's something up there that 'll help them think so—so don't you lose no time, Jim, but just shove off for the big water as fast as ever you can."

(83) I never felt easy till the raft was two mile below there

and out in the middle of the Mississippi. Then we hung up our signal lantern, and judged that we was free and safe once more. I hadn't had a bite to eat since yesterday, so Jim he got out some corn-dodgers and buttermilk, and pork and cabbage and greens—there ain't nothing in the world so good when it's cooked right—and whilst I eat my supper we talked and had a good time. I was powerful glad to get away from the feuds, and so was Jim to get away from the swamp. We said there warn't no home like a raft, after all. Other places do seem so cramped[47] up and smothery[48], but a raft don't. You feel mighty free and easy and comfortable on a raft.

[47] cramped /kræmpt/ *adj.* 狭窄拥挤的；缺少自由活动空间的

[48] smothery /ˈsmʌðərɪ/ *adj.* 透不过气的；令人窒息的

精华赏析

在前一章中，我们讲到"流浪小说"这个题材，通常来说，流浪小说的主人公为男性。因为一个女子，即使是彪悍勇猛的女子，在流浪探险的旅途中也会有诸多不便之处。在欧洲的流浪文学中，冒险和浪漫是这一类故事不可缺少的两大要素，从来都是密不可分的。为了增加故事的可读性和人物塑造的多样性，作者们会安排一些浪漫邂逅的情节，往往是身世孤苦的可怜女子或是背景显赫的美貌女子与流浪的男主人公相遇并一见钟情，在海誓山盟一番后，却又被迫分离，以保证男主人公继续历险的后续情节。例如，拜伦的《唐璜》中就塑造了一系列在男主人公的游历中出现的女子形象，海黛、古尔佩霞、俄国女皇凯瑟琳等。

当然，现实主义风格的作品对于这类刻意渲染暧昧、风流、艳遇的情节，散发淫靡气息的创作风格嗤之以鼻。但是现实主义作品并不回避对女性问题的探索。相反，通过刻画不同的女性形象，现实主义作家往往把对女性的关注放到了一个非常严肃的地位。

在《哈克贝利·费恩历险记》中，马克·吐温笔下的男主人公一个是十三四岁的少年，一个是深受奴役、渴望自由的黑奴，人物的设置决定小说中不会有大篇幅刻画的女性形象。在小说前几章，唯一出场的女性是哈克的监护人道格拉斯寡妇和她的妹妹——吉姆的主人沃森小姐。而这两个人物形象，是美国南方社会道德规范的象征，她们竭力想把哈克教化成一个符合社会道德规范的"文明人"和虔诚温顺的"羔羊"，这完全是违背哈克天性的。道格拉斯寡妇姐妹的形象是刻板的、程式化的，缺乏人性的生动和温度，哈克虽不厌恶，但也不认同。而在第十七、十八这两章"打冤家"的情节中，我们惊喜地发现，格伦基福特家两位小姐极大地吸引了哈克的注意力，尽管其中一位已经逝去。

哀美琳小姐是这个家族中早逝的女儿，读者对她的认知都来自哈克对她创作的炭画和诗歌的介绍。这位不幸早逝的小姐钟情的是哀婉、悲伤、略带神秘气息的绘画和挽诗。且看她画作的内容,墓碑、哭泣是主题,画中人要么着黑要么穿素,画作中透露着浓郁的死亡气息,看得哈克烦躁不安,心神不宁,认为"以她的脾性,在坟墓里也许会开心些"。她总是在别人死后,尸骨未寒之际便送来挽诗,有一次为了一个逝者名字的押韵,耽搁了些功夫,去晚了,她从此消瘦下去,竟然丢了性命。在哀美琳这一人物形象的刻画上,马克·吐温是花费了颇多心思和笔墨的,她实际上是十九世纪美国南方种植园文化急剧衰败的一个缩影。作为美国早期殖民扩张的产物,南方种植园经济是以黑人奴隶为主要劳动力的农奴经济,沿袭传统手工劳作模式,生产效率非常低下。而内战前的美国北部,资本主义工商业得到了迅速发展,从某种程度上说,南方的奴隶制种植园经济已经成为美国社会的一颗赘瘤,受到北方工商业的巨大冲击。哀美琳小姐描绘死亡主题的画作和挽歌,象征了摇摇欲坠、无力回天的南方奴隶制种植园经济行将灭亡的必然趋势。

与她纤弱、忧伤的姐妹不同,索菲亚小姐温柔可爱,对待爱情问题表现出了更多的勇气和主见。她全无美国南方贵族家庭大小姐的傲慢与偏见,依然爱上与自己家族有世仇的哈尼。她机智勇敢,在当时社会不允许女子抛头露面的情况下,利用去教堂做礼拜的机会与自己的情人传递信息,相约私奔。对于索菲亚这一人物形象,通过哈克之嘴,马克·吐温表达了肯定态度。在枪战中,哈克仍不忘询问索菲亚和哈尼的情况,当得知二人已经过了河,平安无事,哈克十分高兴("I was glad of that")。索菲亚无疑是封闭保守的美国南方父权制社会的一个叛逆者,是北方资本主义工商业快速发展催生的一个异类,体现了十九世纪美国南方种植园经济制度下女性自我意识的成长和进步。她的存在,虽无摧枯拉朽之力,却是对男权社会下女性被统治、被歧视、被禁锢的社会现状的有力申诉。同时,我们也应看到,索菲亚的私奔导致了两个家族更深的仇恨以及更惨烈的厮杀,她的父兄为此送命。这是索菲亚为了追求恋爱自由所付出的代价,更是一个落后的旧制度彻底坍塌前必须要经历的撕裂之痛。

阅读思考

1. 有人认为格伦基福特家的索菲亚小姐明知自己的行为会带来悲剧性的后果,仍然任性出逃,其私奔行为是莽撞、自私、愚蠢的行为。请你从女性主义文学批评的角度评论这种观点。

2. 马克·吐温的小说鲜有深刻、饱满、个性鲜明的女性形象,评论界很多声音认为其在描写女性方面贫乏、缺乏深度。你怎么认为?

EXERCISE III

I. Oral presentation.

1. 假设你和同学邀请学校的美国外教 Elva 去都江堰吃饭,请参考以下表达模拟对话。

(1)点餐:

A table for…, please.

What's good?

What's special for today?

Do you have any…?

What soup do you have today?

(2)表达感谢:

Everything was wonderful.

It couldn't have been better.

2. 假设你在美国留学。你和同学们在春假的时候到海边野餐,你们各自带了自己国家有特色的食物,请相互介绍自己国家的美食。

II. Choose the correct words to complete the sentences.

1. A man was seen _____ around outside the factory just before the fire started.

A. prowling B. creeping C. crawling D. sliding

2. He grabbed her arm and _____ her out of the room.

A. walked B. stepped C. hushed D. hustled

3. We _____ down the grassy slope.

A. slipped B. glided C. crept D. slid

4. The plane was _____ out of control.

A. flying B. spinning C. losing D. climbing

5. He _____ and yawned lazily.

A. laughed B. stood C. stretched D. moved

6. Military intervention will only ______ the conflict even further.

A. aggravate B. add C. let D. run

7. The skill to _____ a boat is very important.

A. push B. paddle C. drive D. saddle

8. I _____ my dress when I was ironing it.

A. tore B. burned C. threw D. scorched

9. Water was _____ around in the bottom of the boat.

   A. spilling   B. slopping   C. slipping   D. sliding

10. She _____ at his sleeve to get his attention.

   A. pulled   B. pushed   C. tugged   D. looked

III. Fill in the blanks with suitable prepositions.

1. The mother found her daughter ____ a fix.
2. The escaped prisoner was said to make _____ the beach.
3. Be careful not to run _____ one of these big cats in the jungle!
4. To make up ____ this shortfall, America needs to have its home businesses succeed.
5. For decades women were expected to stay at home and wait _____ men hand and foot.

IV. Answer the following questions.

Questions on the content

1. In Chapter XIII, when Huck began to worry about the men in the wreck, what did he do? Why did Huck say he might come to be a murderer himself?
2. What did Huck and Jim talk about in Chapter XIV? How did Jim make comment on King Solomon?
3. Where were Huck and Jim going to in Chapter XV? What happened in the fog?
4. In Chapter XVI, when Jim said it made him all over trembly and feverish to be so close to freedom, how did Huck feel? And why?
5. In Paragraph 9 of Chapter XVI "My conscience got to stirring me up hotter than ever…", what does "conscience" refer to here?
6. In Chapter XVII, why were the whole family on alert? How many members in this big family, and who were they?
7. How did Buck explain "the feud" to Huck in Chapter XVIII? What could you get from it?
8. Who was dead in Chapter XVIII?

Questions on the structure and style

1. Why is the first-person narrative used in this story? What advantage does the first-person narrative have?
2. What is the function and main idea of Chapter XIV?
3. How does the author portray the characters of Huck, Jim and Col. Grangerford? Illustrate your point with examples.
4. Do you think Huck is a "round character" ? Illustrate your reasons.
5. What do you know about Buck's family? What does the author think of the southern aristocracy?

V. Choose the best translation of the expressions in bold in the following sentences.

1. The fifth night below St. Louis we had a big storm after midnight, with a power of thunder and lightning, and the rain **poured down in a solid sheet.** (Chapter XII)

   A. 用坚固的一片倒下来　　B. 一大片倾倒下来
   C. 铺天盖地倾泻下来　　D. 凝固的一片倾泻下来

2. Seegars, I bet you—and cost five cents apiece, **solid cash**. (Chapter XII)

   A. 实心硬币　　B. 可靠的现钞　　C. 纯现金　　D. 顶呱呱的现钞

3. That was all right as far as it went, but the towhead warn't sixty yards long and the minute I flew by the foot of it I shot out into **the solid white fog,** and hadn't no more idea which way I was going than a dead man. (Chapter XV)

   A. 扎实的白雾　　B. 白茫茫的浓雾　　C. 纯白的大雾　　D. 连续不断的白雾

4. Wake up by and by, and look to see what done it, and maybe see a steamboat coughing along up stream, so far off towards the other side you couldn't tell nothing about her only whether she was stern-wheel or side-wheel; then for about an hour there wouldn't be nothing to hear not nothing to see—just **solid lonesomeness**. (Chapter XIX)

   A. 一片凝固的孤寂　　B. 安全的孤寂　　C. 持续的孤寂　　D. 真实的孤寂

5. I begun to think how dreadful it was, even for murderers, to be in such a **fix**. (Chapter XIII)

   A. 办法　　B. 绝境　　C. 结果　　D. 位置

6. "The first light we see we'll land a hundred yards below it or above it, in a place where it's a good hiding-place for you and the skiff, and then I'll go and **fix up some kind of a yarn**, and get somebody to go for that gang and get them out of their scrape, so they can be hung when their time comes." (Chapter XIII)

   A. 修补一种纱线　　B. 解决某种纱线问题　　C. 胡编乱诌一通　　D. 确定用哪种纱线

7. He said that when I went in the Texas and he crawled back to get on the raft and found her gone he nearly died, because he judged it was all up with him anyway **it could be fixed**; for if he didn't get saved he would get drownded… (Chapter XIV)

   A. 它能够被解决　　B. 它能够被修补好　　C. 他自己可完了　　D. 它能够被固定好

8. I read considerable to Jim about kings and dukes, and earls and such, and how gaudy they dressed, and **how much style they put on**, and called each other your majesty, and your grace and your lordship and so on, 'stead of mister… (Chapter XIV)

   A. 他们穿上多时髦的衣服　　B. 他们穿的款式有多少
   C. 他们穿的风格有多少　　D. 他们的派头有多大

9. And wouldn't he **throw style** into it? —wouldn't he spread himself, nor nothing? (Chapter XII)

   A. 耍花招　　B. 加上自己的风格　　C. 发挥他的风度　　D. 过他那时髦生活

10. "Well, **you're innocent, ain't you!** Does three hundred dollars lay around every day for people to pick up? (Chapter XI)

A. 你可真是太天真了　　B. 你可真是太无辜了
C. 你可真是太率真了　　D. 你可真是头脑太简单了

VI. Rhetorical devices in writing.

Distinguish the rhetorical devices in the following sentences and discuss their functions in English writing.

1. And in about a minute I come a-booming down on a cut bank with smoky ghosts of big trees on it.
2. So we would put in the day, lazying around, listening to the stillness.
3. He was sunshine most always.
4. And they bowed the least bit in the world and said thank you.
5. Away on the bank on t'other side of the river, being a woodyard, likely, and piled by them cheats so you can throw a dog through it anywhere.
6. Not a sound anywheres—perfectly still—just like the whole world was asleep, only sometimes the bullfrogs a-cluttering, maybe.
7. Every time he got money he got drunk; and every time he got drunk he raised Cain around town; and every time he raised Cain he got jailed.
8. What had poor Miss Watson done to you that you could see her nigger go off right under your eyes and never say one single word? What did that poor old woman do to you that you could treat her so mean?
9. We struck for the stern of the texas.
10. And when they come to look at that spare room, they had to take soundings before they could navigate it.

CHAPTER XIX

导读:远离了是非之地,哈克和吉姆继续乘坐木筏子顺流而下,木筏子上的生活平静而自由,令人向往。这一天,上岸觅食的哈克偶遇一老一少,这俩人衣衫褴褛、穷困潦倒,被人追赶如丧家之犬。不承想,其貌不扬的俩人竟然大有来头……

(1) TWO or three days and nights went by; I reckon I might say they swum by, they slid along so quiet and smooth and lovely. Here is the way we put in the time. It was a monstrous big river down there—sometimes a mile and a half wide; we run nights, and laid up and hid daytimes; soon as night was most gone we stopped navigating and tied up—nearly always in the dead water under a towhead; and then cut young cottonwoods and willows, and hid the raft with them. Then we set out the lines. Next we slid into the river and had a swim, so as to freshen up and cool off; then we set down on the sandy bottom where the water was about knee deep, and watched the daylight come. Not a sound anywheres—perfectly still—just like the whole world was asleep, only sometimes the bullfrogs a-cluttering, maybe. The first thing to see, looking away over the water, was a kind of dull line[1]—that was the woods on t'other side; you couldn't make nothing else out; then a pale place in the sky; then more paleness spreading around; then the river softened up away off, and warn't black any more, but gray;[2] you could see little dark spots drifting along ever so far away—trading scows[3], and such things; and long black streaks—rafts; sometimes you could hear a sweep screaking; or jumbled up voices, it was so still, and sounds come so far; and by and by you could see a streak on the water which you know by the look of the streak

[1] 此处指对岸的树映照在水面上若隐若现的轮廓。

[2] 远处的水面亮了些,灰蒙蒙的,不再是黑乎乎一片。

[3] **scow** /skaʊ/ *n.* 平底船

that there's a snag there in a swift current which breaks on it and makes that streak look that way;[4] and you see the mist curl up off of the water, and the east reddens up, and the river, and you make out a log-cabin in the edge of the woods, away on the bank on t'other side of the river, being a woodyard, likely, and piled by them cheats so you can throw a dog through it anywheres;[5] then the nice breeze springs up, and comes fanning you from over there, so cool and fresh and sweet to smell on account of the woods and the flowers; but sometimes not that way, because they've left dead fish laying around, gars[6] and such, and they do get pretty rank[7]; and next you've got the full day, and everything smiling in the sun, and the song-birds just going it!

(2) A little smoke couldn't be noticed now, so we would take some fish off of the lines and cook up a hot breakfast. And afterwards we would watch the lonesomeness of the river, and kind of lazy along, and by and by lazy off to sleep. Wake up by and by, and look to see what done it, and maybe see a steamboat coughing along up-stream, so far off towards the other side you couldn't tell nothing about her only whether she was a stern-wheel or side-wheel[8]; then for about an hour there wouldn't be nothing to hear nor nothing to see—just solid lonesomeness[9]. Next you'd see a raft sliding by, away off yonder, and maybe a galoot on it chopping, because they're most always doing it on a raft; you'd see the axe flash and come down—you don't hear nothing; you see that axe go up again, and by the time it's above the man's head then you hear the *k'chunk*!—it had took all that time to come over the water. So we would put in the day, lazying around, listening to the stillness[10]. Once there was a thick fog, and the rafts and things that went by was beating tin pans so the steamboats wouldn't run over them. A scow or a raft went by so close we could hear them talking and cussing and laughing—heard them plain; but we couldn't see no sign of them; it made you feel crawly[11]; it was like spirits carrying on that way in the air. Jim said he believed it was spirits; but I says:

(3) "No; spirits wouldn't say, 'Dern the dern fog.'"

(4) Soon as it was night out we shoved; when we got

[4] 不一会儿,你会看到水面上一道水纹,从那水纹的样子你就会知道,那里一定竖着什么东西,激流冲击而去,就被分成那样的纹路。

[5] 木料是按体积计算价格。堆在一起的木料之间的空隙越大,体积越大,卖的价钱就越高。这里说木料中间的空隙大得能扔过去条狗,是夸张(hyperbole)和讽刺(sarcasm)的用法。

[6] gar /gaː/ *n.* 雀鳝鱼(一种生活在美国南部及中美洲的凶猛食肉淡水鱼)

[7] rank /ræŋk/ *adj.* 难闻的;恶臭的

[8] 安装于舷侧的明轮叫边轮(side-wheel),安装于船尾的叫尾轮(stern-wheel)。

[9] 这里使用了"移位修饰法"(transferred epithet)的修辞手法。

[10] 这里使用了"矛盾修饰法"(oxymoron)的修辞手法。

[11] crawly /ˈkrɔli/ *adj.* 吓人的

her out to about the middle we let her alone, and let her float wherever the current wanted her to; then we lit the pipes, and dangled our legs in the water, and talked about all kinds of things—we was always naked, day and night, whenever the mosquitoes would let us—the new clothes Buck's folks made for me was too good to be comfortable, and besides I didn't go much on clothes, nohow[12].

(5) Sometimes we'd have that whole river all to ourselves for the longest time. Yonder was the banks and the islands, across the water; and maybe a spark—which was a candle in a cabin window; and sometimes on the water you could see a spark or two—on a raft or a scow, you know; and maybe you could hear a fiddle[13] or a song coming over from one of them crafts. It's lovely to live on a raft. We had the sky up there, all speckled[14] with stars, and we used to lay on our backs and look up at them, and discuss about whether they was made or only just happened. Jim he allowed they was made, but I allowed they happened; I judged it would have took too long to *make* so many. Jim said the moon could a *laid* them; well, that looked kind of reasonable, so I didn't say nothing against it, because I've seen a frog lay most as many, so of course it could be done. We used to watch the stars that fell, too, and see them streak down.[15] Jim allowed they'd got spoiled and was hove out of the nest.[16]

(6) Once or twice of a night we would see a steamboat slipping along in the dark, and now and then she would belch[17] a whole world of sparks up out of her chimbleys[18], and they would rain down in the river and look awful pretty; then she would turn a corner and her lights would wink out and her powwow[19] shut off and leave the river still again; and by and by her waves would get to us, a long time after she was gone, and joggle[20] the raft a bit, and after that you wouldn't hear nothing for you couldn't tell how long, except maybe frogs or something.

(7) After midnight the people on shore went to bed, and then for two or three hours the shores was black—no more sparks in the cabin windows. These sparks was our clock—the first one that showed again meant morning was coming, so we

[12] **nohow** /ˈnəʊˌhaʊ/ *adv.* (口) 绝不；毫不；一点也不

[13] **fiddle** /ˈfɪdl/ *n.* 小提琴

[14] **speckled** /ˈspekld/ *adj.* 布满斑点的

[15] 这里指流星。

[16] 吉姆认为这些蛋坏掉了，才被月亮从窝里给扔出去了。(上文吉姆认为星星是月亮下的蛋，所以才有此说。hove，即 heaved，意为"扔、抛"。)

[17] **belch** /beltʃ/ *v.* 喷出；吐出

[18] 即 chimneys

[19] **powwow** /ˈpauwau/ *n.* (俚) 会议；商谈；此处指喧闹的声音。

[20] **joggle** /ˈdʒɒgl/ *v.* 轻摇；摇动

hunted a place to hide and tie up right away.[21]

（8）One morning about daybreak I found a canoe and crossed over a chute to the main shore—it was only two hundred yards—and paddled about a mile up a crick amongst the cypress[22] woods, to see if I couldn't get some berries. Just as I was passing a place where a kind of a cowpath crossed the crick, here comes a couple of men tearing up the path as tight as they could foot it.[23] *I* thought I was a goner[24], for whenever anybody was after anybody I judged it was *me*—or maybe Jim. I was about to dig out from there in a hurry, but they was pretty close to me then, and sung out and begged me to save their lives—said they hadn't been doing nothing, and was being chased for it—said there was men and dogs a-coming. They wanted to jump right in, but I says:

（9）"Don't you do it. I don't hear the dogs and horses yet; you've got time to crowd through the brush and get up the crick a little ways; then you take to the water and wade down to me and get in—that'll throw the dogs off the scent."

（10）They done it, and soon as they was aboard I lit out[25] for our towhead, and in about five or ten minutes we heard the dogs and the men away off, shouting. We heard them come along towards the crick, but couldn't see them; they seemed to stop and fool around a while; then, as we got further and further away all the time, we couldn't hardly hear them at all; by the time we had left a mile of woods behind us and struck the river, everything was quiet, and we paddled over to the towhead and hid in the cottonwoods and was safe.

（11）One of these fellows was about seventy or upwards, and had a bald head and very gray whiskers. He had an old battered-up[26] slouch hat[27] on, and a greasy blue woollen shirt, and ragged old blue jeans britches stuffed into his boot-tops, and home-knit galluses[28]—no, he only had one. He had an old long-tailed blue jeans coat with slick brass buttons flung over his arm[29], and both of them had big, fat, ratty-looking carpet-bags.

（12）The other fellow was about thirty, and dressed about as ornery. After breakfast we all laid off and talked, and the

[21] 开头这几段是描绘密西西比河风光的名段。文笔细腻、感情真挚，生动刻画了密西西比河的秀美风光和木筏上自由散漫的生活，充分揭示了作者对昔日河上水手经历的无比怀念。

[22] cypress /ˈsaɪprəs/ *n.* 柏树

[23] 两个人朝这边飞奔而来。

[24] goner /ˈgɒnə(r)/ *n.* 垂死之人；快完蛋的人

[25] light out:（美俚）匆匆离去

[26] battered-up: 破旧的；磨损的

[27] 宽边软帽

[28] galluses /ˈgæləsɪz/ *n.* 吊裤带

[29] 燕尾服

first thing that come out was that these chaps didn't know one another.

(13) "What got you into trouble?" says the baldhead to t'other chap.

(14) "Well, I'd been selling an article to take the tartar[30] off the teeth —and it does take it off, too, and generly the enamel[31] along with it—but I stayed about one night longer than I ought to, and was just in the act of sliding out when I ran across you on the trail this side of town, and you told me they were coming, and begged me to help you to get off. So I told you I was expecting trouble myself, and would scatter out *with* you. That's the whole yarn[32]—what's yourn?"

(15) "Well, I'd ben a-running' a little temperance[33] revival thar 'bout a week, and was the pet of the women folks, big and little, for I was makin' it mighty warm for the rummies, I *tell* you, and takin' as much as five or six dollars a night—ten cents a head[34], children and niggers free—and business a-growin' all the time, when somehow or another a little report got around last night that I had a way of puttin' in my time with a private jug[35] on the sly[36]. A nigger rousted[37] me out this mornin', and told me the people was getherin' on the quiet[38] with their dogs and horses, and they'd be along pretty soon and give me 'bout half an hour's start, and then run me down if they could; and if they got me they'd tar and feather me and ride me on a rail[39], sure. I didn't wait for no breakfast—I warn't hungry."

(16) "Old man," said the young one, "I reckon we might double-team[40] it together; what do you think?"

(17) "I ain't undisposed. What's your line—mainly?"

(18) "Jour printer[41] by trade; do a little in patent[42] medicines; theater-actor—tragedy, you know; take a turn to mesmerism[43] and phrenology[44] when there's a chance; teach singing-geography[45] school for a change; sling a lecture sometimes—oh, I do lots of things—most anything that comes handy, so it ain't work. What's your lay?"

(19) "I've done considerble in the doctoring way in my time. Layin' on o' hands is my best holt[46]—for cancer and paral-

30 **tartar** /ˈtɑːtə(r)/ *n.* 牙垢

31 **enamel** /ɪˈnæml/ *n.* 牙釉质

32 **yarn** /jɑːn/ *n.* (夸张或编造的)故事

33 **temperance** /ˈtempərəns/ *n.* 戒酒;禁酒

34 **a head**: 这里使用了"提喻"(synecdoche)的修辞手法。

35 **jug**: 这里指"酒",使用了转喻(metonymy)的修辞手法。

36 **on the sly**: 偷偷地

37 **roust** /raʊst/ *v.* 唤醒

38 **on the quiet**: 私下里;暗中

39 浑身涂满柏油、沾上羽毛在当时是一种严厉的私刑,tar and feather 引申为"严厉惩罚"。另外,骑木杠也是当时流行的一种私刑。

40 两人防守,双人包夹,此处指"合伙"。

41 打零工的印刷工,马克·吐温年轻时曾从事过这种工作。

42 **patent** /ˈpætnt/ *adj.* 专利的

43 **mesmerism** /ˈmesməˌrɪzəm/ *n.* 催眠术

44 **phrenology** /frəˈnɒlədʒi/ *n.* 颅相学

45 当时一些学校把地理知识编成歌谣来教学生,便于记忆。

46 把手放到病人患处(治病)是我的拿手好戏。

ysis[47], and sich things; and I k'n tell a fortune pretty good when I've got somebody along to find out the facts for me.[48] Preachin's my line, too, and workin' camp-meetin's, and missionaryin' around."

(20) Nobody never said anything for a while; then the young man hove a sigh[49] and says:

(21) "Alas!"

(22) "What 're you alassin' about?" says the bald-head.

(23) "To think I should have lived to be leading such a life, and be degraded down into such company." And he begun to wipe the corner of his eye with a rag.

(24) "Dern your skin, ain't the company good enough for you?" says the baldhead, pretty pert[50] and uppish[51].

(25) "Yes, it IS good enough for me; it's as good as I deserve; for who fetched me so low when I was so high? I did myself. I don't blame *you*, gentlemen—far from it; I don't blame anybody. I deserve it all. Let the cold world do its worst; one thing I know—there's a grave somewhere for me. The world may go on just as it's always done, and take everything from me—loved ones, property, everything; but it can't take that. Some day I'll lie down in it and forget it all, and my poor broken heart will be at rest." He went on a-wiping.

(26) "Drot your pore broken heart," says the baldhead; "what are you heaving your pore broken heart at *us* f'r? *We* hain't done nothing."

(27) "No, I know you haven't. I ain't blaming you, gentlemen. I brought myself down—yes, I did it myself. It's right I should suffer—perfectly right—I don't make any moan."

(28) "Brought you down from whar? Whar was you brought down from?"

(29) "Ah, you would not believe me; the world never believes—let it pass—'tis no matter. The secret of my birth—"

(30) "The secret of your birth! Do you mean to say—"

(31) "Gentlemen," says the young man, very solemn, "I will reveal it to you, for I feel I may have confidence in you. By rights I am a duke!"

[47] **paralysis** /pəˈræləsɪs/ *n.* 麻痹；瘫痪

[48] 此句话幽默之中暗含嘲讽，暗示此人是个无赖、骗子。

[49] **heave a sigh**: 叹了一口气（hove 为 heave 的过去式）

[50] **pert** /pɜːt/ *adj.* 无理的；鲁莽的

[51] **uppish** /ˈʌpɪʃ/ *adj.* 傲慢的；盛气凌人

(32) Jim's eyes bugged out when he heard that; and I reckon mine did, too. Then the baldhead says: "No! you can't mean it?"

(33) "Yes. My great-grandfather, eldest son of the Duke of Bridgewater, fled to this country about the end of the last century, to breathe the pure air of freedom; married here, and died, leaving a son, his own father dying about the same time. The second son of the late duke seized the titles and estates—the infant real duke was ignored. I am the lineal descendant of that infant—I am the rightful Duke of Bridgewater; and here am I, forlorn[52], torn from my high estate, hunted of men, despised by the cold world, ragged, worn, heart-broken, and degraded to the companionship of felons[53] on a raft!"

(34) Jim pitied him ever so much, and so did I. We tried to comfort him, but he said it warn't much use, he couldn't be much comforted; said if we was a mind to acknowledge him, that would do him more good than most anything else; so we said we would, if he would tell us how. He said we ought to bow when we spoke to him, and say "Your Grace," or "My Lord," or "Your Lordship"—and he wouldn't mind it if we called him plain "Bridgewater," which, he said, was a title anyway, and not a name; and one of us ought to wait on him at dinner, and do any little thing for him he wanted done.

(35) Well, that was all easy, so we done it. All through dinner Jim stood around and waited on him, and says, "Will yo' Grace have some o' dis or some o' dat?" and so on, and a body could see it was mighty pleasing to him.

(36) But the old man got pretty silent by and by—didn't have much to say, and didn't look pretty comfortable over all that petting that was going on around that duke. He seemed to have something on his mind. So, along in the afternoon, he says:

(37) "Looky here, Bilgewater[54]," he says, "I'm nation sorry for you, but you ain't the only person that's had troubles like that."

(38) "No?"

(39) "No you ain't. You ain't the only person that's ben

[52] forlorn /fəˈlɔːn/ *adj.* 孤苦的；凄凉的

[53] felon /ˈfelən/ *n.* 犯人；罪人

[54] 光头的流浪汉把对方的名字念成了"bilgewater"，意为"舱底的积水，又脏又臭"。

snaked down wrongfully out'n a high place."

(40) "Alas!"

(41) "No, you ain't the only person that's had a secret of his birth." And, by jings, *he* begins to cry.

(42) "Hold! What do you mean?"

(43) "Bilgewater, kin I trust you?" says the old man, still sort of sobbing.

(44) "To the bitter death!" He took the old man by the hand and squeezed it, and says, "That secret of your being: speak!"

(45) "Bilgewater, I am the late Dauphin[55]!"

(46) You bet you, Jim and me stared this time. Then the duke says:

(47) "You are what?"

(48) "Yes, my friend, it is too true—your eyes is lookin' at this very moment on the pore disappeared Dauphin, Looy the Seventeen, son of Looy the Sixteen and Marry Antonette[56]."

(49) "You! At your age! No![57] You mean you're the late Charlemagne[58]; you must be six or seven hundred years old, at the very least."

(50) "Trouble has done it, Bilgewater, trouble has done it; trouble has brung these gray hairs and this premature balditude. Yes, gentlemen, you see before you, in blue jeans and misery, the wanderin', exiled, trampled-on[59], and sufferin' rightful King of France."

(51) Well, he cried and took on so that me and Jim didn't know hardly what to do, we was so sorry—and so glad and proud we'd got him with us, too. So we set in, like we done before with the duke, and tried to comfort *him*. But he said it warn't no use, nothing but to be dead and done with it all could do him any good; though he said it often made him feel easier and better for a while if people treated him according to his rights, and got down on one knee to speak to him, and always called him "Your Majesty," and waited on him first at meals, and didn't set down in his presence till he asked them. So Jim and me set to majestying him, and doing this and that and t'other

[55] **Dauphin** /ˈdɔːfɪn/ *n.*（旧）法国皇太子

[56] 本应为 Louis the Sixteen 和 Marie Antoinette，此人连法国国王和王后的名字都没记准确。

[57] 路易十七生于1785年，如果活到小说故事发生的1840年，应有50多岁，故与此人年龄不符。

[58] 即查理曼大帝，曾是法兰克国王。

[59] **trampled-on**：被践踏的；被蹂躏的

for him, and standing up till he told us we might set down. This done him heaps of good, and so he got cheerful and comfortable. But the duke kind of soured on him, and didn't look a bit satisfied with the way things was going; still, the king acted real friendly towards him, and said the duke's great-grandfather and all the other Dukes of Bilgewater was a good deal thought of by *his* father, and was allowed to come to the palace considerable; but the duke stayed huffy[60] a good while, till by and by the king says:

(52) "Like as not we got to be together a blamed long time on this h-yer raft, Bilgewater, and so what's the use o' your bein' sour? It 'll only make things on-comfortable. It ain't my fault I warn't born a duke, it ain't your fault you warn't born a king—so what's the use to worry? Make the best o' things the way you find 'em, says I—that's my motto[61]. This ain't no bad thing that we've struck here—plenty grub and an easy life—come, give us your hand, duke, and le's all be friends."

(53) The duke done it, and Jim and me was pretty glad to see it. It took away all the uncomfortableness and we felt mighty good over it, because it would a been a miserable business to have any unfriendliness on the raft; for what you want, above all things, on a raft, is for everybody to be satisfied, and feel right and kind towards the others.

(54) It didn't take me long to make up my mind that these liars warn't no kings nor dukes at all, but just low-down humbugs[62] and frauds. But I never said nothing, never let on; kept it to myself; it's the best way; then you don't have no quarrels, and don't get into no trouble. If they wanted us to call them kings and dukes, I hadn't no objections, 'long as it would keep peace in the family; and it warn't no use to tell Jim, so I didn't tell him. If I never learnt nothing else out of pap, I learnt that the best way to get along with his kind of people is to let them have their own way.

[60] huffy /ˈhʌfi/ *adj.* 生气的；发怒的

[61] motto /ˈmɒtəʊ/ *n.* 座右铭；格言

[62] humbug /ˈhʌmbʌg/ *n.* 谎言；骗人的把戏

精华赏析

"So I slid out and slipped off up the road, and there warn't anybody at the church, except maybe a hog or two, for there warn't any lock on the door, and hogs likes a puncheon floor in summer-time because it's cool. If you notice, most folks don't go to church only when they've got to; but a hog is different." 第十八章中这段文字讲的是哈克受索菲亚小姐所托去教堂取回她"遗忘"在那里的《圣经》,返回教堂时看到的情景。我想大家在读到这段文字的时候一定会忍俊不禁,哈哈笑出声来吧。

之所以发笑,是因为教堂向来是神圣、严肃的地方,怎能容许猪这种污秽肮脏的畜生在里面纳凉午休呢?在这里,故事的发展与观众的预期产生了巨大的反差,而作者正是恰当地运用了这个反差,营造出一种幽默诙谐的效果,同时也嘲讽了宗教"一本正经"的虚伪本质:虔诚信徒眼里神圣不可侵犯的圣洁场所,竟成了青年男女传递情书、幽会私通之地,成了被视为不洁之物的猪消暑纳凉的场所——岂不好笑?

这种手法叫作"情景反讽"(situational irony),是反讽(irony)的一种重要类型,被广泛运用在文学创作中。情景反讽是"意图与结果之间出现反差,而且这个反差恰恰是意图的反面"(赵毅衡,2011:8),它在文学作品中的运用能极大地增强故事的戏剧性和可读性。比较典型的一个情景反讽例子是莫泊桑的短篇小说《项链》。马蒂尔德本是一个小职员的妻子,为了能风光地参加晚会,向朋友借了一串钻石项链。谁知在回家的路上,项链意外丢失,马蒂尔德只能借钱买了新项链还给朋友。为了还债,她节衣缩食,辛苦劳作,由一个年轻美丽的少妇变成了一个双手粗糙、容颜衰老的妇女。十年后债还清了,谁知却得知当年向朋友借的项链是一条廉价的假项链!这里,"意图与结果之间的反差"无疑推动了故事情节的发展,加强了戏剧冲突,揭示了故事的主题。

在《哈克贝利·费恩历险记》中,作者也设置了大量的情景反讽。除了上文提到的"教堂取信"这一情节,我们再举一、二例加以分析。在小说第五章,哈克的老爸第一次登场,就给人留下了深刻印象。为了讹诈钱财,他搞得全镇鸡犬不宁,人仰马翻,最后被告上法院,谁料新上任的法官不了解情况,竟奢望能感化这个厚颜无耻的老酒鬼。于是,新法官为老头添置新衣,设宴款待,诚心诚意劝他戒酒,感动得老酒鬼涕泪横流,赌咒发誓,甚至签下契约,保证从此滴酒不沾,洗心革面,重新做人。哈克老爸的这一番慷慨陈词打动了新法官夫妻,大家哭作一团。读者读到这里,估计也会被感染,指望老头儿从此能改掉恶习,承担起做父亲的责任吧。没承想这感人的场景没过多久,当夜这老家伙就偷偷溜出新法官为他安排的房间,用新添置的衣服换了一壶酒,喝得烂醉如泥、人事不省。哈克老爸的言行不一,大大超出了读者的心理预期,这种巨大的落差所形成的奇特的喜剧效果正是情景反讽的魅力所在。作者通过这一系列的落差,生动刻画了一个卑鄙、肮脏、下贱、嗜酒如命、反复无常的老酒鬼形象,令人拍案叫绝。

在本章中,哈克偶然搭救了两名被人追逐的流浪汉。这两人其貌不扬,破衣烂衫,走街串巷,没个正经事儿做,但二人自诩为落难的"公爵"和"国王"!单纯的哈克和老实的吉姆真是惊得下巴都要掉下来了,于是鞍前马后,尽心服侍。"So Jim and me set to majestying him, and doing this and that and t'other for him, and standing up till he told us we might set down."不过没过多久,哈克就发现了这俩人的真实面目——"It didn't take me long to make up my mind that these liars warn't no kings nor dukes at all, but just low-down humbugs and frauds."情景反讽的运用使故事情节一波三折,读者的心情也跟着跌宕起伏,作者也成功塑造了两个出身社会底层的、无耻、狡诈的滑稽流浪汉形象,给人留下了深刻印象。

在《哈克贝利·费恩历险记》中,情景反讽的运用非常普遍,成为该书语言风格的一大特色。这一手法的成功运用,增加了小说的趣味性和戏剧性,推动了故事情节的发展,也完成了作者批判、讽刺的表达需要。我们在阅读文学作品的过程中,准确掌握情景反讽这一写作手法,能帮助我们更深刻地理解作品,把握作者的"言外之意",从而极大地提升我们的阅读体验。

阅读思考

1. 区分言语反讽、情景反讽和戏剧反讽。

2. 欧·亨利的小说以"欧·亨利式结尾"闻名,其实也是情景反讽的运用,试以《警察与赞美诗》为例,分析情景反讽的艺术效果。

CHAPTER XX

导读：哈克和吉姆的木筏昼伏夜出，引起“国王”和“公爵”的注意，吉姆是逃跑的黑奴吗？哈克编了个好故事蒙混过去，“公爵”说他得好好盘算一下，怎样才能白天也赶路。夜里狂风暴雨骤然而至，第二天雨过天晴，木筏子路过一个巴掌大的小镇，“国王”“公爵”和哈克登了岸，两位老爷大显身手，狠狠地捞了一笔。

(1) THEY asked us considerable many questions; wanted to know what we covered up the raft that way for, and laid by in the daytime instead of running—was Jim a runaway nigger? Says I:

(2) "Goodness sakes! would a runaway nigger run *south*?"

(3) No, they allowed he wouldn't. I had to account for things some way, so I says:

(4) "My folks was living in Pike County, in Missouri, where I was born, and they all died off but me and pa and my brother Ike. Pa, he 'lowed he'd break up and go down and live with Uncle Ben, who's got a little one-horse place[1] on the river, forty-four mile below Orleans. Pa was pretty poor, and had some debts; so when he'd squared up[2] there warn't nothing left but sixteen dollars and our nigger, Jim. That warn't enough to take us fourteen hundred mile, deck passage[3] nor no other way. Well, when the river rose pa had a streak of luck[4] one day; he ketched this piece of a raft; so we reckoned we'd go down to Orleans on it. Pa's luck didn't hold out; a steamboat run over the forrard[5] corner of the raft one night, and we all went overboard and dove under the wheel; Jim and me come up all right, but pa was drunk, and Ike was only four years old, so they never come up no more. Well, for the next day or two we had considerable

1 非常小的地方；巴掌大的地方

2 勇敢面对、正视，此处意为“还清债务”。

3 统舱，指轮船上设有较多铺位，能容纳许多乘客的大舱。

4 一点儿好运气

5 即 forward

trouble, because people was always coming out in skiffs and trying to take Jim away from me, saying they believed he was a runaway nigger. We don't run daytimes no more now; nights they don't bother us."

(5) The duke says:

(6) "Leave me alone to cipher out[6] a way so we can run in the daytime if we want to. I'll think the thing over—I'll invent a plan that'll fix it. We'll let it alone for to-day, because of course we don't want to go by that town yonder in daylight—it mightn't be healthy."

(7) Towards night it begun to darken up and look like rain; the heat lightning was squirting[7] around low down in the sky, and the leaves was beginning to shiver—it was going to be pretty ugly, it was easy to see that. So the duke and the king went to overhauling[8] our wigwam, to see what the beds was like. My bed was a straw tick[9] better than Jim's, which was a corn-shuck tick[10]; there's always cobs[11] around about in a shuck tick, and they poke into you and hurt; and when you roll over the dry shucks sound like you was rolling over in a pile of dead leaves; it makes such a rustling that you wake up. Well, the duke allowed he would take my bed; but the king allowed he wouldn't. He says:

(8) "I should a reckoned the difference in rank would a sejested to you that a corn-shuck bed warn't just fitten for me to sleep on. Your Grace 'll take the shuck bed yourself."

(9) Jim and me was in a sweat again for a minute, being afraid there was going to be some more trouble amongst them; so we was pretty glad when the duke says:

(10) "'Tis my fate to be always ground into the mire[12] under the iron heel of oppression. Misfortune has broken my once haughty[13] spirit; I yield, I submit; 'tis my fate. I am alone in the world—let me suffer; can bear it."

(11) We got away as soon as it was good and dark. The king told us to stand well out towards the middle of the river, and not show a light till we got a long ways below the town. We come in sight of the little bunch of lights by and by—that

[6] cipher out: (美)想出;算出

[7] squirt /skwɜːt/ v. 喷出;喷射

[8] overhaul /ˈəʊvəhɔːl/ v. 检修;改造

[9] straw tick: 草褥

[10] 塞着玉米棒皮的垫褥

[11] cob /kɒb/ n. 玉米芯

[12] mire /ˈmaɪə(r)/ n. 泥潭;泥沼

[13] haughty /ˈhɔːtɪ/ adj. 傲慢的;高傲的

was the town, you know—and slid by, about a half a mile out, all right. When we was three-quarters of a mile below we hoisted[14] up our signal lantern; and about ten o'clock it come on to rain and blow and thunder and lighten like everything; so the king told us to both stay on watch till the weather got better; then him and the duke crawled into the wigwam and turned in[15] for the night. It was my watch below till twelve, but I wouldn't a turned in anyway if I'd had a bed, because a body don't see such a storm as that every day in the week, not by a long sight. My souls, how the wind did scream along! And every second or two there'd come a glare that lit up the white-caps[16] for a half a mile around, and you'd see the islands looking dusty through the rain, and the trees thrashing around in the wind; then comes a *h-whack*!—bum! bum! bumble-umble-um-bum-bum-bum-bum—and the thunder would go rumbling and grumbling away, and quit—and then *rip* comes another flash and another sockdolager[17]. The waves most washed me off the raft sometimes, but I hadn't any clothes on, and didn't mind. We didn't have no trouble about snags; the lightning was glaring and flittering around so constant that we could see them plenty soon enough to throw her head this way or that and miss them.[18]

(12) I had the middle watch, you know, but I was pretty sleepy by that time, so Jim he said he would stand the first half of it for me; he was always mighty good that way, Jim was. I crawled into the wigwam, but the king and the duke had their legs sprawled around so there warn't no show for me; so I laid outside—I didn't mind the rain, because it was warm, and the waves warn't running so high now. About two they come up again, though, and Jim was going to call me; but he changed his mind, because he reckoned they warn't high enough yet to do any harm; but he was mistaken about that, for pretty soon all of a sudden along comes a regular ripper and washed me overboard. It most killed Jim a-laughing. He was the easiest nigger to laugh that ever was, anyway.

(13) I took the watch, and Jim he laid down and snored away; and by and by the storm let up for good and all; and the

[14] hoist /hɒɪst/ *v.* 升起；举起，抬高

[15] turn in: 上床睡觉

[16] 这里指的是白色的浪花。

[17] sockdolager /sɒkˈdɒlədʒə/ *n.* 决定性的打击

[18] 这是描写雷电、暴雨的经典名段，写出了雷电交加、狂风怒吼、恶浪翻滚的惊心动魄的气氛。其中，拟声词(onomatopoeia)的使用极大地增强了语言的感染力。除此之外，"rumbling"和"grumbling"这两个单词押韵(rhyme)，形象地刻画了雷声渐息的节奏感和韵律感，十分生动。

first cabin-light that showed I rousted him out, and we slid the raft into hiding quarters for the day.

(14) The king got out an old ratty deck of cards after breakfast, and him and the duke played seven-up[19] a while, five cents a game. Then they got tired of it, and allowed they would "lay out a campaign," as they called it. The duke went down into his carpetbag, and fetched up a lot of little printed bills and read them out loud. One bill said, "The celebrated Dr. Armand de Montalban, of Paris," would "lecture on the Science of Phrenology" at such and such a place, on the blank day of blank, at ten cents admission, and "furnish charts of character at twenty-five cents apiece." The duke said that was *him*. In another bill he was the "world-renowned Shakespearian tragedian, Garrick the Younger[20], of Drury Lane, London[21]." In other bills he had a lot of other names and done other wonderful things, like finding water and gold with a "divining-rod," "dissipating[22] witch spells," and so on. By and by he says:

(15) "But the histrionic[23] muse is the darling. Have you ever trod the boards[24], Royalty?"

(16) "No," says the king.

(17) "You shall, then, before you're three days older, Fallen Grandeur[25]," says the duke. "The first good town we come to we'll hire a hall and do the sword fight in *Richard III*[26] and the balcony scene in *Romeo and Juliet*. How does that strike you?"

(18) "I'm in, up to the hub, for anything that will pay, Bilgewater; but, you see, I don't know nothing about play-actin', and hain't ever seen much of it. I was too small when pap used to have 'em at the palace. Do you reckon you can learn me?"

(19) "Easy!"

(20) "All right. I'm jist a-freezn' for something fresh, anyway. Le's commence right away."

(21) So the duke he told him all about who Romeo was and who Juliet was, and said he was used to being Romeo, so the king could be Juliet.

(22) "But if Juliet's such a young gal, duke, my peeled head and my white whiskers is goin' to look oncommon odd on

[19] 一种纸牌游戏,先得七分者胜。

[20] 指的是扮演莎士比亚戏剧出名的大卫·迦里克,此处"公爵"是冒充迦里克之子行骗。

[21] 伦敦德鲁里巷,伦敦皇家剧院就坐落在该街上。

[22] dissipate /ˈdɪsɪpeɪt/ *v.* 驱散;消失

[23] histrionic /ˌhɪstriˈɒnɪk/ *adj.* 表演的;戏剧的

[24] trod the boards: 登台演戏

[25] 下台的国王,很明显这里"公爵"是打趣"国王"落难,以反击自己被对方称为"Bilgewater"(舱底的污水)。

[26]《理查三世》和后面的《罗密欧和朱丽叶》都是莎士比亚的名剧。

her, maybe."

(23) "No, don't you worry; these country jakes won't ever think of that. Besides, you know, you'll be in costume, and that makes all the difference in the world; Juliet's in a balcony, enjoying the moonlight before she goes to bed, and she's got on her night-gown and her ruffled nightcap. Here are the costumes for the parts."

(24) He got out two or three curtain-calico[27] suits, which he said was meedyevil[28] armor for Richard III. and t'other chap, and a long white cotton nightshirt and a ruffled nightcap to match. The king was satisfied; so the duke got out his book and read the parts over in the most splendid spread-eagle way, prancing[29] around and acting at the same time, to show how it had got to be done; then he give the book to the king and told him to get his part by heart.

(25) There was a little one-horse town[30] about three mile down the bend, and after dinner the duke said he had ciphered out his idea about how to run in daylight without it being dangersome for Jim; so he allowed he would go down to the town and fix that thing. The king allowed he would go, too, and see if he couldn't strike something. We was out of coffee, so Jim said I better go along with them in the canoe and get some.

(26) When we got there there warn't nobody stirring; streets empty, and perfectly dead and still, like Sunday. We found a sick nigger sunning himself in a back yard, and he said everybody that warn't too young or too sick or too old was gone to camp-meeting[31], about two mile back in the woods. The king got the directions, and allowed he'd go and work that camp-meeting for all it was worth[32], and I might go, too.

(27) The duke said what he was after was a printing-office. We found it; a little bit of a concern, up over a carpenter shop—carpenters and printers all gone to the meeting, and no doors locked. It was a dirty, littered-up place, and had ink marks, and handbills with pictures of horses and runaway niggers on them, all over the walls. The duke shed his coat and said he was all right now. So me and the king lit out for the camp-meeting.

[27] calico /'kælɪkəʊ/ *n.* 印花布

[28] 即 medieval

[29] prance /prɑːns/ *v.* 腾跃；欢蹦乱跳；昂首阔步

[30] one-horse town: 小镇

[31] camp-meeting: 信徒的野营集会

[32] 好好利用这个野营集会。这里指“国王”企图打着宗教的幌子骗取钱财。

(28) We got there in about a half an hour fairly dripping, for it was a most awful hot day. There was as much as a thousand people there from twenty mile around. The woods was full of teams and wagons, hitched everywheres, feeding out of the wagon-troughs and stomping to keep off the flies. There was sheds made out of poles and roofed over with branches, where they had lemonade and gingerbread to sell, and piles of watermelons and green corn and such-like truck.

(29) The preaching was going on under the same kinds of sheds, only they was bigger and held crowds of people. The benches was made out of outside slabs of logs, with holes bored in the round side to drive sticks into for legs.[33] They didn't have no backs. The preachers had high platforms to stand on at one end of the sheds. The women had on sun-bonnets; and some had linsey-woolsey frocks[34], some gingham[35] ones, and a few of the young ones had on calico. Some of the young men was barefooted, and some of the children didn't have on any clothes but just a tow-linen[36] shirt. Some of the old women was knitting, and some of the young folks was courting on the sly.

(30) The first shed we come to the preacher was lining out a hymn. He lined out two lines, everybody sung it, and it was kind of grand to hear it, there was so many of them and they done it in such a rousing way; then he lined out two more for them to sing—and so on. The people woke up more and more, and sung louder and louder; and towards the end some begun to groan, and some begun to shout. Then the preacher begun to preach, and begun in earnest, too; and went weaving first to one side of the platform and then the other, and then a-leaning down over the front of it, with his arms and his body going all the time, and shouting his words out with all his might; and every now and then he would hold up his Bible and spread it open, and kind of pass it around this way and that, shouting, "It's the brazen serpent in the wilderness[37]! Look upon it and live!" And people would shout out, "Glory!—A-a-*men*!" And so he went on, and the people groaning and crying and saying amen:

(31) "Oh, come to the mourners' bench[38]! come, black with

[33] 板凳是用劈开的圆木最外面的那块木板做成。平的那面做凳子面儿，圆的那面钻上几个洞，插上几根棍儿当凳子腿儿。

[34] 一种亚麻毛织品做成的连身裙（frock /frɒk/ *n.* 连衣裙）

[35] gingham /ˈgɪŋəm/ *n.* 格子棉布

[36] 短纤维亚麻布

[37] 铜蛇的典故出自《旧约·民数记》。以色列人跟随摩西出埃及，一路受了很多苦难，因此对上帝和摩西产生埋怨和反叛。后来他们被毒蛇所咬，许多人因此丧生，摩西向上帝求情宽恕他们，造出一只铜蛇，被咬的人只要注视铜蛇就能活。

[38] 前排专供忏悔者坐的板凳。

sin! (*amen*!) come, sick and sore! (*amen*!) come, lame and halt and blind! (*amen*!) come, pore and needy, sunk in shame! (*a-a-men*!) come, all that's worn and soiled[39] and suffering! —come with a broken spirit! come with a contrite[40] heart! come in your rags and sin and dirt! the waters that cleanse is free, the door of heaven stands open—oh, enter in and be at rest!" (*a-a-men! glory, glory hallelujah!*)

[39] soiled：这里指堕落的人。

[40] contrite /kənˈtraɪt/ *adj*. 忏悔的；懊悔的

(32) And so on. You couldn't make out what the preacher said any more, on account of the shouting and crying. Folks got up everywheres in the crowd, and worked their way just by main strength to the mourners' bench, with the tears running down their faces; and when all the mourners had got up there to the front benches in a crowd, they sung and shouted and flung themselves down on the straw, just crazy and wild.

(33) Well, the first I knowed the king got a-going, and you could hear him over everybody; and next he went a-charging up on to the platform, and the preacher he begged him to speak to the people, and he done it. He told them he was a pirate—been a pirate for thirty years out in the Indian Ocean—and his crew was thinned out considerable last spring in a fight, and he was home now to take out some fresh men, and thanks to goodness he'd been robbed last night and put ashore off of a steamboat without a cent, and he was glad of it; it was the blessedest thing that ever happened to him, because he was a changed man now, and happy for the first time in his life; and, poor as he was, he was going to start right off and work his way back to the Indian Ocean, and put in the rest of his life trying to turn the pirates into the true path; for he could do it better than anybody else, being acquainted with all pirate crews in that ocean; and though it would take him a long time to get there without money, he would get there anyway, and every time he convinced a pirate he would say to him, "Don't you thank me, don't you give me no credit; it all belongs to them dear people in Pokeville camp-meeting, natural brothers and benefactors[41] of the race, and that dear preacher there, the truest friend a pirate ever had!"

[41] benefactor /ˈbenɪfæktə(r)/ *n*. 捐助者；恩人

(34) And then he busted into tears, and so did everybody.

Then somebody sings out, "Take up a collection for him, take up a collection!" Well, a half a dozen made a jump to do it, but somebody sings out, "Let *him* pass the hat around!" Then everybody said it, the preacher too.

(35) So the king went all through the crowd with his hat swabbing[42] his eyes, and blessing the people and praising them and thanking them for being so good to the poor pirates away off there; and every little while the prettiest kind of girls, with the tears running down their cheeks, would up and ask him would he let them kiss him for to remember him by; and he always done it; and some of them he hugged and kissed as many as five or six times—and he was invited to stay a week; and everybody wanted him to live in their houses, and said they'd think it was an honor; but he said as this was the last day of the camp-meeting he couldn't do no good, and besides he was in a sweat to get to the Indian Ocean right off and go to work on the pirates.

(36) When we got back to the raft and he come to count up he found he had collected eighty-seven dollars and seventy-five cents. And then he had fetched away a three-gallon jug of whisky, too, that he found under a wagon when he was starting home through the woods. The king said, take it all around, it laid over any day he'd ever put in in the missionarying line.[43] He said it warn't no use talking, heathens don't amount to shucks alongside of pirates to work a camp-meeting with.[44]

(37) The duke was thinking *he'd* been doing pretty well till the king come to show up, but after that he didn't think so so much. He had set up and printed off two little jobs for farmers in that printing-office—horse bills—and took the money, four dollars. And he had got in ten dollars' worth of advertisements for the paper, which he said he would put in for four dollars if they would pay in advance—so they done it. The price of the paper was two dollars a year, but he took in three subscriptions for half a dollar apiece on condition of them paying him in advance; they were going to pay in cordwood and onions as usual, but he said he had just bought the concern and knocked down the price as low as he could afford it, and was going to

[42] swab /swɒb/ *v.* 擦拭

[43] 今天是他传教生涯中收获最大的一天了。

[44] 不信教的人就跟海盗一样,搞野营布道会对他们压根儿不起作用。(heathen /ˈhiːðn/ *n.* 异教徒;未开化的人)

run it for cash. He set up a little piece of poetry, which he made, himself, out of his own head—three verses—kind of sweet and saddish—the name of it was, "Yes, crush, cold world, this breaking heart" —and he left that all set up and ready to print in the paper, and didn't charge nothing for it. Well, he took in nine dollars and a half, and said he'd done a pretty square day's work for it.[45]

(38) Then he showed us another little job he'd printed and hadn't charged for, because it was for us. It had a picture of a runaway nigger with a bundle on a stick over his shoulder, and "$200 reward" under it. The reading was all about Jim, and just described him to a dot[46]. It said he run away from St. Jacques' plantation, forty mile below New Orleans, last winter, and likely went north, and whoever would catch him and send him back he could have the reward and expenses.

(39) "Now," says the duke, "after to-night we can run in the daytime if we want to. Whenever we see anybody coming we can tie Jim hand and foot with a rope, and lay him in the wigwam and show this handbill and say we captured him up the river, and were too poor to travel on a steamboat, so we got this little raft on credit from our friends and are going down to get the reward. Handcuffs and chains would look still better on Jim, but it wouldn't go well with the story of us being so poor. Too much like jewelry.[47] Ropes are the correct thing—we must preserve the unities, as we say on the boards.[48]"

(40) We all said the duke was pretty smart, and there couldn't be no trouble about running daytimes. We judged we could make miles enough that night to get out of the reach of the powwow we reckoned the duke's work in the printing office was going to make in that little town; then we could boom right along if we wanted to.

(41) We laid low[49] and kept still, and never shoved out till nearly ten o'clock; then we slid by, pretty wide away from the town, and didn't hoist our lantern till we was clear out of sight of it.

(42) When Jim called me to take the watch at four in the

[45] 这一段通过"公爵"之口介绍了印刷工的日常工作。马克·吐温的经验来自他年轻时的经历。他幼年家贫,在他父亲去世后辍学到印刷厂做了一名学徒。

[46] to a dot:丝毫不差

[47] 给吉姆戴上手铐、脚镣更应景,不过我们不是穷嘛,戴手铐、脚镣就跟戴上了珠宝首饰一样不匹配。

[48] 我们要遵守"三一律",就像戏台上常说的那样。(三一律:西方古典主义戏剧结构理论,要求戏剧创作在时间、地点和情节三者之间保持一致。)

[49] lie low:潜伏;隐匿;不露声色,避免引起别人的注意(非正式场合人们经常忽略lay和lie的区别)

morning, he says:

(43) "Huck, does you reck'n we gwyne to run acrost any mo' kings on dis trip?"

(44) "No," I says, "I reckon not."

(45) "Well," says he, "dat's all right, den. I doan' mine one er two kings, but dat's enough. Dis one's powerful drunk, en de duke ain' much better."

(46) I found Jim had been trying to get him to talk French, so he could hear what it was like; but he said he had been in this country so long, and had so much trouble, he'd forgot it.

精华赏析

在课堂教学中,同学们拿到一个文本进行分析时,往往注重语言层面的特征和差异,如语音上的变异,选词上的不同,句式结构上的变化,等等,仿佛这是文本分析的全部内容。其实不然,文本背后往往隐藏着大量的非语言信息,这些信息决定语言形式的差异,并影响文本意义的产生。我们以本章"公爵"和"国王"的一个对话为例:

Duke: "But the histrionic muse is the darling. Have you ever trod the boards, Royalty?"

King: "No."

Duke: "You shall, then, before you're three days older, Fallen Grandeur," says the duke. "The first good town we come to we'll hire a hall and do the sword fight in *Richard III* and the balcony scene in *Romeo and Juliet*. How does that strike you?"

King: "I'm in, up to the hub, for anything that will pay, Bilgewater; but, you see, I don't know nothing about play-actin', and hain't ever seen much of it. I was too small when pap used to have 'em at the palace. Do you reckon you can learn me?"

Duke: "Easy!"

King: "All right. I'm jist a-freezn' for something fresh, anyway. Le's commence right away."

(So the duke he told him all about who Romeo was and who Juliet was, and said he was used to being Romeo, so the king could be Juliet.)

King: "But if Juliet's such a young gal, duke, my peeled head and my white whiskers is goin' to look oncommon odd on her, maybe."

Duke: "No, don't you worry; these country jakes won't ever think of that. Besides, you know, you'll be in costume, and that makes all the difference in the world; Juliet's in a balcony, enjoying the moonlight before she goes to bed, and she's got on her night-gown and her ruffled nightcap. Here are the costumes for the parts."

我们已经在上面的对话中标出了口语化及语言不规范之处，从中可以清楚地看到，在语言风格及特征上，很明显"国王"使用的语言最不规范，口语化风格也最明显。首先是在语法结构上存在诸多错误，如用双重否定来表示肯定陈述（I don't know nothing about play-actin'…），主谓不一致（… my white whiskers is goin' to…），用形容词来修饰形容词（oncommon odd）等。其次，"国王"的话语在发音上也呈现出鲜明的特点，下面我们重点对"国王"的发音特征进行分析，以期有更多有趣的发现。

"国王"的发音有个明显特征是把很多单词中的语音 /ŋ/ 读作 /n/，如把"acting（/ˈæktɪŋ/）"读作"actin'（/ˈæktɪn/）"，"going（/ˈɡəʊɪŋ/）"读作"goin'（/ˈɡəʊɪn/）"，"freezing（/ˈfriːzɪŋ/）"读作"freezn'（/ˈfriːzn/）"。从发音部位的角度来说，辅音 /ŋ/ 的发音位置在舌根及软腭处，发这个音时需要抬高舌根抵住软腭，这种软腭紧张的发音感觉可以在美声唱法（软腭上提）中找到痕迹。相对于发音位置在齿龈部位的辅音 /n/，/ŋ/ 的发音难度相对较大。而"just（/dʒʌst/）"中的元音"/ʌ/"相比"jist（/dʒɪst/）"中的元音"/ɪ/"舌位更低，口型更大，因此发音更费劲。此外，"国王"的发音中还有个有趣的现象，"let's"中的辅音 /t/ 被省略，"them"中省略掉了"th"的发音 /ð/。这种随意"偷工减料"的话语风格使得"国王"的话语特征鲜明且个性十足。

相比于"国王"句子结构简单散乱、发音漏洞百出的口语化风格，"公爵"的话语则要讲究许多：语法正确、规范，句子结构完整，句式也更复杂、严谨。由定语从句、状语从句和非谓语动词结构组成的复合句的使用，与"国王"简单、破碎的句式立即形成了鲜明的对照。"公爵"话语中最为明显的一个特征体现在用词上，使用了"the histrionic muse""trod the boards""Royalty""Grandeur"（法语词）等词汇，语体正式、考究、华丽，甚至略显陈旧、浮夸。这些词或许能在老电影或者诗歌、戏剧中觅得踪迹，但出现在两个流浪汉的日常对话中，就显得有些奇怪了。

通过对比"国王"和"公爵"的话语风格，我们很容易觉察到二者的鲜明差异。正如一位老师在课堂上的话语风格和他与家人、朋友聊天时的风格截然不同，一个学生在和老师就某个学术问题进行讨论时的说话方式与他和室友玩笑嬉闹时的话语风格也绝不会相同。当然差异本身并不是我们探究的最终目的，我们渴望了解的是，究竟是什么导致了语言风格的巨大差异？

我们已经熟悉了"语境"的概念，知道语言交际存在不同的情景类型（situation type），如上面提到的教师给学生上课、教师与亲友聊天、学生与老师探讨学术问题、学生与室友嬉闹等。在不同的情境中，人们的话语方式和风格也不同，会产生不同的语言变体。这些语言变体既可以体现在语音层，也可以体现在词汇层，当然也可以体现在语法层。

系统功能学派的创始人韩礼德在语境的基础上提出来语域（register）的概念。我们可以把语域看作情景类型的总称，或者说语言变体就是不同类别的语域。那么，语域是如何影响语言,产生语言变体的呢?韩礼德认为影响语言变体的语境因素可归纳为三部分:语场(field)、语旨(tenor)、语式(mode)。简单地说,语场指的是交际过程中实际发生的事,以及参与者所从事的活动,其中语言活动是重要组成部分,包括谈话主题;语旨是指谁是参与者,以及参与者的性质、社会地位和角色;语式指语言交际的渠道或媒介,如是说还是写,是即席的,还是有准备的,包括修辞方式。(张德禄,1987)

回到"国王"和"公爵"的对话中,现在我们已经明白,两人不同的话语风格是受语域的影响。我们如果探究一下造成两人不同语言变体的具体因素,就会发现语言绝不是孤立的音、词、句的存在,它的社会属性是如此强烈,甚至影响语言意义的产生。

首先,从语场的角度来分析,"国王"和"公爵"商量戏剧演出的事,谈论的是莎翁名剧《罗密欧与朱丽叶》,这就不难理解为什么"公爵"的话语中会出现大量华丽、浮夸、正式的词了——这正是戏剧语言的风格。一个经常出演莎剧的演员,把剧本里的台词搬到日常对话中,尤其谈的还是关于戏剧的话题,就不足为怪了。其次,从语旨的角度来说,"国王"是一个走街串巷、一无所长、以行骗谋生的流浪汉。他劝别人戒酒,自己却嗜酒如命;他自称行医,但最拿手的是把手按到病人的病患处,然后念念有词的鬼把戏;他说自己擅长算命,前提是得有人帮他把算命人的事情打听清楚——"国王"这样的身份背景倒和他错误连篇、偷工减料的话语风格绝配。而"公爵"呢,还记得他是如何介绍自己的吗?流浪印刷工、悲剧演员、做过催眠、看相、教书、演讲,与"国王"荒唐的行当相比,"公爵"倒是有些真正的技能,至少他受过教育,这也与他的话语风格相匹配。尤为有趣的是两人在对话中的角色关系。虽然都靠行骗为生,"公爵"更有优越感,毕竟,演戏可是他的专长;而"国王"对此却一无所知。所以我们不难发现,"公爵"控制话轮的转换,决定话轮的开启和结束。这让他在语言表达上更加自信,表现为使用较长的句子和相对复杂的句式结构等。最后从语式的角度来谈,"国王"和"公爵"两人不熟悉,算是第一次碰面,彼此都心存戒备,在话语上表现为多处问句的出现,例如:"Have you ever trod the boards, Royalty?" "How does that strike you?" "Do you reckon you can learn me?" 这些试探性的问句体现出双方内心对彼此身份认同的不确定性。表示建议的句子"Le's commence right away."和表示不确定的词"maybe",也体现了交谈者双方心理距离的存在。

你不会想到,一个简单的对话背后还隐藏着如此海量的信息吧。在文学作品中,语言是刻画人物的重要手段。一个优秀的作者总是能用恰当的语言准确、形象地勾勒出一个个活灵活现的人物。从语言学的角度对文学文本进行解析,给我们提供了一种更加客观的方法,可以带我们走进诗歌、戏剧、小说、散文等文学作品中的广袤天地。

术语解说

语言变体：在系统功能学派看来，语境可以分为文化语境（context of culture）和情景语境（context of situation）。人们在不同语境中，因服务于不同的交际目的，会在语言形式上产生诸多差异，这种受语境支配形成的差异就是语言变体。

话轮转换：话轮（turn）是会话中说话人和听话人完成一个角色转换的过程。在动态交际过程中，交际参与者保持说话人和听话人之间角色的不断转换，称为话轮转换（turn-taking）。

阅读思考

1. 语境和文学文本之间的关系是什么？
2. 用系统功能语言学的"语域"理论分析你感兴趣的某一堂课的老师的语言风格。

CHAPTER XXI

导读：为了计划中的演出，“国王”和“公爵”在木筏上尽心尽力地排练。他们决定在路过的阿肯色州的一个小村镇里演出，于是三人上岸张贴演出海报。哈克一边在街上闲逛，一边打量着这个村镇里破败的房屋和慵懒的村民，无意中竟目睹了一桩凶杀案……

(1) IT was after sun-up now, but we went right on and didn't tie up. The king and the duke turned out by and by looking pretty rusty; but after they'd jumped overboard and took a swim it chippered[1] them up a good deal. After breakfast the king he took a seat on the corner of the raft, and pulled off his boots and rolled up his britches, and let his legs dangle in the water, so as to be comfortable, and lit his pipe, and went to getting his *Romeo and Juliet* by heart. When he had got it pretty good him and the duke begun to practice it together. The duke had to learn him over and over again how to say every speech; and he made him sigh, and put his hand on his heart, and after a while he said he done it pretty well; "only," he says, "you mustn't bellow out *Romeo*! that way, like a bull—you must say it soft and sick and languishy[2], so—R-o-o-meo! that is the idea; for Juliet's a dear sweet mere child of a girl, you know, and she doesn't bray[3] like a jackass[4]."

(2) Well, next they got out a couple of long swords that the duke made out of oak laths, and begun to practice the sword fight—the duke called himself Richard III; and the way they laid on and pranced around the raft was grand to see. But by and by the king tripped and fell overboard, and after that they took a rest, and had a talk about all kinds of adventures they'd had in

[1] chipper /ˈtʃɪpə(r)/ v. (使)鼓起精神；(使)高兴起来

[2] 即 languish (/ˈlæŋgwɪʃ/ v. 失去活力；变得衰弱；受煎熬)

[3] bray /breɪ/ v. (驴子)嘶叫；以刺耳的高声讲话

[4] jackass /ˈdʒækæs/ n. 笨蛋；傻瓜

other times along the river.

(3) After dinner the duke says:

(4) "Well, Capet[5], we'll want to make this a first-class show, you know, so I guess we'll add a little more to it. We want a little something to answer encores[6] with, anyway."

(5) "What's onkores, Bilgewater?"

(6) The duke told him, and then says:

(7) "I'll answer by doing the Highland fling[7] or the sailor's hornpipe[8]; and you—well, let me see—oh, I've got it—you can do Hamlet's soliloquy[9]."

(8) "Hamlet's which?"

(9) "Hamlet's soliloquy, you know; the most celebrated thing in Shakespeare. Ah, it's sublime[10], sublime! Always fetches the house. I haven't got it in the book—I've only got one volume—but I reckon I can piece it out from memory. I'll just walk up and down a minute, and see if I can call it back from recollection's vaults."

(10) So he went to marching up and down, thinking, and frowning horrible every now and then; then he would hoist up his eyebrows; next he would squeeze his hand on his forehead and stagger back and kind of moan; next he would sigh, and next he'd let on to drop a tear. It was beautiful to see him. By and by he got it. He told us to give attention. Then he strikes a most noble attitude, with one leg shoved forwards, and his arms stretched away up, and his head tilted back, looking up at the sky; and then he begins to rip and rave[11] and grit his teeth[12]; and after that, all through his speech, he howled, and spread around, and swelled up his chest, and just knocked the spots out of any acting ever I see before. This is the speech—I learned it, easy enough, while he was learning it to the king:

(11) To be, or not to be; that is the bare bodkin
(12) That makes calamity of so long life;
(13) For who would fardels bear, till Birnam Wood do come to Dunsinane,
(14) But that the fear of something after death
(15) Murders the innocent sleep,
(16) Great nature's second course,

[5] 卡佩家族是法国贵族，于987—1328年统治法国，即卡佩王朝。上一章中“国王”说自己是法国皇子，故“公爵”如此称呼他。

[6] encore /ˈɒŋkɔː(r)/ *n.*（演出结束后）加演的节目；（观众喊的）再来一个

[7] 苏格兰高地舞

[8] 号笛舞（水手传统单人舞）

[9] soliloquy /səˈlɪləkwi/ *n.* 独白

[10] sublime /səˈblaɪm/ *adj.* 宏伟壮丽的；令人赞叹的

[11] rave /reɪv/ *v.* 咆哮；怒吼

[12] grit one's teeth:（生气时）咬牙切齿；咬紧牙关

(17) And makes us rather sling the arrows of outrageous fortune
(18) Than fly to others that we know not of.
(19) There's the respect must give us pause;
(20) Wake Duncan with thy knocking! I would thou couldst;
(21) For who would bear the whips and scorns of time,
(22) The oppressor's wrong, the proud man's contumely,
(23) The law's delay, and the quietus which his pangs might take,
(24) In the dead waste and middle of the night, when churchyards yawn
(25) In customary suits of solemn black,
(26) But that the undiscovered country from whose bourne no traveler returns,
(27) Breathes forth contagion on the world,
(28) And thus the native hue of resolution, like the poor cat i' the adage,
(29) Is sicklied o'er with care,
(30) And all the clouds that lowered o'er our housetops,
(31) With this regard their currents turn awry,
(32) And lose the name of action.
(33) 'Tis a consummation devoutly to be wished.
(34) But soft you, the fair Ophelia:
(35) Ope not thy ponderous and marble jaws,
(36) But get thee to a nunnery—go![13]

(37) Well, the old man he liked that speech, and he mighty soon got it so he could do it first-rate. It seemed like he was just born for it; and when he had his hand in and was excited, it was perfectly lovely the way he would rip and tear and rair up behind when he was getting it off.

(38) The first chance we got the duke he had some show bills printed; and after that, for two or three days as we floated along, the raft was a most uncommon lively place, for there warn't nothing but sword fighting and rehearsing—as the duke called it—going on all the time. One morning, when we was pretty well down the State of Arkansaw, we come in sight of a little one-horse town in a big bend; so we tied up about three-quarters of a mile above it, in the mouth of a crick which was shut in like a tunnel by the cypress trees, and all of us but Jim took the canoe and went down there to see if there was any chance in that place for our show.

(39) We struck it mighty lucky; there was going to be a

[13]"公爵"背诵的这段哈姆雷特的"独白"颠三倒四，谬误百出，夹杂了莎士比亚的《麦克白》和《查理三世》等剧的词句。另外，东拼西凑篡改名剧是十九世纪喜剧惯用的手段。

circus there that afternoon, and the country people was already beginning to come in, in all kinds of old shackly wagons, and on horses. The circus would leave before night, so our show would have a pretty good chance. The duke he hired the courthouse, and we went around and stuck up our bills. They read like this:

(40) Shaksperean Revival!!!
(41) Wonderful Attraction!
(42) For One Night Only!
(43) The world renowned tragedians,
(44) David Garrick the Younger[14], of Drury Lane Theatre London,
(45) and
(46) Edmund Kean the elder[15], of the Royal Haymarket Theatre,
(47) Whitechapel, Pudding Lane, Piccadilly, London, and the
(48) Royal Continental Theatres, in their sublime
(49) Shaksperean Spectacle entitled
(50) The Balcony Scene
(51) in
(52) Romeo and Juliet!!!
(53) Romeo...............Mr. Garrick
(54) Juliet.................Mr. Kean
(55) Assisted by the whole strength of the company!
(56) New costumes, new scenes, new appointments!
(57) Also:
(58) The thrilling, masterly, and blood-curdling
(59) Broad-sword conflict
(60) In Richard III!!!
(61) Richard III.............Mr. Garrick
(62) Richmond.............Mr. Kean
(63) Also:
(64) (by special request)
(65) Hamlet's Immortal Soliloquy!!
(66) By The Illustrious Kean!
(67) Done by him 300 consecutive nights in Paris!
(68) For One Night Only,
(69) On account of imperative European engagements!
(70) Admission 25 cents; children and servants, 10 cents.

(71) Then we went loafing around town. The stores and houses was most all old, shackly, dried up frame concerns that hadn't ever been painted; they was set up three or four foot

14 "公爵"此处冒充著名莎剧演员大卫·迦里克之子行骗。

15 爱德蒙·基恩(1787—1833),英国著名悲剧演员,擅演莎剧。

above ground on stilts[16], so as to be out of reach of the water when the river was over-flowed. The houses had little gardens around them, but they didn't seem to raise hardly anything in them but jimpson-weeds, and sunflowers, and ash piles, and old curled-up boots and shoes, and pieces of bottles, and rags, and played-out tinware. The fences was made of different kinds of boards, nailed on at different times; and they leaned every which way, and had gates that didn't generly have but one hinge[17]—a leather one. Some of the fences had been white-washed some time or another, but the duke said it was in Clumbus' time, like enough. There was generly hogs in the garden, and people driving them out.

(72) All the stores was along one street. They had white domestic awnings[18] in front, and the country people hitched their horses to the awning-posts. There was empty drygoods boxes under the awnings, and loafers roosting[19] on them all day long whittling[20] them with their Barlow knives[21]; and chawing tobacco, and gaping and yawning and stretching—a mighty ornery lot. They generly had on yellow straw hats most as wide as an umbrella, but didn't wear no coats nor waistcoats, they called one another Bill, and Buck, and Hank, and Joe, and Andy, and talked lazy and drawly[22], and used considerable many cuss words. There was as many as one loafer leaning up against every awning-post, and he most always had his hands in his britches-pockets, except when he fetched them out to lend a chaw of tobacco or scratch. What a body was hearing amongst them all the time was:

(73) "Gimme a chaw 'v tobacker, Hank."

(74) "Cain't; I hain't got but one chaw left. Ask Bill."

(75) Maybe Bill he gives him a chaw; maybe he lies and says he ain't got none. Some of them kinds of loafers never has a cent in the world, nor a chaw of tobacco of their own. They get all their chawing by borrowing; they say to a fellow, "I wisht you'd len' me a chaw, Jack, I jist this minute give Ben Thompson the last chaw I had" —which is a lie pretty much everytime; it don't fool nobody but a stranger; but Jack ain't no stranger, so he says:

(76) "*You* give him a chaw, did you? So did your sister's

[16] stilt /stɪlt/ *n.* 支柱

[17] hinge /hɪndʒ/ *n.* 铰链；合页

[18] awning /ˈɔːnɪŋ/ *n.* (门窗上面的)遮阳棚；雨篷

[19] roost /ruːst/ *v.* 栖息

[20] whittle /ˈwɪtl/ *v.* 削(木头)

[21] 一种坚实而廉价的小折刀

[22] drawly /ˈdrɔːli/ *adj.* 拉长语调的

cat's grandmother. You pay me back the chaws you've awready borry'd off'n me, Lafe Buckner, then I'll loan you one or two ton of it, and won't charge you no back intrust, nuther."

(77) "Well, I *did* pay you back some of it wunst."

(78) "Yes, you did—'bout six chaws. You borry'd store tobacker and paid back nigger-head."

(79) Store tobacco is flat black plug, but these fellows mostly chaws the natural leaf twisted. When they borrow a chaw they don't generly cut it off with a knife, but set the plug in between their teeth, and gnaw[23] with their teeth and tug at the plug with their hands till they get it in two; then sometimes the one that owns the tobacco looks mournful at it when it's handed back, and says, sarcastic:

(80) "Here, gimme the *chaw*, and you take the *plug*."

(81) All the streets and lanes was just mud; they warn't nothing else *but* mud—mud as black as tar and nigh[24] about a foot deep in some places, and two or three inches deep in *all* the places. The hogs loafed and grunted around everywheres. You'd see a muddy sow[25] and a litter of pigs come lazying along the street and whollop[26] herself right down in the way, where folks had to walk around her, and she'd stretch out and shut her eyes and wave her ears whilst the pigs was milking her, and look as happy as if she was on salary[27]. And pretty soon you'd hear a loafer sing out, "Hi! SO boy! sick him, Tige!" and away the sow would go, squealing[28] most horrible, with a dog or two swinging to each ear, and three or four dozen more a-coming; and then you would see all the loafers get up and watch the thing out of sight, and laugh at the fun and look grateful for the noise. Then they'd settle back again till there was a dog fight. There couldn't anything wake them up all over, and make them happy all over, like a dog fight—unless it might be putting turpentine[29] on a stray dog and setting fire to him, or tying a tin pan to his tail and see him run himself to death.

(82) On the river front some of the houses was sticking out over the bank, and they was bowed and bent, and about ready to tumble in,[30] The people had moved out of them. The bank

[23] gnaw /nɔː/ *v.* 咬；啃

[24] nigh /naɪ/ *adv.* 几乎；差不多

[25] sow /saʊ/ *n.* 母猪

[26] 即 wallow（/ˈwɒləʊ/ *v.* 在水或烂泥里打滚；翻滚）

[27] 瞧它一副悠闲快活的样子，好像靠领薪水过日子一样无忧无虑。（这里使用了拟人的修辞手法。）

[28] squeal /skwiːl/ *v.* 尖声长叫

[29] turpentine /ˈtɜːpəntaɪn/ *n.* 松脂；松节油

[30] 有些临河的房子，朝着河岸倒过去，弯腰鞠躬一样，都快塌到河里去了。

was caved[31] away under one corner of some others, and that corner was hanging over. People lived in them yet, but it was dangersome, because sometimes a strip of land as wide as a house caves in at a time. Sometimes a belt of land a quarter of a mile deep will start in and cave along and cave along till it all caves into the river in one summer. Such a town as that has to be always moving back, and back, and back, because the river's always gnawing at it.

(83) The nearer it got to noon that day the thicker and thicker was the wagons and horses in the streets, and more coming all the time. Families fetched their dinners with them from the country, and eat them in the wagons. There was considerable whisky drinking going on, and I seen three fights. By and by somebody sings out:

(84) "Here comes old Boggs!—in from the country for his little old monthly drunk; here he comes, boys!"[32]

(85) All the loafers looked glad; I reckoned they was used to having fun out of Boggs. One of them says:

(86) "Wonder who he's a-gwyne to chaw up this time. If he'd a-chawed up all the men he's ben a-gwyne to chaw up in the last twenty year he'd have considerable ruputation now."

(87) Another one says, "I wisht old Boggs 'd threaten me, 'cuz then I'd know I warn't gwyne to die for a thousan' year."

(88) Boggs comes a-tearing along on his horse, whooping and yelling like an Injun[33], and singing out:

(89) "Cler the track, thar. I'm on the waw-path, and the price uv coffins is a-gwyne to raise."

(90) He was drunk, and weaving about in his saddle; he was over fifty year old, and had a very red face. Everybody yelled at him and laughed at him and sassed[34] him, and he sassed back, and said he'd attend to them and lay them out in their regular turns, but he couldn't wait now because he'd come to town to kill old Colonel Sherburn, and his motto was, "Meat first, and spoon vittles to top off on."[35]

(91) He see me, and rode up and says:

(92) "Whar'd you come f'm, boy? You prepared to die?"

(93) Then he rode on. I was scared, but a man says:

[31] cave /keɪv/ v. (使)塌陷;倒塌

[32] 下面讲述的凶杀案取材于发生在马克·吐温家乡汉尼拔(Hannibal)的真实案件,彼时马克·吐温才十岁,其父是经办此案的治安法官。

[33] Injun /ˈɪndʒən/ n. 印第安人

[34] sass /sæs/ v.(美国口语)对(某人)粗鲁无礼(sass back:与某人顶嘴)

[35] "先吃肉,临了再来几勺汤。"

(94) "He don't mean nothing; he's always a-carryin' on like that when he's drunk. He's the best naturedest old fool in Arkansaw—never hurt nobody, drunk nor sober[36]."

(95) Boggs rode up before the biggest store in town, and bent his head down so he could see under the curtain of the awning and yells:

(96) "Come out here, Sherburn! Come out and meet the man you've swindled[37]. You're the houn'[38] I'm after, and I'm a-gwyne to have you, too!"

(97) And so he went on, calling Sherburn everything he could lay his tongue to, and the whole street packed with people listening and laughing and going on. By and by a proud-looking man about fifty-five—and he was a heap the best dressed man in that town, too—steps out of the store, and the crowd drops back on each side to let him come. He says to Boggs, mighty ca'm and slow—he says:

(98) "I'm tired of this, but I'll endure it till one o'clock. Till one o'clock, mind—no longer. If you open your mouth against me only once after that time you can't travel so far but I will find you."

(99) Then he turns and goes in. The crowd looked mighty sober; nobody stirred, and there warn't no more laughing. Boggs rode off blackguarding[39] Sherburn as loud as he could yell, all down the street; and pretty soon back he comes and stops before the store, still keeping it up. Some men crowded around him and tried to get him to shut up, but he wouldn't; they told him it would be one o'clock in about fifteen minutes, and so he *must* go home—he must go right away. But it didn't do no good. He cussed away with all his might, and throwed his hat down in the mud and rode over it, and pretty soon away he went a-raging down the street again, with his gray hair a-flying. Everybody that could get a chance at him tried their best to coax[40] him off of his horse so they could lock him up and get him sober; but it warn't no use—up the street he would tear again, and give Sherburn another cussing. By and by somebody says:

(100) "Go for his daughter!—quick, go for his daughter; sometimes he'll listen to her. If anybody can persuade him, she can."

[36] sober /ˈsəʊbə(r)/ *adj.* 未醉的；头脑清醒的

[37] swindle /ˈswɪndl/ *v.* 诈骗

[38] 即 hound（/haʊnd/ *n.* 猎狗）

[39] blackguard /ˈblægɑːd/ *v.* 辱骂；捣乱

[40] coax /kəʊks/ *v.* 哄劝；劝诱

(101) So somebody started on a run. I walked down street a ways and stopped. In about five or ten minutes here comes Boggs again, but not on his horse. He was a-reeling across the street towards me, bare-headed, with a friend on both sides of him a-holt of his arms and hurrying him along. He was quiet, and looked uneasy; and he warn't hanging back any, but was doing some of the hurrying himself. Somebody sings out:

(102) "Boggs!"

(103) I looked over there to see who said it, and it was that Colonel Sherburn. He was standing perfectly still in the street, and had a pistol raised in his right hand—not aiming it, but holding it out with the barrel tilted up towards the sky. The same second I see a young girl coming on the run, and two men with her. Boggs and the men turned round to see who called him, and when they see the pistol the men jumped to one side, and the pistol-barrel come down slow and steady to a level—both barrels cocked[41]. Boggs throws up both of his hands and says, "O Lord, don't shoot!" Bang! goes the first shot, and he staggers back, clawing[42] at the air—bang! goes the second one, and he tumbles backwards on to the ground, heavy and solid, with his arms spread out. That young girl screamed out and comes rushing, and down she throws herself on her father, crying, and saying, "Oh, he's killed him, he's killed him!" The crowd closed up around them, and shouldered and jammed one another, with their necks stretched, trying to see, and people on the inside trying to shove them back and shouting, "Back, back! give him air, give him air!"

(104) Colonel Sherburn he tossed his pistol on to the ground, and turned around on his heels and walked off.

(105) They took Boggs to a little drug store, the crowd pressing around just the same, and the whole town following, and I rushed and got a good place at the window, where I was close to him and could see in. They laid him on the floor and put one large Bible under his head, and opened another one and spread it on his breast; but they tore open his shirt first, and I seen where one of the bullets went in. He made about a dozen

[41] cock /kɒk/ *v.* 扣上扳机;准备射击

[42] claw /klɔː/ *v.*(用爪子或指甲)抓;挠

long gasps, his breast lifting the Bible up when he drawed in his breath, and letting it down again when he breathed it out—and after that he laid still; he was dead. Then they pulled his daughter away from him, screaming and crying, and took her off. She was about sixteen, and very sweet and gentle looking, but awful pale and scared.

(106) Well, pretty soon the whole town was there, squirming[43] and scrouging[44] and pushing and shoving to get at the window and have a look, but people that had the places wouldn't give them up, and folks behind them was saying all the time, "Say, now, you've looked enough, you fellows; 'tain't right and 'tain't fair for you to stay thar all the time, and never give nobody a chance; other folks has their rights as well as you."

(107) There was considerable jawing back,[45] so I slid out, thinking maybe there was going to be trouble. The streets was full, and everybody was excited. Everybody that seen the shooting was telling how it happened, and there was a big crowd packed around each one of these fellows, stretching their necks and listening. One long, lanky[46] man, with long hair and a big white fur stovepipe hat on the back of his head, and a crooked-handled cane, marked out the places on the ground where Boggs stood and where Sherburn stood, and the people following him around from one place to t'other and watching everything he done, and bobbing their heads to show they understood, and stooping a little and resting their hands on their thighs[47] to watch him mark the places on the ground with his cane; and then he stood up straight and stiff where Sherburn had stood, frowning and having his hat-brim down over his eyes, and sung out, "Boggs!" and then fetched his cane down slow to a level, and says "Bang!" staggered backwards, says "Bang!" again, and fell down flat on his back. The people that had seen the thing said he done it perfect; said it was just exactly the way it all happened. Then as much as a dozen people got out their bottles and treated him.

(108) Well, by and by somebody said Sherburn ought to be lynched[48]. In about a minute everybody was saying it; so away they went, mad and yelling, and snatching down every clothes-line they come to to do the hanging with.

[43] squirm /skwɜːm/ v.（因紧张、疼痛）来回扭动；坐卧不宁

[44] scrouge /skraʊdʒ/ v. 挤；推

[45] 前面的人纷纷还嘴回击

[46] lanky /ˈlæŋkɪ/ adj. 瘦长的

[47] thigh /θaɪ/ n. 大腿

[48] lynch /lɪntʃ/ v. 处以私刑

精华赏析

在关于马克·吐温及《哈克贝利·费恩历险记》的研究中,人们反复提到的是本书中方言土语及口语化语言的大量使用,使小说充满浓郁的地方色彩,散发出独特魅力。《哈克贝利·费恩历险记》在语言上的这种独特风格,是相对于常规的语言风格而言的,因此可以被视为对常规语言的变异或者偏离。

"作家在写作的过程中往往努力使自己的语言与众不同,只有超出平常的语言才能引人入胜,才能体现自己的风格。因此在分析作品的时候,就要分析作品中的变异。变异的总和就是作品的独特的风格。"(刘世生,2006:26)就变异的形式而言,我们一般可以区分语音层、书写层、词汇层、语法层以及意义层的变异。就本书而言,语音层的非常规现象俯拾皆是,例如把"just"读作"jist","haven't"读作"hain't","and"读作"en","that's"读作"dat's"等,这是本书语言最具特色的地方之一。语音层的变异忠实而有趣地描述了人物的真实生活场景,使人物妙趣横生,充满异乡情调,极富艺术感染力。

上面所举的语音层的变异在书写上的体现——"jist""hain't""en""dat's"等便可被视为书写层的变异。另外,书写层的变异还包括文本在排版、印刷、大小写、斜体和标点等语相学范畴上的非常规现象。这一点在诗歌中较为常见,如卡明斯(e. e. cummings)的诗歌"1 (a"在字母排列上的奇思妙想,而狄金森诗歌中大量出现的破折号除了表现韵律上的起伏跌宕外,还具有视觉上的审美价值。《哈克贝利·费恩历险记》中书写层的变异主要体现在斜体的使用上,例如本章中马克·吐温在描写小镇居民懒散、邋遢的生活日常时写道"Here, gimme the *chaw*, and you take the *plug*."借人一片烟叶,一口恨不得咬去一大半,作者通过"chaw"和"plug"的前后对比,形象地刻画了当地居民猥琐龌龊、爱贪小便宜的可笑嘴脸。

词汇层的变异包括新造词、方言词及古语词的使用,例如本书第十九章中单词"powwow"来源于美洲土著的一种风俗,该词的使用就极具地方特色。第十八章里"preforeordestination"是马克·吐温新造的词,由"predestination"(预定论)和"foreordination"(命中注定)合并而成,这种非常规的词汇的使用可谓寓意深远。

语法变异在本书中也很典型,例如用双重否定表示否定意义、表示复数概念的名词或代词后面跟单数谓语动词等,在此不再赘述。

语义层的变化主要是指语义的"非理性",常见于诗歌分析中。此外语义层的变异还包括语篇变异(涉及语篇的衔接与连贯、信息结构、话轮转换等)和语用变异(如违背会话原则、关联、礼貌以及面子的情况)。(刘世生,2006)例如本章中Boggs那句威风凛凛的"I'm on the waw-path, and the price uv coffins is a-gwyne to raise."这句话本意是说"棺材的价格要上涨了",似乎与当时的会话情景并无关联。Boggs这句话要表达的是"你们都让开点道儿,否则就是找死！”（想找死的人多了，棺材价格自然就高了！）可见此处语义在语用层的变异是为了顾及面子而对会话原则的违背。

在文体学研究的领域里，除了“变异说”之外，一种更加普遍的文体观是把语言的非常规现象看作是相对日常标准语言的“凸出”。我们都有这样的经验，当欣赏一幅画时，我们的注意力往往集中在画中最核心的内容上，而起衬托作用的背景往往会被忽略或遗忘，这是因为在视觉艺术中立体需要与背景区分开来。在文体分析中，语言的变异偏离“凸出”于日常标准语言这个“背景”，所以更加容易为人识别，这种现象被称为“前景化”。

在日常生活中，即使是一个诗人，也不会满口噫、兮、欤、哉，一个戏曲演员也不会天天把“梦回莺啭，乱煞年光遍”这样的词儿挂在嘴边。文学语言区别于日常生活语言就是因为它的“文学性”（literariness）。人类认知过程中存在“自动化”（automation）这一特征，换句话说，人们对生活中的许多事情（包括语言）习以为常，并不觉得有什么独特之处。而文学创作正是通过文学语言制造“陌生化”（defamiliarization），“让人们带着一种新的眼光去看事物，使人感到新鲜、惊异、陌生，从而产生强烈的美感。”（刘世生，2006：35）

《哈克贝利·费恩历险记》中语言的“前景化”现象正是这部作品语言风格的独特之处，使它在世界文学浩如烟海的作品中熠熠生辉，散发出独特魅力。马克·吐温在描写地域民俗、刻画人物上的独特语言技巧，甚至引发了美国文学语言的革命，深刻影响了二十世纪的美国文学。福克纳更是把马克·吐温当作第一个名副其实的美国作家，认为以后所有的美国作家都是他的传人。

术语解说

语相学：也叫字位学（graphology），研究对象为书面语（包括印刷体和手写体）中字体、字号、排版、标点、斜体、字母大小写以及特殊符号等在文本中的运用，分析其对文本理解产生的作用及效果。

阅读思考

1. 语言变异对文本的作用是什么？
2. 除了语言层面的变异和偏离，《哈克贝利·费恩历险记》中还表现出哪些非语言层面的前景化特征？

CHAPTER XXII

导读:舍伯恩开枪打死挑衅的博格斯后,镇上的居民纷纷朝舍伯恩家涌去,要求用私刑处罚舍伯恩。然而舍伯恩看透了这群人的懦弱和愚蠢,镇定地击溃了这帮乌合之众的心理防线。人群四分五裂,很快便夺路而逃。哈利便又溜去看镇上马戏团的表演,节目十分精彩。而此时,"国王"和"公爵"正在筹备着他们当晚的演出。

(1) THEY swarmed up towards Sherburn's house, a-whooping and yelling and raging like Injuns, and everything had to clear the way or get run over and tromped to mush, and it was awful to see. Children was heeling it ahead of the mob, screaming and trying to get out of the way; and every window along the road was full of women's heads, and there was nigger boys in every tree, and bucks and wenches[1] looking over every fence; and as soon as the mob would get nearly to them they would break and skaddle back out of reach. Lots of the women and girls was crying and taking on, scared most to death.

(2) They swarmed up in front of Sherburn's palings as thick as they could jam together, and you couldn't hear yourself think for the noise. It was a little twenty-foot yard. Some sung out "Tear down the fence! tear down the fence!" Then there was a racket of ripping and tearing and smashing, and down she goes[2], and the front wall of the crowd begins to roll in like a wave.

(3) Just then Sherburn steps out on to the roof of his little front porch, with a double-barrel gun[3] in his hand, and takes his stand, perfectly calm and deliberate, not saying a word. The racket stopped, and the wave sucked back.

(4) Sherburn never said a word—just stood there, looking

[1] buck /bʌk/ *n.* 年轻的印第安人或黑人
wench /wɛntʃ/ *n.* 少妇,乡下姑娘
此处buck和wench并列,指男男女女们。

[2] 此处使用了倒装句表强调,正常语序应为"and she goes down","she"实际指的是栅栏,画线部分的句意为:栅栏被推倒了。这个倒装句渲染了这伙人来势汹汹的气氛。

[3] a double-barrel gun: 双筒散弹枪

down. The stillness was awful creepy[4] and uncomfortable. Sherburn run his eye slow along the crowd; and wherever it struck the people tried a little to out-gaze him, but they couldn't; they dropped their eyes and looked sneaky. Then pretty soon Sherburn sort of laughed; not the pleasant kind, but the kind that makes you feel like when you are eating bread that's got sand in it.

(5) Then he says, slow and scornful:

(6) "The idea of *you* lynching[5] anybody! It's amusing. The idea of you thinking you had pluck enough to lynch a *man*[6]! Because you're brave enough to tar and feather poor friendless cast-out women that come along here, did that make you think you had grit enough to lay your hands on a *man*? Why, a *man's* safe in the hands of ten thousand of your kind — as long as it's daytime and you're not behind him.

(7) "Do I know you?[7] I know you clear through I was born and raised in the South, and I've lived in the North; so I know the average all around. The average man's a coward. In the North he lets anybody walk over him that wants to, and goes home and prays for a humble spirit to bear it.[8] In the South one man all by himself, has stopped a stage full of men in the daytime, and robbed the lot. Your newspapers call you a brave people so much that you think you are braver than any other people—whereas you're just AS brave, and no braver. Why don't your juries hang murderers? Because they're afraid the man's friends will shoot them in the back, in the dark—and it's just what they *would* do.

(8) "So they always acquit; and then a *man* goes in the night, with a hundred masked cowards at his back and lynches the rascal. Your mistake is, that you didn't bring a man with you; that's one mistake, and the other is that you didn't come in the dark and fetch your masks. You brought PART of a man—Buck Harkness, there—and if you hadn't had him to start you, you'd a taken it out in blowing.[9]

(9) "You didn't want to come. The average man don't like trouble and danger. *You* don't like trouble and danger. But if

[4] creepy /'kri:pi/ *adj.* 诡异的；令人毛骨悚然的

[5] lynch /lɪntʃ/ *v.* 处以私刑；以私刑绞死

[6] 本段使用了类文本手段（paratextual），"you""man"均为斜体，起强调作用。原文中这样的"类文本手段"较多，通常都是起强调作用。

[7] 反问（rhetorical question）

[8] 北方人会让任何想从他身上踩过去的人得逞，然后自己灰溜溜回家，关起门来祈祷上帝赐予自己谦卑精神来承受这一切。

[9] 你们只能带来巴克·哈克尼斯这个半吊子的货色——瞧，他就在那呢。要不是他鼓动你们过来，你们早就像风中散沙一样四处散了。

only *half* a man—like Buck Harkness, there—shouts 'Lynch him! lynch him!' you're afraid to back down—afraid you'll be found out to be what you are—*cowards*—and so you raise a yell, and hang yourselves on to that half-a-man's coat-tail, and come raging up here, swearing what big things you're going to do. The pitifulest thing out is a mob; that's what an army is—a mob; they don't fight with courage that's born in them, but with courage that's borrowed from their mass, and from their officers. But a mob without any *man* at the head of it is *beneath* pitifulness. Now the thing for *you* to do is to droop your tails and go home and crawl in a hole. If any real lynching's going to be done it will be done in the dark, Southern fashion; and when they come they'll bring their masks, and fetch a *man* along. Now *leave*—and take your half-a-man with you" —tossing his gun up across his left arm and cocking[10] it when he says this.

(10) The crowd washed back sudden, and then broke all apart, and went tearing off every which way, and Buck Harkness he heeled it after them, looking tolerable cheap[11]. I could a stayed if I wanted to, but I didn't want to.[12]

(11) I went to the circus and loafed around the back side till the watchman went by, and then dived in under the tent. I had my twenty-dollar gold piece and some other money, but I reckoned I better save it, because there ain't no telling how soon you are going to need it, away from home and amongst strangers that way. You can't be too careful. I ain't opposed to spending money on circuses when there ain't no other way, but there ain't no use in *wasting* it on them.

(12) It was a real bully circus. It was the splendidest[13] sight that ever was when they all come riding in, two and two, a gentleman and lady, side by side, the men just in their drawers and undershirts, and no shoes nor stirrups, and resting their hands on their thighs easy and comfortable—there must a been twenty of them—and every lady with a lovely complexion, and perfectly beautiful, and looking just like a gang of real sure-enough[14] queens, and dressed in clothes that cost millions of dollars, and just littered with diamonds. It was a powerful fine

[10] cock /kɒk/ *v.* 扣上扳机

[11] 此处大意为"看起来十分可笑"。

[12] 此句中，a 应为 have。另外，此处可明确看出哈克内心对于人群讨伐舍伯恩事件的态度。

[13] splendid 的最高级形式应为 most splendid，此处为语法错误。

[14] sure-enough 在此处意为"如假包换的，货真价实的"。

sight; I never see anything so lovely. And then one by one they got up and stood, and went a-weaving around the ring so gentle and wavy and graceful, the men looking ever so tall and airy and straight, with their heads bobbing and skimming along, away up there under the tent-roof, and every lady's rose-leafy dress flapping soft and silky around her hips, and she looking like the most loveliest parasol[15].

[15] **parasol** /ˈpærəsɒl/ *n.* 阳伞

(13) And then faster and faster they went, all of them dancing, first one foot out in the air and then the other, the horses leaning more and more, and the ringmaster going round and round the center-pole, cracking his whip and shouting "Hi!—hi!" and the clown cracking jokes behind him; and by and by all hands dropped the reins, and every lady put her knuckles on her hips and every gentleman folded his arms, and then how the horses did lean over and hump themselves! And so one after the other they all skipped off into the ring, and made the sweetest bow I ever see, and then scampered out, and everybody clapped their hands and went just about wild.

(14) Well, all through the circus they done the most astonishing things; and all the time that clown carried on so it most killed the people. The ringmaster[16] couldn't ever say a word to him but he was back at him quick as a wink with the funniest things a body ever said; and how he ever *could* think of so many of them, and so sudden and so pat, was what I couldn't noway understand. Why, I couldn't a thought of them in a year. And by and by a drunk man tried to get into the ring—said he wanted to ride; said he could ride as well as anybody that ever was. They argued and tried to keep him out, but he wouldn't listen, and the whole show come to a standstill. Then the people begun to holler at him and make fun of him, and that made him mad, and he begun to rip and tear[17]; so that stirred up the people, and a lot of men begun to pile down off of the benches and swarm towards the ring, saying, "Knock him down! throw him out!" and one or two women begun to scream. So, then, the ringmaster he made a little speech, and said he hoped there wouldn't be no disturbance, and if the man would promise he wouldn't make no

[16] **ringmaster** /ˈrɪŋmɑːstə/ *n.* 表演指导者;马戏演出指挥

[17] **rip and tear**: 横冲直撞

more trouble he would let him ride if he thought he could stay on the horse. So everybody laughed and said all right, and the man got on. The minute he was on, the horse begun to rip and tear and jump and cavort around, with two circus men hanging on to his bridle trying to hold him, and the drunk man hanging on to his neck, and his heels flying in the air every jump, and the whole crowd of people standing up shouting and laughing till tears rolled down. And at last, sure enough, all the circus men could do, the horse broke loose, and away he went like the very nation, round and round the ring, with that sot laying down on him and hanging to his neck, with first one leg hanging most to the ground on one side, and then t'other one on t'other side, and the people just crazy. It warn't funny to me, though; I was all of a tremble to see his danger. But pretty soon he struggled up astraddle and grabbed the bridle, a-reeling this way and that; and the next minute he sprung up and dropped the bridle and stood! and the horse a-going like a house afire too. He just stood up there, a-sailing around as easy and comfortable as if he warn't ever drunk in his life—and then he begun to pull off his clothes and sling them. He shed them so thick they kind of clogged up the air, and altogether he shed seventeen suits. And, then, there he was, slim and handsome, and dressed the gaudiest and prettiest you ever saw, and he lit into that horse with his whip and made him fairly hum—and finally skipped off, and made his bow and danced off to the dressing-room, and everybody just a-howling with pleasure and astonishment.[18]

(15) Then the ringmaster he see how he had been fooled, and he *was* the sickest ringmaster you ever see, I reckon. Why, it was one of his own men! He had got up that joke all out of his own head, and never let on to nobody. Well, I felt sheepish enough to be took in so, but I wouldn't a been in that ringmaster's place, not for a thousand dollars. I don't know; there may be bullier circuses than what that one was, but I never struck them yet. Anyways, it was plenty good enough for *me*; and wherever I run across[19] it, it can have all of MY custom every time.

[18] 第11—15段生动详细地记叙了哈克观看的一个马戏团表演,其中,单第14段就超过了500词。在这部作品里,哈克在漂流途中亲眼目睹了密西西比河流域的美国现实社会众生相。从这些人、事、物的描写中,我们也可以一窥当年美国社会的真实面貌。

[19] **run across**: 偶然碰见;穿过

(16) Well, that night we had *our* show; but there warn't only about twelve people there—just enough to pay expenses. And they laughed all the time, and that made the duke mad; and everybody left, anyway, before the show was over, but one boy which was asleep. So the duke said these Arkansaw lunkheads[20] couldn't come up to Shakespeare; what they wanted was low comedy—and maybe something ruther worse than low comedy, he reckoned. He said he could size their style. So next morning he got some big sheets of wrapping paper and some black paint, and drawed off some handbills, and stuck them up all over the village. The bills said:

[20] lunkhead /ˈlʌŋkhed/ *n.* 呆子;笨蛋

(17) AT THE COURT HOUSE!
(18) FOR 3 NIGHTS ONLY!
(19) The World-Renowned Tragedians
(20) DAVID GARRICK THE YOUNGER!
(21) AND
(22) EDMUND KEAN THE ELDER!
(23) Of the London and Continental
(24) Theatres,
(25) In their Thrilling Tragedy of
(26) THE KING'S CAMELEOPARD,
(27) OR
(28) THE ROYAL NONESUCH ! ! !
(29) Admission 50 cents.

(30) Then at the bottom was the biggest line of all, which said:

(31) LADIES AND CHILDREN NOT ADMITTED.[21]

[21] 妇孺严禁入内。

(32) "There," says he, "if that line don't fetch[22] them, I don't know Arkansaw!"

[22] fetch /fetʃ/ *v.* 取来

精华赏析

在这一章中我们重点分析下马克·吐温笔下小镇上人们的众生相。在第二十一章中舍伯恩杀死了博格斯。到了这一章,镇上的人一窝蜂似的涌向舍伯恩的住所要找他算账,起初他们看起来气势汹汹，“一路上大喊大骂，赛过印第安人。不管是什么东西都得闪开让道，要不然就被撞倒在地，踩得个稀巴烂，让人看了也怪害怕的”。可当这群人看到舍伯恩端着上了膛的双管枪，听了他威风凛凛的一番话后，就立刻被吓跑了。刚来的时候让人觉得势不可挡，可是没两下“这一大群人突然像潮水似的往后退去，乱纷纷就朝四下里飞奔”。马克·吐温通过这前后的强烈对比，把一群乌合之众刻画得淋漓尽致。

在这本小说中陆地和河流是相对立的，陆地上充满欺诈、凶残、暴力和死亡。比如“国王”和“公爵”的欺诈，南方贵族的仇杀，第二十一章中的凶杀案等都发生在陆地上。而小说中的河流却代表着宁静、纯洁、和谐、生机和活力。陆地和河流的意象在后面的精华赏析中还会有详细分析。这一章中我们重点分析下象征欺诈、凶残、暴力和死亡的陆地上人们的众生相。小说中除了塑造“国王”“公爵”这两个最具代表性的江湖骗子形象外，还花了大量笔墨描写了陆地上人们的众生相。

一、游手好闲的镇上人

在第二十一章中哈克他们在镇上四处闲逛，看到在沿街商铺前堆放的空木箱上赖着这样一群人，“手里拿着巴洛牌小折刀，在空木箱上来回乱削，嘴里咀嚼着烟叶子，同时还在张口打哈欠，伸伸懒腰——真是好一伙流氓。……他们唠扯起来，总是慢声慢气，拖拖沓沓，还搀着好多骂人的脏话。这样的流氓可多着呢，在每一根遮篷支柱旁边，至少就有这么一个流氓歪靠着。他差不多老让两只手插在裤兜里，只有在借别人烟叶子，或是瘙痒的时候，才把手掏出来”。从这里我们看到像这样游手好闲的人在这镇上还不是少数呢，他们非常贫穷，可是他们的贫穷完全不值得同情，全是因为自身的懒惰造成的，他们懒得说话，懒得连手都不愿从兜里掏出来，每天无精打采地混日子。除了贫穷、懒惰以外，他们还是一群残忍的家伙，为了找乐子，觉得看母猪被狗追咬都还不够，还会“给一条迷路的狗浇上松节油，点上一把火，或是在狗尾巴上拴上一只洋铁皮锅子，看着它跑累了，断了气，这时也许他们才过瘾哩”。

可以这样说，这是一群因懒惰而导致贫困的人，他们的生活毫无生气与活力，他们的内心除了空虚就只剩下残忍。

二、冷漠的“看客”

在第二十一章中博格斯被杀后有两段话详细地描写了镇上人们的反应。熙熙攘攘围了一群人，可没几个人真心关心博格斯的死活，更没有人为他的死感到悲痛，镇上的人赶过来只是来看热闹的，他们相互之间推推搡搡，想抢占一个好位置，看得清楚点。还有一个细高个、披着长头发的人活灵活现地表演了一下凶杀案的全过程，“凡是亲眼看见过的人，都说他表演得呱呱叫，跟刚发生的情景一模一样。于是，就有几十个人掏出自己的酒瓶来，请他干一杯”。这场凶杀案成了镇上人的一场精彩表演和热闹聚会。这不由得让我们想起了鲁迅的《示众》，讲的是大街上的一群人看犯人被示众的场景。鲁迅的这篇小说写得很奇，整篇都描写小巷里的人看犯人被示众，可是全文从头到尾都没有提到示众的犯人，只是大家在看，可看的是谁，看的这个犯人是男是女，其高矮胖瘦，我们一无所知。这正是鲁迅的高明之处，全文的主旨就是想告诉大家，所有来观看的人对犯人的命运是完全冷漠的。冷漠就是这篇小说的主旨。鲁迅对“看客”心态进行了无情的批判。我们不难发现，《示众》和本书第二十一章的描写有异曲同工之妙,马克·吐温和鲁迅共同描写了麻木、冷漠的"看客"形象。"看客"们的精神世界是空虚无聊的,内心是冷漠麻木的,别人的生死与他们毫无关系。

三、欺软怕硬的乌合之众

在这一章中借舍伯恩的话批判了一群欺软怕硬的乌合之众。舍伯恩嘲笑他们这群人的胆量只够捉弄流落至此地的那些可怜的弃妇们,用私刑欺负这些手无寸铁的妇女,给她们身上涂柏油、插羽毛。可是要碰上个身强力壮的男人,他们就什么也做不了了。这群乌合之众在骨子里都是贪生怕死的,哪怕被人从头上跨过去,他们也只能回家做祷告。他们习惯了逆来顺受,却要欺压弱小无助的人以获得心理上的平衡。舍伯恩还讽刺说这样一群人要是组成陪审团也是胆小如鼠,罔顾正义与法律的。"你们的陪审团为什么不敢把杀人犯都判处绞刑呢?就是因为他们害怕杀人犯的亲友们会在暗头里开枪打死他们……"。这样一群怕惹麻烦,怕冒风险的人组成的军队也是一样的乌合之众。"说到底,军队也一样——都是乌合之众;他们打起仗来,不是靠他们天生就有的勇气,而是全仗着人多势众,还有不少指挥官罢了"。从平头老百姓到陪审团,再到军队,都是欺软怕硬、贪生怕死的乌合之众。

马克·吐温对陆地上的人和事进行了无情的批判,揭露了社会生活中的种种丑恶现象:尔虞我诈、贪生怕死、冷漠无情等。可是小说不只是揭露丑恶,它还给了我们一个希望,那就是哈克。哈克纯洁、诚实,看遍陆地上种种丑恶后,仍能用一颗真诚善良的心对待他人、帮助他人,这是多么难能可贵。

经典文学作品最可贵之处不只是揭露黑暗,而是让人们看到光明和希望。正如威廉·福克纳在诺贝尔奖颁奖典礼上的致辞所说的那样"当最后一块无用的礁石在血红色的、死气沉沉的黄昏中伫立,世界末日的钟声在它上空渐渐远去时,仍然会有一个声音,那是人类仍然在用微弱但永不停息的声音说话。我拒绝接受这种情景。我相信人类不会仅仅存在,他还将胜利。人类是不朽的,这不是因为万物当中仅仅他拥有发言权,而是因为他有一个灵魂,一种有同情心、牺牲精神和忍耐力的精神。诗人、作家的责任就是书写这种精神。他们有权力升华人类的心灵,使人类回忆起过去曾经使他无比光荣的东西——勇气、荣誉、希望、自尊、同情、怜悯和牺牲,从而帮助人类生存下去。诗人的声音不应该仅仅成为人类历史的记录,更应该成为人类存在与胜利的支柱和栋梁"。

阅读思考

1. 你还读到过哪些书中的河流和这本小说中的河流有着相同的象征意义?

2. 经典文学作品对你的意义是什么?

CHAPTER XXIII

导读:在这一章中,"国王"和"公爵"忙活了半天的演出在当晚如期进行。并无真本领的两人,靠着噱头把观众骗进来后,利用他们不甘心上当的心态继续行骗,只用了三个晚上就赚到了一大笔钱。在两个骗子睡着后,哈克和吉姆聊起了天。

(1) WELL, all day him and the king was hard at it, rigging up[1] a stage and a curtain and a row of candles for footlights; and that night the house was jam full of men in no time. When the place couldn't hold no more, the duke he quit tending door and went around the back way and come on to the stage and stood up before the curtain and made a little speech, and praised up this tragedy, and said it was the most thrillingest one that ever was; and so he went on a-bragging[2] about the tragedy, and about Edmund Kean the Elder, which was to play the main principal part in it; and at last when he'd got everybody's expectations up high enough, he rolled up the curtain, and the next minute the king come a-prancing[3] out on all fours, naked; and he was painted all over, ring-streaked-and-striped, all sorts of colors, as splendid as a rainbow. And—but never mind the rest of his outfit; it was just wild, but it was awful funny. The people most killed themselves laughing; and when the king got done capering and capered off behind the scenes, they roared and clapped and stormed and haw-hawed till he come back and done it over again, and after that they made him do it another time. Well, it would make a cow laugh to see the shines that old idiot cut.[4]

(2) Then the duke he lets the curtain down, and bows to the people, and says the great tragedy will be performed only two nights more, on accounts of pressing London engagements,

[1] rig up: 安装

[2] brag /bræg/ v. 吹牛

[3] prance /prɑːns/ v. 昂首阔步;以后脚腾跃;欢腾

[4] 其实,就算一头牛看到这老笨蛋演得这么精彩也会哈哈大笑的。

where the seats is all sold already for it in Drury Lane; and then he makes them another bow, and says if he has succeeded in pleasing them and instructing them, he will be deeply obleeged if they will mention it to their friends and get them to come and see it.

（3）Twenty people sings out:

（4）"What, is it over? Is that *all*?"

（5）The duke says yes. Then there was a fine time. Everybody sings out, "Sold!" and rose up mad, and was a-going for that stage and them tragedians. But a big, fine looking man jumps up on a bench and shouts:

（6）"Hold on! Just a word, gentlemen." They stopped to listen. "We are sold—mighty badly sold. But we don't want to be the laughing stock[5] of this whole town, I reckon, and never hear the last of this thing as long as we live. NO. What we want is to go out of here quiet, and talk this show up, and sell the REST of the town! Then we'll all be in the same boat. Ain't that sensible?"（"You bet it is!—the jedge is right!" everybody sings out.）[6] "All right, then—not a word about any sell. Go along home, and advise everybody to come and see the tragedy."

（7）Next day you couldn't hear nothing around that town but how splendid that show was.[7] House was jammed again that night, and we sold this crowd the same way. When me and the king and the duke got home to the raft we all had a supper; and by and by, about midnight, they made Jim and me back her out and float her down the middle of the river, and fetch her in and hide her about two mile below town.

（8）The third night the house was crammed again—and they warn't new-comers this time, but people that was at the show the other two nights. I stood by the duke at the door, and I see that every man that went in had his pockets bulging, or something muffled up under his coat—and I see it warn't no perfumery, neither, not by a long sight. I smelt sickly eggs by the barrel, and rotten cabbages, and such things; and if I know the signs of a dead cat being around, and I bet I do, there was sixty-four of them went in. I shoved in there for a minute, but it

[5] laughing stock：笑料；笑柄

[6] 此处，Ain't 应为 Isn't；jedge 应为 judge，这里指站出来发言的这个人。

[7] 通常，我们认为双重否定表示肯定。然而在古英语以及非正式口语体中，许多时候双重否定只是起到了强调否定概念的作用，并不表达肯定的含义。这种情况在这部作品中大量存在。

was too various for me; I couldn't stand it. Well, when the place couldn't hold no more people the duke he give a fellow a quarter and told him to tend door for him a minute, and then he started around for the stage door, I after him; but the minute we turned the corner and was in the dark he says:

(9) "Walk fast now till you get away from the houses, and then shin[8] for the raft like the dickens[9] was after you!"

(10) I done it, and he done the same.[10] We struck the raft at the same time, and in less than two seconds we was gliding down stream, all dark and still, and edging towards the middle of the river, nobody saying a word. I reckoned the poor king was in for a gaudy time of it with the audience, but nothing of the sort; pretty soon he crawls out from under the wigwam[11], and says:

(11) "Well, how'd the old thing pan out[12] this time, duke?" He hadn't been up-town at all.

(12) We never showed a light till we was about ten mile below the village. Then we lit up and had a supper, and the king and the duke fairly laughed their bones loose over the way they'd served them people.

(13) The duke says:

(14) "Greenhorns, flatheads! I knew the first house would keep mum and let the rest of the town get roped in; and I knew they'd lay for us the third night, and consider it was *their* turn now. Well, it is their turn, and I'd give something to know how much they'd take for it. I *would* just like to know how they're putting in their opportunity. They can turn it into a picnic if they want to—they brought plenty provisions[13]."

(15) Them rapscallions took in four hundred and sixty-five dollars in that three nights. I never see money hauled in by the wagon-load like that before.

(16) By and by, when they was asleep and snoring, Jim says:[14]

(17) "Don't it s'prise you de way dem kings carries on, Huck?"

(18) "No," I says, "it don't."

(19) "Why don't it, Huck?"

[8] shin /ʃɪn/ *v.* 攀爬;快步走

[9] dickens /ˈdɪkɪnz/ *n.* 魔鬼

[10] 此处本应为 I have done it, and he has done the same. 此处省略了助动词 have 和 has,属于口语中不规范的省略句式。

[11] wigwam /ˈwɪgwæm/ *n.* 棚屋;简陋小屋

[12] pan out: 成功;奏效

[13] provision /prəˈviʒn/ *n.*(pl.) 食品

[14] 第 17—30 段哈克和吉姆两人的对话有着特殊的意义。在见识了"国王"和"公爵"的招摇撞骗后,吉姆突然开始主动和哈克探讨起"国王"的行事风格。他说道,"咱们遇到的这国王是个混蛋流氓,事实如此,就是不折不扣的混蛋流氓。"(第 21 段)这样的话在那个时代背景下由黑奴吉姆说出,无疑具有特别的象征意义。而哈克之后的回答更可窥得作者对于当时美国社会当权者的批判态度——"依我来看,所有的国王差不多都是流氓。"(第 22 段)。

(20) "Well, it don't, because it's in the breed. I reckon they're all alike,"

(21) "But, Huck, dese kings o' ourn is reglar rapscallions; dat's jist what dey is; dey's reglar rapscallions."

(22) "Well, that's what I'm a-saying; all kings is mostly rapscallions, as fur as I can make out."

(23) "Is dat so?"

(24) "You read about them once—you'll see. Look at Henry the Eight; this 'n 's a Sunday-school Superintendent[15] to *him*. And look at Charles Second, and Louis Fourteen, and Louis Fifteen, and James Second, and Edward Second, and Richard Third, and forty more; besides all them Saxon heptarchies[16] that used to rip around so in old times and raise Cain. My, you ought to seen old Henry the Eight[17] when he was in bloom. He was a blossom. He used to marry a new wife every day, and chop off her head next morning. And he would do it just as indifferent as if he was ordering up eggs. 'Fetch up Nell Gwynn,' he says. They fetch her up. Next morning, 'Chop off her head!' And they chop it off. 'Fetch up Jane Shore,' he says; and up she comes, Next morning, 'Chop off her head'—and they chop it off. 'Ring up Fair Rosamun.' Fair Rosamun answers the bell. Next morning, 'Chop off her head.' And he made every one of them tell him a tale every night; and he kept that up till he had hogged a thousand and one tales that way, and then he put them all in a book, and called it Domesday Book—which was a good name and stated the case. You don't know kings, Jim, but I know them; and this old rip of ourn is one of the cleanest I've struck in history. Well, Henry he takes a notion he wants to get up some trouble with this country. How does he go at it—give notice?—give the country a show? No. All of a sudden he heaves all the tea in Boston Harbor overboard, and whacks out a declaration of independence, and dares them to come on. That was HIS style—he never give anybody a chance. He had suspicions of his father, the Duke of Wellington. Well, what did he do? Ask him to show up? No—drownded him in a butt of mamsey, like a cat. S'pose people left money laying around where he was—what did he

[15] 主日学校校监

[16] heptarchy /ˈheptɑːkɪ/ *n.* 七王国；七国联盟

[17] Henry the Eight 指的是亨利八世——亨利七世和王后伊丽莎白的第三个孩子，他曾经历六次婚姻，其情人以及王后有多位来自波林家族，著名电影《波林家的女孩》便触及这段历史。亨利八世在位期间，拥有空前强大的专制权力，为资本主义的进一步发展壮大创造了有利条件。

do? He collared it. S'pose he contracted to do a thing, and you paid him, and didn't set down there and see that he done it—what did he do? He always done the other thing. S'pose he opened his mouth—what then? If he didn't shut it up powerful quick he'd lose a lie every time. That's the kind of a bug Henry was; and if we'd a had him along 'stead of our kings he'd a fooled that town a heap worse than ourn done. I don't say that ourn is lambs, because they ain't, when you come right down to the cold facts; but they ain't nothing to *that* old ram, anyway. All I say is, kings is kings, and you got to make allowances. Take them all around, they're a mighty ornery lot. It's the way they're raised." [18]

（25）"But dis one do *smell* so like de nation, Huck."

（26）"Well, they all do, Jim. We can't help the way a king smells; history don't tell no way."

（27）"Now de duke, he's a tolerble likely man in some ways."

（28）"Yes, a duke's different. But not very different. This one's a middling hard lot for a duke. When he's drunk there ain't no near-sighted man could tell him from a king."

（29）"Well, anyways, I doan' hanker for no mo' un um, Huck. Dese is all I kin stan'."

（30）"It's the way I feel, too, Jim. But we've got them on our hands, and we got to remember what they are, and make allowances. Sometimes I wish we could hear of a country that's out of kings."

（31）What was the use to tell Jim these warn't real kings and dukes? It wouldn't a done no good; and, besides, it was just as I said: you couldn't tell them from the real kind.[19]

（32）I went to sleep, and Jim didn't call me when it was my turn. He often done that.[20] When I waked up just at daybreak he was sitting there with his head down betwixt his knees, moaning and mourning to himself. I didn't take notice nor let on. I knowed what it was about. He was thinking about his wife and his children, away up yonder, and he was low and homesick; because he hadn't ever been away from home before in his life;

[18] 第19段大篇幅的语言描写是哈克的独白，比较完整地反映了哈克的观点、态度，从而呈现了哈克这个人物的性格特征。我们从中可看出三点：第一，哈克对于规则制定者或者说统治者，并不认同；第二，哈克是一个比较有见识的孩子，他提到了许多历史事件和人物，并从中得出了自己独立的观点、看法，这对于那个时代哈克这样的孩子来说是十分可贵的；第三，来自哈克视角的对于当权者的不认可，事实上也反映了作者对于当时社会制度的批判态度。

[19] 本段对于哈克的心理描写是比较重要的，它和第24段以及更前面哈克对吉姆所说的对于当权者的看法形成呼应。吉姆谈的是他们遇到的"国王"，而哈克所说的则是所有的国王，因为"you couldn' t tell them from the real kind"。此处的心理描写更进一步揭示了这部作品中所蕴含的批判现实主义精神。

[20] 这句简单的记叙，看似一笔带过，实则和段尾哈克在心中对吉姆的一句话总结形成呼应。两处都着墨不多，但都反映出了此时哈克对吉姆的评价。随着

and I do believe he cared just as much for his people as white folks does for their'n. It don't seem natural, but I reckon it's so. He was often moaning and mourning that way nights, when he judged I was asleep, and saying, "Po' little 'Lizabeth! po' little Johnny! it's mighty hard; I spec' I ain't ever gwyne to see you no mo', no mo'!" He was a mighty good nigger, Jim was.[21]

(33) But this time I somehow got to talking to him about his wife and young ones; and by and by he says:[22]

(34) "What makes me feel so bad dis time 'uz bekase I hear sumpn over yonder on de bank like a whack, er a slam, while ago, en it mine me er de time I treat my little 'Lizabeth so ornery. She warn't on'y 'bout fo' year ole, en she tuck de sk'yarlet fever, en had a powful rough spell; but she got well, en one day she was a-stannin' aroun', en I says to her, I says:

(35) "'Shet de do'.'

(36) "She never done it; jis' stood dah, kiner smilin' up at me. It make me mad; en I says agin, mighty loud, I says:

(37) "'Doan' you hear me? Shet de do'!'[23]

(38) "She jis stood de same way, kiner smilin' up. I was a-bilin'! I says:

(39) "'I lay I MAKE you mine!'

(40) "En wid dat I fetch' her a slap side de head dat sont her a-sprawlin'. Den I went into de yuther room, en 'uz gone 'bout ten minutes; en when I come back dah was dat do' a-stannin' open YIT, en dat chile stannin' mos' right in it, a-lookin' down and mournin', en de tears runnin' down. My, but I WUZ mad! I was a-gwyne for de chile, but jis' den—it was a do' dat open innerds—jis' den, 'long come de wind en slam it to, behine de chile, ker-BLAM!—en my lan', de chile never move'! My breff mos' hop outer me; en I feel so—so—I doan' know *how* I feel. I crope out, all a-tremblin', en crope aroun' en open de do' easy en slow, en poke my head in behine de chile, sof' en still, en all uv a sudden I says POW! jis' as loud as I could yell. *She never budge!* Oh, Huck, I bust out a-cryin' en grab her up in my arms, en say, 'Oh, de po' little thing! De Lord God Amighty fogive po' ole Jim, kaze he never gwyne to fogive hisself as long's he live!'

接触增多,哈克越来越看到吉姆身上的优点,并记在心里,这为之后哈克最终选择同那个时代普遍的社会道德规范决裂,帮助黑奴吉姆,埋下了伏笔。

[21] 参见批注20。

[22] 本章花了大量篇幅写哈克和吉姆在"国王"以及"公爵"睡着后的聊天,多个段落都是两人的对话。这些对话总的来说分为两部分,第一部分探讨对于"国王"的看法,我们前面已作过分析;至于第二部分,则是吉姆的回忆(第34—40段)。

[23] 此处应为Don't you hear me? Shut the door!

[24] 本段是对吉姆的语言描写段落,也是吉姆的独白段落,比较集中地反映了本章中哈克和吉姆的第二部分谈话的内容(参见批注22)。在这一部分对话中,吉姆回忆了此前因为过失而给女儿造成伤害的事情。这样长篇的独白段落可以比较完整地表现出吉姆这个人物的特征。具体来说,我们可以总结出两点:一是从表达而言,不规范的口语化用词和不规范的省略发音比较多,许多词汇甚至都不是单词,而是语音仿写。这样的表达

Oh, she was plumb deef en dumb, Huck, plumb deef en dumb—en I'd ben a-treat'n her so!" [24]

习惯和吉姆的社会地位、文化背景、受教育程度是符合的;二是从内容而言,吉姆忆及曾经伤害女儿时所表现出的痛苦、悔恨,体现出了他善良、温和、爱家人的性格特质。

精华赏析

这部作品大胆呈现出了不同于经典欧洲文学形式的、美国文学独有的新形式,标志着美国文学独立于欧洲文学的发端。符合传统语法规则的,有着浓郁美国本土特色的语言风格是美国文学独立的标志,也使得美国文学有了自己的鲜明特色。下面,我们就从三个方面来说明这部作品独特的语言风格。

一、"双重否定" 的使用

在语法学习中,我们一直熟记于心的一个规律是"双重否定等于肯定"。然而我们根据上下文语境不难推断出,这部作品中许多出现双重否定的地方实际上表达的仍然是否定性的含义,例如:"…and I see it warn't no perfumery"(第 8 段),"… but they ain't nothing to that old ram, anyway"(第 24 段),"… history don't tell no way"(第 26 段),等等。类似的情况在这部作品中可以说是随处可见。而放眼实际的日常交流抑或是影视剧中的对话片段,我们发现这样的现象也并不鲜见。

其实,双重否定句并非只表达肯定含义,而是分为三种类型:肯定型双重否定句、强调型双重否定句、委婉型双重否定句,分别执行三种功能:肯定、强调、委婉。我们这里探讨的就是第二种情况。在这类句子中,一个否定词对另一个否定词起到意义上的强调作用,即"否定 + 否定 = 强调否定"。这样的双重否定句常见于古代英语和现代英语口语。(张宏国,2004)

二、含有语法错误以及拼写错误等表达的使用

在这本书中,时态不一致,主谓不一致,人称、时态、数的错误等语法错误以及各种拼写错误,也比比皆是。

语法错误:如"when they was asleep and snoring, Jim says…"(第 16 段),"It don't seem natural"(第 32 段),"I knowed what it was about"(第 32 段)等。

拼写错误:如 deef 指 deaf, g'yirls 指 girls;又如"You bet it is! — the jedge is right!"(第 6 段)中 jedge 实为 judge;又比如"Doan' you hear me? Shet de do'!"(第 34 段)中 shet 实为 shut。

事实上,类似的错误表达几乎俯拾皆是,究其原因,并不是因为作者马克·吐温文法不精,或是他写作中有所疏忽。错误的表达本身就是作者用以塑造人物,凸显人物特征的一种手段。借由这样的方式,当时美国现实社会中混迹于底层而性格各异的一个个没有接受过

正规的语言训练,缺乏系统的教育经历的人物形象,跃然纸上。

三、口语化的表达方式的使用

这部作品是以主人公哈克的第一人称视角讲述的漂流故事,有着大量的人物对话描写,这就使其必然带有口语化的语言风格。我们从单词的选用,到不规范的、口语化的、省略发音的词汇形式,再到句式结构,都可看出这一点。例如,大量使用常见于口语的不规范词汇形式,如,用 warn't 指 wasn't 和 weren't;比如,使用不规范的、口语化的、省略发音的词汇形式,如,have 大量简写为 a,用 'em 代 them,又如之前提过的 "Doan' you hear me? Shet de do'!" 中以 Doan' 代 don't,以 de 代 the,以 do' 代 door 的情况;以及使用口语化的句式结构,如,"I done it, and he done the same" (第 10 段)等。

我们要读懂这本极具美国本土语言特色的小说,把握其语言特征可以说是必须的。《哈克贝利·费恩历险记》这本书以极具美国本土特色的语言风格向读者呈现出了一个个毫不教条、真实可信、血肉丰满的人物形象,进而反映出一个真实生动的美国社会。

阅读思考

1. 在本章的最后一段中,哈克和吉姆聊了一些什么内容?
2. 从本章最后一段的聊天中可以看出吉姆有什么样的性格特质?

CHAPTER XXIV

导读：哈克、吉姆、“公爵”和“国王”一行，乘小船继续前行。两个骗子计划再去另一个镇上试试运气，于是朝着小镇附近停靠的一艘大轮船出发，意欲伪装成从大城市乘轮船到达小镇的外地人。途中，他们偶遇要搭轮船前往奥尔良的一名年轻人，聊天时了解到附近镇上一位名叫彼得的村民刚刚去世，彼得临死前想再见自己在外地的兄弟们一面，却未能遂愿。彼得给这两位未及见上最后一面的兄弟——威廉和哈维，和生活在本地的已逝兄弟乔治的女儿们，留下了一笔遗产。

(1) NEXT day, towards night, we laid up under a little willow towhead out in the middle, where there was a village on each side of the river, and the duke and the king begun to lay out a plan for working them towns. Jim he spoke to the duke, and said he hoped it wouldn't take but a few hours, because it got mighty heavy and tiresome to him when he had to lay all day in the wigwam tied with the rope. You see, when we left him all alone we had to tie him, because if anybody happened on to him all by himself and not tied it wouldn't look much like he was a runaway nigger, you know. So the duke said it *was* kind of hard to have to lay roped all day, and he'd cipher out[1] some way to get around it.

(2) He was uncommon bright, the duke was, and he soon struck it. He dressed Jim up in King Lear's outfit—it was a long curtain-calico[2] gown, and a white horse-hair wig and whiskers[3]; and then he took his theater paint and painted Jim's face and hands and ears and neck all over a dead, dull, solid blue, like a man that's been drownded nine days. Blamed if he warn't the horriblest[4] looking outrage I ever see. Then the duke took and wrote out a sign on a shingle so:

[1] cipher out: 算出；想出

[2] calico /ˈkælɪkəʊ/ *n.*（美）印花棉布；（英）白棉布

[3] whiskers /ˈhwɪskəz/ *n.* 胡须，腮须（whisker 的复数）

[4] 应为 most horrible

(3) Sick Arab—but harmless when not out of his head.

(4) And he nailed that shingle to a lath[5], and stood the lath up four or five foot in front of the wigwam. Jim was satisfied. He said it was a sight better than lying tied a couple of years every day, and trembling all over every time there was a sound. The duke told him to make himself free and easy, and if anybody ever come meddling[6] around, he must hop out of the wigwam, and carry on a little, and fetch a howl or two like a wild beast, and he reckoned they would light out and leave him alone. Which was sound enough judgment; but you take the average man, and he wouldn't wait for him to howl. Why, he didn't only look like he was dead, he looked considerable more than that.

(5) These rapscallions wanted to try the Nonesuch[7] again, because there was so much money in it, but they judged it wouldn't be safe, because maybe the news might a worked along down by this time. They couldn't hit no project that suited exactly; so at last the duke said he reckoned he'd lay off and work his brains an hour or two and see if he couldn't put up something on the Arkansaw village; and the king he allowed he would drop over to t'other village without any plan, but just trust in Providence[8] to lead him the profitable way—meaning the devil, I reckon. We had all bought store clothes where we stopped last; and now the king put his'n on, and he told me to put mine on. I done it, of course. The king's duds[9] was all black, and he did look real swell and starchy. I never knowed how clothes could change a body before. Why, before, he looked like the orneriest old rip that ever was; but now, when he'd take off his new white beaver and make a bow and do a smile, he looked that grand and good and pious that you'd say he had walked right out of the ark, and maybe was old Leviticus[10] himself. Jim cleaned up the canoe, and I got my paddle ready. There was a big steamboat laying at the shore away up under the point, about three mile above the town—been there a couple of hours, taking on freight. Says the king:

(6) "Seein' how I'm dressed, I reckon maybe I better arrive down from St. Louis or Cincinnati, or some other big place. Go

5 lath /lɑːθ/ n. 板条；瘦人

6 meddle /ˈmedl/ v. 干预；瞎弄

7 nonesuch /ˈnɒnsʌtʃ/ n. 极为优秀的人；无双的人或物；无可匹敌者(此处指之前的演出——王室异兽。)

8 Providence /ˈprɒvɪd(ə)ns/ n. 上帝

9 duds /dʌdz/ n. 衣服；行李

10 Leviticus /liˈvitikəs/ n.《利未记》(《圣经·旧约全书》中的一卷，共27章，记载了利未族的祭司团所需谨守的一切律例。)

for the steamboat, Huckleberry; we'll come down to the village on her."

(7) I didn't have to be ordered twice to go and take a steamboat ride. I fetched the shore a half a mile above the village, and then went scooting along the bluff bank in the easy water. Pretty soon we come to a nice innocent-looking young country jake setting on a log swabbing[11] the sweat off of his face, for it was powerful warm weather; and he had a couple of big carpet-bags by him.

(8) "Run her nose in shore," says the king. I done it. "Wher' you bound for, young man?"

(9) "For the steamboat; going to Orleans."

(10) "Git aboard," says the king. "Hold on a minute, my servant 'll he'p you with them bags. Jump out and he'p the gentleman, Adolphus" —meaning me, I see.[12]

(11) I done so, and then we all three started on again. The young chap was mighty thankful; said it was tough work toting his baggage such weather. He asked the king where he was going, and the king told him he'd come down the river and landed at the other village this morning, and now he was going up a few mile to see an old friend on a farm up there. The young fellow says:

(12) "When I first see you I says to myself, 'It's Mr. Wilks, sure, and he come mighty near getting here in time.' But then I says again, 'No, I reckon it ain't him, or else he wouldn't be paddling up the river.' You *ain't* him, are you?"

(13) "No, my name's Blodgett—Elexander Blodgett—*reverend* Elexander Blodgett, I s'pose I must say, as I'm one o' the Lord's poor servants. But still I'm jist as able to be sorry for Mr. Wilks for not arriving in time, all the same, if he's missed anything by it—which I hope he hasn't." [13]

(14) "Well, he don't miss any property by it, because he'll get that all right; but he's missed seeing his brother Peter die—which he mayn't mind, nobody can tell as to that—but his brother would a give anything in this world to see *him* before he died; never talked about nothing else all these three weeks;

[11] **swab** /swɒb/ *v.* 擦拭

[12] Adolphus 是"国王"编造的人名,指的是他的"仆人"——哈克。此处"国王"装模作样地指挥"仆人"哈克提行李,煞有介事,十分自然,实为行骗老手。

[13] 本段为"国王"和年轻人的对话。"国王"给自己随口编了一个新名字,并声称自己是一名牧师——上帝的仆人"the Lord' s poor servants"。谎言信手拈来,极为熟练,如果真有这样的仆人的话,上帝估计也会气死吧。本章中有大量"国王"的直接引语,将骗子无耻又滑稽的形象塑造得活灵活现。

hadn't seen him since they was boys together—and hadn't ever seen his brother William at all—that's the deef and dumb one—William ain't more than thirty or thirty-five. Peter and George were the only ones that come out here; George was the married brother; him and his wife both died last year. Harvey and William's the only ones that's left now; and, as I was saying, they haven't got here in time."

(15) "Did anybody send 'em word?"

(16) "Oh, yes; a month or two ago, when Peter was first took; because Peter said then that he sorter felt like he warn't going to get well this time. You see, he was pretty old, and George's g'yirls was too young to be much company for him, except Mary Jane, the red-headed one; and so he was kinder lonesome after George and his wife died, and didn't seem to care much to live. He most desperately wanted to see Harvey—and William, too, for that matter—because he was one of them kind that can't bear to make a will. He left a letter behind for Harvey, and said he'd told in it where his money was hid, and how he wanted the rest of the property divided up so George's g'yirls would be all right—for George didn't leave nothing. And that letter was all they could get him to put a pen to."

(17) "Why do you reckon Harvey don't come? Wher' does he live?"

(18) "Oh, he lives in England—Sheffield—preaches there—hasn't ever been in this country. He hasn't had any too much time—and besides he mightn't a got the letter at all, you know."

(19) "Too bad, too bad he couldn't a lived to see his brothers, poor soul. You going to Orleans, you say?"

(20) "Yes, but that ain't only a part of it. I'm going in a ship, next Wednesday, for Ryo Janeero, where my uncle lives."

(21) "It's a pretty long journey. But it'll be lovely; wisht[14] I was a-going. Is Mary Jane the oldest? How old is the others?"

(22) "Mary Jane's nineteen, Susan's fifteen, and Joanna's about fourteen—that's the one that gives herself to good works and has a hare-lip."

[14] 应为 wished

(23) "Poor things! to be left alone in the cold world so."

(24) "Well, they could be worse off. Old Peter had friends, and they ain't going to let them come to no harm. There's Hobson, the Babtis' preacher; and Deacon Lot Hovey, and Ben Rucker, and Abner Shackleford, and Levi Bell, the lawyer; and Dr. Robinson, and their wives, and the widow Bartley, and—well, there's a lot of them; but these are the ones that Peter was thickest with, and used to write about sometimes, when he wrote home; so Harvey 'll know where to look for friends when he gets here."

(25) Well, the old man went on asking questions till he just fairly emptied that young fellow. Blamed if he didn't inquire about everybody and everything in that blessed town, and all about the Wilkses; and about Peter's business—which was a tanner; and about George's—which was a carpenter; and about Harvey's—which was a dissentering[15] minister; and so on, and so on. Then he says:

(26) "What did you want to walk all the way up to the steamboat for?"

(27) "Because she's a big Orleans boat, and I was afeard she mightn't stop there. When they're deep they won't stop for a hail. A Cincinnati boat will, but this is a St. Louis one."

(28) "Was Peter Wilks well off?"

(29) "Oh, yes, pretty well off. He had houses and land, and it's reckoned he left three or four thousand in cash hid up som'ers."

(30) "When did you say he died?"

(31) "I didn't say, but it was last night."

(32) "Funeral to-morrow, likely?"

(33) "Yes, 'bout the middle of the day."

(34) "Well, it's all terrible sad; but we've all got to go, one time or another. So what we want to do is to be prepared; then we're all right."

(35) "Yes, sir, it's the best way. Ma used to always say that."

(36) When we struck the boat she was about done loading,

[15] **dissent** /dɪˈsent/ *v.* 不同意；对东正教教义不遵循
dissenter /dɪˈsentə(r)/ *n.* 持异议者；反对者
此处应该使用 dissenting，表“非国教派的，不信奉国教的”之意。

and pretty soon she got off. The king never said nothing about going aboard, so I lost my ride, after all. When the boat was gone the king made me paddle[16] up another mile to a lonesome place, and then he got ashore and says:

(37) "Now hustle back, right off, and fetch the duke up here, and the new carpet-bags. And if he's gone over to t'other side, go over there and git him. And tell him to git himself up regardless. Shove[17] along, now."

(38) I see what *he* was up to; but I never said nothing, of course. When I got back with the duke we hid the canoe, and then they set down on a log, and the king told him everything, just like the young fellow had said it—every last word of it. And all the time he was a-doing it he tried to talk like an Englishman; and he done it pretty well, too, for a slouch. I can't imitate him, and so I ain't a-going to try to; but he really done it pretty good. Then he says:

(39) "How are you on the deef and dumb[18], Bilgewater?"

(40) The duke said, leave him alone for that;[19] said he had played a deef and dumb person on the histronic boards. So then they waited for a steamboat.

(41) About the middle of the afternoon a couple of little boats come along, but they didn't come from high enough up the river; but at last there was a big one, and they hailed her. She sent out her yawl, and we went aboard, and she was from Cincinnati; and when they found we only wanted to go four or five mile they was booming mad, and gave us a cussing[20], and said they wouldn't land us. But the king was ca'm. He says:

(42) "If gentlemen kin afford to pay a dollar a mile apiece to be took on and put off in a yawl, a steam-boat kin afford to carry 'em, can't it?"

(43) So they softened down and said it was all right; and when we got to the village they yawled[21] us ashore. About two dozen men flocked down when they see the yawl a-coming, and when the king says:

(44) "Kin any of you gentlemen tell me wher' Mr. Peter Wilks lives?" they give a glance at one another, and nodded

[16] paddle /ˈpæd(ə)l/ v. 划桨；戏水；涉水

[17] shove /ʃʌv/ v. 挤；撞；猛推

[18] 此处应为 deaf and dumb，指又聋又哑。这里使用了头韵（alliteration）的修辞手法。

[19] 公爵说，只管交给他就是了。

[20] cuss /kʌs/ v. 诅咒；咒骂

[21] yawl /jɔːl/ v. 驾驶船载小艇（小帆船）

their heads, as much as to say, "What d' I tell you?" Then one of them says, kind of soft and gentle:

(45) "I'm sorry sir, but the best we can do is to tell you where he *did* live yesterday evening."

(46) Sudden as winking the ornery old cretur went an to smash, and fell up against the man, and put his chin on his shoulder, and cried down his back, and says:

(47) "Alas[22], alas, our poor brother—gone, and we never got to see him; oh, it's too, too hard!" [23]

(48) Then he turns around, blubbering, and makes a lot of idiotic signs to the duke on his hands, and blamed if he didn't drop a carpet-bag and bust out a-crying. If they warn't the beatenest lot, them two frauds, that ever I struck.

(49) Well, the men gathered around and sympathized with them, and said all sorts of kind things to them, and carried their carpet-bags up the hill for them, and let them lean on them and cry, and told the king all about his brother's last moments, and the king he told it all over again on his hands to the duke, and both of them took on about that dead tanner like they'd lost the twelve disciples. Well, if ever I struck anything like it, I'm a nigger. It was enough to make a body ashamed of the human race.[24]

[22] alas /ə'læs/ *int.* 唉(表悲伤、遗憾、恐惧、关切等语气)

[23] 本段及本章接近尾声的多个段落均为"国王"和"公爵"两人商量如何敛财的对话,使用了大量直接引语。此处的直接引语将骗子的无耻、贪婪生动直观地呈现在读者面前。

[24] 呃,我发誓我要是见过这么不要脸的玩意儿,就让我变成个黑奴吧。这可真是足以让任何人都为之羞愧的人性的堕落啊。

精华赏析

人类一直有着一种崇拜英雄的情结,几乎深入血液。早期人类生产力水平低下,靠天吃饭,所以崇拜神,敬畏各种自然之力;随着科技的发展,虽然生产力水平日益增长,人类却依然怀有这样的英雄情结,普遍在内心深处渴望成为某种意义上的英雄,或是希冀着能有某位英雄拯救自己于水火。前者常见于各类励志文学以及影视作品,后者更是许多热卖的美国大片所钟爱的主题,例如,"钢铁侠""蜘蛛侠""绿灯侠"……

而所谓的"反英雄",顾名思义,指违反了常规,颠覆了人们传统认知的"英雄"。"反英雄"的形象事实上和"英雄"的形象一样,常常出现在各种神话传说、文学以及影视作品中,例如,大闹天宫的孙悟空;又如,闹海的哪吒;还如,许多不畏强权揭竿起义的英雄好汉……而这部作品中的主人公哈克贝利·费恩,便是美国文学史上最早的反英雄形象之一。即便是今天，我们读到这部作品中的许多情节时，也常常会感叹于哈克的“不同于常人”。例如，寡妇道格拉斯收养哈克，心疼他的漂泊，给他稳定的生活，教他礼仪，让他接受教育，然而他却觉得浑身不自在，无聊至极，甚至“恨不得死了算了”（本书第一章）。又比如，哈克逃学厌学；还比如，哈克对于沃森小姐口中的“bad place”——地狱，充满了向往，反而对于遵守各种社会礼仪、规则，按部就班地去生活，感到十分痛苦；再比如，哈克对之前得到的一笔巨款——六千金币，并不看重，甚至急于将这笔钱送给撒切尔法官。读到这里，我想，不论是书中的法官撒切尔，还是作为读者的我们都免不了大吃一惊吧，那可是六千金币啊！

哈克是个“好孩子”吗？他不爱读书，常常逃学，行、走、坐、卧，皆不合礼仪。那哈克是个“乖孩子”吗？他热爱漂泊，宁愿漂流在衣食不定的密西西比河上，也不愿意安稳地生活在寡妇道格拉斯家中。哈克选择漂流，一部分是因为酗酒父亲的暴虐，更大的原因是他并不喜欢循规蹈矩的生活，甚至到了故事的结尾处，他仍然拒绝被萨利姨妈收养、教化，于是偷偷溜走。那么，哈克是个“坏孩子”吗？他生活在社会的底层，却对金钱不甚在意，为了避免麻烦还迫不及待地将自己获得的大笔财富赠予他人；他机智、勇敢、心地善良，保护了单纯的玛丽·珍妮姐妹，更重要的是，他一路保护并帮助了一个被当时的社会制度压迫在社会最底层的黑人奴隶——吉姆。

这样的一个人物形象，无论是从二十世纪欧洲抑或美国的社会价值标准的角度来看，还是用当今世界的眼光来审视，都颇有些离经叛道，也都很难简单地去界定他是一个“好孩子”或“坏孩子”。然而，有一点却十分确定，我们在惊讶于哈克之不走寻常路的同时，也必须承认他的聪明机智；我们在得出哈克并非传统意义上的“好孩子”这个结论的同时，也很难否认他善良、富有正义感又勇敢。我们发现，在哈克的心中，他与许多当时美国主流的价值观以及行为规范都无法产生共鸣，而是有着自己的基于直觉和体验的价值认定标准；然而，他又具备着传统主流价值观所一直倡导的诸如“善良、正直、聪慧”这样的可贵品质。

简而言之，一方面，哈克身上具备着一般英雄所具备的一些可贵优秀的品质，却又在某些方面，其所想所为和当时的社会通行规则、价值取向所认定的想法和做法背道而驰……而这，正是一个“反英雄”的典型特征。哈克身上这种“反英雄”的特征，这种对于当时美国社会通行社会规范、道德价值取向的“反叛”，增强了本书的现实批判意义，深化了作品的主题。可以说，哈克这位“反英雄”主人公之于当时美国社会制度和规范的反叛，正是这部作品具有深刻的现实批判意义，成为一部伟大的文学作品的重要原因之所在。

术语解说

反英雄：所谓反英雄，指的是“在人物和世界的关系上都是被现实压倒的人物，他们虽然具有善良的品质，但是他们实现自己理想的任何努力都受到生活的讽刺，使他们在世界上不是扮演小丑的角色，就是成为无能为力的受难者。”（贾中华，1997）但尽管消极、滑稽、荒谬，他们还是有着一些传统英雄的特点：“他们都是追求高尚品质的探索者，他们虽然在思想和行动上缺少重大的旨趣，然而都因为追求人的尊严而获得了高尚的品格……他们总是丢不掉自己的信念：生活的价值取决于它的尊严，而不是取决于它的成功。”（郭宏安，1983：484）

阅读思考

1. 你认为从本章中“国王”的直接引语部分可以看出他有怎样的性格特征？

2. 找出几处“国王”说话时的行为动作描写，并分析这类描写对于塑造人物起到了什么样的作用。

EXERCISE IV

I. Oral presentation.

1. 在本书第十九章中，哈克和吉姆遇到了“公爵”和“国王”两人，两个骗子策划了演出以骗取钱财。请选取你喜爱的一部戏剧或者影视作品中的片段，或者自拟剧本，进行演出。
2. 假设你和同学参加了赴美暑假夏令营。你们都是《哈克贝利·费恩历险记》的书迷，于是两人决定按照哈克漂流的路线旅行。请参考以下表达和你的朋友商量旅游攻略，并陈述理由。

   How much is the fare to…?

   Is there a bus/flight/ship to…?

   Can we get to… on the bus/flight/ship?

   When will… stop for lunch?

   How many stops are there on the way to…?

   Where can we buy…?

II. Choose the correct words to complete the sentences.

1. He sat on the edge with his legs _____ over the side.
   A. dangling　B. shaking　C. swinging　D. moving
2. Our camping trip was _____ by bad weather.
   A. spilled　B. slipped　C. slid　D. spoiled
3. He _____ into the water to push the boat out.
   A. wandered　B. waded　C. wondered　D. swam
4. After a long siege, the town was forced to _____.
   A. move　B. yield　C. collapse　D. break
5. Although I soon ____ him of my innocence, I think he still has serious doubts about my sanity.
   A. reminded　B. believed　C. convinced　D. persuaded
6. We manage to _____ six people into the car.
   A. convince　B. squeeze　C. push　D. pull
7. After lunch, she watched, listened and ____ Bobby into talking about himself.
   A. persuaded　B. take　C. coated　D. coaxed
8. People _____ to the stores, buying up everything in sight.
   A. swarmed　B. swam　C. slipped　D. glided
9. No computer can _____ the complex functions of the human brain.
   A. take　B. damage　C. imitate　D. destroy

10. He tried to ____ the alarm clock by putting it under his pillow.
    A. throw   B. reduce   C. destroy   D. muffle

III. Fill in the blanks with suitable prepositions.

1. You have to account _____ what you did yesterday.
2. Students were asked to learn these poems _____ heart.
3. There would be great change in this place _____ no time.
4. The supermarket was packed _____ people who wanted to buy fresh water.
5. They succeeded _____ finishing this project after a year's hard work.

IV. Answer the following questions.

Questions on the content

1. What the figures of speech are in this sentence "We used to watch the stars that fell, too, and see them streak down. Jim allowed they'd got spoiled and was hove out of the nest." ? (Chapter XIX)
2. Do you know the real identity of the king and the duke?
3. What kind of man were the king and the duck? How were the king and the duke contrasted with Huck and Jim in every aspect?
4. In Chapter XXI, why did the king and the duke rehearse together?
5. From Paragraph 71 to 72 in Chapter XXI, what do you know about this town?
6. In Chapter XXII, why did people swarm up towards Sherburn's house? What happened later?
7. In fact it's a terrible show. But "Next day you couldn't hear nothing around that town but how splendid that show was." Why? (Chapter XXII)
8. Why did the king go on asking question till he just fairly emptied that young fellow? What was the king's plan? (Chapter XXIV)

Questions on the structure and style

1. What are the characteristics of the language used by the king?
2. There are many ironies in this novel. Try to point them out. Are all of them used appropriately and effectively in this novel? Illustrate your ideas with examples.
3. What are the striking characteristics of Mark Twain's writing style in this novel?
4. What is the main idea of Chapter XXII? In this chapter, what do you know about people in this town? Why did the crowd wash back sudden?
5. What is the plot of Chapter XXI? When does the plot reach its climax in this chapter?

V. Translate the following sentences into Chinese by using division.

1. We judged we could make miles enough that night to get out of the reach of the powwow we reckoned the duke's work in the printing office was going to make in that little town; then we could boom right along if we wanted to. (Chapter XX)

2. We come to a little flat piece of land which as dry and very thick with trees and bushed and vine. (Chapter XVIII)
3. …and they all went in a big parlor that had a new rag carpet on the floor, and got together in a corner that was out of range of the front windows—there warn't none on the side. (Chapter XVII)
4. He stormed right along, and said any man that pretended to be an Englishman and couldn't imitate the lingo no better than what he did was a fraud and a liar. (Chapter XXV)
5. He was the softest, glidingest, stealthiest man I ever see; and there warn't no more smile to him than there is to a ham. (Chapter XXVII)
6. I says to myself I reckon a body that ups and tells the truth when he is in a tight place is taking considerable many resks, though I ain't had no experience, and can't say for certain; but it looks so to me, anyway; and yet here's a case where I's blest if it don't look to me like the truth is better and actualy safer than a lie. (Chapter XXVIII)
7. When he got a-front of us he lifts his hat ever so gracious and dainty, like it was the lid of a box that had butterflies asleep in I and he didn't want to disturb them. (Chapter XXXIII)
8. And what's more—if I was one of them I would see a man in Jericho before I would drop my business and come to him for the rubbing of an old tin lamp. (Chapter III)
9. Anyhow, there's one thing—there's more honor in getting him out through a lot of difficulties and dangers, where there warn't one of them furnished to you by people who it was their duty to furnish them, and you had to contrive them all out of your own head. (Chapter XXXV)
10. Poor thing, many's the time I made myself go up to the little room that used to be hers and get out her poor old scrapbook and read in it when her pictures had been aggravating me and I had soured on her a little. (Chapter XVII)

VI. Sensory details in writing.

A descriptive essay is generally developed through sensory details including sight, hearing, taste, smell and touch, which can actually visualize the things being described. In Chapter XX, there is a successful description of storm on the Mississippi with multiple sensory details.

Sensory details of sight:

And every second or two there'd come a glare that lit up the white-caps for a half a mile around, and you'd see the islands looking dusty through the rain, and the trees thrashing around in the wind.

Sensory details of hearing:

Then comes a *h-whack*!—bum! bum! bumble-umble-um-bum-bum-bum-bum—and the thunder would go rumbling and grumbling away, and quit—and then *rip* comes another flash and another sockdolager.

Writing task: describe a pleasant night scene in the countryside with multiple sensory details.

CHAPTER XXV

导读:"国王""公爵"以及哈克和吉姆一行,顺利到达了彼得所在的村子。由此,拉开了一场他们伪装成为"威廉"和"哈维"——彼得的两位身在外地的兄弟,来骗取遗产的大戏。四人的到来令聚集的人群激动起来,人们簇拥着他们一同来到彼得的家,见到了彼得的三个侄女。两个骗子开始哭天抢地,极尽所能地表演,赢得了几乎所有人的信任。

(1) THE news was all over town in two minutes, and you could see the people tearing down on the run from every which way, some of them putting on their coats as they come. Pretty soon we was in the middle of a crowd, and the noise of the tramping[1] was like a soldier march. The windows and dooryards was full; and every minute somebody would say, over a fence:

(2) "Is it *them*?"

(3) And somebody trotting along with the gang would answer back and say:

(4) "You bet it is."

(5) When we got to the house the street in front of it was packed, and the three girls was standing in the door. Mary Jane *was* red-headed, but that don't make no difference,[2] she was most awful beautiful, and her face and her eyes was all lit up like glory, she was so glad her uncles was come. The king he spread his arms, and Mary Jane she jumped for them, and the hare-lip[3] jumped for the duke, and there they *had* it! Everybody most, leastways women, cried for joy to see them meet again at last and have such good times.

(6) Then the king he hunched the duke private—I see him do it—and then he looked around and see the coffin, over in

[1] **tramp** /'træmpiŋ/ *v.* (长途)跋涉;踩;踏

[2] 此处又是双重否定并不表示肯定的一个例子。实际指的是玛丽·珍妮的红发并不影响她的美貌。

[3] **hare lip**: 唇裂;兔唇

the corner on two chairs; so then him and the duke, with a hand across each other's shoulder, and t'other hand to their eyes, walked slow and solemn[4] over there, everybody dropping back to give them room, and all the talk and noise stopping, people saying "Sh!" and all the men taking their hats off and drooping their heads, so you could a heard a pin fall. And when they got there they bent over and looked in the coffin, and took one sight, and then they bust out a-crying so you could a heard them to Orleans,[5] most; and then they put their arms around each other's necks, and hung their chins over each other's shoulders; and then for three minutes, or maybe four, I never see two men leak the way they done.[6] And, mind you, everybody was doing the same; and the place was that damp I never see anything like it. Then one of them got on one side of the coffin, and t'other on t'other side, and they kneeled down and rested their foreheads on the coffin, and let on to pray all to themselves. Well, when it come to that it worked the crowd like you never see anything like it, and everybody broke down and went to sobbing right out loud[7]—the poor girls, too; and every woman, nearly, went up to the girls, without saying a word, and kissed them, solemn, on the forehead, and then put their hand on their head, and looked up towards the sky, with the tears running down, and then busted out and went off sobbing and swabbing, and give the next woman a show. I never see anything so disgusting.

(7) Well, by and by the king he gets up and comes forward a little, and works himself up and slobbers[8] out a speech, all full of tears and flapdoodle[9] about its being a sore trial for him and his poor brother to lose the diseased, and to miss seeing diseased alive after the long journey of four thousand mile, but it's a trial that's sweetened and sanctified to us by this dear sympathy and these holy tears, and so he thanks them out of his heart and out of his brother's heart, because out of their mouths they can't, words being too weak and cold, and all that kind of rot and slush[10], till it was just sickening; and then he blubbers[11] out a pious goody-goody Amen, and turns himself loose and goes to crying fit to bust.

[4] **solemn** /ˈsɒləm/ *adj.* 庄严的；严肃的；隆重的；郑重的

[5] 此处使用了夸张手法（hyperbole），两个骗子戏演得之夸张，骗人时之倾尽全力，和作者语言风格之幽默均可见一斑。

[6] 注意此处动词用的是leak，哈克心中对二人眼泪的态度不言自明。这一句话描述两个骗子假装痛苦流泪，举止夸张。

[7] 此处记叙两个骗子假装哀恸悼念的一系列动作和周围人的反应。注意，谈及周围群众反应时，作者使用了动词work，这个词虽简单但十分传神地表明了俩骗子装模作样的言行是为了达到其目的——煽动围观群众的情绪，博取信任。

[8] **slobber** /ˈslɒbə/ *v.* 流口水；情不自禁地说

[9] **flapdoodle** /ˈflæpduːd(ə)l/ *n.* 瞎话；梦话；胡说

[10] **slush** /slʌʃ/ *n.* 烂泥；污水；胡说八道

[11] **blubber** /ˈblʌbə/ *v.* 哭泣；又哭又闹

(8) And the minute the words were out of his mouth somebody over in the crowd struck up the doxolojer, and everybody joined in with all their might, and it just warmed you up and made you feel as good as church letting out. Music is a good thing; and after all that soul-butter and hogwash[12] I never see it freshen up things so, and sound so honest and bully.

(9) Then the king begins to work his jaw again,[13] and says how him and his nieces would be glad if a few of the main principal friends of the family would take supper here with them this evening, and help set up with the ashes of the diseased; and says if his poor brother laying yonder could speak he knows who he would name, for they was names that was very dear to him, and mentioned often in his letters; and so he will name the same, to wit, as follows, vizz.:—Rev. Mr. Hobson, and Deacon Lot Hovey, and Mr. Ben Rucker, and Abner Shackleford, and Levi Bell, and Dr. Robinson, and their wives, and the widow Bartley.

(10) Rev. Hobson and Dr. Robinson was down to the end of the town a-hunting together—that is, I mean the doctor was shipping a sick man to t'other world, and the preacher was pinting him right. Lawyer Bell was away up to Louisville on business. But the rest was on hand, and so they all come and shook hands with the king and thanked him and talked to him; and then they shook hands with the duke and didn't say nothing, but just kept a-smiling and bobbing their heads like a passel[14] of sapheads whilst he made all sorts of signs with his hands and said "Goo-goo—goo-goo-goo" all the time, like a baby that can't talk.

(11) So the king he blattered[15] along, and managed to inquire about pretty much everybody and dog in town, by his name, and mentioned all sorts of little things that happened one time or another in the town, or to George's family, or to Peter. And he always let on that Peter wrote him the things; but that was a lie: he got every blessed one of them out of that young flathead[16] that we canoed up to the steamboat.

(12) Then Mary Jane she fetched the letter her father left behind, and the king he read it out loud and cried over it. It give

[12] hogwash /ˈhɒgwɒʃ/ *n.* 猪食；废话

[13] 此处再度使用了动词work，表现出"国王"不走心的胡说八道。马克·吐温高超写作技巧之一大特点，便是能用简单常见的词汇生动形象地记叙事件，描绘景物，刻画人物。

[14] passel /ˈpæs(ə)l/ *n.* 一批；一群

[15] blatter /ˈblætə/ *v.* 唠叨；滔滔不绝地说

[16] flathead /ˈflæthed/ *n.* 傻瓜，容易受骗的人

the dwelling-house and three thousand dollars, gold, to the girls; and it give the tanyard (which was doing a good business), along with some other houses and land (worth about seven thousand), and three thousand dollars in gold to Harvey and William, and told where the six thousand cash was hid, down cellar. So these two frauds said they'd go and fetch it up, and have everything square and above-board[17]; and told me to come with a candle. We shut the cellar door behind us, and when they found the bag they spilt it out on the floor, and it was a lovely sight, all them yaller-boys[18]. My, the way the king's eyes did shine! He slaps the duke on the shoulder and says:

(13) "Oh, *this* ain't bully nor noth'n! Oh, no, I reckon not! Why, Billy, it beats the Nonesuch, *don't* it?"

(14) The duke allowed it did. They pawed the yaller-boys, and sifted them through their fingers and let them jingle down on the floor; and the king says:

(15) "It ain't no use talkin'; bein' brothers to a rich dead man and representatives of furrin heirs that's got left is the line for you and me, Bilge. Thish yer comes of trust'n to Providence. It's the best way, in the long run. I've tried 'em all, and ther' ain't no better way."

(16) Most everybody would a been satisfied with the pile, and took it on trust; but no, they must count it. So they counts it, and it comes out four hundred and fifteen dollars short. Says the king:

(17) "Dern him, I wonder what he done with that four hundred and fifteen dollars?"

(18) They worried over that awhile, and ransacked all around for it. Then the duke says:

(19) "Well, he was a pretty sick man, and likely he made a mistake—I reckon that's the way of it. The best way's to let it go, and keep still about it. We can spare it."

(20) "Oh, shucks, yes, we can *spare* it. I don't k'yer noth'n 'bout that[19]—it's the *count* I'm thinkin' about. We want to be awful square and open and above-board here, you know. We want to lug this h-yer money up stairs and count it before

[17] 此处意为“公开公平地”俩骗子嘴上说得道貌岸然，实际心里想的却都是如何霸占遗产。

[18] yaller的意思为“黄色的”，这里yaller-boys指的是黄灿灿的金币。

[19] 这句话其实应写为“I don't care nothing about that”，表达否定的含义。

everybody—then ther' ain't noth'n suspicious. But when the dead man says ther's six thous'n dollars, you know, we don't want to—"

(21) "Hold on," says the duke. "Le's make up the deffisit," and he begun to haul out yaller-boys out of his pocket.

(22) "It's a most amaz'n' good idea, duke—you *have* got a rattlin' clever head on you," says the king. "Blest if the old Nonesuch ain't a heppin' us out agin," and *he* begun to haul out yaller-jackets and stack them up.

(23) It most busted them, but they made up the six thousand clean and clear.[20]

(24) "Say," says the duke, "I got another idea. Le's go up stairs and count this money, and then take and GIVE IT TO THE GIRLS."

(25) "Good land, duke, lemme hug you! It's the most dazzling idea 'at ever a man struck. You have cert'nly got the most astonishin' head I ever see. Oh, this is the boss dodge, ther' ain't no mistake 'bout it. Let 'em fetch along their suspicions now if they want to—this 'll lay 'em out."

(26) When we got up-stairs everybody gethered around the table, and the king he counted it and stacked it up, three hundred dollars in a pile—twenty elegant little piles. Everybody looked hungry at it, and licked their chops. Then they raked[21] it into the bag again, and I see the king begin to swell himself up for another speech. He says:

(27) "Friends all, my poor brother that lays yonder[22] has done generous by them that's left behind in the vale of sorrers. He has done generous by these yer poor little lambs that he loved and sheltered, and that's left fatherless and motherless. Yes, and we that knowed him knows that he would a done MORE generous by 'em if he hadn't ben afeard o' woundin' his dear William and me. Now, *wouldn't* he? Ther' ain't no question 'bout it in MY mind. Well, then, what kind o' brothers would it be that 'd stand in his way at sech a time? And what kind o' uncles would it be that 'd rob—yes, ROB—sech poor sweet lambs as these 'at he loved so at sech a time? If I know

[20] **bust** /bʌst/ *v.* 使破产；猛烈打击
本句中 clean and clear 使用了头韵（alliteration）的修辞手法，渲染了两个骗子决定补齐钱财差额以获取充分信任的决心。

[21] **rake** /reɪk/ *v.* 用耙子耙；（用树枝或手指甲）刮擦

[22] **yonder** /ˈjɒːndə/ *adv.* （过时语言或方言）那里，在那边

William—and I *think* I do—he—well, I'll jest ask him." He turns around and begins to make a lot of signs to the duke with his hands, and the duke he looks at him stupid and leather-headed a while; then all of a sudden he seems to catch his meaning, and jumps for the king, goo-gooing with all his might for joy, and hugs him about fifteen times before he lets up.[23] Then the king says, "I knowed it; I reckon *that*'ll convince anybody the way *he* feels about it. Here, Mary Jane, Susan, Joanner, take the money—take it *all*. It's the gift of him that lays yonder, cold but joyful."[24]

(28) Mary Jane she went for him, Susan and the hare-lip went for the duke, and then such another hugging and kissing I never see yet. And everybody crowded up with the tears in their eyes, and most shook the hands off of them frauds, saying all the time:

(29) "You *dear* good souls!—how lovely!—how could you!"

(30) Well, then, pretty soon all hands got to talking about the diseased again, and how good he was, and what a loss he was, and all that; and before long a big iron-jawed man worked himself in there from outside, and stood a-listening and looking, and not saying anything; and nobody saying anything to him either, because the king was talking and they was all busy listening. The king was saying—in the middle of something he'd started in on—

(31) "—they bein' partickler friends o' the diseased. That's why they're invited here this evenin'; but tomorrow we want all to come—everybody; for he respected everybody, he liked everybody, and so it's fitten that his funeral orgies[25] sh'd be public."

(32) And so he went a-mooning on and on, liking to hear himself talk, and every little while he fetched in his funeral orgies again, till the duke he couldn't stand it no more; so he writes on a little scrap of paper, "OBSEQUIES[26], you old fool," and folds it up, and goes to goo-gooing and reaching it over people's heads to him. The king he reads it and puts it in his

[23] 这部分的动作描写十分传神。老奸巨猾的"国王"向"公爵"疯狂暗示,"公爵"开始没明白其用意,最后恍然大悟、手舞足蹈起来……两个骗子为诈得遗产而绞尽脑汁的滑稽嘴脸被表现得生动自然。

[24] 本段大部分内容是"国王"向人群发表的一场演讲的第一部分,可视为"国王"的独白。从中我们可看出两点:第一,"国王"假话连篇却说得"情真意切";第二,口语化表达和错误表达较多。前者进一步揭示了"国王"满口谎言,毫无底线,实为行骗老手的真相;后者从言谈方面暗示了"国王"的文化水平并不高,不可能是真国王的事实。

[25] orgy /ˈɔːdʒɪ/ *n.* 狂欢;放荡 此处 funeral orgies 指殡葬酒宴。

[26] obsequies /ˈɒbsɪkwɪz/ *n.* 葬礼;葬仪

pocket, and says:

(33) "Poor William, afflicted as he is, his *heart's* aluz right. Asks me to invite everybody to come to the funeral—wants me to make 'em all welcome. But he needn't a worried—it was jest what I was at."

(34) Then he weaves along again, perfectly calm, and goes to dropping in his funeral orgies again every now and then, just like he done before. And when he done it the third time he says:

(35) "I say orgies, not because it's the common term, because it ain't—obsequies bein' the common term—but because orgies is the right term. Obsequies ain't used in England no more now—it's gone out. We say orgies now in England. Orgies is better, because it means the thing you're after more exact. It's a word that's made up out'n the Greek ORGO, outside, open, abroad; and the Hebrew JEESUM, to plant, cover up; hence in TER. So, you see, funeral orgies is an open er public funeral."

(36) He was the *worst* I ever struck. Well, the iron-jawed man he laughed right in his face. Everybody was shocked. Everybody says, "Why, *doctor*!" and Abner Shackleford says:

(37) "Why, Robinson, hain't you heard the news? This is Harvey Wilks."

(38) The king he smiled eager, and shoved out his flapper, and says:

(39) "Is it my poor brother's dear good friend and physician? I—"

(40) "Keep your hands off of me!" says the doctor. "*You* talk like an Englishman, *don't* you? It's the worst imitation I ever heard. *You* Peter Wilks's brother! You're a fraud, that's what you are!" [27]

(41) Well, how they all took on! They crowded around the doctor and tried to quiet him down, and tried to explain to him and tell him how Harvey'd showed in forty ways that he *was* Harvey, and knowed everybody by name, and the names of the very dogs, and begged and BEGGED him not to hurt Harvey's feelings and the poor girl's feelings, and all that. But it warn't no

[27] 本段中，医生就第35段中"国王"卖弄的"学问"当众提出了质疑。这既为后来的情节发展做了铺垫，同时也引导读者们从骗子的语言表达中寻找漏洞。

use; he stormed right along, and said any man that pretended to be an Englishman and couldn't imitate the lingo no better than what he did, was a fraud and a liar. The poor girls was hanging to the king and crying; and all of a sudden the doctor ups and turns on *them*. He says:

(42) "I was your father's friend, and I'm your friend; and I warn you as a friend, and an honest one that wants to protect you and keep you out of harm and trouble, to turn your backs on that scoundrel and have nothing to do with him, the ignorant tramp, with his idiotic Greek and Hebrew, as he calls it. He is the thinnest kind of an impostor—has come here with a lot of empty names and facts which he picked up somewheres, and you take them for *proofs*, and are helped to fool yourselves by these foolish friends here, who ought to know better. Mary Jane Wilks, you know me for your friend, and for your unselfish friend, too. Now listen to me; turn this pitiful rascal out—I *beg* you to do it. Will you?"

(43) Mary Jane straightened herself up, and my, but she was handsome! She says:

(44) "*Here* is my answer." She hove[28] up the bag of money and put it in the king's hands, and says, "Take this six thousand dollars, and invest for me and my sisters any way you want to, and don't give us no receipt for it."

(45) Then she put her arm around the king on one side, and Susan and the hare-lip done the same on the other. Everybody clapped their hands and stomped on the floor like a perfect storm, whilst the king held up his head and smiled proud. The doctor says:

(46) "All right; I wash *my* hands of the matter. But I warn you all that a time 's coming when you're going to feel sick whenever you think of this day." And away he went.

(47) "All right, doctor," says the king, kinder mocking him; "we'll try and get 'em to send for you;" which made them all laugh, and they said it was a prime good hit.

[28] **hove** /həʊv/ *v.*（用力）举起（heave 的过去式及过去分词）

精华赏析

在本章中,哈克被迫同“国王”“公爵”一起来到一处村落,去欺骗刚刚过世的村民彼得的侄女,以诈取遗产。在从世仇的争斗中逃脱,重回密西西比河继续漂流之后,这是哈克又一次较长时间地呆在陆地上。事实上,整个故事的发展脉络,似乎都遵循着这样的模式,上岸历经各种遭遇,尔后又重回河上继续漂流……那么这部作品中一次又一次出现的“陆地”“河流”,是否仅仅只是“陆地”与“河流”呢?从原型分析和象征意象的角度来看,答案当然是否定的。

“原型”的对应英文为archetype,从词源上来说,该词来自希腊语中的arche(原初)和typo(形式)。“原型批评”是文学批评中一个非常重要的流派,加拿大文学评论家诺思罗普·弗莱(Northrop Frye)是其创始人。他认为原型是一种典型或反复出现的意象。(朱立元,1998)简单地说,当文学作品中反复出现某种特定人物、主题、意象、情景时,文学评论家们通常认为这并非偶然,而是具有特定的象征意义,这些反复出现的象征意象被视为原型。

这部作品讲述了哈克和吉姆沿密西西比河漂流历险的故事。整部作品是以主人公哈克的第一人称视角来讲述的。在和吉姆漂流历险的过程中,哈克目睹了当时美国社会的种种现实,看到了腐败、伪善,看到了人们的贪婪无耻、下流卑鄙,也看到了人们的善良、热情……在描写整个历险之旅过程中哈克的种种经历和见闻时,马克·吐温融入了许多特殊的象征意象,例如:河流、陆地、木筏、漂流等。这些反复出现的意象都并非偶然,而是各自具有特定的象征意义。接下来,我们就具体分析这部作品中的一些原型及其象征意义。

一、水的意象

纵观古今,无论在东方文化抑或西方文化当中,“水”似乎总有着一种巨大且神秘的力量。比如中国人认为“上善若水,有容乃大”“水可载舟,亦可覆舟”;又比如《圣经》中记载说洪水袭来,世界末日,一切归零……似乎冥冥中,对于“水”的敬畏,成为了人类具有的一种共通的、无意识的心理。这或许是因为在科技十分落后的原始时期,“水”这种自然之力过于强大也过于重要。人类必须毗水而居,才能够生活耕种;而当洪水暴雨来袭之时,人类又往往徒遭其害,难于还手。无论是出于什么样的原因,这种人类共通的,超越了时空、文化差异的心理感受,使得“水”成为文学作品中一个常见的原型。

通过分析文本,我们发现,哈克逃离暴戾的父亲,依靠的是密西西比河;哈克想要寻求新的自由生活,选择了在密西西比河上漂流;哈克从世仇械斗中幸运逃出,又回到了密西西比河上;哈克在以为摆脱卑鄙贪财的“国王”和“公爵”后,第一件事便是寻找吉姆重新继续密西西比河上的漂流之旅。这条大河似乎象征着希望与自由。虽然在河上也曾遭遇危险,但是哈克和吉姆在一次次经历各种磨难后,总是重新回到大河的怀抱,怀着希望,继续追寻着向往的自由生活。

二、陆地的意象

作为与"水"相对立的一个意象，这部作品中的"陆地"意象对于主人公们而言又意味着什么呢？通过分析文本我们不难发现，开始漂流之前，在"陆地"生活中，哈克面对的是酗酒暴虐的父亲，是刻板无趣的道格拉斯寡妇；在开始漂流历险的行程后，在一次次回到"陆地"上的经历中，哈克遇到的是贪婪狡诈的"国王"和"公爵"，看到的是为了家族纷争世代械斗滥杀的暴行，他甚至还不得不同两个骗子一起去欺骗善良的玛丽·珍妮姐妹以诈取钱财。

哈克似乎总是急于从陆地生活中遭遇的这一次次欺诈、暴行、争斗中脱身，期望着能够重新踏上密西西比河，继续追求自由的探索之旅。至此，"陆地"的象征意义逐渐清晰起来，它代表着大河的对立面，象征着与充满美好、自由、希望的生活完全相反的一种生活。

三、木筏的意象

读过本书的人恐怕都很难忽视不断出现在故事各个情节发展阶段的木筏。逃离父亲时，哈克依靠的是木筏；漂流的进程中，每次上岸时，哈克往往需要先把木筏藏起来以备继续漂流之需；离开陆地重回大河之时，哈克又需要先找到木筏，方能继续他的历险之旅……这不断出现的"木筏"，也并非偶然，同样具有特定的象征意义。

事实上，大河和木筏的组合，也许已经足以引发读者们产生某种联想——世界末日之后，行驶在广袤的、肆虐后终于平静下来的洪流之上，承载着整个世界仅存的人类和动物生命，以及人类未来全部希望的诺亚方舟。这部作品中的木筏，就像诺亚方舟一般，为哈克提供庇护，供哈克休憩，载着哈克和吉姆，奔向希望和自由。在本书的第十八章结尾处，从家族宿仇械斗中逃生的哈克在回到木筏之后，感叹道"别的地方似乎总是那么别扭、那么沉闷，但木筏上不会。在木筏上，你只会感到极其自由、放松和舒服。"重新继续漂流生活后，在本书第十九章开篇伊始，行文的节奏变得舒缓，出现了大段的景物和心理描写。文中写到，哈克感觉"两三天就这么过去了，过得是那么宁静、舒心、美好，我或许应该说，这日子像水一般流淌着就漂过去了"。又写到，"一丝微风从对面岸上拂来，带着凉意，是如此清新、甜蜜，夹杂着树木花朵的芬芳"。从这些文本细节中可看出，"木筏"的存在仿若救世的诺亚方舟，承载着希望和安宁，是哈克和吉姆追寻梦想和希望的途径。

"一千个读者心中有一千个哈姆雷特"，每个读者心中对文学作品里的细节可能会有不同的阅读联想。那又是什么使得处于不同的时间、空间、有着不同背景、来自不同文化的读者们，在阅读文学作品时对某些细节产生高度相似的联想呢？这种人类无意识的、共通的心理机制，使得我们在差异化的阅读体验当中呈现出共性，产生共鸣，也是文学欣赏当中不可缺失的一个重要前提。人们分析具体原型意象的象征意义时，观点有时不尽相同，但是挖掘并把握这些原型的象征意义，对于我们更好地理解作品，深刻解读细节，体味作者的真实创作意图，是十分重要的。

术语解说

诺思罗普·弗莱：诺思罗普·弗莱（Northrop Frye）（1912—1991）是二十世纪加拿大著名美学家和文学理论家。他深入地探索了西方文化的神话本质，系统地建立了以神话—原型为核心的文学类型批评和美学理论，为加拿大以及整个世界的文学、美学理论的发展作出了卓越的贡献。弗莱认为，有些常见的自然景象，如大海、森林等，在文学作品中反复出现，就不能被看作是"巧合"。相反，这种反复显示了自然界中的某种联系，而文学则模仿这种联系。（朱立元，1998）

阅读思考

1. 在本章的第 27 段，"He turns around and begins to make a lot of signs to the duke with his hands, and the duke he looks at him stupid and leather-headed a while; then all of a sudden he seems to catch his meaning, and jumps for the king, goo-gooing with all his might for joy, and hugs him about fifteen times before he lets up." 这句话中，"公爵" 突然明白了 "国王" 的什么意图呢？

2. 请解释第 35 段的内容，并谈谈从本段中可以看出 "国王" 有怎样的性格特征。

CHAPTER XXVI

导读：罗宾逊医生对哈克一行人的身份提出了质疑，但他的质疑声很快被淹没了，善良的女孩子们也选择相信“国王”和“公爵”及哈克一行人。当晚，假“哈维”和“威廉”以及侄女们共同享用了一顿大餐，而哈克则和兔唇女孩在厨房吃饭。在两人的交谈中，哈克露出马脚，差点被识破，这时善良单纯的玛丽·珍妮过来责备了兔唇女孩，并让她向哈克道歉。哈克深为玛丽·珍妮姐妹的善意和信任所感动，下定决心偷藏那六千块钱，为女孩子们保住这笔遗产。然而，藏钱却并没有那么容易。

(1) WELL, when they was all gone the king he asks Mary Jane how they was off for spare rooms, and she said she had one spare room, which would do for Uncle William, and she'd give her own room to Uncle Harvey, which was a little bigger, and she would turn into the room with her sisters and sleep on a cot[1]; and up garret[2] was a little cubby, with a pallet[3] in it. The king said the cubby would do for his valley—meaning me.

(2) So Mary Jane took us up, and she showed them their rooms, which was plain but nice. She said she'd have her frocks and a lot of other traps took out of her room if they was in Uncle Harvey's way, but he said they warn't. The frocks[4] was hung along the wall, and before them was a curtain made out of calico that hung down to the floor. There was an old hair trunk in one corner, and a guitar-box in another, and all sorts of little knickknacks and jimcracks around, like girls brisken up a room with. The king said it was all the more homely and more pleasanter for these fixings, and so don't disturb them. The duke's room was pretty small, but plenty good enough, and so was my cubby[5].

(3) That night they had a big supper, and all them men and

[1] cot /kɒt/ n. 简易床；轻便小床

[2] garret /ˈgærət/ n. 阁楼；顶楼

[3] pallet /ˈpælɪt/ n. 简陋小床

[4] frock /frɒk/ n. 连衫裙

[5] cubby /ˈkʌbi/ n. 小房间

women was there, and I stood behind the king and the duke's chairs and waited on them, and the niggers waited on the rest. Mary Jane she set at the head of the table, with Susan alongside of her, and said how bad the biscuits was, and how mean the preserves was, and how ornery[6] and tough the fried chickens was—and all that kind of rot, the way women always do for to force out compliments; and the people all knowed everything was tiptop[7], and said so—said "How *do* you get biscuits to brown so nice?" and "Where, for the land's sake, *did* you get these amaz'n pickles?" and all that kind of humbug[8] talky-talk, just the way people always does at a supper, you know.[9]

(4) And when it was all done me and the hare-lip had supper in the kitchen off of the leavings, whilst the others was helping the niggers clean up the things. The hare-lip she got to pumping me about England, and blest if I didn't think the ice was getting mighty thin sometimes.[10] She says:

(5) "Did you ever see the king?"

(6) "Who? William Fourth? Well, I bet I have—he goes to our church." I knowed he was dead years ago, but I never let on[11]. So when I says he goes to our church, she says:

(7) "What—regular?"

(8) "Yes—regular. His pew's right over opposite ourn—on t'other side the pulpit."

(9) "I thought he lived in London?"

(10) "Well, he does. Where *would* he live?"

(11) "But I thought *you* lived in Sheffield?" [12]

(12) I see I was up a stump[13]. I had to let on to get choked with a chicken bone, so as to get time to think how to get down again.[14] Then I says:

(13) "I mean he goes to our church regular when he's in Sheffield. That's only in the summer time, when he comes there to take the sea baths."

(14) "Why, how you talk—Sheffield ain't on the sea."

(15) "Well, who said it was?"

(16) "Why, you did."

(17) "I *didn't* nuther."

[6] **ornery** /'ɔːrnərɪ/ *adj.* 坏脾气的;低劣的

[7] **tiptop** /'tɪp'tɒp/ *n.* 极好;绝顶

[8] **humbug** /'hʌmbʌg/ *n.* 骗子;欺骗;谎话

[9] 这一句话比较长,也十分有趣,着墨不多却将人们在餐桌上虚情假意的谦虚展现得淋漓尽致。而最后的 you know 暗示着哈克对这一套社会人之间的社交把戏了然于心。

[10] 此处为暗喻(metaphor),借"如履薄冰"之意来形容此时哈克害怕谎言被识破的慌乱。

[11] **let on**: 放在心上;假装

[12] 本章中哈克和兔唇女孩在厨房的对话十分有趣。女孩怀疑哈克一行人的真假,不断询问相关信息,哈克则胡编乱造,疲于应对。这句话就是女孩质疑哈克的其中一句。这样的当面质疑在整个对话中不止一次,我们从这个不断地"撒谎——被质疑,圆谎——又被质疑"的过程中可以看出当时哈克窘迫慌乱的心理状态,再和后面第二十八章中哈克为了保护女孩们的遗产而撒谎时的状态进行比较,人物的性格特征就更为清晰了。同时,马克·吐温幽默的写作风格也在这看似简单的对话描写中得到体现。

[13] **up a stump**: 处境尴尬

(18) "You did!"

(19) "I didn't."

(20) "You did."

(21) "I never said nothing of the kind."

(22) "Well, what *did* you say, then?"

(23) "Said he come to take the sea *baths*—that's what I said."

(24) "Well, then, how's he going to take the sea baths if it ain't on the sea?"

(25) "Looky here," I says; "did you ever see any Congress-water?"

(26) "Yes."

(27) "Well, did you have to go to Congress to get it?"

(28) "Why, no."

(29) "Well, neither does William Fourth have to go to the sea to get a sea bath."

(30) "How does he get it, then?"

(31) "Gets it the way people down here gets Congress-water—in barrels. There in the palace at Sheffield they've got furnaces, and he wants his water hot. They can't bile that amount of water away off there at the sea. They haven't got no conveniences for it."

(32) "Oh, I see, now. You might a said that in the first place and saved time."

(33) When she said that I see I was out of the woods[15] again, and so I was comfortable and glad. Next, she says:

(34) "Do you go to church, too?"

(35) "Yes—regular."

(36) "Where do you set?"

(37) "Why, in our pew[16]."

(38) "*Whose* pew?"

(39) "Why, OURN—your Uncle Harvey's."

(40) "His'n? What does *he* want with a pew?"

(41) "Wants it to set in. What did you *reckon* he wanted with it?"

(42) "Why, I thought he'd be in the pulpit."

(43) Rot him, I forgot he was a preacher. I see I was up a stump again, so I played another chicken bone and got another

[14] 这一句中，哈克遭到兔唇女孩质疑后，慌乱之下谎称被鸡骨头卡住喉咙来打岔。用和话题不相关的事情来扰乱话题违反了“合作原则”中的“相关性原则”，这样的做法往往具有特殊的交际目的。此处，哈克的目的显然是想要用不相干的事情打岔，蒙混过关。（“合作原则”详见第二十八章的“精华赏析”。）

[15] out of the woods：脱离险境；脱离困境

[16] pew /pjuː/ *n.* 座位；教堂内的靠背长凳

think.[17] Then I says:

(44) "Blame it, do you suppose there ain't but one preacher to a church?"

(45) "Why, what do they want with more?"

(46) "What!—to preach before a king? I never did see such a girl as you. They don't have no less than seventeen."

(47) "Seventeen! My land! Why, I wouldn't set out such a string as that, not if I *never* got to glory. It must take 'em a week."

(48) "Shucks[18], they don't *all* of 'em preach the same day—only *one* of 'em."

(49) "Well, then, what does the rest of 'em do?"

(50) "Oh, nothing much. Loll around, pass the plate—and one thing or another. But mainly they don't do nothing."

(51) "Well, then, what are they *for*?"

(52) "Why, they're for *style*. Don't you know nothing?"

(53) "Well, I don't *want* to know no such foolishness as that. How is servants treated in England? Do they treat 'em better 'n we treat our niggers?"

(54) "NO! A servant ain't nobody there. They treat them worse than dogs."

(55) "Don't they give 'em holidays, the way we do, Christmas and New Year's week, and Fourth of July?"

(56) "Oh, just listen! A body could tell *you* hain't ever been to England by that. Why, Hare-l—why, Joanna, they never see a holiday from year's end to year's end; never go to the circus, nor theater, nor nigger shows, nor nowheres."

(57) "Nor church?"

(58) "Nor church."

(59) "But *you* always went to church."[19]

(60) Well, I was gone up again. I forgot I was the old man's servant. But next minute I whirled[20] in on a kind of an explanation how a valley[21] was different from a common servant and *had* to go to church whether he wanted to or not, and set with the family, on account of its being the law. But I didn't do it pretty good, and when I got done I see she warn't satisfied. She says:

[17] 此处哈克编造的谎言再度露出了破绽，同第12段一样，重复出现的"鸡骨头卡喉咙"情节带来了极其幽默的表达效果。哈克越是窘迫，读来就越是可爱有趣。

[18] **shucks** /ʃʌks/ *int.* (表示窘迫或失望)唉，糟了；(表示不满)呸

[19] 这是哈克的话又一次被女孩发现漏洞。从"合作原则"会话的分析角度来看，这种情况属于会话一方多次直接质疑对方所说内容是否符合"质量原则"。这样的处理方式给会话带来了特殊的交际效果。此处则是凸显了哈克的紧张感，影响了对话的节奏，并带来了幽默的效果。

[20] **whirl** /wɜːl/ *v.* 旋转；(思绪)混乱

[21] 此处指的是哈克充当的"国王"随从的角色

(61) "Honest injun[22], now, hain't you been telling me a lot of lies?"

(62) "Honest injun," says I.

(63) "None of it at all?"

(64) "None of it at all. Not a lie in it," says I.

(65) "Lay your hand on this book and say it."

(66) I see it warn't nothing but a dictionary, so I laid my hand on it and said it. So then she looked a little better satisfied, and says:

(67) "Well, then, I'll believe some of it; but I hope to gracious[23] if I'll believe the rest."

(68) "What is it you won't believe, Joe?" says Mary Jane, stepping in with Susan behind her. "It ain't right nor kind for you to talk so to him, and him a stranger and so far from his people. How would you like to be treated so?"

(69) "That's always your way, Maim—always sailing in to help somebody before they're hurt. I hain't done nothing to him. He's told some stretchers[24], I reckon, and I said I wouldn't swallow it all; and that's every bit and grain I *did* say. I reckon he can stand a little thing like that, can't he?"

(70) "I don't care whether 'twas little or whether 'twas big; he's here in our house and a stranger, and it wasn't good of you to say it. If you was in his place it would make you feel ashamed; and so you oughtn't to say a thing to another person that will make *them* feel ashamed."

(71) "Why, Maim, he said—"

(72) "It don't make no difference what he *said*—that ain't the thing. The thing is for you to treat him *kind*, and not be saying things to make him remember he ain't in his own country and amongst his own folks."

(73) I says to myself, THIS is a girl that I'm letting that old reptle[25] rob her of her money!

(74) Then Susan *she* waltzed in; and if you'll believe me, she did give Hare-lip hark from the tomb!

(75) Says I to myself, and this is *another* one that I'm letting him rob her of her money!

(76) Then Mary Jane she took another inning, and went in sweet and lovely again—which was her way; but when she got

[22] honest injun: 真诚地

[23] gracious /ˈgreɪʃəs/ *adj.* 亲切的；高尚的；和蔼的

[24] stretcher /ˈstretʃər/ *n.* 担架；延伸器
这里是指编造的夸大事实的谎言。

[25] 此处应为reptile(/ˈreptaɪl/ *n.* 爬行动物；卑鄙的人)。此处指试图骗走金币的骗子，属于暗喻(metaphor)。reptile这个词生动形象，足见哈克心中的厌恶。与此同时，一个虽然所学有限，言语粗陋，但是善良有正义感的孩子的形象也跃然纸上。

done there warn't hardly anything left o' poor Hare-lip. So she hollered.

(77) "All right, then," says the other girls; "you just ask his pardon."

(78) She done it, too; and she done it beautiful. She done it so beautiful it was good to hear; and I wished I could tell her a thousand lies, so she could do it again.

(79) I says to myself, this is *another* one that I'm letting him rob her of her money. And when she got through they all jest laid themselves out to make me feel at home and know I was amongst friends. I felt so ornery and low down and mean that I says to myself, my mind's made up; I'll hive that money for them or bust.

(80) So then I lit out—for bed, I said, meaning some time or another. When I got by myself I went to thinking the thing over. I says to myself, shall I go to that doctor, private, and blow on these frauds? No—that won't do. He might tell who told him; then the king and the duke would make it warm for me[26]. Shall I go, private, and tell Mary Jane? No—I dasn't do it. Her face would give them a hint, sure; they've got the money, and they'd slide right out and get away with it. If she was to fetch in help I'd get mixed up in the business before it was done with, I judge. No; there ain't no good way but one. I got to steal that money, somehow; and I got to steal it some way that they won't suspicion that I done it. They've got a good thing here, and they ain't a-going to leave till they've played this family and this town for all they're worth, so I'll find a chance time enough. I'll steal it and hide it; and by and by, when I'm away down the river, I'll write a letter and tell Mary Jane where it's hid. But I better hive it tonight if I can, because the doctor maybe hasn't let up as much as he lets on he has; he might scare them out of here yet.[27]

(81) So, thinks I, I'll go and search them rooms. Upstairs the hall was dark, but I found the duke's room, and started to paw around it with my hands; but I recollected it wouldn't be much like the king to let anybody else take care of that money

[26] make it hot for sb: 弄得某人日子不好过;采用敌视态度使待人呆不下去
这里原文使用的是make it warm for sb,分析上下文可知其大意仍是为难哈克,让他的日子不好过。

[27] 整段内容都是哈克在下定决心要帮助女孩子们保住遗产后,暗暗思考并计划筹谋的心理描写。作为一个孩子,他思维缜密,观察细致,计划周全。超出年龄的机智使得聪明勇敢的人物形象更加鲜明,也从侧面反映出人物的善良。

but his own self; so then I went to his room and begun to paw around there. But I see I couldn't do nothing without a candle, and I dasn't light one, of course. So I judged I'd got to do the other thing—lay for them and eavesdrop. About that time I hears their footsteps coming, and was going to skip under the bed; I reached for it, but it wasn't where I thought it would be; but I touched the curtain that hid Mary Jane's frocks, so I jumped in behind that and snuggled in amongst the gowns, and stood there perfectly still.

(82) They come in and shut the door; and the first thing the duke done was to get down and look under the bed. Then I was glad I hadn't found the bed when I wanted it. And yet, you know, it's kind of natural to hide under the bed when you are up to[28] anything private. They sets down then, and the king says:

(83) "Well, what is it? And cut it middlin' short, because it's better for us to be down there a-whoopin' up the mournin' than up here givin' 'em a chance to talk us over."

(84) "Well, this is it, Capet. I ain't easy; I ain't comfortable. That doctor lays on my mind. I wanted to know your plans. I've got a notion, and I think it's a sound one."

(85) "What is it, duke?"

(86) "That we better glide out of this before three in the morning, and clip it down the river with what we've got. Specially, seeing we got it so easy—GIVEN back to us, flung at our heads, as you may say, when of course we allowed to have to steal it back. I'm for knocking off and lighting out[29]."

(87) That made me feel pretty bad. About an hour or two ago it would a been a little different, but now it made me feel bad and disappointed,[30] The king rips out and says:

(88) "What! And not sell out the rest o' the property? March off like a passel of fools and leave eight or nine thous'n' dollars' worth o' property layin' around jest sufferin' to be scooped in?—and all good, salable stuff, too."

(89) The duke he grumbled; said the bag of gold was enough, and he didn't want to go no deeper—didn't want to rob a lot of orphans of *everything* they had.

[28] **up to**: 忙于……；在做……

[29] **light out**: 本意指熄灯，这里指匆匆离开，溜走。

[30] 此处哈克听到"公爵"建议提前溜走，很是担心。从情节设置上来说，这里的事件走向和哈克计划的不一样，这类节外生枝的情节设置增加了悬念，也使得故事更引人入胜。

(90) "Why, how you talk!" says the king. "We sha'n't rob 'em of nothing at all but jest this money. The people that *buys* the property is the suff'rers; because as soon 's it's found out 'at we didn't own it—which won't be long after we've slid—the sale won't be valid, and it 'll all go back to the estate. These yer orphans 'll git their house back agin, and that's enough for *them*; they're young and spry, and k'n easy earn a livin'. *They* ain't a-goin to suffer. Why, jest think—there's thous'n's and thous'n's that ain't nigh so well off. Bless you, *they* ain't got noth'n' to complain of." [31]

(91) Well, the king he talked him blind; so at last he give in, and said all right, but said he believed it was blamed foolishness to stay, and that doctor hanging over them. But the king says:

(92) "Cuss the doctor! What do we k'yer for *him*? Hain't we got all the fools in town on our side? And ain't that a big enough majority in any town?"

(93) So they got ready to go down stairs again. The duke says:

(94) "I don't think we put that money in a good place."

(95) That cheered me up. I'd begun to think I warn't going to get a hint of no kind to help me. The king says:

(96) "Why?"

(97) "Because Mary Jane 'll be in mourning from this out; and first you know the nigger that does up the rooms will get an order to box these duds up and put 'em away; and do you reckon a nigger can run across money and not borrow some of it?"

(98) "Your head's level agin, duke," says the king; and he comes a-fumbling under the curtain two or three foot from where I was. I stuck tight to the wall and kept mighty still, though quivery; and I wondered what them fellows would say to me if they catched me; and I tried to think what I'd better do if they did catch me.[32] But the king he got the bag before I could think more than about a half a thought, and he never suspicioned I was around.[33] They took and shoved the bag through a rip in the straw tick that was under the feather-bed, and crammed it in a foot or two amongst the straw and said it was all right now, because a nigger only makes up the feather-bed, and don't turn

[31] 整段为"国王"的大段独白,将自己和"公爵"诈取遗产的行为说得冠冕堂皇,有情有义。在会话中,大段独白往往表示说话人在会话中处于比较强势的地位。这里"国王"掌控着话题,强势地说服"公爵"放弃提前溜走的想法。这样的"强势"是因为骗子们的行为真的无可厚非吗?当然不是,不过是因为贪婪,想要骗更多的钱而已。"国王"之厚颜无耻可谓被刻画得淋漓尽致了。

[32] 这是一处行为和心理描写。在这里充分渲染了情势之紧张。

[33] 然而,我根本还来不及多想,"国王"就拿到了钱袋子,他一点儿也没怀疑我就在他身旁。

over the straw tick only about twice a year, and so it warn't in no danger of getting stole now.

(99) But I knowed better. I had it out of there before they was half-way down stairs. I groped along up to my cubby, and hid it there till I could get a chance to do better. I judged I better hide it outside of the house somewheres, because if they missed it they would give the house a good ransacking: I knowed that very well. Then I turned in, with my clothes all on; but I couldn't a gone to sleep if I'd a wanted to, I was in such a sweat to get through with the business. By and by I heard the king and the duke come up; so I rolled off my pallet and laid with my chin at the top of my ladder, and waited to see if anything was going to happen. But nothing did.

(100) So I held on till all the late sounds had quit and the early ones hadn't begun yet; and then I slipped down the ladder.

精华赏析

在上一章的赏析中，我们探讨了原型的象征意象。大家或许注意到了，在我们具体讨论的几个意象中，"水" 和 "陆地" 是彼此对立的一组意象。在本章的赏析部分，我们来探讨一下 "二元对立"。

"二元对立" 最初是一个哲学概念，相关观点在古希腊时期就已存在，其代表人物是柏拉图。后来，著名语言学家、结构主义语言学的创始人索绪尔（Saussure）提出了一系列彼此对立的概念用以阐释结构主义语言学的理论体系，其中包括：能指（Signifier）与所指（Signified）；历时（Diachronic）与共时（Synchronic）；语言（Langue）与言语（Parole）等。再后来，语言学中的 "二元对立" 原则引起了西方文学评论家们的广泛重视，将其应用于诗歌的赏析解读，以及小说的文本解读当中。（方汉泉，2004）比如，"野火烧不尽，春风吹又生" 就是一句典型的呈现出二元对立关系的诗句，中国古典诗歌出于对仗工整的要求，二元对立的概念和关系绝非罕见；又比如，在文学作品中，善恶，黑白，生死，虚实等，都是常见的二元对立的逻辑概念关系。

接下来，我们探讨一下这部作品中存在的一些二元对立关系。

一、"水" 与 "陆地" 的二元对立

正如我们在上一章的精华赏析部分提到过的，哈克在漂流的过程中，依托着 "大河" 追求自由,憧憬希望,寻求庇护,而每一次踏上“陆地”似乎总是遭遇争斗,欺诈,痛苦……于是,我们认为在这部作品中,“水”隐喻着自由,希望和精神世界的美好,而“陆地”则代表着其对立面:争斗,欺诈和现实世界的痛苦等。

二、黑人与白人的二元对立

小说的故事围绕着白人孩子哈克和黑人奴隶吉姆的漂流历险展开。这两个不同肤色主要人物的设定,绝非偶然。这部作品涉及种族主义和奴隶制的话题已成为一种共识。从一开始,两位主人公都生活艰辛,一个是因为父亲酗酒虐待,一个是因为奴隶的身份。然而两人明显的差异是一黑一白。在当时的历史背景下,即使是生活在社会最底层的白人男孩哈克,对于黑奴吉姆也是有资格轻视的。我们看到在本书的第十五章,哈克和吉姆在大雾中失散,当他们终于又见面时,哈克捉弄了吉姆,谎称没有大雾,也没有岛屿,一切都没有发生,吉姆只是打了一个瞌睡,还说这一切肯定是吉姆在做梦……吉姆思考了半天,终于想明白是被哈克捉弄了后十分伤心。此时文中写到,“足足十五分钟后,我才鼓足了勇气朝这个黑人低头认错”。从这里可以清晰地看出哈克和吉姆身份处境的一种对立的不平等关系。而在十六章中,哈克备受“良心”的谴责,决定择机告发逃跑的黑奴吉姆,以及后来,吉姆被“国王”和“公爵”私自卖掉后,哈克最初想到帮助吉姆的方式,是给吉姆的主人写信。可以说,直到第三十一章,白人孩子哈克和黑人奴隶吉姆一直处于一种基于肤色的对立关系当中,他始终处于是否告发吉姆的心理斗争中。但哈克最终决定自己想办法救出吉姆,这意味着他选择同现实世界中的通行社会规则决裂。可以说,这个故事在黑人和白人二元对立的关系中,产生冲突,发展变化,最终融合。

三、儿童与成年人的二元对立

许多文学评论家都注意到了这部作品中的主人公哈克是一名儿童。这种设定同样有着其特殊意义。作为读者的我们,在阅读这部作品时也必定时常感叹哈克小小年纪,却如此聪明、机智、勇敢。当他面对酗酒成性的父亲的虐待时,当他机智应对搜捕者的盘查保护吉姆时,当他面对看似体面正派的两个家族之间永无休止的争斗杀戮时,当他面对“国王”和“公爵”的卑鄙无耻和狡猾时,当他帮助保护善良的玛丽·珍妮姐妹时……凡此种种,他的机智、果决、勇敢、善良在成年人的种种不堪的映衬之下,越发鲜活生动,熠熠生辉。

没有黑,哪有白?若无生,何谈死?“二元对立”关系的存在十分普遍,在阅读文本分析作品时,如果能够借助这种规律把握作者的深层意图,对我们往往是十分有益的。

阅读思考

1. 试找出哈克和兔唇女孩的对话中存在漏洞的地方。
2. 第 87 段中提到哈克感觉很糟,请问是为什么?

CHAPTER XXVII

导读：好不容易从“公爵”和“国王”那里把钱偷出来的哈克，趁着大家都睡着打算溜出去藏钱。然而就在他经过大厅时，突然听见有人下楼，迫于无奈，他暂时将钱藏进了“棺材”。举行完葬礼后，“公爵”和“国王”急着拍卖产业拿钱走人，于是谎称要带着“侄女们”离开此地，共同生活。到了拍卖日一大早，“公爵”和“国王”发现钱不见了。

(1) I CREPT to their doors and listened; they was snoring. So I tiptoed along, and got down stairs all right. There warn't a sound anywheres. I peeped[1] through a crack of the dining-room door, and see the men that was watching the corpse all sound asleep on their chairs. The door was open into the parlor[2], where the corpse was laying, and there was a candle in both rooms. I passed along, and the parlor door was open; but I see there warn't nobody in there but the remainders of Peter; so I shoved on[3] by; but the front door was locked, and the key wasn't there. Just then I heard somebody coming down the stairs, back behind me. I run in the parlor and took a swift look around, and the only place I see to hide the bag was in the coffin. The lid was shoved along about a foot, showing the dead man's face down in there, with a wet cloth over it, and his shroud on. I tucked[4] the money-bag in under the lid, just down beyond where his hands was crossed, which made me creep[5], they was so cold, and then I run back across the room and in behind the door.[6]

(2) The person coming was Mary Jane. She went to the coffin, very soft, and kneeled down and looked in; then she put up her handkerchief, and I see she begun to cry, though I couldn't hear her, and her back was to me. I slid out, and as I

[1] peep /pi:p/ v. 窥视；偷看

[2] parlor /ˈpɑ:lə/ n. 会客室

[3] shove on: 推着（前行）

[4] tuck /tʌk/ v. 使折叠；收拢

[5] creep /kri:p/ v. 起鸡皮疙瘩

[6] 我把钱袋塞在棺材盖板下面，刚好碰到尸体交叉的双手，他的手冰凉冰凉的，我起了一身鸡皮疙瘩。然后我绕回客厅，躲在门后。这一段描写很是生动有趣，着墨不多，用词简单，但让人如临其境。

passed the dining-room I thought I'd make sure them watchers hadn't seen me; so I looked through the crack, and everything was all right. They hadn't stirred.

(3) I slipped up to bed, feeling ruther blue, on accounts of the thing playing out that way after I had took so much trouble and run so much resk about it. Says I, if it could stay where it is, all right; because when we get down the river a hundred mile or two I could write back to Mary Jane, and she could dig him up again and get it; but that ain't the thing that's going to happen; the thing that's going to happen is, the money 'll be found when they come to screw on the lid. Then the king 'll get it again, and it 'll be a long day before he gives anybody another chance to smouch it from him. Of course I WANTED to slide down and get it out of there, but I dasn't try it. Every minute it was getting earlier now, and pretty soon some of them watchers would begin to stir, and I might get catched—catched with six thousand dollars in my hands that nobody hadn't hired me to take care of. I don't wish to be mixed up in no such business as that, I says to myself.

(4) When I got down stairs in the morning the parlor was shut up, and the watchers was gone. There warn't nobody around but the family and the widow Bartley and our tribe. I watched their faces to see if anything had been happening, but I couldn't tell.

(5) Towards the middle of the day the undertaker[7] come with his man, and they set the coffin in the middle of the room on a couple of chairs, and then set all our chairs in rows, and borrowed more from the neighbors till the hall and the parlor and the dining-room was full. I see the coffin lid was the way it was before, but I dasn't go to look in under it, with folks around.

(6) Then the people begun to flock in[8], and the beats and the girls took seats in the front row at the head of the coffin, and for a half an hour the people filed[9] around slow, in single rank, and looked down at the dead man's face a minute, and some dropped in a tear, and it was all very still and solemn[10], only the girls and the beats holding handkerchiefs to their eyes and

[7] undertaker /'ʌndəteɪkə/ n. 承办人;殡仪业人员

[8] flock in: 成群地走进;涌来

[9] file /faɪl/ v. 列队行进

[10] 此处意为“安静又肃穆”。这里使用了头韵(alliteration)修辞,起强调渲染作用。

keeping their heads bent, and sobbing a little. There warn't no other sound but the scraping of the feet on the floor and blowing noses—because people always blows them more at a funeral than they do at other places except church.

(7) When the place was packed full the undertaker he slid around in his black gloves with his softy soothering ways, putting on the last touches, and getting people and things all ship-shape[11] and comfortable, and making no more sound than a cat. He never spoke; he moved people around, he squeezed in late ones, he opened up passageways, and done it with nods, and signs with his hands. Then he took his place over against the wall. He was the softest, glidingest, stealthiest man I ever see; and there warn't no more smile to him than there is to a ham.[12]

(8) They had borrowed a melodeum[13]—a sick one; and when everything was ready a young woman set down and worked it, and it was pretty skreeky and colicky[14], and everybody joined in and sung, and Peter was the only one that had a good thing, according to my notion. Then the Reverend Hobson opened up, slow and solemn, and begun to talk; and straight off the most outrageous row busted out in the cellar a body ever heard; it was only one dog, but he made a most powerful racket, and he kept it up right along; the parson he had to stand there, over the coffin, and wait—you couldn't hear yourself think. It was right down awkward, and nobody didn't seem to know what to do. But pretty soon they see that long-legged undertaker make a sign to the preacher as much as to say, "Don't you worry—just depend on me." Then he stooped[15] down and begun to glide along the wall, just his shoulders showing over the people's heads. So he glided along, and the powwow and racket getting more and more outrageous all the time; and at last, when he had gone around two sides of the room, he disappears down cellar. Then in about two seconds we heard a whack, and the dog he finished up with a most amazing howl or two, and then everything was dead still, and the parson begun his solemn talk where he left off.[16] In a minute or two here comes this undertaker's back and shoulders gliding along

[11] **ship-shape** /ˈʃɪpʃeɪp/ *adj.* 井井有条的

[12] 他是我见过最温柔，行动最流畅，做事最安静的人了。而且他脸上一直没有任何笑容，和火腿似的，一板一眼的。这里对于丧礼承办人的描述很有趣，我们也禁不住在脑海里描绘他的形象。根据描述，他业务熟练是必然的，脸上没有一点笑容，是因为丧礼的缘故还是因为性格的缘故呢？读者似乎和哈克融为一体，打量着这个丧礼承办人的言行表情，可能产生类似的疑问。以第一人称叙述的故事往往具有这样神奇的感染力。

[13] 此处应为melodeon(/mɪˈləʊdɪən/ *n.* 簧风琴的一种；手风琴的一种)

[14] **colicky** /ˈkɒːlɪki/ *adj.* 疝气痛的；肚腹绞痛的

[15] **stoop** /stuːp/ *v.* 弯腰

[16] 丧礼承办人再度出场了。在牧师开始讲话时，一条狗不识趣儿地开始吠叫。正当情况变得尴尬时，丧

the wall again; and so he glided and glided around three sides of the room, and then rose up, and shaded his mouth with his hands, and stretched his neck out towards the preacher, over the people's heads, and says, in a kind of a coarse whisper, "HE HAD A RAT!" Then he drooped down and glided along the wall again to his place. You could see it was a great satisfaction to the people, because naturally they wanted to know. A little thing like that don't cost nothing, and it's just the little things that makes a man to be looked up to and liked. There warn't no more popular man in town than what that undertaker was.

礼承办人很快示意交给他解决。他以一贯的流畅姿态滑离众人视线进入地窖，一声响动后，狗发出凄厉的嚎叫声，然后一切都安静了下来。

如果说，第7段提到的丧礼承办人精于业务却面无笑容的原因我们还不清楚的话，这一部分描写其实已经回答了我们的疑问。我们应该都明白发生了什么。一个极端务实能干，但是冷血无情的人物形象无形中就被巧妙地塑造了出来。

(9) Well, the funeral sermon[17] was very good, but pison long and tiresome; and then the king he shoved in and got off some of his usual rubbage[18], and at last the job was through, and the undertaker begun to sneak up on[19] the coffin with his screw-driver. I was in a sweat then, and watched him pretty keen. But he never meddled at all; just slid the lid along as soft as mush, and screwed it down tight and fast. So there I was! I didn't know whether the money was in there or not. So, says I, s'pose somebody has hogged that bag on the sly?—now how do I know whether to write to Mary Jane or not? S'pose she dug him up and didn't find nothing, what would she think of me? Blame it, I says, I might get hunted up and jailed; I'd better lay low and keep dark, and not write at all; the thing's awful mixed now; trying to better it, I've worsened it a hundred times, and I wish to goodness I'd just let it alone, dad fetch the whole business![20]

[17] **sermon** /'sɜːmən/ *n.* 布道；训诫；冗长的讲话

[18] 应该为 rubbish，指"国王"那套编造的鬼话。

[19] **sneak up on**: 悄悄接近，慢慢到来

[20] 哈克看见有人要开启棺材，心中十分紧张，全身冒汗。各种想法飞快闪过他的脑海，他左思右想之后怕得要命，不由得后悔，希望自己当初没有决定帮助玛丽·珍妮姐妹。

这里对哈克的心理描写使得情节发展更扣人心弦，也使得哈克这个人物形象更加真实可信。他此时的紧张，他的害怕，他的后悔，都使得哈克这个人物更加可爱。

(10) They buried him, and we come back home, and I went to watching faces again—I couldn't help it, and I couldn't rest easy. But nothing come of it; the faces didn't tell me nothing.

(11) The king he visited around in the evening, and sweetened everybody up, and made himself ever so friendly; and he give out the idea that his congregation over in England would be in a sweat about him, so he must hurry and settle up the estate right away and leave for home. He was very sorry he was so pushed, and so was everybody; they wished he could stay longer, but they said they could see it couldn't be done. And he said of course him and William would take the girls home

with them; and that pleased everybody too, because then the girls would be well fixed and amongst their own relations; and it pleased the girls, too—tickled them so they clean forgot they ever had a trouble in the world; and told him to sell out as quick as he wanted to, they would be ready. Them poor things was that glad and happy it made my heart ache to see them getting fooled and lied to so, but I didn't see no safe way for me to chip in[21] and change the general tune.

(12) Well, blamed if the king didn't bill the house and the niggers and all the property for auction straight off—sale two days after the funeral; but anybody could buy private beforehand if they wanted to.

(13) So the next day after the funeral, along about noontime, the girls' joy got the first jolt[22]. A couple of nigger traders come along, and the king sold them the niggers reasonable, for three-day drafts[23] as they called it, and away they went, the two sons up the river to Memphis, and their mother down the river to Orleans. I thought them poor girls and them niggers would break their hearts for grief; they cried around each other, and took on so it most made me down sick to see it. The girls said they hadn't ever dreamed of seeing the family separated or sold away from the town. I can't ever get it out of my memory, the sight of them poor miserable girls and niggers hanging around each other's necks and crying; and I reckon I couldn't a stood it all, but would a had to bust out and tell on our gang if I hadn't knowed the sale warn't no account and the niggers would be back home in a week or two.[24]

(14) The thing made a big stir in the town, too, and a good many come out flatfooted and said it was scandalous[25] to separate the mother and the children that way. It injured the frauds some; but the old fool he bulled right along, spite of all the duke could say or do, and I tell you the duke was powerful uneasy.

(15) Next day was auction day. About broad day[26] in the morning the king and the duke come up in the garret and woke me up, and I see by their look that there was trouble. The king

[21] **chip in**: 插嘴；集资 此处指插手帮助女孩子们脱困。

[22] **jolt** /dʒəʊlt; dʒɒlt/ *n.* 颠簸，摇晃；一阵强烈的感情（如震惊）

[23] **draft** /dræft/ *n.* 汇票；草稿 这里 three-day drafts 指的是三天到期的付现支票。

[24] 这几句大多为对哈克的心理描写。中间穿插有少量女孩子们的语言描写。这里的心理描写和第9段的心理描写形成对比。之前哈克还十分后悔不该帮女孩子们，这里想的又都是女孩子们该有多伤心难过，而自己又是如何不忍心。这样的心理变化和对比使人物更为真实丰满的同时，也突出了哈克的善良。

[25] **scandalous** /ˈskændələs/ *adj.* 可耻的；诽谤性的

[26] "broad daylight" 指光天化日，大白天。此处 "broad day" 应该指的是天刚亮的时候。

says:

(16) "Was you in my room night before last?"

(17) "No, your majesty" —which was the way I always called him when nobody but our gang warn't around.

(18) "Was you in there yisterday er last night?"

(19) "No, your majesty."

(20) "Honor bright, now —no lies."

(21) "Honor bright, your majesty, I'm telling you the truth. I hain't been a-near your room since Miss Mary Jane took you and the duke and showed it to you."

(22) The duke says:

(23) "Have you seen anybody else go in there?"

(24) "No, your grace, not as I remember, I believe."

(25) "Stop and think."

(26) I studied awhile and see my chance; then I says:

(27) "Well, I see the niggers go in there several times." [27]

(28) Both of them gave a little jump, and looked like they hadn't ever expected it, and then like they *had*. Then the duke says:

(29) "What, all of them?"

(30) "No—leastways, not all at once—that is, I don't think I ever see them all come *out* at once but just one time."

(31) "Hello! When was that?"

(32) "It was the day we had the funeral. In the morning. It warn't early, because I overslept. I was just starting down the ladder, and I see them."

(33) "Well, go on, *go* on! What did they do? How'd they act?"

(34) "They didn't do nothing. And they didn't act anyway much, as fur as I see. They tiptoed away; so I seen, easy enough, that they'd shoved in there to do up your majesty's room, or something, s'posing you was up; and found you WARN'T up, and so they was hoping to slide out of the way of trouble without waking you up, if they hadn't already waked you up."

(35) "Great guns, *this* is a go!" says the king; and both of them looked pretty sick and tolerable silly. They stood there

[27] 已知前情的我们心知肚明发生了什么。哈克这个回答就是故意将"国王"和"公爵"引入歧途,以洗脱自己的嫌疑。

a-thinking and scratching their heads a minute, and the duke he bust into a kind of a little raspy chuckle, and says:

(36) "It does beat all how neat the niggers played their hand. They let on to be *sorry* they was going out of this region! And I believed they *was* sorry, and so did you, and so did everybody. Don't ever tell *me* any more that a nigger ain't got any histrionic talent. Why, the way they played that thing it would fool *anybody*. In my opinion, there's a fortune in 'em. If I had capital and a theater, I wouldn't want a better lay-out than that—and here we've gone and sold 'em for a song[28]. Yes, and ain't privileged to sing the song yet. Say, where IS that song—that draft?"

(37) "In the bank for to be collected. Where *would* it be?"

(38) "Well, *that*'s all right then, thank goodness."

(39) Says I, kind of timid-like:

(40) "Is something gone wrong?"

(41) The king whirls on me and rips out[29]:

(42) "None o' your business! You keep your head shet, and mind y'r own affairs—if you got any. Long as you're in this town don't you forgit *that*—you hear?" Then he says to the duke, "We got to jest swaller it and say noth'n': mum's the word for US.[30]"

(43) As they was starting down the ladder the duke he chuckles again, and says:

(44) "Quick sales *and* small profits! It's a good business—yes."

(45) The king snarls[31] around on him and says:

(46) "I was trying to do for the best in sellin' 'em out so quick. If the profits has turned out to be none, lackin' considable, and none to carry, is it my fault any more'n it's yourn?"

(47) "Well, *they'd* be in this house yet and we *wouldn't* if I could a got my advice listened to." [32]

(48) The king sassed[33] back as much as was safe for him, and then swapped around and lit into *me* again. He give me down the banks for not coming and *telling* him I see the niggers come out of his room acting that way—said any fool would

[28] 此处指以很便宜的价格售卖。

[29] rip out: 扯掉;狠狠地发出

[30] mum /mʌm/ *adj.* 沉默的;守密的
此处意为"为了我们自己(骗子们)而保持沉默,一字也不提"。

[31] snarl /snɑːl/ *v.* (狗)龇牙狂吠;咆哮着说

[32] 第44—47段这番对话是在两个骗子已经决定对丢钱的事情保持沉默之后发生的。俩人稍有余力便开始彼此挤兑讽刺。因为他们的组合行骗本来就是利益驱使,并没有真情意,一旦事关利益便只剩彼此指责。

[33] sass /sæs/ *v.* 跟……顶嘴;对……说无礼的话

a *knowed* something was up. And then waltzed in and cussed *himself* awhile, and said it all come of him not laying late and taking his natural rest that morning, and he'd be blamed if he'd ever do it again. So they went off a-jawing; and I felt dreadful glad I'd worked it all off on to the niggers, and yet hadn't done the niggers no harm by it.

精华赏析

这部小说中有大量景物描写。在这样一部有大河原型和漂流原型的作品中,关于密西西比河以及沿途流域的景物描写可以说是无法避免的。事实上,马克·吐温在这部作品中所作的景物描写远远超出了"必须涉及"的写作内容的范畴。景物描写不仅仅是整个故事展开的背景,也不仅仅是烘托气氛,呼应人物心理,而是实实在在地参与到了人物的塑造,情节的发展当中去。接下来,我们将选取书中三段景物描写来加以阐述、解读。

一、正式开始漂流前的一段景物描写

为了逃离父亲而假装死亡的哈克躲到了杰克逊岛上,遇到了逃跑的黑奴吉姆。在本书的第九章中,哈克和吉姆发现了岛上的一个山洞,两人将木筏上的东西搬到山洞里,打算暂居山洞中。天黑后,突然下起雨来……马克·吐温花了不少的篇幅来描绘此时的情景,长达二百余词。文中这样写道,"天很快就黑了下来,并且开始电闪雷鸣……然后马上就开始下起雨来,雨下得很大。我从没见过刮这么大的风……雨又急又密,远处的树木看起来模模糊糊的……一阵狂风吹来,树木都吹折了腰,然后树叶泛白的背面又纷纷被狂风忽地朝天吹翻卷过来……这时,一声惊雷炸裂开来,轰隆隆,呼噜噜地从天上劈了下来……"

整段描写生词不多,却十分形象,让人如临其境。我们还应注意到,这段描写的场景发生在哈克刚逃离了父亲,暂避在杰克逊岛的时候,而这个时候,哈克还未正式开始踏上密西西比河的漂流之旅。此时的这一大段风雨雷电的场景描写,不仅是自然场景的描述,更暗喻着即将开始漂流历险的哈克和吉姆将要遇到的艰难险阻。那在狂风中被蹂躏得东倒西歪的树木,那劈裂的惊雷,那密密的大雨,都预示着前行的道路中可能会遇到的各种惊心动魄的瞬间。

二、关于迷雾的一段景物描写

在本书的第十五章中,哈克和吉姆继续漂流。然而,很快河上起了大雾,哈克想要把木筏拴在河边的小树上,不料,一个激流涌过,小树被连根拔起,带着木筏在浓雾中漂得不知去向……哈克和吉姆就此失散……"我撞到一处陡峭的河岸,岸上耸立着高大的,影影绰绰,阴森森的树木"……"眨眼的工夫,一切又都笼罩在寂静的浓雾中了,我安安静静地坐着,听着自己心跳的声音,心大约跳了一百下,我一动也没动。"之后,哈克和吉姆终于碰面,吉姆欣喜不已，哈克却捉弄了吉姆谎称这一切都是吉姆在做梦，吉姆气愤地指责哈克，哈克低头向黑奴吉姆认错。

这一部分描写同样具有特殊象征意义。这段描写出现在哈克和吉姆离开杰克逊岛之后，两个人开始一同漂流不久，此时两人之间自然还没能更多地了解彼此和形成深厚的感情。这浓厚的迷雾正如两人未知的、充满了不确定性的将来，它令身处其中的人们心生恐惧，然而最终哈克和吉姆还是会合在了一起，这也暗示了两人最终将结下牢固的友谊，同舟共济。同时，这里哈克捉弄吉姆，受到吉姆指责后向吉姆认错的情节也十分重要，这是哈克内心有别于社会道德的道德认知开始形成的初期。

三、逃离家族宿仇争斗后的一段景物描写

在第十八章的结尾，哈克机智地摆脱了家族宿仇的争斗后和吉姆会合，两人十分高兴，重新踏上了漂流之旅。在第十九章开篇伊始，出现了大篇幅的景物描写，整个叙事节奏舒缓了下来，“两三天就这么过去了，过得是那么宁静，舒心，美好，我或许应该说，这日子像水一般流淌着就漂过去了”……又写到，“一丝微风从对面岸上拂来，带着凉意，是如此清新，甜蜜，夹杂着树木花朵的芬芳”……“然而也不总是那样，因为有时候他们会把尖嘴鱼之类的死鱼丢得到处都是，臭不可闻。然后，天就全亮了，万物在阳光下微笑，鸟儿也都唱起歌来。”

在这一段文字中我们可以看到，阳光和煦，微风拂面，连空气都散发着清新的草木香气……景随心生，这和谐、美好、沐浴着阳光和花木芬芳的场景，只有摆脱了烦恼，心情放松下来的哈克和吉姆才可感受得到。因此，此处的景物描写事实上反映的是此时哈克和吉姆的心情，暗示着两人内心的喜悦以及对接下来的探险旅程所怀揣的美好憧憬和希望。另外，我们还应该注意到，这段文字中也提及“然而也不总是那样，因为有时候他们会把尖嘴鱼之类的死鱼丢得到处都是，臭不可闻”。但接着，“天就全亮了，万物在阳光下微笑，鸟儿也都唱起歌来”。这也似乎预示着尽管前路仍有艰险，但最终哈克和吉姆将迎来他们所向往的生活。

文学作品中的景物描写常常承载着塑造人物，建构情节的功能。优秀文学作品中的景物描写，常常能够于无形中令人物和主题深入读者内心，感动读者，使得读者和书中人物感同身受。马克·吐温的这部《哈克贝利·费恩历险记》之所以广受赞誉，他高超的写作技巧是其中一个非常重要的原因。这部作品词句简单，但人物鲜活可信，情景动人，情节生动有趣，这些都体现出了作者四两拨千斤的高超写作技巧。

阅读思考

1. 本章中提到了丧礼承办人这一人物，请问你怎么看待这个人物，请用书中相关细节支撑你的观点。

2. 你认为哈克是一个什么样的孩子？请在本章中找出相关细节支持你的观点。

CHAPTER XXVIII

导读:哈克把“国王”和“公爵”糊弄过去后,发现玛丽·珍妮在暗自伤心。原来,拍卖家产时,两个骗子将家里黑奴母女卖给了不同人家,而致亲情阻隔,玛丽·珍妮为此伤心不已。看到此情此景,哈克再也不忍继续欺骗,便将真相和盘托出。之后,玛丽·珍妮按照哈克的计划离开,为掩人耳目哈克谎称她是去拜访病人。随后,“国王”和“公爵”按照计划急着拍卖女孩子们的家产,可就在拍卖接近尾声时,不速之客出现了。

(1) BY and by it was getting-up time. So I come down the ladder and started for down-stairs; but as I come to the girls' room the door was open, and I see Mary Jane setting by her old hair trunk, which was open and she'd been packing things in it—getting ready to go to England. But she had stopped now with a folded gown in her lap, and had her face in her hands, crying. I felt awful bad to see it; of course anybody would. I went in there and says:

(2) "Miss Mary Jane, you can't a-bear to see people in trouble, and I can't—most always. Tell me about it."

(3) So she done it. And it was the niggers—I just expected it. She said the beautiful trip to England was most about spoiled for her; she didn't know *how* she was ever going to be happy there, knowing the mother and the children warn't ever going to see each other no more—and then busted out[1] bitterer than ever, and flung up her hands, and says:

(4) "Oh, dear, dear, to think they ain't *ever* going to see each other any more!"

(5) "But they *will*—and inside of two weeks—and I *know* it!" says I.

(6) Laws[2], it was out before I could think! And before I

[1] bust out: 爆发

[2] 此处为感叹词,意思类似于“天呐”。

could budge[3] she throws her arms around my neck and told me to say it *again*, say it *again*, say it *again*![4]

(7) I see I had spoke too sudden and said too much, and was in a close place[5]. I asked her to let me think a minute; and she set there, very impatient and excited and handsome, but looking kind of happy and eased-up, like a person that's had a tooth pulled out. So I went to studying it out[6]. I says to myself, I reckon a body that ups and tells the truth when he is in a tight place[7] is taking considerable many resks, though I ain't had no experience, and can't say for certain; but it looks so to me, anyway; and yet here's a case where I'm blest if it don't look to me like the truth is better and actuly SAFER than a lie. I must lay it by in my mind, and think it over some time or other, it's so kind of strange and unregular. I never see nothing like it. Well, I says to myself at last, I'm a-going to chance it; I'll up and tell the truth this time, though it does seem most like setting down on a kag of powder and touching it off just to see where you'll go to.

(8) Then I says:

(9) "Miss Mary Jane, is there any place out of town a little ways where you could go and stay three or four days?"

(10) "Yes; Mr. Lothrop's. Why?"

(11) "Never mind why yet. If I'll tell you how I know the niggers will see each other again inside of two weeks—here in this house—and PROVE how I know it—will you go to Mr. Lothrop's and stay four days?"

(12) "Four days!" she says; "I'll stay a year!"

(13) "All right," I says, "I don't want nothing more out of *you* than just your word—I druther have it than another man's kiss-the-Bible.[8] "She smiled and reddened up very sweet, and I says, "If you don't mind it, I'll shut the door—and bolt it."

(14) Then I come back and set down again, and says:

(15) "Don't you holler[9]. Just set still and take it like a man. I got to tell the truth, and you want to brace up[10], Miss Mary, because it's a bad kind, and going to be hard to take, but there ain't no help for it. These uncles of yourn ain't no uncles at all; they're a couple of frauds—regular dead-beats[11]. There, now

[3] budge /bʌdʒ/ v. 挪动；改变态度或意见

[4] 第4—6段是关于玛丽·珍妮的语言以及行为描写。字数不多，用词简单，但是一个单纯、善良、真诚的女孩子形象一下就出来了。

[5] 陷入艰难境地

[6] 原指仔细研究，此处指仔细思考如何向玛丽·珍妮解释。

[7] in a tight place: 处于困境

[8] 西方有亲吻圣经宣誓的传统，此处指，哈克认为玛丽·珍妮说话比别人亲吻圣经发誓更值得信赖。

[9] holler /'hɒlə/ v. 发牢骚；叫喊；抱怨

[10] brace up: 下定决心；打起精神

[11] dead-beat: 流浪汉 此处意为"流氓，坏蛋"。

we're over the worst of it, you can stand the rest middling easy."

(16) It jolted her up like everything, of course;[12] but I was over the shoal[13] water now, so I went right along, her eyes a-blazing higher and higher all the time, and told her every blame thing, from where we first struck that young fool going up to the steamboat, clear through to where she flung herself on to the king's breast at the front door and he kissed her sixteen or seventeen times—and then up she jumps, with her face afire[14] like sunset, and says:

(17) "The brute! Come, don't waste a minute—not a SECOND—we'll have them tarred and feathered, and flung in the river!"

(18) Says I:

(19) "Cert'nly. But do you mean BEFORE you go to Mr. Lothrop's, or—"

(20) "Oh," she says, "what am I THINKING about!" she says, and set right down again. "Don't mind what I said—please don't—you WON'T, now, *will* you?" Laying her silky hand on mine in that kind of a way that I said I would die first. "I never thought, I was so stirred up," she says; "now go on, and I won't do so any more. You tell me what to do, and whatever you say I'll do it."

(21) "Well," I says, "it's a rough gang, them two frauds, and I'm fixed so I got to travel with them a while longer, whether I want to or not—I druther not tell you why; and if you was to blow on[15] them this town would get me out of their claws, and I'd be all right; but there'd be another person that you don't know about who'd be in big trouble. Well, we got to save HIM, hain't we? Of course. Well, then, we won't blow on them."[16]

(22) Saying them words put a good idea in my head. I see how maybe I could get me and Jim rid of the frauds; get them jailed here, and then leave. But I didn't want to run the raft in the daytime without anybody aboard to answer questions but me; so I didn't want the plan to begin working till pretty late to-night. I says:

(23) "Miss Mary Jane, I'll tell you what we'll do, and you won't have to stay at Mr. Lothrop's so long, nuther. How fur is it?"

[12] jolt /dʒəʊlt/ *v.* 猛推;使颠簸;使震惊,使觉醒
毫无疑问,这个真相对于她来说无异于天崩地裂。

[13] shoal /ʃəʊl/ *n.* 浅滩;沙洲

[14] afire /ə'faɪə/ *adj.* 燃烧着(的);着火(的)

[15] blow on: 吹凉(食物)
此处指"告发"。

[16] 这一段语言描写的是哈克向玛丽·珍妮解释他的计划安排,同时也从侧面再度展现了这个孩子的聪明和考虑周全。

(24) "A little short of four miles—right out in the country, back here."

(25) "Well, that'll answer. Now you go along out there, and lay low till nine or half-past to-night, and then get them to fetch you home again—tell them you've thought of something. If you get here before eleven put a candle in this window, and if I don't turn up wait *till* eleven, and *then* if I don't turn up it means I'm gone, and out of the way, and safe. Then you come out and spread the news around, and get these beats jailed."

(26) "Good," she says, "I'll do it."

(27) "And if it just happens so that I don't get away, but get took up along with them, you must up and say I told you the whole thing beforehand, and you must stand by me all you can."

(28) "Stand by you![17] indeed I will. They sha'n't touch a hair of your head!" she says, and I see her nostrils spread and her eyes snap when she said it, too.[18]

(29) "If I get away I sha'n't be here," I says, "to prove these rapscallions ain't your uncles, and I couldn't do it if I *was* here. I could swear they was beats and bummers, that's all, though that's worth something. Well, there's others can do that better than what I can, and they're people that ain't going to be doubted as quick as I'd be. I'll tell you how to find them. Gimme a pencil and a piece of paper. There—'Royal Nonesuch, Bricksville.' Put it away, and don't lose it. When the court wants to find out something about these two, let them send up to Bricksville and say they've got the men that played the Royal Nonesuch, and ask for some witnesses—why, you'll have that entire town down here before you can hardly wink, Miss Mary. And they'll come a-biling[19], too."

(30) I judged we had got everything fixed about right now. So I says:

(31) "Just let the auction go right along, and don't worry. Nobody don't have to pay for the things they buy till a whole day after the auction on accounts of the short notice, and they ain't going out of this till they get that money; and the way we've fixed it the sale ain't going to count, and they ain't going

[17] **stand by**: 支持;袖手旁观;准备;站在旁边

此处意为"支持你"。

[18] 我看见她说这番话时,鼻孔微张,眼神坚定。前两句中,玛丽·珍妮表态说她一定会坚决支持哈克,不让人动他一根毫毛。此处对玛丽·珍妮的动作描写实为揭示她此时的心理状态,她斗志昂扬,下定了决心要保护哈克。

[19] **bile** /baɪl/ *n.* 胆汁;愤怒

to get no money. It's just like the way it was with the niggers—it warn't no sale, and the niggers will be back before long. Why, they can't collect the money for the *niggers* yet—they're in the worst kind of a fix, Miss Mary."

(32) "Well," she says, "I'll run down to breakfast now, and then I'll start straight for Mr. Lothrop's."

(33) "Deed, *that* ain't the ticket,[20] Miss Mary Jane," I says, "by no manner of means; go BEFORE breakfast."

(34) "Why?"

(35) "What did you reckon I wanted you to go at all for, Miss Mary?"

(36) "Well, I never thought—and come to think, I don't know. What was it?"

(37) "Why, it's because you ain't one of these leather-face[21] people. I don't want no better book than what your face is.[22] A body can set down and read it off like coarse print. Do you reckon you can go and face your uncles when they come to kiss you good-morning, and never—"

(38) "There, there, don't! Yes, I'll go before breakfast—I'll be glad to. And leave my sisters with them?"

(39) "Yes; never mind about them. They've got to stand it yet a while. They might suspicion something if all of you was to go. I don't want you to see them, nor your sisters, nor nobody in this town; if a neighbor was to ask how is your uncles this morning your face would tell something. No, you go right along, Miss Mary Jane, and I'll fix it with all of them. I'll tell Miss Susan to give your love to your uncles and say you've went away for a few hours for to get a little rest and change, or to see a friend, and you'll be back to-night or early in the morning."

(40) "Gone to see a friend is all right, but I won't have my love given to them."

(41) "Well, then, it sha'n't be." It was well enough to tell HER so—no harm in it. It was only a little thing to do, and no trouble; and it's the little things that smooths people's roads the most, down here below;[23] it would make Mary Jane comfortable, and it wouldn't cost nothing. Then I says: "There's one more

[20] ticket为暗喻用法(metaphor),意指"行之有效的办法"。此处是说哈利认为玛丽·珍妮想早饭后再离开是行不通的。

[21] 厚脸皮的人

[22] 此处仍为双重否定表达否定的意义。原句大致为"I don't want better book than what your face is",字面意思为"我找不到比你的脸更好的书了",实际是说,玛丽·珍妮太容易将心事表现在脸上,就好像白纸黑字印在书上那么一目了然。

[23] 往往就是一些小事情处理得好,才让人们脚下的人生道路顺畅起来。这句话是哈克心里的一句总结,一个十三四岁的孩子的人生经验。今天听来仍然不无道理。

thing—that bag of money."

(42) "Well, they've got that; and it makes me feel pretty silly to think *how* they got it."

(43) "No, you're out, there. They hain't got it."

(44) "Why, who's got it?"

(45) "I wish I knowed, but I don't. I *had* it, because I stole it from them; and I stole it to give to you; and I know where I hid it, but I'm afraid it ain't there no more. I'm awful sorry, Miss Mary Jane, I'm just as sorry as I can be; but I done the best I could; I did honest. I come nigh getting caught, and I had to shove it into the first place I come to, and run—and it warn't a good place."

(46) "Oh, stop blaming yourself—it's too bad to do it, and I won't allow it—you couldn't help it; it wasn't your fault. Where did you hide it?"

(47) I didn't want to set her to thinking about her troubles again; and I couldn't seem to get my mouth to tell her what would make her see that corpse laying in the coffin with that bag of money on his stomach. So for a minute I didn't say nothing; then I says:

(48) "I'd ruther not *tell* you where I put it, Miss Mary Jane, if you don't mind letting me off[24]; but I'll write it for you on a piece of paper, and you can read it along the road to Mr. Lothrop's, if you want to. Do you reckon that 'll do?"[25]

(49) "Oh, yes."

(50) So I wrote: "I put it in the coffin. It was in there when you was crying there, away in the night. I was behind the door, and I was mighty sorry for you, Miss Mary Jane."

(51) It made my eyes water a little to remember her crying there all by herself in the night, and them devils laying there right under her own roof, shaming her and robbing her; and when I folded it up and give it to her I see the water come into her eyes, too; and she shook me by the hand, hard, and says:

(52) "GOOD-bye. I'm going to do everything just as you've told me; and if I don't ever see you again, I sha'n't ever forget you. and I'll think of you a many and a many a time, and I'll PRAY for you, too!"—and she was gone.

(53) Pray for me! I reckoned if she knowed me she'd take

[24] **let off**: 允许离开;准许……暂停工作;宽恕

[25] 第47和第48段说的是哈克因为不忍心告诉玛丽·珍妮他把钱藏在叔叔彼得的棺木里,而大费周章地安排写在纸上事后告知。哈克的善良、细心再一次体现在细节中。

a job that was more nearer her size.[26] But I bet she done it, just the same—she was just that kind. She had the grit to pray for Judus if she took the notion—there warn't no back-down to her, I judge.[27] You may say what you want to, but in my opinion she had more sand in her than any girl I ever see; in my opinion she was just full of sand[28]. It sounds like flattery, but it ain't no flattery. And when it comes to beauty—and goodness, too—she lays over them all. I hain't ever seen her since that time that I see her go out of that door; no, I hain't ever seen her since, but I reckon I've thought of her a many and a many a million times, and of her saying she would pray for me; and if ever I'd a thought it would do any good for me to pray for HER, blamed if I wouldn't a done it or bust.

(54) Well, Mary Jane she lit out the back way, I reckon; because nobody see her go. When I struck Susan and the hare-lip, I says:

(55) "What's the name of them people over on t'other side of the river that you all goes to see sometimes?"

(56) They says:

(57) "There's several; but it's the Proctors, mainly."

(58) "That's the name," I says; "I most forgot it. Well, Miss Mary Jane she told me to tell you she's gone over there in a dreadful hurry—one of them's sick."

(59) "Which one?"

(60) "I don't know; leastways, I kinder forget; but I thinks it's—"

(61) "Sakes alive, I hope it ain't HANNER?"

(62) "I'm sorry to say it," I says, "but Hanner's the very one."

(63) "My goodness, and she so well only last week! Is she took bad?"

(64) "It ain't no name for it. They set up with[29] her all night, Miss Mary Jane said, and they don't think she'll last many hours."

(65) "Only think of that, now! What's the matter with her?"

(66) I couldn't think of anything reasonable, right off that way, so I says:

(67) "Mumps[30]."

[26] 我猜她要是知道我其实是个什么样的人,她就会做更符合她身份的事了。这里是指哈克认为玛丽·珍妮十分善良,知道自己曾经做过"坏事",会鄙弃自己而不再为自己祈祷。

[27] 但我打赌她还是会为我祈祷的——她就是那样一种人,一旦下定决心,就算是犹大她也会为他祈祷的。她从来不会食言,我就是这么觉得的。

[28] 这里指玛丽·珍妮充满了勇气,浑身是胆。

[29] set up with: 向……提供……
此处指陪护、看护生病的人。

[30] mumps /mʌmps/ *n.* 流行性腮腺炎

(68) "Mumps your granny! They don't set up with people that's got the mumps." [31]

(69) "They don't, don't they? You better bet they do with *these* mumps. These mumps is different. It's a new kind, Miss Mary Jane said."

(70) "How's it a new kind?"

(71) "Because it's mixed up with other things."

(72) "What other things?"

(73) "Well, measles[32], and whooping-cough, and erysiplas, and consumption, and yaller janders, and brain-fever, and I don't know what all."

(74) "My land! And they call it the MUMPS? "

(75) "That's what Miss Mary Jane said."

(76) "Well, what in the nation do they call it the MUMPS for?"

(77) "Why, because it is the mumps. That's what it starts with."

(78) "Well, ther' ain't no sense in it. A body might stump his toe, and take pison, and fall down the well, and break his neck, and bust his brains out, and somebody come along and ask what killed him, and some numskull[33] up and say, 'Why, he stumped his TOE.' Would ther' be any sense in that? NO. And ther' ain't no sense in *this*, nuther. Is it ketching?"

(79) "Is it KETCHING[34]? Why, how you talk. Is a HARROW[35] catching—in the dark? If you don't hitch on to one tooth, you're bound to on another, ain't you? And you can't get away with that tooth without fetching the whole harrow along, can you? Well, these kind of mumps is a kind of a harrow, as you may say—and it ain't no slouch of a harrow, nuther, you come to get it hitched on good."

(80) "Well, it's awful, I think," says the hare-lip. "I'll go to Uncle Harvey and—"

(81) "Oh, yes," I says, "I *would*. OF COURSE I would. I wouldn't lose no time."

(82) "Well, why wouldn't you?"

(83) "Just look at it a minute, and maybe you can see. Hain't your uncles obleegd to get along home to England as fast as they can? And do you reckon they'd be mean enough to go

[31] 腮腺炎个屁！得腮腺炎的人不用人看护。玛丽·珍妮离开后，哈克遇到了兔唇女孩和苏珊。两人询问玛丽·珍妮离开的原因，为了保证计划的顺利进行，哈克向她们撒了谎。这几个对话段落都是哈克对女孩子们撒谎的内容。和第二十六章中与兔唇女孩在厨房聊天时的对话类似，都有违反"合作原则"的地方。例如，这一句就被女孩子们当场揭穿所说并非事实，明显违反了"质的原则"。然而和第二十六章不同的是，这里哈克撒谎完全是为了保护女孩子们而不是为了蒙混过关。（"合作原则"详见本章"精华赏析"。）

[32] measle /ˈmiːzl/ *n.* 麻疹

[33] numskull /ˈnʌmskʌl/ *n.* 傻瓜；笨蛋（同 numbskull）

[34] 此处应为 catching，这里是双关（pun）的用法。既指疾病有传染性，也指耙子扎人。

[35] harrow /ˈhærəʊ/ *n.* 耙

off and leave you to go all that journey by yourselves? *You* know they'll wait for you. So fur, so good.[36] Your uncle Harvey's a preacher, ain't he? Very well, then; is a *preacher* going to deceive a steamboat clerk? is he going to deceive a *ship clerk*?—so as to get them to let Miss Mary Jane go aboard? Now *you* know he ain't. What *will* he do, then? Why, he'll say, 'It's a great pity, but my church matters has got to get along the best way they can; for my niece has been exposed to the dreadful pluribus-unum mumps, and so it's my bounden duty to set down here and wait the three months it takes to show on her if she's got it.' But never mind, if you think it's best to tell your uncle Harvey—"[37]

(84) "Shucks, and stay fooling around here when we could all be having good times in England whilst we was waiting to find out whether Mary Jane's got it or not? Why, you talk like a muggins."

(85)" Well, anyway, maybe you'd better tell some of the neighbors."

(86) "Listen at that, now. You do beat all for natural stupidness. Can't you *see* that THEY'D go and tell? Ther' ain't no way but just to not tell anybody at *all*."

(87) "Well, maybe you're right—yes, I judge you ARE right."

(88) "But I reckon we ought to tell Uncle Harvey she's gone out a while, anyway, so he won't be uneasy about her?"

(89) "Yes, Miss Mary Jane she wanted you to do that. She says, 'Tell them to give Uncle Harvey and William my love and a kiss, and say I've run over the river to see Mr.'—Mr.—what IS the name of that rich family your uncle Peter used to think so much of?—I mean the one that—"

(90) "Why, you must mean the Apthorps, ain't it?"

(91) "Of course; bother them kind of names, a body can't ever seem to remember them, half the time, somehow. Yes, she said, say she has run over for to ask the Apthorps to be sure and come to the auction and buy this house, because she allowed her uncle Peter would ruther they had it than anybody else; and she's going to stick to them till they say they'll come, and then, if she ain't too tired, she's coming home; and if she is, she'll be home in the morning anyway. She said, don't say nothing about the

[36] 应为so far, so good,意为"到目前为止一切顺利;到目前还好"。

[37] 这部分说的是哈克向苏珊和兔唇女孩解释自己为什么没有去告诉"叔叔们"玛丽·珍妮离家的事情。

这段话有176词,比较长,有违背"合作原则"中"量的原则"之嫌。(详见本章"精华赏析"。)然而,我们分析文本可发现,这可能是基于两个原因:(1)因为哈克太想让对方相信自己的谎言而解释得太多太细;(2)哈克实际意图是想让女孩子们替他向"叔叔们"撒谎,以保证计划的顺利进行,所以附加了很多额外信息。

我们可以将哈克这一次和女孩子们撒谎的对话和第二十六章中哈克向兔唇女孩撒谎胡说时的那番话进行比较。这一次,哈克准备得更为充分,也没有出现所说内容明显和话题"不相关"的情况。

Proctors, but only about the Apthorps—which 'll be perfectly true, because she is going there to speak about their buying the house; I know it, because she told me so herself."

(92) "All right," they said, and cleared out to lay for their uncles, and give them the love and the kisses, and tell them the message.

(93) Everything was all right now. The girls wouldn't say nothing because they wanted to go to England; and the king and the duke would ruther Mary Jane was off working for the auction than around in reach of Doctor Robinson. I felt very good; I judged I had done it pretty neat—I reckoned Tom Sawyer couldn't a done it no neater himself. Of course he would a throwed more style into it, but I can't do that very handy, not being brung up to it.[38]

(94) Well, they held the auction in the public square, along towards the end of the afternoon, and it strung along[39], and strung along, and the old man he was on hand and looking his level pisonest, up there longside of the auctioneer, and chipping in a little Scripture now and then, or a little goody-goody saying of some kind, and the duke he was around goo-gooing for sympathy all he knowed how, and just spreading himself generly.

(95) But by and by the thing dragged through, and everything was sold—everything but a little old trifling lot[40] in the graveyard. So they'd got to work that off—I never see such a girafft as the king was for wanting to swallow *everything*. Well, whilst they was at it a steamboat landed, and in about two minutes up comes a crowd a-whooping and yelling and laughing and carrying on, and singing out:

(96) "HERE'S your opposition line! here's your two sets o' heirs to old Peter Wilks—and you pays your money and you takes your choice!"

[38] 这一段是对哈克的心理描写。回答完女孩子们的疑问后,哈克在心中暗暗地总结评价了一番自己的安排。正如哈克所期望的,女孩子们因为急于跟着"叔叔们"回到英国生活而按照哈克的意思就玛丽·珍妮离家的原因对"叔叔们"撒了谎;而"国王"和"公爵"也巴不得玛丽·珍妮拍卖的那天不在场,因为这样她就不会受到罗宾逊医生的影响。一切都如哈克所期望的一般顺利,他对自己的表现十分满意,洋洋得意地想着,汤姆·索亚也不能干得更漂亮了……读者朋友们,你们对哈克的表现还满意吗?

[39] **string along**: 欺骗;跟随 此处指拍卖延迟、拖延。

[40] **trifling** /ˈtraɪflɪŋ/ *adj.* 微不足道的

lot /lɒt/ n. 份额;命运;阄 这里 trifling lot 指的是墓地上一些零碎的小东西。

精华赏析

马克·吐温作品的一大特色是幽默的语言风格。在《哈克贝利·费恩历险记》中,这一点体现得十分突出。在本书中,无论是天真的童稚话语,还是极富地方特色的美国口语,以及黑人语言等,都传递出了许多幽默的元素。在本章当中,玛丽·珍妮因为两个骗子将家里的黑奴母女卖给了不同人家,导致亲情阻隔,而伤心不已。哈克深为玛丽·珍妮的善良所感动,再也不忍继续欺骗,于是将真相和盘托出。哈克定下计划,先让玛丽·珍妮离开家三四天,然后他再来对付"国王"和"公爵"。为了解释玛丽·珍妮的离开,哈克谎称她去拜访病人。在这一部分,我们将主要以在玛丽·珍妮离开后哈克撒谎以掩人耳目的对话部分为例,用"合作原则"的理论来集中分析讨论马克·吐温的语言幽默。

"合作原则"(Cooperative Principle,简称 CP),是由美国著名语言哲学家格赖斯(Grice)在 1975 年提出的。格赖斯认为,人们在交际过程中,对话双方彼此合作,遵循着某一原则,以求共同有效地完成交际任务。这一原则包含四条准则九条细则(何学德,2005),我们将其总结如下:

(1)量的准则(The Maxim of Quantity)

1)所说的话应该满足交际所需的信息量

2)所说的话不应超出交际所需的信息量

(2)质的准则(The Maxim of Quality)

1)不要说自知是虚假的话

2)不要说缺乏足够证据的话

(3)关系准则(The Maxim of Relation)

所说的话必须相关

(4)方式准则(The Maxim of Manner)

1)避免晦涩

2)避免歧义

3)简练

4)要有条理

然而,在实际言语交际中,人们却常常故意违反"合作原则"以达到特别的交际目的。在本章中,哈克面对苏珊和兔唇女孩的询问,东拉西扯,胡诌了各种漏洞百出的理由。这部分对话很有意思,接下来,我们就用这四条准则对这一部分对话进行具体分析。

首先,关于量的准则。这一部分对话从本章第 55 段一直持续到本章第 91 段,对话内容长达 900 余词。其中,除了苏珊和兔唇女孩寥寥数语的询问,绝大部分都是哈克的解释。试想,正常情况下回答此类问题绝不至于达到近 1 000 词,这甚至远远超过了一篇专业八级英语作文的字数要求,明显违反了量的准则。而哈克之所以提供了远远超过所需的信息量,一则是因为他说的并非事实,反而解释得过多;二则是因为他说这番话真正的意图是让两个女孩同意就玛丽·珍妮离家的原因去向“国王”和“公爵”撒谎,以保证计划的顺利实施。此时,违反“量的准则”恰恰暗示了哈克心中藏有不同于表面的其他意图。

其次,关于质的准则。在长达几百词的解释中,哈克说了许多他自己以及作为读者的我们都心知肚明的假话,他给出的解释也是漏洞百出,这些都明显违反了质的准则。读者在读到哈克胡扯玛丽·珍妮的朋友得了腮腺炎被看出漏洞,于是又继续东拉西扯,胡诌这是一种“新的腮腺炎”,并且这种“新的腮腺炎”还会带来“麻疹,百日咳,丹毒,肺病,黄疸病,脑膜炎”的并发症时,恐怕会忍俊不禁,如果真有人集这许多种并不相干的疾病于一身的话,也算是百病缠身了吧。在读到这些明显不合逻辑的地方时,我们在感慨这个不过十三四岁的小孩子之聪明大胆的同时,由于深知哈克“满嘴跑火车”是为了帮助保护善良的玛丽·珍妮姐妹,也就更能真切地体会到这个混迹于社会底层的白人孩子身上所具有的善良勇敢的可贵品质。此时,这些违反了“质的原则”的假话,反而句句都传递出哈克的真诚善意,并且由于和真实情况反差巨大,产生了一种极其诙谐幽默的效果。

再次,关于关系准则。本章中哈克向兔唇女孩和苏珊解释玛丽·珍妮离开家的原因时虽然东拉西扯,解释显得有些牵强,但还算不上典型的“不相关”的情况。与本章的这番对话相比,在第二十六章中,哈克与兔唇女孩在厨房里聊天的那番对话出现了更为典型的违反“相关性原则”的现象。事实上,我们在批注中已经提过,哈克在那一次的对话中,两次假装被鸡骨头卡到喉咙来脱困,“鸡骨头卡住喉咙”的小插曲明显和他们所谈的话题毫无关系,但恰好是只有这样才能实现哈克真正的交际目的——转移话题,摆脱被发现漏洞的困境。

最后,当以上三条准则被违反之时,很明显方式准则也已经被违反了。哈克的解释废话连篇,毫无简练可言,并且漏洞百出,逻辑牵强,他用和话题完全不相干的事情来打岔的时候,自然也谈不上简练或有条理。

然而,正是在违反了“合作原则”之后,哈克的整个表现显得滑稽又可爱,读者们忍俊不禁的同时,考虑到哈克真正的用意是如此善良,恐怕又难免会对这个人物油然而生几分喜爱和敬佩吧。

阅读思考

1. 试比较本章中哈克对兔唇女孩以及苏珊撒谎时的对话以及第二十六章中哈克在厨房对兔唇女孩撒谎时的对话,分析其异同。

2. 请谈谈你对哈克贝利·费恩制定的帮助玛丽·珍妮姐妹计划的看法,并给出细节支持你的观点。

CHAPTER XXIX

导读:正当"国王"和"公爵"忙着拍卖姑娘们的产业时,人群拥着两个陌生人出现了,这两人声称自己是真正的哈维和威廉。由于双方都称对方是冒牌货,于是,此前就质疑"国王"和"公爵"身份的医生,同刚从外地回来的律师,以及目睹"国王"一行人上岸的证人一起,提出了一系列问题让双方对质。最终,大家决定开棺验尸以辨真伪。然而,就在开棺时,又发生了让大家意想不到的情况。

(1) THEY was fetching a very nice-looking old gentleman along, and a nice-looking younger one, with his right arm in a sling. And, my souls[1], how the people yelled and laughed, and kept it up. But I didn't see no joke about it, and I judged it would strain the duke and the king some to see any. I reckoned they'd turn pale. But no, nary a pale did THEY turn. The duke he never let on he suspicioned what was up, but just went a goo-gooing around, happy and satisfied, like a jug that's googling out buttermilk; and as for the king, he just gazed and gazed down sorrowful on them new-comers like it give him the stomach-ache in his very heart to think there could be such frauds and rascals in the world.[2] Oh, he done it admirable.[3] Lots of the principal people gethered around the king, to let him see they was on his side. That old gentleman that had just come looked all puzzled to death. Pretty soon he begun to speak, and I see straight off he pronounced LIKE an Englishman—not the king's way, though the king's *was* pretty good for an imitation. I can't give the old gent's words, nor I can't imitate him; but he turned around to the crowd, and says, about like this:

(2) "This is a surprise to me which I wasn't looking for; and I'll acknowledge, candid and frank, I ain't very well

[1] 此处表达感叹,大意为"天呐"。

[2] 这一处对"国王"和"公爵"的行为描写十分精彩。因为"真正的"哈维和威廉出现了,哈克以为冒牌货"国王"和"公爵"肯定会吓得脸都白了。但事实上,"公爵"脸上丝毫看不出担忧,反而看起来得意又高兴;而"国王"呢,"心痛地"看着新来的这两个人,神情悲悯,仿佛在感叹世间怎么会有这样的无赖。这里,哈克以及读者的心理预期和实际情况相差甚远,这种巨大反差带来了强烈的戏剧效果,两个骗子的厚颜无耻和高超演技实在令人惊叹。

[3] 哦,他演得可真够精彩的啊!

fixed to meet it and answer it; for my brother and me has had misfortunes; he's broke his arm, and our baggage got put off at a town above here last night in the night by a mistake. I am Peter Wilks' brother Harvey, and this is his brother William, which can't hear nor speak—and can't even make signs to amount to much, now't he's only got one hand to work them with. We are who we say we are; and in a day or two, when I get the baggage, I can prove it. But up till then I won't say nothing more, but go to the hotel and wait."

(3) So him and the new dummy started off; and the king he laughs, and blethers[4] out:

(4) "Broke his arm—*very* likely, AIN'T it?—and very convenient, too, for a fraud that's got to make signs, and ain't learnt how. Lost their baggage! That's MIGHTY good!—and mighty ingenious—under the CIRCUMSTANCES!"

(5) So he laughed again; and so did everybody else, except three or four, or maybe half a dozen. One of these was that doctor; another one was a sharp-looking gentleman, with a carpet-bag of the old-fashioned kind made out of carpet-stuff,[5] that had just come off of the steamboat and was talking to him in a low voice, and glancing towards the king now and then and nodding their heads—it was Levi Bell, the lawyer that was gone up to Louisville; and another one was a big rough husky[6] that come along and listened to all the old gentleman said, and was listening to the king now. And when the king got done this husky up and says:

(6) "Say, looky here; if you are Harvey Wilks, when'd you come to this town?"

(7) "The day before the funeral, friend," says the king.

(8) "But what time o' day?"

(9) "In the evenin'—'bout an hour er two before sundown."

(10) "*How'd* you come?"

(11) "I come down on the Susan Powell from Cincinnati."

(12) "Well, then, how'd you come to be up at the Pint in the *mornin'*—in a canoe?"

(13) "I warn't up at the Pint in the mornin'."

[4] blether /ˈbleðər/ *v.* 胡说

[5] 另外一位是名老绅士，他目光锐利，手里拿着一个用毛毯做的老式旅行袋。情节发展至此，律师出场了。他的出场伴随着对他的外貌描写，而人物特征便已可从中显示一二了。

[6] husky /ˈhʌskɪ/ *n.* 强壮结实之人

(14) "It's a lie." [7]

(15) Several of them jumped for him and begged him not to talk that way to an old man and a preacher.

(16) "Preacher be hanged, he's a fraud and a liar. He was up at the Pint that mornin'. I live up there, don't I? Well, I was up there, and he was up there. I see him there. He come in a canoe, along with Tim Collins and a boy."

(17) The doctor he up and says:

(18) "Would you know the boy again if you was to see him, Hines?"

(19) "I reckon I would, but I don't know. Why, yonder he is, now. I know him perfectly easy."

(20) It was me he pointed at. The doctor says:

(21) "Neighbors, I don't know whether the new couple is frauds or not; but if *these* two ain't frauds, I am an idiot, that's all. I think it's our duty to see that they don't get away from here till we've looked into this thing. Come along, Hines; come along, the rest of you. We'll take these fellows to the tavern and affront them with t'other couple, and I reckon we'll find out *something* before we get through." [8]

(22) It was nuts for the crowd, though maybe not for the king's friends; so we all started. It was about sundown. The doctor he led me along by the hand, and was plenty kind enough, but he never let go my hand.

(23) We all got in a big room in the hotel, and lit up some candles, and fetched in the new couple. First, the doctor says:

(24) "I don't wish to be too hard on these two men, but I think they're frauds, and they may have complices[9] that we don't know nothing about. If they have, won't the complices get away with that bag of gold Peter Wilks left? It ain't unlikely. If these men ain't frauds, they won't object to sending for that money and letting us keep it till they prove they're all right—ain't that so?"

(25) Everybody agreed to that. So I judged they had our gang in a pretty tight place right at the outstart. But the king he only looked sorrowful, and says:

[7] 第6—14段这几句对话，讲述的是一位曾亲睹"国王"一行人乘木筏上岸的村民主动站出来和"国王"对质。此前对于两个骗子的身份无论是否有疑问，人们都没有实质性的证据，这里是第一次有人拿出实证。在情节发展上，这是一个比较重要的细节。

[8] 乡亲们，我现在还不知道新来的那两个人是不是骗子，但如果我看不出这两个家伙是骗子，我就太愚蠢了，事实就是如此。我认为我们有责任确保在把事情调查清楚之前，这两人不会逃脱。来吧，海因斯，大家伙儿都一起去吧。我们应该把这几个人带到客栈去，让他们和其他人对质。我想，不用花太大力气我们就能发现一些蛛丝马迹。

这个段落是对医生的语言描写，是一段医生的独白。从中能看出三点：(1)医生的逻辑清晰，表达简洁；(2)医生的语言表达比较规范，而且口语中的缩略用词或发音没有什么错误；(3)医生此时在争取话语权，控制局面。作者在这里通过对医生的语言描写塑造了这个人物。

[9] complice /ˈkɒmplɪs/ *n.* 同谋者；帮凶

(26)"Gentlemen, I wish the money was there, for I ain't got no disposition[10] to throw anything in the way of a fair, open, out-and-out investigation[11] o' this misable business; but, alas, the money ain't there; you k'n send and see, if you want to."

(27)"Where is it, then?"

(28)"Well, when my niece give it to me to keep for her I took and hid it inside o' the straw tick o' my bed, not wishin' to bank it for the few days we'd be here, and considerin' the bed a safe place, we not bein' used to niggers, and suppos'n' 'em honest, like servants in England. The niggers stole it the very next mornin' after I had went down stairs; and when I sold 'em I hadn't missed the money yit, so they got clean away with it. My servant here k'n tell you 'bout it, gentlemen."

(29) The doctor and several said "Shucks!" and I see nobody didn't altogether believe him. One man asked me if I see the niggers steal it. I said no, but I see them sneaking out[12] of the room and hustling away, and I never thought nothing, only I reckoned they was afraid they had waked up my master and was trying to get away before he made trouble with them. That was all they asked me. Then the doctor whirls on me and says:

(30)"Are *you* English, too?"

(31) I says yes; and him and some others laughed, and said, "Stuff!"[13]

(32) Well, then they sailed in[14] on the general investigation, and there we had it, up and down, hour in, hour out, and nobody never said a word about supper, nor ever seemed to think about it — and so they kept it up, and kept it up; and it *was* the worst mixed-up thing you ever see. They made the king tell his yarn[15], and they made the old gentleman tell his'n; and anybody but a lot of prejudiced chuckleheads would a *seen* that the old gentleman was spinning truth and t'other one lies. And by and by they had me up to tell what I knowed. The king he give me a left-handed look out of the corner of his eye, and so I knowed enough to talk on the right side.[16] I begun to tell about Sheffield, and how we lived there, and all about the English Wilkses, and so on; but I didn't get pretty fur till the doctor begun to laugh;

[10] **disposition** /dɪspəˈzɪʃ(ə)n/ *n.* 性情

[11] 这里指"公开、公正、公平地进行调查"。

[12] **sneak out**: 开溜;偷偷摸摸地走

[13] 此处为咒骂的语言。

[14] **sail in**: 仪态万方地走进来;劲头十足地行动起来;毅然出面

[15] **yarn** /jɑːn/ *n.* 奇谈;故事

[16] "国王"悄悄给我使了一个眼色,我马上就明白该怎么说话了。这里的行为描写将哈克的机灵劲儿十分传神地呈现了出来。

and Levi Bell, the lawyer, says:

(33) "Set down, my boy; I wouldn't strain myself if I was you. I reckon you ain't used to lying, it don't seem to come handy; what you want is practice. You do it pretty awkward." [17]

(34) I didn't care nothing for the compliment, but I was glad to be let off, anyway. [18]

(35) The doctor he started to say something, and turns and says:

(36) "If you'd been in town at first, Levi Bell—"

(37) The king broke in and reached out his hand, and says:

(38) "Why, is this my poor dead brother's old friend that he's wrote so often about?"

(39) The lawyer and him shook hands, and the lawyer smiled and looked pleased, and they talked right along[19] awhile, and then got to one side and talked low; and at last the lawyer speaks up and says:

(40) "That'll fix it. I'll take the order and send it, along with your brother's, and then they'll know it's all right."

(41) So they got some paper and a pen, and the king he set down and twisted his head to one side, and chawed[20] his tongue, and scrawled[21] off something; and then they give the pen to the duke—and then for the first time the duke looked sick. But he took the pen and wrote. So then the lawyer turns to the new old gentleman and says:

(42) "You and your brother please write a line or two and sign your names."

(43) The old gentleman wrote, but nobody couldn't read it. The lawyer looked powerful astonished, and says:

(44) "Well, it beats *me*[22]—and snaked a lot of old letters out of his pocket, and examined them, and then examined the old man's writing, and then THEM again; and then says: "These old letters is from Harvey Wilks; and here's *these* two handwritings, and anybody can see they didn't write them" (the king and the duke looked sold and foolish, I tell you, to see how the lawyer had took them in), "and here's *this* old gentleman's hand writing, and anybody can tell, easy enough, *He* didn't write

[17] 尽管哈克十分聪明机灵，但毕竟年纪尚小，所见所知有限，更重要的是他对于撒谎并不像“国王”和“公爵”那般心安理得。律师很快便发现了破绽。

[18] 这句语言描写实在是太过有趣。对于律师揭穿自己谎言的事儿，哈克认为这是一种夸赞，因为律师说“他不常，也不擅长撒谎”。在读了许多哈克聪明机智，考虑周全的计划安排后，再读到这句话，一个天真、单纯、孩子气的哈克的形象一下就打动了读者的心，让我们记起，他毕竟还只是一个孩子。

[19] right along: 不停地；继续地；不断地

[20] chaw /tʃɔː/ *v.* 咀嚼（烟草）

[21] scrawl /skrɔːl/ *v.* 马马虎虎（或潦草）地写

[22] 此处意为“这可难倒我了”。

them—fact is, the scratches he makes ain't properly *writing* at all. Now, here's some letters from—"

(45) The new old gentleman says:

(46) "If you please, let me explain. Nobody can read my hand but my brother there—so he copies for me. It's *his* hand you've got there, not mine."

(47) "*Well*!" says the lawyer, "this IS a state of things. I've got some of William's letters, too; so if you'll get him to write a line or so we can com—"

(48) "He *can't* write with his left hand," says the old gentleman. "If he could use his right hand, you would see that he wrote his own letters and mine too. Look at both, please—they're by the same hand."

(49) The lawyer done it, and says:

(50) "I believe it's so—and if it ain't so, there's a heap[23] stronger resemblance than I'd noticed before, anyway. Well, well, well! I thought we was right on the track of a slution, but it's gone to grass, partly. But anyway, one thing is proved—*these* two ain't either of 'em Wilkses" —and he wagged[24] his head towards the king and the duke.

(51) Well, what do you think? That muleheaded old fool wouldn't give in *then*! Indeed he wouldn't. Said it warn't no fair test. Said his brother William was the cussedest joker in the world, and hadn't tried to write — *he* see William was going to play one of his jokes the minute he put the pen to paper. And so he warmed up and went warbling[25] right along till he was actuly beginning to believe what he was saying *himself*; but pretty soon the new gentleman broke in, and says:

(52) "I've thought of something. Is there anybody here that helped to lay out[26] my br—helped to lay out the late Peter Wilks for burying?"

(53) "Yes," says somebody, "me and Ab Turner done it. We're both here."

(54) Then the old man turns towards the king, and says:

(55) "Perhaps this gentleman can tell me what was tattooed on his breast?"

[23] heap /hiːp/ *n.* 堆；许多；累积

[24] wag /wæg/ *v.*（动物尾巴）来回摇摆；来回摇动（竖立的手指）

[25] warble /ˈwɔːrbl/ *v.* 鸟鸣；用柔和的颤声唱
此处是指“国王”滔滔不绝地编造谎言。

[26] lay out：展示；安排
此处指的是“装殓（去世的彼得）”。

(56) Blamed if the king didn't have to brace up mighty quick, or he'd a squshed down like a bluff bank that the river has cut under, it took him so sudden; and, mind you, it was a thing that was calculated to make most *anybody* sqush[27] to get fetched such a solid one as that without any notice, because how was HE going to know what was tattooed on the man? He whitened a little; he couldn't help it; and it was mighty still in there, and everybody bending a little forwards and gazing at him. Says I to myself, *now* he'll throw up the sponge[28]—there ain't no more use. Well, did he? A body can't hardly believe it, but he didn't. I reckon he thought he'd keep the thing up till he tired them people out, so they'd thin out[29], and him and the duke could break loose and get away. Anyway, he set there, and pretty soon he begun to smile, and says:

(57) "Mf! It's a *very* tough question, AIN'T it! *Yes*, sir, I k'n tell you what's tattooed on his breast. It's jest a small, thin, blue arrow—that's what it is; and if you don't look clost, you can't see it. *Now* what do you say—hey?"

(58) Well, I never see anything like that old blister for clean out-and-out cheek.[30]

(59) The new old gentleman turns brisk[31] towards Ab Turner and his pard, and his eye lights up like he judged he'd got the king *this* time, and says:

(60) "There—you've heard what he said! Was there any such mark on Peter Wilks' breast?"

(61) Both of them spoke up and says:

(62) "We didn't see no such mark."

(63) "Good!" says the old gentleman. "Now, what you *did* see on his breast was a small dim P, and a B (which is an initial he dropped when he was young), and a W, with dashes between them, so: P—B—W" —and he marked them that way on a piece of paper. "Come, ain't that what you saw?"

(64) Both of them spoke up again, and says:

(65) "No, we *didn't*. We never seen any marks at all."

(66) Well, everybody *was* in a state of mind now, and they sings out:

[27] 这个词并不存在,这里可能指的是squash,原意为"挤压,粉碎"。

[28] throw up the sponge: 放弃;投降认输

[29] thin out: 使稀薄;使稀疏此处指人们松懈下来。

[30] out-and-out: 彻头彻尾的
天呐,我可真是从没见过这么厚颜无耻之人。
这里是暗喻(metaphor)用法。

[31] brisk /brɪsk/ *adj.* 敏锐的;轻快的

(67) "The whole BILIN' of 'm 's frauds! Le's duck 'em! le's drown 'em! le's ride 'em on a rail!" and everybody was whooping[32] at once, and there was a rattling powwow. But the lawyer he jumps on the table and yells, and says:

(68) "Gentlemen—*gentlemen*! Hear me just a word—just a SINGLE word—if you PLEASE! There's one way yet—let's go and dig up the corpse and look."

(69) That took them.

(70) "Hooray!"[33] they all shouted, and was starting right off; but the lawyer and the doctor sung out:

(71) "Hold on, hold on! Collar all these four men and the boy, and fetch THEM along, too!"

(72) "We'll do it!" they all shouted; "and if we don't find them marks we'll lynch the whole gang!"

(73) I *was* scared, now, I tell you. But there warn't no getting away, you know. They gripped us all, and marched us right along, straight for the graveyard, which was a mile and a half down the river, and the whole town at our heels[34], for we made noise enough, and it was only nine in the evening.

(74) As we went by our house I wished I hadn't sent Mary Jane out of town; because now if I could tip her the wink she'd light out and save me, and blow on our dead-beats.

(75) Well, we swarmed along down the river road, just carrying on like wildcats; and to make it more scary the sky was darking up, and the lightning beginning to wink and flitter, and the wind to shiver amongst the leaves. This was the most awful trouble and most dangersome I ever was in; and I was kinder stunned; everything was going so different from what I had allowed for; stead of being fixed so I could take my own time if I wanted to, and see all the fun,[35] and have Mary Jane at my back to save me and set me free when the close-fit come, here was nothing in the world betwixt me and sudden death but just them tattoo-marks. If they didn't find them—

(76) I couldn't bear to think about it; and yet, somehow, I couldn't think about nothing else. It got darker and darker, and it was a beautiful time to give the crowd the slip; but that big

[32] whoop /'hu:p/ *v.* 高叫

[33] hooray /hʊ'reɪ/ *int.*（表喜悦、赞同等）好极了；万岁

[34] at one's heels: 紧随；紧跟在某人的后面

[35] take one's own time: 从容不迫，这里指的是哈克本以为他能够轻轻松松地看着“国王”和“公爵”出丑，没想到自己也受到了牵连。

husky had me by the wrist—Hines—and a body might as well try to give Goliar[36] the slip. He dragged me right along, he was so excited, and I had to run to keep up.

(77) When they got there they swarmed into the graveyard and washed over it like an overflow. And when they got to the grave they found they had about a hundred times as many shovels as they wanted, but nobody hadn't thought to fetch a lantern. But they sailed into digging anyway by the flicker of the lightning, and sent a man to the nearest house, a half a mile off, to borrow one.

(78) So they dug and dug like everything; and it got awful dark, and the rain started, and the wind swished[37] and swushed along, and the lightning come brisker and brisker, and the thunder boomed; but them people never took no notice of it, they was so full of this business; and one minute you could see everything and every face in that big crowd, and the shovelfuls of dirt sailing up out of the grave, and the next second the dark wiped it all out, and you couldn't see nothing at all.[38]

(79) At last they got out the coffin and begun to unscrew the lid, and then such another crowding and shouldering and shoving as there was, to scrouge[39] in and get a sight, you never see; and in the dark, that way, it was awful. Hines he hurt my wrist dreadful pulling and tugging so, and I reckon he clean forgot I was in the world, he was so excited and panting.

(80) All of a sudden the lightning let go a perfect sluice[40] of white glare, and somebody sings out:

(81) "By the living jingo,[41] here's the bag of gold on his breast!"

(82) Hines let out a whoop, like everybody else, and dropped my wrist and give a big surge to bust his way in and get a look, and the way I lit out and shinned for the road in the dark there ain't nobody can tell.

(83) I had the road all to myself, and I fairly flew—leastways, I had it all to myself except the solid dark, and the now-and-then glares, and the buzzing of the rain, and the thrashing[42] of the wind, and the splitting of the thunder; and sure as

[36] 此处应该是goliath [/gə'laɪəθ/ *n.* 巨人;哥利亚(圣经中被大卫杀死的巨人)]
此处指海因斯死死抓住哈克,令他难以脱逃。

[37] swish /swɪʃ/ *v.* 鞭打;使发出沙沙声

[38] 这一段中,前三行和最后一行为景物描写,一片漆黑中,风雨雷电大作;其余则是对哈克的心理描写。在这个段落里,情景交融,寓情于景,以景抒情,表现了哈克此时绝望迷茫的心情。

[39] scrouge /skraʊdʒ/ *v.* 推;挤

[40] sluice /slu:s/ *n.* 水闸;洗矿槽
这里指的是一道白色闪电的亮光。

[41] 此处表强烈的感叹,大意为"我的老天啊,上帝啊"。

[42] thrash /θræʃ/ *v.* 打;逆行;猛烈摆动

you are born I did clip it along![43]

(84) When I struck the town I see there warn't nobody out in the storm, so I never hunted for no back streets, but humped[44] it straight through the main one; and when I begun to get towards our house I aimed my eye and set it. No light there; the house all dark—which made me feel sorry and disappointed, I didn't know why. But at last, just as I was sailing by, FLASH comes the light in Mary Jane's window! and my heart swelled up sudden, like to bust; and the same second the house and all was behind me in the dark, and wasn't ever going to be before me no more in this world. She *was* the best girl I ever see, and had the most sand.

(85) The minute I was far enough above the town to see I could make the towhead[45], I begun to look sharp for a boat to borrow, and the first time the lightning showed me one that wasn't chained I snatched it and shoved. It was a canoe, and warn't fastened with nothing but a rope. The towhead was a rattling big distance off, away out there in the middle of the river, but I didn't lose no time; and when I struck the raft at last I was so fagged[46] I would a just laid down to blow and gasp if I could afforded it. But I didn't. As I sprung aboard I sung out:

(86) "Out with you, Jim, and set her loose! Glory be to goodness, we're shut of them!"

(87) Jim lit out, and was a-coming for me with both arms spread, he was so full of joy; but when I glimpsed him in the lightning my heart shot up in my mouth and I went overboard backwards; for I forgot he was old King Lear and a drownded A-rab all in one, and it most scared the livers and lights out of me. But Jim fished me out, and was going to hug me and bless me, and so on, he was so glad I was back and we was shut of the king and the duke,[47] but I says:

(88) "Not now; have it for breakfast, have it for breakfast! Cut loose and let her slide!"

(89) So in two seconds away we went a-sliding down the river, and it *did* seem so good to be free again and all by ourselves on the big river, and nobody to bother us.[48] I had to skip

[43] 这一段不长，却有近三行都是景物描写。这些景物描写从侧面反映了此时此景下哈克的心情。

[44] hump /hʌmp/ *v.* 隆起；急速行进
这里是指哈克弓起身子快速行走。

[45] towhead /ˈtəʊhed/ *n.* 沙洲

[46] fagged /fæɡd/ *adj.* 累坏的

[47] 看见哈克回来，吉姆十分高兴，他将哈克从水里捞起来，拥抱、安抚他。本章中吉姆这唯一的一次出场，寥寥数语，几个动作，却表现出了吉姆对哈克真切的关心。

[48] 哈克和吉姆重逢，回到大河之上，再获自由，十分高兴。这里暗示哈克内心渴望远离人类文明社会的纷争与欺诈，憧憬能够亲近大自然的自由生活。

around a bit, and jump up and crack my heels a few times—I couldn't help it; but about the third crack I noticed a sound that I knowed mighty well, and held my breath and listened and waited; and sure enough, when the next flash busted out over the water, here they come!—and just a-laying to their oars and making their skiff hum! It was the king and the duke.

(90) So I wilted[49] right down on to the planks then, and give up; and it was all I could do to keep from crying.

[49] **wilt** /wɪlt/ *v.* 枯萎;凋谢;变得萎靡不振;失去自信

精华赏析

在本章中,"国王"和"公爵"忙着拍卖姑娘们的产业时,两个陌生人出现了,声称自己是真正的哈维和威廉。人们于是提出了一系列问题让双方对质。最终,大家决定开棺验尸以辨真伪。然而,就在开棺时,又发生了让大家意想不到的情况,哈克则趁乱偷偷溜走去和吉姆会合。这连续几个章节讲述的都是哈克、吉姆同骗子"国王"和"公爵"一路上的经历。在这个过程中,哈克亲眼见识了两个骗子的无耻卑鄙、冷酷无情。在本章结尾处,本来以为摆脱两个骗子终于可以和吉姆继续回到密西西比河上漂流的哈克,欣喜不已,谁料想,两个骗子又出现在了他眼前。

这一段情节是否让大家觉得有一些眼熟?在本书的第十八章中,哈克见识了两个家族因为家族间的世仇而持续多年彼此械斗仇杀,在章节的结尾处,好不容易逃脱出来的哈克回到船上和吉姆重逢继续漂流,吉姆开心地迎接他,两人都十分高兴,重新开始了自由的漂流生活。并且在接下来的第十九章开篇,作者还进行了大篇幅的景物描写,以景抒情,寓情于景,充分表现出哈克当时的惬意快乐。

这两段情节何其相似!似乎,哈克总是在岸上经历和见识人类文明社会里存在的卑鄙、残忍和纷争,然而他总是急于摆脱这一切,渴望回到密西西比河上继续他自由的漂流生活。他渴望回到大自然之中,去休养生息、感受生活的芳甜美好。于是我们可以有这样一种假设,那就是哈克内心似乎一直渴望着远离人类文明社会的争斗欺诈,向往回到大自然的怀抱,过自由的生活。在类似情节反复出现的同时,人类文明社会丑陋贪婪的一面和大自然质朴美好的一面形成了鲜明的对比,从这种对比中,我们可以清晰地看出这部作品中暗含的生态主义思想。

"生态批评"(ecocriticism)是由美国批评家威廉·鲁克特(William Rueckert)于1978年在一篇论文中首次提出的术语。从字面上看,这个术语是将生态学范畴的一些理念引入文学批评中,这一类文学批评方式必然强调自然和环境的因素。有一些学者强调"生态批评”并非简单的生态加上文学的组合，而是更深层次的融合，意味着一种更为以生物为中心的世界观（王岳川，2009）。我们在此不进行更多细致全面的探讨，只分析这部作品中体现出生态批评思想的一些细节。

一、质朴天真的哈克

其实，我们在前面分析人物的时候已经多次提到过，本书主人公哈克的身上有着许多和当时主流社会规范、主流价值观不一样的地方，算得上是当时的一个小小“反叛者”。比如，在第一章中我们看到，“寡妇在生活的方方面面都很规矩十分讲究，我实在受不了时就出来，重新穿上我的破衣烂衫，又睡在糖桶里，觉得轻松又自在。”类似细节描述十分常见，于是我们明白，从一开始，哈克就不喜欢受社会规范约束，对金钱缺乏占有欲望，他朴拙的原生态的价值取向，从根本上就和当时人类社会文明所推崇的价值观相背离。比起受到人类社会文明的约束教化，他更喜欢放松自由的生活。可以说，马克·吐温一开始设定的主人公哈克贝利·费恩就不是一个认同并乖乖接受社会文明教化的所谓规矩人。

之后在漂流历险的过程中，哈克在岸上见到的、感受到的、经历的，大多是人类文明社会中的欺诈、贪婪和争斗；可是每每回到大河上他就感到舒适、愉快。这类细节我们前面已经提过，就不再多说了。从这些我们不难看出，从一开始就并不喜欢受到人类文明社会约束的哈克，在漂流的过程中，进一步认识了当时的美国社会现实，也进一步见识了人类文明社会中的虚伪丑陋的一面，他一次次迫不及待地逃离人类文明社会，向往回到大河之上，回到大自然的怀抱，只有那样的生活才能够让他感到愉快轻松。

总的来说，哈克排斥当时的人类社会文明规范，喜欢亲近大自然，向往自由生活，并在漂流历险的过程中，进一步成长、成熟。可以说，质朴天真，热爱大自然，渴望自由生活的哈克是这部作品中生态主义思想的一个象征。

二、美好的庇护所——大自然

我们前面从各个角度探讨过密西西比河对于哈克，对于这部作品而言的特殊象征意义。比起充满了争斗和欺诈贪婪的人类文明社会，哈克显然更喜欢自由自在地生活在大自然的怀抱中。在密西西比河上漂流的日子，虽然动荡，也遭遇过危险，可是我们读不到生活在道格拉斯寡妇家时哈克那种难受，憋闷得要死的心理描写。我们多次提到了逃离家族宿仇争斗的哈克在继续漂流后，在本书第十九章开篇的那几段景物描写。这部分描写节奏舒缓，鸟语花香……寓情于景，以景抒情，读者能从这样的景物描写中充分感受到大自然对哈克的意义，就如同令人心安的美好的庇护所一般，供哈克和吉姆逃离纷争，休养身心，追寻希望。

在本书的最后，哈克不愿意被萨利阿姨领养，不愿意被她教化成一个文明人，于是选择了又一次离开人类文明社会。这个细节有着非常强的象征性意义，大自然之于哈克，是天性，也是最终的归宿。

三、人类社会的争斗、欺诈、虚伪

大河上的漂流生活和人类文明社会的生活作为相对立的一组象征概念一直贯穿于这部作品。我们要明白，书中写到的家族间的争斗杀戮也好，卑鄙无耻的“国王”和“公爵”也好，这些人物和事件都是人类文明社会中的一个个缩影，哈克厌恶的不是某一个人、某一件事,而是在人类文明社会中的社会人为了谋求私利,抑或为了遵循某种社会规范,又或是被社会通行价值观所驱使而做出的各种丑恶行径。这部作品的写作背景是工业文明发展极快,迅速发展的科学技术和各种机器极大地改变着人类社会的时期。在那样一个变革的时代,工业文明和科技发展带来的人和人、人和自然关系的异化凸显。马克·吐温在多部作品中表达过对童年时代自然与人和谐共处的快乐生活的怀念,他对现代工业文明所带来的这种变化是十分抗拒的。

可以说,大河生活和人类文明社会生活在书中的鲜明对比,正体现了作者将人类文明和自然生态的差异直接展示在读者面前,希望读者去直观地感受丑恶和美好的创作意图,体现了这部作品中的生态主义批评思想。

四、蓄奴制度的残忍罪恶

十九世纪美国南方种植园经济十分发达,使得南方的奴隶制更加盛行。然而,在自然生态法则中,不同肤色并没有高低贵贱之分。当时的西方文明社会强行划分三六九等,将黑人视为低劣的种族,视其理应为奴,正是当时人类文明社会的又一个丑恶的表现。在这部作品中,主人公——十三四岁的白人小男孩哈克贝利·费恩,在一路的漂流历险中,从一开始戏弄黑奴吉姆,随时想要告发吉姆,到后来越来越多地感受到吉姆身上的善良温情,看到吉姆的聪明才智,体会到吉姆对自己的真情后,最终选择了为了吉姆而和人类文明社会道德规则决裂。他最终决定背弃蓄奴制度,自己想办法救出吉姆的做法,有着很强的象征意义。

哈克一路上关于是否遵循社会通行规范告发逃跑黑奴吉姆,还是继续帮助他逃离的思想斗争,象征着人类社会文明和自然生态思想的斗争。最终,哈克选择了遵从内心直觉感受和经验,而和人类文明社会的普遍价值规范决裂,这正是这部作品生态主义思想的又一重要体现。

十九世纪工业文明的日益发展,人和人、人和自然关系的异化,使得当时的人类文明价值体系与一直热爱着儿童时期人与自然之间和谐关系的马克·吐温所认同的价值取向相背离。在这部作品中,他将对当时人类文明社会价值走向的批判,以及对自然生态的向往热爱,糅合在了许多细节中。

术语解说

生态批评:"生态学"一词,是由希腊语 oicos(房子、住所)派生而来,最早出现在德语中,即 die Okologie,英语为 the ecology。生态主义并非横空出世,其思想渊源与十八世纪开始的浪漫主义运动有着分不开的关系。1858 年,美国作家梭罗在《瓦尔登湖》一书中阐释了自己的人与自然和谐的观念。他从生态平衡的角度反对喧嚣的城市,而赞美有着树林和溪流的自然世界。

一般认为,"生态批评"这一概念由美国批评家威廉·鲁克特首次提出。他的《文学与生态学:一次生态批评实验》一文在《衣阿华评论》1978年冬季号上刊出,通过"生态批评"概念明确地将"文学与生态学结合起来"。对"生态批评"的定义,言人人殊,难有定论。米歇尔·P.布兰奇等人在《阅读大地》中说:隐含(且通常明确包含)在这种新批评方式诸多作为之中的是一种对文化变化的呼唤。生态批评不只是对文学中的自然进行分析的一种手段,它还意味着走向一种更为生物中心的世界观。正如女权主义和非裔美国文学批评呼唤一种文化变化,即通过揭露早期观点的狭隘性而努力促成一种更具包容性的世界观一样,生态批评通过考察我们关于自然世界之文化假定的狭隘性如何限制了我们展望一个生态方面可持续发展的人类社会的能力而呼唤文化的改变。(王岳川,2009)

阅读思考

1. 请找出本书中除本章外三处"寓情于景""借景抒情"的描写。
2. 请找出本章中关于医生和律师的一些动作描写细节,并分析其对人物塑造的作用。

CHAPTER XXX

导读：本以为摆脱了"国王"和"公爵"的哈克，跑到沙洲和吉姆会合，打算重回大河，继续漂流生活。然而，"国王"和"公爵"却突然出现。哈克大失所望之余，机智地编造理由洗清了自己偷钱的嫌疑。尔后，两个骗子开始彼此怀疑对方偷了钱，闹得不可开交。

(1) WHEN they got aboard the king went for me, and shook me by the collar, and says:[1]

(2) "Tryin' to give us the slip, was ye, you pup[2]! Tired of our company, hey?"

(3) I says:

(4) "No, your majesty, we warn't—PLEASE don't, your majesty!"

(5) "Quick, then, and tell us what *was* your idea, or I'll shake the insides out o' you!"

(6) "Honest, I'll tell you everything just as it happened, your majesty. The man that had a-holt of me was very good to me, and kept saying he had a boy about as big as me that died last year, and he was sorry to see a boy in such a dangerous fix; and when they was all took by surprise by finding the gold, and made a rush for the coffin, he lets go of me and whispers[3], 'Heel it now, or they'll hang ye, sure!' and I lit out. It didn't seem no good for *me* to stay—I couldn't do nothing, and I didn't want to be hung if I could get away. So I never stopped running till I found the canoe; and when I got here I told Jim to hurry, or they'd catch me and hang me yet, and said I was afeard you and the duke wasn't alive now, and I was awful sorry, and so was Jim, and was awful glad when we see you coming; you may ask Jim if I didn't."

1 本章几乎都是对话描写。在上一章的结尾，新的哈维和威廉出现后，人们为辨明真伪，决定开棺，哈克趁乱溜走。然而两个骗子也成功脱困，并找到了哈克。在经过短暂的对哈克的质疑后，两人开始说出心中真正的想法——怀疑对方。本章主要内容正是这番精彩的骗子之间彼此指责，互相讥讽的对话。仔细分析这部分对话，对于理解人物，理清情节发展细节，体会作者的写作技巧，是很有必要的。（详见本章"精华赏析"）

2 pup /pʌp/ *n.* 小狗；幼畜

3 whisper /ˈwɪspə/ *v.* 低声地说；私下说

(7) Jim said it was so; and the king told him to shut up, and said, "Oh, yes, it's *mighty* likely!" and shook me up again, and said he reckoned he'd drownd me. But the duke says:

(8) "Leggo the boy, you old idiot! Would *you* a done any different? Did you inquire around for *him* when you got loose? I don't remember it." [4]

(9) So the king let go of me, and begun to cuss that town and everybody in it. But the duke says:

(10) "You better a blame' sight give *yourself* a good cussing, for you're the one that's entitled to[5] it most. You hain't done a thing from the start that had any sense in it, except coming out so cool and cheeky[6] with that imaginary blue-arrow mark. That *was* bright—it was right down bully; and it was the thing that saved us. For if it hadn't been for that they'd a jailed us till them Englishmen's baggage come—and then—the penitentiary[7], you bet! But that trick took 'em to the graveyard, and the gold done us a still bigger kindness; for if the excited fools hadn't let go all holts and made that rush to get a look we'd a slept in our cravats[8] to-night—cravats warranted to WEAR, too—longer than *we'd* need 'em."

(11) They was still a minute—thinking; then the king says, kind of absent-minded[9] like:

(12) "Mf! And we reckoned the *niggers* stole it!"

(13) That made me squirm[10]!

(14) "Yes," says the duke, kinder slow and deliberate and sarcastic, "*We* did."

(15) After about a half a minute the king drawls[11] out:

(16) "Leastways[12], I did."

(17) The duke says, the same way:

(18) "On the contrary, I did."

(19) The king kind of ruffles[13] up, and says:

(20) "Looky here, Bilgewater, what'r you referrin' to?"

(21) The duke says, pretty brisk:[14]

(22) "When it comes to that, maybe you'll let me ask, what was *you* referring to?"

(23) "Shucks!" says the king, very sarcastic; "but I don't

[4] 第1—8段是这部分对话的第1个话题——质疑哈克。这个话题持续时间较短，对话回合不多，因为两个骗子相互间并不信任，他们真正怀疑的都是对方。

[5] (be) entitled to: 有权享有；有……的资格

[6] cheeky /ˈtʃiːkɪ/ *adj.* 无耻的；厚脸皮的

[7] penitentiary /ˌpenɪˈtenʃəri/ *n.* 监狱；宗教裁判官；宗教裁判所；教养所

[8] cravat /krəˈvæt/ *n.* 领带；领巾；领结

[9] absent-minded *adj.* 心不在焉的；健忘的；出神的

[10] squirm /skwɜːm/ *v.* 扭动；羞愧；不舒服

[11] drawl /drɔːl/ *v.* (拉长调)慢吞吞地说

[12] leastways /ˈliːstweɪz/ *adv.* 无论如何；至少

[13] ruffle /ˈrʌfl/ *v.* (使)起伏不平；(使某人)变得不平静，生气

[14] 注意此处"公爵"说话的方式。brisk这里是指说话语气犀利、强势。

know—maybe you was asleep, and didn't know what you was about."

(24) The duke bristles up now, and says:

(25) "Oh, let *up* on[15] this cussed nonsense; do you take me for a blame' fool? Don't you reckon I know who hid that money in that coffin?"

(26) "*Yes*, sir! I know you *do* know, because you done it yourself!"

(27) "It's a lie!" —and the duke went for him. The king sings out:

(28) "Take y'r hands off!—leggo my throat!—I take it all back!"

(29) The duke says: "Well, you just own up[16], first, that you *did* hide that money there, intending to give me the slip one of these days, and come back and dig it up, and have it all to yourself."

(30) "Wait jest a minute, duke—answer me this one question, honest and fair; if you didn't put the money there, say it, and I'll b'lieve you, and take back everything I said."

(31) "You old scoundrel[17], I didn't, and you know I didn't. There, now!"

(32) "Well, then, I b'lieve you. But answer me only jest this one more—now *don't* git mad; didn't you have it in your mind to hook the money and hide it?"

(33) The duke never said nothing for a little bit; then he says:[18]

(34) "Well, I don't care if I *did*, I didn't *do* it, anyway. But you not only had it in mind to do it, but you *done* it."

(35) "I wisht I never die if I done it, duke, and that's honest. I won't say I warn't goin' to do it, because I *was*; but you—I mean somebody—got in ahead o' me."

(36) "It's a lie! You done it, and you got to *say* you done it, or—"[19]

(37) The king began to gurgle[20], and then he gasps out:

(38) "'Nough!—I *own up*!"

(39) I was very glad to hear him say that; it made me feel

[15] **let up on**: 减少压力；宽容对待

[16] **own up**: *v.* 坦白；爽快承认

[17] **scoundrel** /ˈskaʊndr(ə)l/ *n.* 恶棍；无赖；流氓

[18] 这里"公爵"短暂地沉默了一下，我们通常认为对话中的沉默是处于弱势的表现。然而这里的沉默是为了思考对策给对方致命一击，并非弱势。

[19] 第10—36段为这部分对话的第2个话题——彼此质疑。该话题为主话题，两个骗子唇枪舌剑，互相指责、讥讽。其间"公爵"说话时作者使用了brisk，bristle等词，而"国王"说话时使用了sing，gurgle等词。分析时请注意这类说话态度、动作的描述，及两人在会话中所处地位等问题。

[20] **gurgle** /ˈɡɜːɡ(ə)l/ *v.* 作汩汩声；作咯咯声

much more easier than what I was feeling before. So the duke took his hands off and says:

(40) "If you ever deny it again I'll drown you. It's *well* for you to set there and blubber[21] like a baby—it's fitten for you, after the way you've acted. I never see such an old ostrich for wanting to gobble[22] everything—and I a-trusting you all the time, like you was my own father. You ought to been ashamed of yourself to stand by and hear it saddled on to a lot of poor niggers, and you never say a word for 'em. It makes me feel ridiculous to think I was soft enough to BELIEVE that rubbage. Cuss you, I can see now why you was so anxious to make up the deffersit—you wanted to get what money I'd got out of the Nonesuch and one thing or another, and scoop it *all*!"[23]

(41) The king says, timid, and still a-snuffling[24]: "Why, duke, it was you that said make up the deffersit; it warn't me."

(42) "Dry up![25] I don't want to hear no more out of you!" says the duke. "And *now* you see what you *got* by it. They've got all their own money back, and all of *ourn* but a shekel or two *besides*. G'long to bed, and don't you deffersit *me* no more deffersits, long 's *you* live!"

(43) So the king sneaked into the wigwam and took to his bottle for comfort, and before long the duke tackled HIS bottle; and so in about a half an hour they was as thick as thieves again, and the tighter they got the lovinger they got, and went off a-snoring in each other's arms. They both got powerful mellow[26], but I noticed the king didn't get mellow enough to forget to remember to not deny about hiding the money-bag again. That made me feel easy and satisfied. Of course when they got to snoring we had a long gabble, and I told Jim everything.

[21] blubber /ˈblʌbə/ *v.* 又哭又闹

[22] gobble /ˈgɒb(ə)l/ *v.* 狼吞虎咽；贪食；咯咯叫

[23] 第37—42段为这部分对话的第3个话题——和解。从第38段可看出，两人的和解是从"国王"的妥协开始的。因为尘埃落定，所以这部分回合不多。本段是一个比较长的独白段落，获胜的"公爵"取得了会话中的绝对优势位置，发表了显示强势地位的长篇独白。

[24] snuffle /ˈsnʌfl/ *v.* 抽鼻子；带鼻音说话

[25] dry up 本意为干涸，此处指让对方住口。

[26] mellow /ˈmeləʊ/ *adj.* 圆润的，柔和的；成熟的；芳醇的 此处指"国王"和"公爵"睡得很熟。

精华赏析

这部作品的一大语言特色就是大量的人物对话。人物形象的塑造,情节的发展推动等,都在会话当中自然而然地铺展开来,向前推进。因此,在理解这部作品时,对大量的会话进行分析,对于更准确地理解人物和情节,把握其微妙的隐含意义,有着非常重要的作用。在在上一章中,哈克巧妙地帮助玛丽·珍妮保住了财物,并偷偷溜走去和吉姆会合,继续漂流。然而,本以为已经摆脱了的"国王"和"公爵"却突然出现,哈克大失所望。然而,"国王"和"公爵"二人却顾不上怀疑哈克,他们互不信任,彼此怀疑,彼此指责,因此产生了大量的对话,而本章主要内容就是两人的这些对话。我们对这部分对话进行会话分析,管中窥豹,能够更直观地体会到马克·吐温写作风格之幽默诙谐,细节描写之巧妙。通过会话分析,我们能够发现在话锋交错中,"国王"和"公爵"是如何发起话题,又如何展开话题,如何回应话题,在会话中处于什么地位,各自地位又以何种方式发生了何种变化,二人内心分别又有着怎样的小盘算等。这部分对话背后所蕴含的这许多信息让人物性格特征更加生动鲜活,而情节发展脉络也会更加清晰明了。接下来,我们将使用会话分析当中的"话轮转换"概念对本章中"国王"和"公爵"在和哈克、吉姆会合后的对话进行分析。

首先,我们先理解一下"话轮转换"这个概念。"话轮",顾名思义,指的就是在会话当中,参与会话者轮流说话的情况,是由美国社会学家哈维·塞克斯(Harvey Sacks)提出的一个重要概念。在使用这个概念对会话进行分析时,需要一个评价框架,不同学者对于这个框架的具体内容看法不尽相同,但整体框架还是大同小异的。在这里我们使用其中一种评价框架,该框架含有以下几个衡量标准:(1)话题提出和控制情况;(2)话轮长度;(3)话轮类型;(4)话语打断和独白现象;(5)话轮控制策略。需要说明的是,第(3)点具体指的是,说话是为了发起新话题,是为了回应对方,是为了打断对方而说,还是为了发表自己的观点等;而第(4)点标准提出的原因,是基于在会话当中,打断或者独白的出现往往是比较粗鲁无礼的,这也意味着说话人在对话当中呈现出强势姿态;第(5)点具体指的是,采用比如铺垫,肢体语气,打断对方说话等与话题无关或者语言以外的方式来调节以及控制会话的话题控制策略。这几种话轮控制策略中,有的显示出温和的姿态,例如进入正题前先进行铺垫,而有的则显示出比较强势的话轮控制姿态,例如打断对方说话。

接下来,我们就来具体看看"国王"和"公爵"的这部分对话。在进行话轮转换分析时,我们通常依据话题进行具体分析。而在这一部分对话中,总的来说,有三个话题:(1)质疑哈克(第1—8段);(2)彼此质疑(第10—36段);(3)和解(第37—43段)。其中,第(2)个话题为主话题。在这几个话题中,我们不考虑哈克所说内容,只分析"国王"和"公爵"的对话。话轮转换的相关数据如下:

话题	（1）质疑哈克		（2）彼此质疑		（3）和解		合计	
人物	国王	公爵	国王	公爵	国王	公爵	国王	公爵
话轮数	3	1	9	10	2	2	14	13
（1）话题提出和控制情况	被控制	控制话题	逐渐势弱	逐渐强势	被控制	控制话题	话题逐渐被公爵控制	
（2）话轮平均长度（词）	12	26	17.9	28.4	14	96	16.1	38.6
（3）话轮类型	发话（2）回应（1）	发话	发话 / 回应 / 打断	发话 / 回应	回应	打断 / 独白	回应 / 发话 / 打断	回应 / 发话 / 打断 / 独白
（4）话语打断和独白次数	0	1 次打断	1 次打断	0	0	1 次打断，1 次独白	1 次打断	2 次打断；1 次独白
（5）话轮控制策略			装作不经意说话 / 讽刺回应 / 打断对方	讽刺说话 / 扑向对方 / 坚定地说 / 高声说话 / 沉默	发出咯咯声 / 喘气（承认）	小心翼翼地说话		

从这张表中，我们可以清晰地看出这部分对话的详细发展进程。下面我们分别就这三个话题当中的话轮转换情况进行分析。

第一个话题为质疑哈克。这部分话轮数很少，"国王"有 3 个话轮，"公爵"只有 1 个话轮；话轮长度也很短，"国王"的话轮平均长度为 12 词，而"公爵"的话轮长度为 26 词。我们看到"公爵"虽然只有 1 个话轮，但却长达 26 词，远超过"国王"，同时，分析文本我们发现这一个话轮是"公爵"打断了"国王"说话。这是因为在这个话题中，"公爵"掌控着话题，他直接打断了"国王"对哈克的质疑，而开始指责"国王"。"国王"的 3 个话轮，虽然有两次发话，但分析文本我们发现这两次都是对哈克发话，1 次"回应"的对象为"公爵"。在这个话题的有限话轮中，从话轮长度、话轮类型以及打断话轮的情况来看，"公爵"都控制着话题。

第二个话题为主话题，二人彼此质疑。双方的话轮数比较平均，"国王" 9 个，"公爵" 10 个。话轮长度也显著增加，"国王"的话轮平均长度为 17.9 词，"公爵"的话轮平均长度为 28.4 词。而在试图取得话题控制权方面，"公爵"率先将指责的矛头指向"国王"。"国王"一开始装模作样地说以为是黑奴偷走了金币，回应话题，而后两人互相讽刺。"公爵"在整个话题中，语气坚决，声音更大，并伴随有扑向"国王"的肢体动作，虽然最后有沉默，但是分析文本我们发现，这个沉默是因为"公爵"在思考对策，并非弱势。反观"国王"，在这部分虽有 1 次打断对方说话，却并非强势，而是强弩之末，垂死挣扎。最终，这个话题在"公爵"斩钉截铁的指责中结束。整个话题当中，双方你来我往，互相争夺话语控制权，"公爵"表现得更为强硬，逐渐掌握话语控制权，"国王"虽有挣扎，却逐渐势弱。

在第三个话题中，"国王"和"公爵"二人达成了和解。二人的和解，是从"国王"承认偷拿了钱开始的，此时的"国王"已经彻底放弃，因此在这一部分的对话中，二人在会话当中的地位相差悬殊。下面，我们就从"话轮转换"分析的角度来获取实际的数据支撑。在这一部分中，两人话轮数一样，各有两个话轮。然而，俩人的话轮长度却差异巨大，"国王"的两个话轮平均长度为 14 词，"公爵"的话轮平均长度达到了 96 词。我们从这已经可以看出"公爵"控制话题的优势。另外，"公爵"的这两个话轮，1 次是打断"国王"说话，1 次是独白，强势尽显。反观"国王"，两个话轮都是回应"公爵"，说话小心翼翼，寥寥数语，彻底落败，完全失去了话语控制权。

总体而言，从话轮个数来看，两人比较平均，"国王"有 14 个话轮，"公爵"有 13 个话轮，这是因为两人在对话中你来我往，各说各话，因此比较平均；而从话轮平均长度来看，"公爵"为 38.6 词，明显超过"国王"的 16.1 词，是"国王"的两倍还多；从话轮类型来看，"公爵"有两次打断，1 次独白。"国王"仅有 1 次打断，而且分析文本我们发现，这 1 次打断实际上是"国王"的挣扎，并非真正处于强势；从话轮控制策略来看，"公爵"的强势一以贯之，而"国王"则在强弱之间变化；从话题变化来看，"国王"在第 1 以及第 3 个话题中都处于明显弱势，在第 2 个话题（主话题）中，两人进行了话语权的争夺，但"国王"渐渐势弱。

文学作品的分析评论一直以来都更多地局限在定性讨论，往往缺乏实实在在的数据支撑。在会话分析中，如果能够引入数据，进行量化观察，往往能帮助我们更清晰地把握人物性格，掌握情节发展脉络，更真切地体味作者的写作技巧，从而了解作者的意图。

术语解说

话轮：哈维·塞克斯（Harvey Sacks）在 1974 年针对谈话话语提出了话轮转换理论（turn-taking model）。这套理论包括话轮构造部分（turn-constructional component）和话轮分配部分（turn-allocation component）。这里话轮的含义实际上是指给予一个说话人说话的权利与义务以及他实际上所说的话语。当然，关于话轮的定义众说纷纭，如对沉默及体态语（body language）以及反馈（feedback）等现象是否属于话轮，就有不同的意见。然而，为了定量分析的方便，从实际出发，我们认为剧本中出现的任何一个话语（utterance）都是一个话轮。用于戏剧文体学的话轮分析框架大致由以下五个方面构成：（1）话题提出和控制情况（the initiation and control of topics）；（2）话轮长度（turn-length）；（3）话轮类型（turn-type）；（4）话语打断和独白现象（interruption and monologue）；（5）话轮控制策略（turn-control strategies）。（李华东，2001）

阅读思考

1. 试分析本章中“公爵”和“国王”间的话轮转换。

2. 试用话轮转换分析框架分析《高级英语》中 *BLACKMAIL* 这一课中侦探和公爵夫人之间的对话。

CHAPTER XXXI

导读：无奈之下，哈克和吉姆只能与两个骗子一同继续漂流。途中，"国王"和"公爵"决定在一个镇子停留并继续行骗赚钱。然而，事与愿违，两人并没有骗到多少钱。之后，二人就开始密谋些什么。到达一个叫比克斯维尔的小村落下游后，"国王"独自一人上岸打探消息，哈克和"公爵"久等"国王"不回，两人于是到镇上去找"国王"，其间，哈克寻机再度溜走，却发现吉姆不见了。

(1) WE dasn't stop again at any town for days and days; kept right along down the river. We was down south in the warm weather now, and a mighty long ways from home. We begun to come to trees with Spanish moss on them, hanging down from the limbs like long, gray beards. It was the first I ever see it growing, and it made the woods look solemn and dismal[1]. So now the frauds reckoned they was out of danger, and they begun to work the villages again.

(2) First they done a lecture on temperance[2]; but they didn't make enough for them both to get drunk on. Then in another village they started a dancing-school; but they didn't know no more how to dance than a kangaroo does; so the first prance they made the general public jumped in and pranced them out of town. Another time they tried to go at yellocution; but they didn't yellocute long till the audience got up and give them a solid good cussing, and made them skip out. They tackled missionarying[3], and mesmerizing[4], and doctoring, and telling fortunes, and a little of everything; but they couldn't seem to have no luck. So at last they got just about dead broke, and laid around the raft as she floated along, thinking and thinking, and never saying nothing, by the half a day at a time, and dreadful

[1] dismal /ˈdɪzməl/ *adj.* 阴沉的；沉闷的

[2] temperance /ˈtempərəns/ *n.* 戒酒

[3] missionary /ˈmɪʃənərɪ/ *n.* 传教士 *adj.* 传教的
此处作为动词使用，应该是一种误用。

[4] mesmerize /ˈmezməraɪz/ *v.* 施催眠术；迷住
此处指两个骗子试图以传教布道的方式骗钱。

blue and desperate.

(3) And at last they took a change and begun to lay their heads together in the wigwam and talk low and confidential[5] two or three hours at a time. Jim and me got uneasy. We didn't like the look of it. We judged they was studying up some kind of worse deviltry[6] than ever. We turned it over and over, and at last we made up our minds they was going to break into somebody's house or store, or was going into the counterfeit-money[7] business, or something. So then we was pretty scared, and made up an agreement that we wouldn't have nothing in the world to do with such actions, and if we ever got the least show we would give them the cold shake and clear out and leave them behind. Well, early one morning we hid the raft in a good, safe place about two mile below a little bit of a shabby village named Pikesville, and the king he went ashore and told us all to stay hid whilst he went up to town and smelt around to see if anybody had got any wind of the Royal Nonesuch there yet. ("House to rob, you *mean*," says I to myself; "and when you get through robbing it you'll come back here and wonder what has become of[8] me and Jim and the raft—and you'll have to take it out in wondering.") And he said if he warn't back by midday the duke and me would know it was all right, and we was to come along[9].

(4) So we stayed where we was. The duke he fretted and sweated around, and was in a mighty sour way. He scolded us for everything, and we couldn't seem to do nothing right; he found fault with[10] every little thing. Something was a-brewing, sure. I was good and glad when midday come and no king; we could have a change, anyway — and maybe a chance for THE chance on top of[11] it. So me and the duke went up to the village, and hunted around there for the king, and by and by we found him in the back room of a little low doggery, very tight, and a lot of loafers bullyragging him for sport, and he a-cussing and a-threatening with all his might, and so tight he couldn't walk, and couldn't do nothing to them. The duke he begun to abuse him for an old fool, and the king begun to sass back, and the minute they was fairly at it I lit out and shook the reefs out of

[5] confidential /ˌkɒnfɪˈdenʃl/ *adj.* 机密的

[6] deviltry /ˈdev(ə)ltrɪ/ *n.* 恶行;残暴(等于 devilry)

[7] counterfeit money: 假币;伪钞

[8] become of: 使遭遇……;……降临于;发生……情况

[9] come along: 出现;一起来;陪伴

[10] find fault with: 不满于

[11] on top of: 另外;紧接着;在……之上

my hind legs[12], and spun down the river road like a deer, for I see our chance; and I made up my mind that it would be a long day before they ever see me and Jim again. I got down there all out of breath but loaded up with joy, and sung out:

(5) "Set her loose, Jim! we're all right now!"

(6) But there warn't no answer, and nobody come out of the wigwam. Jim was gone! I set up a shout—and then another—and then another one; and run this way and that in the woods, whooping and screeching; but it warn't no use—old Jim was gone. Then I set down and cried; I couldn't help it. But I couldn't set still long. Pretty soon I went out on the road, trying to think what I better do, and I run across a boy walking, and asked him if he'd seen a strange nigger dressed so and so, and he says:

(7) "Yes."

(8) "Whereabouts[13]?" says I.

(9) "Down to Silas Phelps' place, two mile below here. He's a runaway nigger, and they've got him. Was you looking for him?"

(10) "You bet I ain't! I run across him in the woods about an hour or two ago, and he said if I hollered he'd cut my livers out—and told me to lay down and stay where I was; and I done it. Been there ever since; afeard to come out."

(11) "Well," he says, "you needn't be afeard no more, becuz they've got him. He run off f'm down South, som'ers."

(12) "It's a good job they got him."

(13) "Well, I *reckon*! There's two hunderd dollars reward on him. It's like picking up money out'n the road."

(14) "Yes, it is—and I could a had it if I'd been big enough; I see him FIRST. Who nailed him?"

(15) "It was an old fellow—a stranger—and he sold out his chance in him for forty dollars, becuz he's got to go up the river and can't wait. Think o' that, now! You bet *I'd* wait, if it was seven year."

(16) "That's me, every time," says I. "But maybe his chance ain't worth no more than that, if he'll sell it so cheap.

[12] 此处指撒开了腿跑。

[13] **whereabouts** /weərə'baʊts/ *n.* 下落；行踪

Maybe there's something ain't straight about it."

(17) "But it IS, though—straight as a string.[14] I see the handbill[15] myself. It tells all about him, to a dot[16]—paints him like a picture, and tells the plantation he's frum, below NewrLEANS. No-sirree[17]-BOB, they ain't no trouble 'bout *that* speculation, you bet you. Say, gimme a chaw tobacker, won't ye?"

(18) I didn't have none, so he left. I went to the raft, and set down in the wigwam to think. But I couldn't come to nothing. I thought till I wore my head sore, but I couldn't see no way out of the trouble. After all this long journey, and after all we'd done for them scoundrels, here it was all come to nothing, everything all busted up and ruined, because they could have the heart to[18] serve Jim such a trick as that, and make him a slave again all his life, and amongst strangers, too, for forty dirty dollars.[19]

(19) Once I said to myself it would be a thousand times better for Jim to be a slave at home where his family was, as long as he'd *got* to be a slave, and so I'd better write a letter to Tom Sawyer and tell him to tell Miss Watson where he was. But I soon give up that notion for two things: she'd be mad and disgusted at his rascality[20] and ungratefulness for leaving her, and so she'd sell him straight down the river again; and if she didn't, everybody naturally despises an ungrateful nigger, and they'd make Jim feel it all the time, and so he'd feel ornery and disgraced. And then think of *me*! It would get all around that Huck Finn helped a nigger to get his freedom; and if I was ever to see anybody from that town again I'd be ready to get down and lick his boots for shame.[21] That's just the way: a person does a low-down thing, and then he don't want to take no consequences of it. Thinks as long as he can hide, it ain't no disgrace. That was my fix exactly. The more I studied about this the more my conscience went to grinding me, and the more wicked and low-down and ornery I got to feeling. And at last, when it hit me all of a sudden that here was the plain hand of Providence slapping me in the face and letting me know my wickedness was being watched all the time from up there in heaven, whilst I was

[14] straight这里应该理解为"坦率,符合事实"。这句话大意为"所说的话完完全全符合实情"。

[15] handbill /ˈhæn(d)bɪl/ *n.* 传单;招贴

[16] to a dot: 丝毫不差地;正确地

[17] sirree /sɪˈriː/ *n.* 先生;用以强调肯定或否定的语句

[18] have the heart to: 忍心做;有勇气做

[19] 从这里开始,出现了多处对哈克的大篇幅心理描写。从这些心理描写中我们可以看出哈克的心理和道德意识观念的变化。哈克和吉姆开始漂流出自偶然,在以后的历险中哈克也多次想要告发逃跑的黑奴吉姆。但是,在共同经历了这么多好的坏的事情之后,哈克发现两个骗子居然狠心地为了肮脏的区区四十块钱就卖掉了吉姆。哈克此时的心理活动已经告诉了读者他内心对吉姆的态度以及两人之间关系的变化。

[20] rascality /rɑːˈskælətɪ/ *n.* 坏事,恶行;卑鄙行为;流氓行为

[21] 整个这一段都是对哈克的心理描写。哈克得知吉姆被卖掉后,心中产生了激

stealing a poor old woman's nigger that hadn't ever done me no harm, and now was showing me there's One that's always on the lookout[22], and ain't a going to allow no such miserable doings to go only just so fur and no further, I most dropped in my tracks I was so scared. Well, I tried the best I could to kinder soften it up somehow for myself by saying I was brung up wicked, and so I warn't so much to blame; but something inside of me kept saying, "There was the Sunday-school, you could a gone to it; and if you'd a done it they'd a learnt you there that people that acts as I'd been acting about that nigger goes to everlasting fire."

(20) It made me shiver. And I about made up my mind to pray, and see if I couldn't try to quit being the kind of a boy I was and be better. So I kneeled down. But the words wouldn't come. Why wouldn't they? It warn't no use to try and hide it from Him. Nor from *me*, neither. I knowed very well why they wouldn't come. It was because my heart warn't right; it was because I warn't square; it was because I was playing double. I was letting *on* to give up sin, but away inside of me I was holding on to the biggest one of all. I was trying to make my mouth *say* I would do the right thing and the clean thing, and go and write to that nigger's owner and tell where he was; but deep down in me I knowed it was a lie, and He knowed it. You can't pray a lie—I found that out.[23]

(21) So I was full of trouble, full as I could be; and didn't know what to do.[24] At last I had an idea; and I says, I'll go and write the letter—and then see if I can pray. Why, it was astonishing, the way I felt as light as a feather right straight off, and my troubles all gone. So I got a piece of paper and a pencil, all glad and excited, and set down and wrote:[25]

(22) Miss Watson, your runaway nigger Jim is down here two mile below Pikesville, and Mr. Phelps has got him and he will give him up for the reward if you send.

(23) HUCK FINN.

(24) I felt good and all washed clean of sin for the first time I had ever felt so in my life, and I knowed I could pray now. But I didn't do it straight off, but laid the paper down and set there

烈的思想斗争。最开始，哈克在情感上无法接受两小骗子的卑鄙又无情的做法；理智上，他立刻开始思考如何帮助吉姆。本段就是哈克理智思考帮助吉姆的对策。哈克首先想到的是告知沃森小姐吉姆的去处。然而他立刻否定了这个想法，一是因为这样一来，吉姆仍然难逃被奴役的命运。二是自己帮助黑奴这样不光彩的事情就会曝光。这两个原因，哪个在此时的哈克心中更为重要呢？显然是第二个。全段388词，从"And then think of me!"这句开始，哈克开始思考第二个理由，并开始深深自责，这一部分就达到了276词。

22 **on the lookout**: 寻找；注意

23 本段一整段仍然是对哈克的心理描写。在本段中，哈克内心十分自责，这份自责是针对他帮助黑奴吉姆逃跑这件事的。他认为自己十分邪恶，心术不正，并试图向上帝祈祷，承诺做"正确"的事，却无法做到。

24 所以我心里乱糟糟的，乱到极点了，不知该怎么办才好。

25 本段仍然是对哈克的心理描写。心乱如麻的哈克下定决心做"正确的事情"，于是开始给沃森小姐写信。

thinking—thinking how good it was all this happened so, and how near I come to being lost and going to hell.[26] And went on thinking. And got to thinking over our trip down the river; and I see Jim before me all the time: in the day and in the night-time, sometimes moonlight, sometimes storms, and we a-floating along, talking and singing and laughing. But somehow I couldn't seem to strike no places to harden me against him, but only the other kind.[27] I'd see him standing my watch on top of his'n, 'stead of calling me, so I could go on sleeping; and see him how glad he was when I come back out of the fog; and when I come to him again in the swamp, up there where the feud was; and such-like times; and would always call me honey, and pet me and do everything he could think of for me, and how good he always was; and at last I struck the time I saved him by telling the men we had small-pox aboard, and he was so grateful, and said I was the best friend old Jim ever had in the world, and the *only* one he's got now; and then I happened to look around and see that paper.[28]

(25) It was a close place. I took it up, and held it in my hand. I was a-trembling, because I'd got to decide, forever, betwixt two things, and I knowed it. I studied a minute, sort of holding my breath, and then says to myself:

(26) "All right, then, I'll *go* to hell" —and tore it up.[29]

(27) It was awful thoughts and awful words, but they was said. And I let them stay said; and never thought no more about reforming. I shoved the whole thing out of my head, and said I would take up wickedness again, which was in my line, being brung up to it, and the other warn't. And for a starter I would go to work and steal Jim out of slavery again; and if I could think up anything worse, I would do that, too; because as long as I was in, and in for good, I might as well go the whole hog[30][31].

(28) Then I set to thinking over how to get at it, and turned over some considerable many ways in my mind; and at last fixed up a plan that suited me. So then I took the bearings[32] of a woody island that was down the river a piece, and as soon as it was fairly dark I crept out with my raft and went for it, and

[26] 这一个对哈克的心理描写段落有两个部分，这是第一个部分。哈克在写完信后，因为做了"正确的事情"，感觉好极了，他没有急着再次开始祈祷，而是开始想自己多么庆幸，因为差一点儿他就迷失了自己，做了要下地狱的事。

[27] 但是，不知怎么的，我总是找不到一件事能让我对他狠下心来，恰恰相反，一想到他，我的心就软下来了。这句是指哈克回想起和吉姆一路的经历，越想越无法狠下心来告发吉姆。

[28] 本段心理描写的第二部分从"And went on thinking."开始。哈克继续想的，都是和吉姆一路上经历的风风雨雨……想到这些，他根本无法狠心告发吉姆，此时，他看到了自己写好的信。

[29] 第25段和第26两段仍然是对哈克的心理描写，也是哈克道德意识完成转变的部分。有趣的是，从第18段到这里，哈克进行了很久的思想斗争，内心各种挣扎，也一度做了"正确的事情"——给沃森小姐写好告发信，并感到十分轻松高兴。但是，此刻，他只想了一分钟，就决定推翻之前的决定，做出了新的选择——下地狱，并撕掉了信。

hid it there, and then turned in. I slept the night through, and got up before it was light, and had my breakfast, and put on my store clothes, and tied up some others and one thing or another in a bundle, and took the canoe and cleared for shore. I landed below where I judged was Phelps's place, and hid my bundle in the woods, and then filled up the canoe with water, and loaded rocks into her and sunk her where I could find her again when I wanted her, about a quarter of a mile below a little steam sawmill that was on the bank.

(29) Then I struck up the road[33], and when I passed the mill I see a sign on it, "Phelps's Sawmill," and when I come to the farm-houses, two or three hundred yards further along, I kept my eyes peeled, but didn't see nobody around, though it was good daylight now. But I didn't mind, because I didn't want to see nobody just yet—I only wanted to get the lay of the land. According to my plan, I was going to turn up there from the village, not from below. So I just took a look, and shoved along, straight for town. Well, the very first man I see when I got there was the duke. He was sticking up a bill for the Royal Nonesuch—three-night performance—like that other time. They had the cheek, them frauds! I was right on him before I could shirk[34]. He looked astonished, and says:

(30) "Hel-lo! Where'd *you* come from?" Then he says, kind of glad and eager, "Where's the raft?—got her in a good place?"

(31) I says:

(32) "Why, that's just what I was going to ask your grace."

(33) Then he didn't look so joyful, and says:

(34) "What was your idea for asking *me*?" he says.

(35) "Well," I says, "when I see the king in that doggery yesterday I says to myself, we can't get him home for hours, till he's soberer; so I went a-loafing around town to put in the time and wait. A man up and offered me ten cents to help him pull a skiff[35] over the river and back to fetch a sheep, and so I went along; but when we was dragging him to the boat, and the man left me a-holt of the rope and went behind him to shove him along, he was too strong for me and jerked loose and run, and we

[30] go the whole hog: 全力以赴；干到底

[31] 这一段是对哈克做出选择后的心理描写段落。和之前作出写信选择之后不同，这一次，哈克决定后，虽然仍然认为自己的想法和决定很可怕，但却不打算更改，还下定决心干到底。将这一段心理描写和前面的思想斗争相比较，我们能够看出哈克内心深处真正的情感倾向和道德价值取向。

[32] take the bearing: 定方位

[33] strike up the road: 上路

[34] shirk /ʃɜːk/ *v.* 推卸；逃避

[35] skiff /skɪf/ *n.* 小艇

after him. We didn't have no dog, and so we had to chase him all over the country till we tired him out. We never got him till dark; then we fetched him over, and I started down for the raft. When I got there and see it was gone, I says to myself, 'They've got into trouble and had to leave; and they've took my nigger, which is the only nigger I've got in the world, and now I'm in a strange country, and ain't got no property no more, nor nothing, and no way to make my living;' so I set down and cried. I slept in the woods all night. But what *did* become of the raft, then?—and Jim—poor Jim!" [36]

(36) "Blamed if I know—that is, what's become of the raft. That old fool had made a trade and got forty dollars, and when we found him in the doggery the loafers had matched half-dollars with him and got every cent but what he'd spent for whisky; and when I got him home late last night and found the raft gone, we said, 'That little rascal has stole our raft and shook us, and run off[37] down the river.'"

(37) "I wouldn't shake my *nigger*, would I?—the only nigger I had in the world, and the only property."

(38) "We never thought of that. Fact is, I reckon we'd come to consider him OUR nigger; yes, we did consider him so—goodness knows we had trouble enough for him. So when we see the raft was gone and we flat broke, there warn't anything for it but to try the Royal Nonesuch another shake. And I've pegged along ever since, dry as a powder-horn[38]. Where's that ten cents? Give it here."

(39) I had considerable money, so I give him ten cents, but begged him to spend it for something to eat, and give me some, because it was all the money I had, and I hadn't had nothing to eat since yesterday. He never said nothing. The next minute he whirls on me and says:

(40) "Do you reckon that nigger would blow on us? We'd skin him if he done that!"

(41) "How can he blow? Hain't he run off?"

(42) "No! That old fool sold him, and never divided with me, and the money's gone."

[36] 在哈克下定决心后，作者对他的心理描写就大幅减少，对话段落开始增加，这自然是因为哈克开始采取实际的营救行动了。本段是哈克见到"公爵"后说的一段话。我们用前面介绍过的"合作原则"来分析：首先，我们当然知道这么长的一段都是假话，违反"质的原则"；其次篇幅太长，内容过细，也违反了"量的原则"。此处，哈克大费周章编故事，就是为了从"公爵"口中套出吉姆的去向。本书中哈克撒谎的次数是比较多的，撒谎时也大多违反了"合作原则"。但谎言和谎言并不相同，他撒谎时的状态、目的也不尽相同。注意比较哈克不同时候的谎言，体会作者对细节的把握。

[37] **run off**: 逃跑

[38] **powder horn**: (牛角制成的)火药筒

此处是指"公爵"说自己口干舌燥。

(43) "*Sold* him?" I says, and begun to cry; "why, he was MY nigger, and that was my money. Where is he?—I want my nigger."

(44) "Well, you can't get your nigger, that's all—so dry up your blubbering.[39] Looky here—do you think *you'd* venture to blow on us? Blamed if I think I'd trust you. Why, if you *was* to blow on us—"

(45) He stopped, but I never see the duke look so ugly out of his eyes before. I went on a-whimpering[40], and says:

(46) "I don't want to blow on nobody; and I ain't got no time to blow, nohow. I got to turn out and find my nigger."

(47) He looked kinder bothered, and stood there with his bills fluttering on his arm, thinking, and wrinkling up his forehead. At last he says:

(48) "I'll tell you something. We got to be here three days. If you'll promise you won't blow, and won't let the nigger blow, I'll tell you where to find him."

(49) So I promised, and he says:

(50) "A farmer by the name of Silas Ph—" and then he stopped. You see, he started to tell me the truth; but when he stopped that way, and begun to study and think again, I reckoned he was changing his mind. And so he was. He wouldn't trust me; he wanted to make sure of having me out of the way the whole three days. So pretty soon he says:[41]

(51) "The man that bought him is named Abram Foster—Abram G. Foster—and he lives forty mile back here in the country, on the road to Lafayette."

(52) "All right," I says, "I can walk it in three days. And I'll start this very afternoon."

(53) "No you wont, you'll start *now*; and don't you lose any time about it, neither, nor do any gabbling by the way. Just keep a tight tongue in your head and move right along, and then you won't get into trouble with US, d'ye hear?"

(54) That was the order I wanted, and that was the one I played for. I wanted to be left free to work my plans.

(55) "So clear out," he says; "and you can tell Mr. Foster whatever you want to. Maybe you can get him to believe that Jim

[39] 此处大意为"你别再哭哭啼啼个没完了"。

[40] whimper /ˈwɪmpə(r)/ *v.* 呜咽;啜泣着说;低声抱怨

[41] 这个段落也是比较有意思的。除了第一句话,本段大部分都是对哈克的心理描写。哈克见"公爵"欲言又止,于是预测他改变主意不会说实话了,事实的确如此。哈克此处的心理活动和前面作思想斗争时完全不同。做完决定后,聪明机灵的哈克又回来了。

is your nigger—some idiots don't require documents—leastways I've heard there's such down South here. And when you tell him the handbill and the reward's bogus[42], maybe he'll believe you when you explain to him what the idea was for getting 'em out. Go 'long now, and tell him anything you want to; but mind you don't work your jaw any *between* here and there."

[42] **bogus** /ˈbəʊgəs/ *n.* 伪币

(56) So I left, and struck for the back country. I didn't look around, but I kinder felt like he was watching me. But I knowed I could tire him out at that. I went straight out in the country as much as a mile before I stopped; then I doubled back through the woods towards Phelps'. I reckoned I better start in on my plan straight off without fooling around, because I wanted to stop Jim's mouth till these fellows could get away. I didn't want no trouble with their kind. I'd seen all I wanted to of them, and wanted to get entirely shut of them.[43]

[43] 我已经受够了那两个骗子，我要和他们一刀两断。

精华赏析

这部受到海明威盛赞的作品，一直以来都在美国文学史上具有里程碑意义。而这本书之所以是一部伟大的作品，一个重要原因便是其中所体现的道德意识及道德价值取向。哈克贝利·费恩的历险漂流过程，事实上是一个道德意识成长的过程，也是一个精神探索的过程。作为一个生活在社会底层的白人孩子，哈克的道德意识最初是什么样的，在漂流过程中，又产生了怎样的变化，最终他做出了怎么样的道德选择……弄清楚这些东西，对于准确理解这部作品的价值取向，把握作者的态度都有着重要的意义。这部作品的基本故事设定是生活在社会最底层的白人孩子哈克和黑人奴隶吉姆的历险漂流组合。因此，接下来我们就从哈克和吉姆之间的关系变化这个角度来分析主人公哈克的道德意识成长过程。

一、开始漂流之前哈克的道德意识

踏上漂流之路之前，哈克常常被酗酒的父亲打骂，缺乏家庭温暖，却也厌恶好心照顾他的寡妇道格拉斯和沃森小姐僵化死板的训诫。可以说，从一开始，他就是一个未被那个时代的社会规范驯化的孩子，是一个小小的“反叛者”。这也为之后他的道德价值取向的成长提供了基础。

作为一个年纪不过十三四岁的白人孩子，他并没有在既往的生活经历中得到许多的疼爱和温暖。他的父亲是一个酒鬼，每日游手好闲，经常在喝醉后打骂他。在踏上漂流历险的旅程之前，哈克就常常居无定所，缺乏家庭温暖。然而，他却并不喜欢待在好心收养他的寡妇道格拉斯家里，不喜欢接受各种礼仪规矩的教化，也不太喜欢上学，常常逃课；他生活动荡，却认为在寡妇家那种规规矩矩的安稳生活十分沉闷无趣，甚至"恨不得死了算了"；他混迹于社会最底层，却对金钱没有强烈的占用欲望，甚至为了摆脱金钱可能带来的麻烦，迫不及待地将之前幸运获得的六千块钱送给了撒切尔法官……可以说，从一开始，哈克就是一个未被当时社会主流价值观和社会规范教化的"反叛者"。

二、哈克的道德意识发展之初

踏上漂流之路以后，随着经历的增长，和吉姆相处的增多，哈克对吉姆的态度和看法发生了变化，他的道德意识也在这个过程中得到成长和发展。一开始，他认为保护逃跑的黑奴是有违正义，违背良心的错误行为，后来在越来越多地认识到吉姆身上的优点，感怀于吉姆的善良温暖后，哈克心中基于直觉和体验的新的道德认知和价值取向开始逐渐形成。

好不容易摆脱了父亲的哈克遇到了逃出来的黑奴吉姆，很自然地和吉姆一同漂泊逃亡。尽管如此，哈克心里却明白维护逃跑的黑奴是"错误的"。在本书的第十六章，当哈克看到吉姆因为可能获得自由而雀跃不已的时候，他内心的想法是"他快要自由了。——那这事儿怪谁呢？当然是怪我了。无论如何，我都无法逃脱良心的指责""可怜的沃森小姐对你这么好，你却眼睁睁看着她的黑奴逃跑，一个字也不说""黑奴就是得寸进尺的"。甚至，在备受负疚感的折磨后，他做出了决定，"现在还不晚——一见到灯光我就划到岸边去告发他。"尽管之后遇到搜捕黑奴的人时，善良的哈克仍然没能狠下心来把吉姆交出去，反而巧妙地撒了个谎，帮助了吉姆，但他其实痛恨自己的"软弱"。面对搜捕者的提问，"我没有马上回答。我想要回答，但就是没法说出口。有那么一两秒钟，我努力鼓起勇气说出来，但我不算个男子汉，我那点勇气还不如兔子。"这时的"反叛者"哈克，对待吉姆是和当时的社会规范以及社会道德观念坚定地站在一起的，认为告发他是自己应该采取的正确行动。

然而，随着相处日久，黑奴吉姆身上的善良温暖和对哈克的真诚照顾与喜爱，不断地触动着哈克。例如，吉姆在见到从家族世仇的械斗中安全归来的哈克时，高兴得一把抱住了他，"上帝保佑你……我以为你已经丝(死)掉了，上帝啊，你又回来了我是多高兴啊。"重新回到船上，见到吉姆的哈克也别提多开心了。两人吃着东西聊着天，哈克感到，"这世上再也没有地方比木筏更好了"。此处提及木筏的时候，使用了"home"一词，表示木筏上有吉姆，有哈克，成为了一个家。

三、哈克的道德意识的成熟

哈克和吉姆一路漂流，到了第三十一章的时候，发生了一件大事。黑奴吉姆被贪财的"国王"和"公爵"以四十块钱的低价卖掉。在得知吉姆被卖后，哈克开始思考帮助吉姆的办法，此时他不得不做出抉择——是遵循社会规范依靠沃森小姐救出吉姆，还是和社会规则决裂，依靠自己。也正是这个契机促使哈克的道德意识和道德取向走向成熟。

得知吉姆被卖后，哈克首先感到的是伤心愤怒，他从情感上接受不了吉姆被这两个卑鄙无情的骗子出卖。继而，他立刻开始思考如何救出吉姆。他首先想到应该遵循社会规范，告知吉姆的前主人——沃森小姐，由她名正言顺地要回黑奴吉姆。然而这样一来，吉姆就必须重新回归奴隶的身份，甚至可能因为之前逃跑的事情而被再度卖掉。与此同时，他帮助黑奴逃跑这样不光彩的事情就会曝光，他将面临巨大的社会舆论指责。哈克因此陷入了深深的自责，开始审视自己的"罪恶"。然而，尽管会受到人们的指责，哈克还是决心"改邪归正"，动笔写就告知沃森小姐吉姆去向的信件，并即刻获得了内心的平静，感到"全身的罪恶都被洗涤干净了"。

然而，他很快又开始回想起这一路漂泊中和吉姆的情谊。哈克想起他们一同在木筏上经历风暴，一同唱歌欢笑，想起吉姆为了让自己多睡一会儿而主动替他值班，想起吉姆在看到从浓雾中回来的自己时，以及看到从两个家族的械斗当中平安归来的自己时，那高兴的样子，想起来吉姆对自己的种种照顾和爱护。哈克左右为难，但仅仅一分钟后，他做出了最终的决定——"那么好吧，就让我下地狱吧。"至此，哈克在现实世界的社会规则和他内心的道德观之间做出了选择。这短短"一分钟"和之前左思右想，进行心理斗争时的举棋不定形成鲜明对比。而哈克之所以能够仅思考一分钟就推翻之前的决定，究其真正的原因，还是因为帮助吉姆获得真正自由的决定才真正符合他内心深处早已存在，只是还未最终成形的道德价值取向。

在哈克道德价值取向成形并逐渐成熟的过程中，我们可以清晰地看出他的变化过程。他仍然因为做了社会规范所不认可的事情而感到深深的内疚自责，甚至在撕掉告发信，做出和社会规则决裂的选择后，仍然认为自己的想法十分可怕。然而可贵的是，即便如此，他却没有像之前那样摇摆不定，反而下定决心，帮助吉姆到底。这不仅仅是因为他和吉姆之间的情谊，更因为他内心深处的那种逐渐成熟的、朴拙的、基于直觉和体验的道德意识使得他坚定于这样的选择。

马克·吐温创作这部作品是在十九世纪七八十年代，但小说中设定的背景是十九世纪四十至六十年代的美国。此时的美国，工业化进程带来的劳资矛盾日益严重，政治腐败，人民生活困苦，蓄奴制和种族歧视所带来的社会问题也已发展到十分紧迫的程度。马克·吐温如此设定，有其特别的用意。经历了内战的美国社会发展到十九世纪八十年代，人们对战争所能带来的新的美好生活的希望有所减退，南方各个州的种族主义势力再度抬头，黑人的生存处境再度恶化。然而包括黑人在内的美国人民，事实上仍然在渴望着，追求着更好的新的世界。而哈克的精神探索之旅，他的道德意识，价值取向发展演变的历程，正是这个时代美国人民内心精神追求的缩影。在这场探索之旅中，在哈克心里，社会道德观念和基于直觉以及体验的新道德观之间的矛盾冲突，也增强了人物的真实度，增加了作品的张力，深化了主题。

阅读思考

1. 本章第 24 段是对哈克的心理描写，共分为两个部分，请问你认为哈克更倾向于第一部分还是第二部分？请陈述理由。

2. 请找出本书中那些可以看出哈克和吉姆之间关系状态，彼此对对方的态度看法的细节。

EXERCISE V

I. Oral presentation.

1. 假设你的朋友就到底是出国留学还是在国内考研究生的问题询问你的意见,请参考以下表达模拟对话。

   If I were you, I would like to...

   What do you think of...

   What about...

   I'd suggest that...

   You might/ may as well...

   The way I see it, you should...

   Might I make a suggestion?

   If I were in your shoes...

   It seems to me that you should...

   Would you be interested in...?

2. 假设你在美国读研究生,并作为留学生代表致辞,介绍自己和自己的家乡,并陈述自己出国留学的理由。可参考使用以下表达。

   I'd be happy to...

   What I am going to talk about...

   I should like to pay tribute to...

   I sincerely hope...

   I look forward to seeing...

   Best wishes for...

   Working together, ...

II. Choose the correct words to complete the sentences.

1. It's _____ that all this damage has been caused by mindless vandalism.

   A. disgusted B. disgusting C. exciting D. excited

2. I had a sore throat and it hurt to _____.

   A. breathe B. laugh C. swallow D. cry

3. Armed troops _____ the hospital yesterday.

   A. helped B. searched C. moved D. went

4. She slipped out of bed and _____ to the window.

A. tiptoed　　B. slid　　C. toted　　D. took

5. Thousands of people _____ to the beach this weekend.

A. flocked　　B. slipped　　C. slid　　D. glided

6. I'm sorry to ____ you all this way in the heat.

A. place　　B. put　　C. drag　　D. drab

7. He sat for hours just ____ into space.

A. glaring　　B. gazing　　C. watching　　D. seeing

8. What _____ me is why he left the country without telling anyone.

A. holds　　B. excites　　C. puzzles　　D. understands

9. The spectators were _____ visibly in the hot sun.

A. shaking　　B. moving　　C. crying　　D. wilting

10. I've been ____ around all day trying to get everything done.

A. staying　　B. talking　　C. rushing　　D. fooling

III. Fill in the blanks with suitable prepositions.

1. Today, we travel through city streets all ____ the world to explore street art.
2. Yesterday she was robbed ____ her purse when she went home.
3. It's really difficult to let go ____ your sad memory.
4. A commission will be set up to look ____ why we failed in this program.
5. Residents who live nearby complain ____ aircraft noise.

IV. Answer the following questions.

Questions on the content

1. How did the king deceive Mary Jane in Chapter XXV?
2. Did Joe believe in Huck? And why?
3. Why did Huck make up his mind to hide that money for the three sisters? (Chapter XXVI)
4. Where did Huck hide the money?
5. Why was Mary Jane sad in Chapter XXVIII? Did Huck tell Mary the truth?
6. Why did people get out the coffin? What did people find in the coffin? (Chapter XXIX)
7. Did the king blame Huck in Chapter XXX?
8. What figures of speech are in this sentence "...for if the excited fools hadn't let go all holts and made that rush to get a look we'd a slept in our cravats to-night—cravats warranted to WEAR, too—longer than *We'd* need 'em." ? (Chapter XXX)

Questions on the structure and style

1. What is/are the theme(s) of the story?

2. Do you see any good qualities in Jim that the king and the duke don't have?
3. Do you see any symbolic implications in River and Land? Explain your point.
4. What details are used to show the villagers' characteristics?
5. Do you think that women are stereotyped or new women characters featured with bright personality and unique charms are created in this novel? Explain your point.

V. Translate the following sentences into Chinese by using explanation or annotation.

1. One morning I happened to turn over the saltcellar at breakfast. I reached some of it as quick as I could to throw over my left shoulder and keep off the bad luck, But Miss Watson was in ahead of me, and crossed me off. (Chapter Ⅳ)
2. Miss Watson's nigger, Jim, had a hairball as big as your fist, which had been took out of the fourth stomach of an ox, and he used to do magic with it. He said there was a spirit inside of it, and it knowed everything. (Chapter Ⅳ)
3. Well, Henry he takes a notion he wants to get up some trouble with this country. How does he go at it—give notice? —give the country a show? No. All of a sudden he heaves all the tea in Boston Harbor overboard, and whacks out a declaration of independence, and dares them to come on. (Chapter XXIII)
4. He had suspicious of his father, the **Duke of Wellington**. Well, what did he do? Ask him to show up? No—drownded himself in a butt of mamsey, like a cat. (Chapter XXIII)
5. Why, before, he looked like the orneriest old rip that ever was; but now, when he'd take off his new white beaver and make a bow and do a smile, he looked that grand and good and pious that you'd say he had walked right out of the ark, and maybe was old **Leviticus** himself. (Chapter XXIV)
6. She had the grit to pray for **Judus** if she took the notion—there warn't no backdown to her, I judge. (Chapter XXVIII)
7. "... I lay you'll be the **Methusalem**-numskull of creation before I ask you—or the likes of you." (Chapter XXXIII)
8. The **Iron Mask** always done that, and it's a blame's good way, too. (Chapter XXXV)
9. Why, look at one of them prisoners in the bottom dungeon of the **Castle Deef**, in the harbor of Marseilles, that dug himself out that way; how long was he at it, you reckon? (Chapter XXXV)
10. "... He's plumb crazy, s' I; it's what I says in the fust place, it's what I says in the middle, 'n' it's what I says last 'n' all the time—the nigger's crazy—crazy's **Nebokoodneezer**, s'I." (Chapter XXXXI)

VI. Summary writing.

Answer the following questions which are based on the murder Huck witnessed in Chapter XX and XXI.

· Where did the murder take place?

· How did Boggs behave when he first appeared in the presence of the crowd?

· How did the crowd react to Boggs?

· What did Boggs do before the biggest store in town?

· How did Sherburn warn Boggs?

· Did Boggs stop his cussing and yelling to Sherburn?

· What did Huck see five or ten minutes later?

· What happened when Boggs appeared again about five or ten minutes later?

· What did the crowd do to Boggs?

· What was the long, lanky man doing at the scene?

· Why did the crowd snatch down every clothes-line they come to?

· How did Sherburn scare off the crowd gathered in front of his house?

Writing task: write a short story based on the above questions.

KEYS TO EXERCISES

EXERCISE Ⅰ

Ⅱ. 1—5 ADBCA　6—10 BCDCB

Ⅲ. 1. out　2. in　3. on; of　4. out of　5. on

V.

1. 烂醉如泥

2. 游手好闲;好逸恶劳

3. 纹丝不动;到处流窜;贼头狗脑;穷凶极恶

4. 趾高气扬

5. 戒酒节欲;洗心革面;重新做人;丢人现眼

6. 深更半夜;贼眉鼠眼;打得火热

7. 虔信上帝;行善积德;神恩无涯;命里注定;乌七八糟

8. 语言辛辣;态度傲慢

9. 孑然一身;孤苦伶仃;显贵家业;走投无路;破衣烂衫;筋疲力尽;丢人现眼

10. 流离颠沛;漂泊异国;遭人践踏;受苦受难

EXERCISE Ⅱ

Ⅱ. 1—5 ACBCD　6—10 ACACD

Ⅲ. 1. to　2. about　3. out　4. in　5. into

V.

1. 他(吉姆)大声嚷嚷,一下子蹦了起来;亮光里只见那头恶蛇还在蠢动,打算再蹿上来咬人。(*n.* → *v.*)

2. 哪知道汤姆·索亚把我踅摸到了,他说他打算搞一个强盗帮;他说我如果先回到寡妇那里,做一个正派人,就可以加入。(*adj.* → *n.*)

3. 我受这种罪虽然只有六七分钟,但是自己觉得好像还要长得多似的。(*n.* → *v.*)

4. 最后,他(老头)跟他的那匹马全都血淋淋地瘸着腿回家转;但是格兰杰福特家族的这些人都得让人抬回家去——他们里头有一个早就死了,另一个转天也死了。(*adj.* →*adv.*; *adj.* → *v.*)

5. …… 这时候,你就听见一声霹雳怪吓人地劈将下来,随后又从天际发出隆隆轰响,一溜歪斜地往地心深处滚下去,有如好几只空木桶,顺着长长的楼梯,欢蹦乱跳地往下滚,你知道。(*adj.* → *adv.*;*v.p.* → *adv.*)

6. 他光着脑袋,跌跌撞撞地穿过大街向我走过来,他两侧都有一个朋友挽着他的胳膊,催着他赶快走。(*adj.* → *adv.*;*prep.* → *v.*)

7. 吉姆拼命地吃,因为他都快要饿死了。等我们把肚子都给填饱了,就懒洋洋地倒下来,仿佛躺死似的。(*prep.* → *adv.*;*v.* → *adv.*)

8. 后来,我们两眼看着孤寂的河面,怪懒洋洋的,没多久就懒洋洋地睡着了。(*n.* → *adj.*;*v.* → *adj.*)

9. 我听了吉姆的这些话,心里挺难过,因为这无异于降低了他的身份。我的良心又把我唤醒,使我感到无比激动,到最后我就对自己的良心说:"别跟我过不去吧——现在还不算太晚——只要一看见灯光,我就划到岸上去告发他。"(*n.* → *v.*)

10. 天底下再也没有比一帮子乌合之众更可怜的了;说到底,军队也一样——都是乌合之众;他们打起仗来,不是靠他们天生就有的勇气,而是全仗着人多势众,还有不少指挥官罢了。可是一伙乌合之众如果没有一条好汉牵头,那就连可怜都谈不上。(*prep.* → *v.*)

EXERCISE III

Ⅱ. 1—5 ADDBC　6—10 ABDBC

Ⅲ. 1. in　2. for　3. into　4. for　5. on

Ⅴ. 1—5 CDBAB　6—10 CCDAD

EXERCISE IV

Ⅱ. 1—5 ADBBC　6—10 BDACD

Ⅲ. 1. for　2. by　3. in　4. with　5. in

Ⅴ.

1. 我们估算着那天夜里准能远远地开出去好多好多英里,尽管由于公爵在印刷所里搞的鬼闹得小镇上满城风雨,我们也管不着了——到那时,我们想要快速前进就快速前进了。

2. 我们来到了一小块平地上,那里地上是干的,长满了大大小小的树木和藤蔓。

3. …… 他们就一块儿走进了一个大客厅,大客厅地板上铺着一块碎布头编成的新地毯。他们全都待在离前窗很远的一个角落里——这里连一个窗子也没有。

4. 他(医生)依然怒不可遏,说凡是冒充英国人而英国话又说得糟透了的人,就准是个骗子,肯定是在扯谎。

5. 他是我见过最温柔,行动最流畅,做事最安静的人了。而且他脸上一直没有任何笑容,和火腿似的,一板一眼的。

6. 我暗自思忖:一个人置身于窘境时,不得不说出实话来,我认为确实是非常冒险的事情;我尽管没有这种经验,不敢说得太肯定,可是不管怎么样,我总觉得就是这么回事;就眼下这件事来说，我总觉得说实话要比说谎话好得多，实际上也稳妥得多。

7. 他来到我们跟前时，就高雅大方地把帽子摘下来，好像轻手轻脚地揭开一只盒子盖，生怕惊动了盒子里头睡着了的蝴蝶似的。

8. 再说——如果说我是妖怪的话，我才不会扔下自己的正经事，冲着擦一下旧铁皮灯的那个人老远跑过去。

9. 但是不管怎么样，有一件事总得先交代清楚——那就是说务必经过一连串艰难险阻的情节，最后把他搭救出来，这才能博得人们更多喝彩；本来那些艰难险阻的情节，应该预先给我们安排好的，可是既然现在没有安排好，我们也就只好自己开动脑筋，把它们通通构思出来。

10. 可怜的姑娘！都好多回了，先是她的一些画惹我生气，使我不免对她有点讨厌，于是，我就情不自禁地来到她原先住的那个房间，把她那本可怜的旧剪贴簿拿过来，尽情观赏一番。

EXERCISE V

Ⅱ. 1—5 BCBAA 6—10 CBCDC

Ⅲ. 1. over 2. of 3. of 4. into 5. of

V.

1. 一天早上，我在吃早餐时，不巧把盐瓶子碰翻了。我赶紧伸过手去，想把那些盐屑撒到左肩膀后面去，免得触霉头。(达芬奇的名画《最后的晚餐》中，犹大碰洒了一碗盐。盐洒了是坏运气或麻烦的征兆。而犹大给耶稣带来的正是麻烦。有些人如果碰洒了盐，就会把盐往肩膀后洒。他们认为，把盐洒到身后可以吓跑一直跟着他们的魔鬼，或者至少在他们逃跑时使魔鬼被弄花了眼。)不料，沃森小姐却抢先拦住了我。

2. 沃森小姐的黑奴吉姆，有一个拳头那样大的毛团，那是从一头牛的第四个胃里取出来的，他常用它来变戏法。他说这毛团里头有一位神仙，它真可以说是无所不知，无所不晓。(此处吉姆迷信的毛团来自非洲伏都教，该教是来自西非的一种民间宗教，现仍流行于海地和其他加勒比海诸岛的黑人中。)

3. 你看，亨利不知怎的突然来了个怪念头，竟跟我们美国捣乱来了。那么，他是怎么着手的——事先打过一声招呼吗？——给我们一个准备的机会了吗？不，全都没有。他突然把所有船上的茶叶，通通给扔到波士顿海湾里去，赶紧做好了一篇独立宣言，看我们还敢不敢怎么的。(此处哈克提到的波士顿倾茶事件，发生在 1773 年，当时北美各州反对英国统治，拒绝缴纳茶税，并将停泊在波士顿海湾内三艘英国船上所载茶叶数百吨，投入海中，三年后，即 1776 年美国人签署了《独立宣言》，宣布独立。此事件与亨利八世毫无关系。)

4. 他对他父亲威灵顿公爵还疑神疑鬼呢。嘿，我说他是怎么着——要他露露面吗？不——他把他扔到一只大酒桶里，像一只猫似的给淹死了。(此处哈克提到的威灵顿公爵是十八世纪的人，不可能是亨利八世的父亲。在大酒桶里淹死的也不是威灵顿公爵，据传是克拉伦斯公爵。)

5. 在这以前,他就像是一个十恶不赦的老废物,可是现在呢,他把他那崭新的白水獭帽子一摘去,俯身一打躬,露齿一笑,瞧他那副神气可真是雍容风雅,虔敬有礼,你会说他是刚从方舟里头走出来的,说不定还是老利未蒂克本人哩。(《利未蒂克》是《圣经·旧约全书》中的一卷,简称《利未记》,记载了虔心敬奉上帝的人所应遵守的法则。哈克把它当作了实有其人的人名,并跟诺亚方舟故事混淆在一起了。)

6. 只要她灵机一动,她甚至会斗胆替犹大祷祝哩,我估摸。(犹大是耶稣门徒之一,也是他把耶稣出卖了。)

7. "……我说,就算你赶明变成玛式撒拉式老傻帽活寿星,我也不会来求你——或是像你这一号蠢货——跟我亲嘴呀。"(玛式撒拉是《圣经·旧约全书·创世纪》中以诺之子,据传享年 969 岁。)

8. 那个铁面人就常常这样做的,那的确也是个好办法。(铁面人是法国著名作家大仲马的小说《布拉日罗纳子爵》中的主人公。小说的一部分被译成英文,书名为《铁面人》。铁面人是法国路易十四统治时期的一个政治犯,被囚禁长达四十余年之久,1703 年死于巴士底狱,史料证明,他的面具是用黑天鹅绒做的,后来的传说却把它变成了铁质的。)

9. 哼,你看看马赛港湾迪弗城堡最末层地牢里头的在押囚犯,他们里头有一个就是采取这种办法挖洞逃跑的。你猜,他总共挖了多长日子?(迪弗城堡是位于法国马赛港湾的一座小岛,为法国国王弗兰西斯一世于 1524 年所建,此后很多年都是法国国家监狱。大仲马的名著《基督山伯爵》中的主人公即被关押在那里。)

10. "……我一开头就是这么说,说到中间我也是这么说,说到最后我始终是这么说——那个黑人准是疯了——疯得就像尼波苦倔哉,我说。"(此处人物把字音念错了,正确的姓名应是尼布甲尼撒二世。他是新巴比伦国王,曾多次发动侵略战争,占领叙利亚、腓尼基和巴勒斯坦,并攻陷过耶路撒冷,且大兴土木,修建了巴比伦城和世界奇观之一的"空中花园"。史书上记载,他曾发过疯。)

REFERENCES

MADDEN D, 1980. A Primer of Novel. Washington: Scarecrow Press.

UNGERER F, SCHMID H J, 1996. An Introduction to Cognitive Linguistics. Harlow Addison Wesley Longman Limited.

LYOTARD J F, 1984. The Post-Modern Conditions. Minneapolis: University of Minnesota Press.

E.M. 福斯特 , 2016. 小说面面观 . 冯涛 , 译 . 上海 : 上海译文出版社 .

方汉泉 , 2004. 二元对立原则及其在文学批评中的运用 . 外语与外语教学 (7):37-41.

弗吉尼亚・伍尔夫 , 1989. 一间自己的屋子 . 王还 , 译 . 北京 : 三联书店 .

弗兰西斯・伯纳特 , 2015. 秘密花园 . 邱晓亮 , 译 . 成都 : 四川文艺出版社 .

郭宏安 , 1983. 萨特研究 . 北京 : 中国社会科学出版社 .

何学德 , 2005. 会话质量 : 合作原则与礼貌原则语境运用研究 . 西南民族大学学报 (人文社科版), 26(11):344-346.

贾中华 , 1997.《奥吉・玛琪历险记》与当代文学中的反英雄形象 . 甘肃社会科学 (4):67-69.

李华东 , 俞东明 , 2001. 从话轮转换看权势关系、性格刻画和情节发展 . 解放军外国语学院学报 , 24(2):26-30.

刘世生 , 朱瑞青 , 2006. 文体学概论 . 北京 : 北京大学出版社 .

马克・吐温 , 2015. 哈克贝利・费恩历险记 . 潘庆舲 , 译 . 北京 : 商务印书馆 .

马克・吐温 , 2005. 马克・吐温作品选——密西西比河(下). 马敬福 , 译 . 贵阳 : 贵州人民出版社 .

邱运华 , 2006. 文学批评方法与案例 . 北京 : 北京大学出版社 .

荣格 , 1987. 心理学与文学 . 冯川 , 苏克 , 译 . 北京 : 三联书店 .

斯达尔夫人 , 1986. 论文学 . 徐继曾 , 译 . 北京 : 人民文学出版社 .

泰纳, 1994.《英国文学史》序言 . 杨烈, 译 .// 伍蠡甫, 胡经之 . 西方文艺理论名著选编 . 北京 : 北京大学出版社 .

王岳川 , 2009. 生态文学与生态批评的当代价值 . 北京大学学报 (哲学社会科学版), 46(2):130-142.

张德禄 , 1987. 语域理论简介 . 现代外语 (4):23-29.

张宏国 , 2004. 英语双重否定句浅说 . 铜陵学院学报 (1):91-93.

赵毅衡, 2016. 符号学原理与推演. 南京: 南京大学出版社.
赵毅衡, 2013a. 当说着被说的时候: 比较叙述学导论. 成都: 四川文艺出版社.
赵毅衡, 2013b. 广义叙述学. 成都: 四川大学出版社.
赵毅衡, 2013c. 苦恼的叙述者. 成都: 四川文艺出版社.
赵毅衡, 2011. 反讽时代: 形式论与文化批评. 上海: 复旦大学出版社.
朱立元, 1998. 弗莱的原型批评美学. 人文杂志 (6):128-134.